ISBN 978-1-4400-8440-9
PIBN 10154306

1 MONTH OF
FREE
READING

at

www.ForgottenBooks.com

By purchasing this book you are eligible for one month membership to ForgottenBooks.com, giving you unlimited access to our entire collection of over 1,000,000 titles via our web site and mobile apps.

To claim your free month visit:

www.forgottenbooks.com/free154306

English
Français
Deutsche
Italiano
Español
Português

www.forgottenbooks.com

Mythology Photography **Fiction**
Fishing Christianity **Art** Cooking
Essays Buddhism Freemasonry
Medicine **Biology** Music **Ancient**
Egypt Evolution Carpentry Physics
Dance Geology **Mathematics** Fitness
Shakespeare **Folklore** Yoga Marketing
Confidence Immortality Biographies
Poetry **Psychology** Witchcraft
Electronics Chemistry History **Law**
Accounting **Philosophy** Anthropology
Alchemy Drama Quantum Mechanics
Atheism Sexual Health **Ancient History**
Entrepreneurship Languages Sport
Paleontology Needlework Islam
Metaphysics Investment Archaeology
Parenting Statistics Criminology
Motivational

THE

ANGEL-MESSIAH

OF

BUDDHISTS, ESSENES, AND CHRISTIANS

BY

ERNEST DE BUNSEN

LONDON

LONGMANS, GREEN, AND CO.

1880

INTRODUCTION.

THE CONCEPTION of an incarnate Angel as Messiah is of Eastern origin, and there is no trace of it in those portions of the Hebrew Scriptures which possibly were written before the Captivity, nor in the first three Gospels. 'The Angel-Messiah' or Melech-Hamoshiach is a compound title which constantly occurs in the Commentaries or Midrashim, the records of Scribal tradition, also in the Targums. Although this Messianic name is not to be found in the Talmud, the latter designates as the Messiah the Angel of God who followed the Israelites in the wilderness, and who is here called the Angel Metatron, or He who stands by the throne (pp. 91, 92, 101, 303). That Angel Paul calls Christ.

It can be shown that this new Messianic conception was introduced into Judaism and into Christianity by the Essenes or Essai, to whom John the Baptist or Ashai, the bather, probably belonged, and who are in the New Testament designated as disciples of John. Jesus opposed the principal doctrines of John, whom he designated as not belonging to his kingdom of heaven, or of the Spirit, which he declared as having already come; whilst the disciples of John had not even heard 'whether there be any Holy Ghost.' The disciples of John the Baptist or Essene must have expected that the Spirit of God would be brought from heaven to earth by Him who should baptize with the Holy Ghost. The Law and the Prophets until John had only prophesied about the future coming of the Spirit of God or the kingdom of heaven, but since the days of John those who entered it did so by force, because it suffered violence, or was violently closed by the Scribes and Pharisees, who 'shut up the kingdom of heaven against men.' Jesus did not sanction, but seems to have even opposed, the doctrine of the Angel-Messiah as promulgated by the Essenes or disciples of John.

Nothing is transmitted to us about the Messianic expectations of the Essenes, and this mysterious fact is best explained by the supposition that their secret tradition referred to an incarnate Angel as the Messiah. This supposition is confirmed by the presumable Messianic expectations of John the Baptist or Essene. As such he could not reveal them, if 'He that should come,' the Tathâgata of Buddhists (p. 342), was to be an incarnate Angel ; for the Essenes were bound by oath not to divulge their doctrines about angels. At the end of the Apostolic age the Essenes can be proved to have believed in Jesus as the Angel-Messiah, and Epiphanius asserts that they never changed their original doctrines (pp. 111–117). A special oath bound the initiated Essene 'not to communicate to any one their doctrines in any other way than he has received them.' Thus innovations were excluded, and it becomes probable that the Essenes in the time of John expected an Angel-Messiah.

The first Jew who can be proved to have applied this new Messianic doctrine to Jesus was Stephen, one of the Greek-speaking Jews, Grecians or Hellenists, some of whom were from Alexandria, where the principal settlements of the Essenian Therapeuts were. We shall try to show that Stephen's doctrine of an Angel-Messiah, which Paul accepted, was an Essenic doctrine.

Paul was probably among the men of Cilicia who took part in the disputations with Stephen; and he was present at the death of the first martyr, previous to his journey to Damascus as leader of the persecution which arose 'because of Stephen.' The latter's co-religionists, distinguished from the Hebrews as Grecians in the Acts, were scattered, whilst the Apostles remained at Jerusalem. Some of the scattered disciples went as far as Antioch; and to this congregation or Church, founded independently from the Apostles at Jerusalem, Paul was introduced by Barnabas. His Epistle, cited as genuine by the unanimous voice of the ancient Church (pp. 323, 324), proves him to have been an Essene and a preacher of Jesus, not as son of David, but as Son of God, as the Angel-Messiah whom the Essenes expected. After the conversion of Paul to the faith of Stephen, which once he destroyed, the new Apostle had accepted some of the doctrines of the universalist Therapeuts. Paul promulgated by his Epistles the faith in Christ as the spiritual Rock which followed the Israelites, that is, as the Angel of whom Stephen had said, almost in the same words, that he had been with the fathers in the wilderness. In this sense Paul says that Christ was the man ' from heaven,' and that all things were by him created.

The principal doctrines and rites of the Essenes can be connected with the East, with Parsism, and especially with Buddhism. Among the doctrines which Essenes and Buddhists had in common was that of the Angel-Messiah. The remarkable parallels in the most ancient records of the lives of Gautama-Buddha and of Jesus

Christ require explanation. They cannot all be attributed to chance or to importation from the West.

We now possess an uninterrupted chain of Buddhist writings in China, 'from at least 100 B.C. to A.D. 600,' according to Professor Beal. In the Chinese version of the Dhammapada, by him translated (No. xxxi. p. 142 f.), Buddha's sermon on 'Falsehood' is fully given, which is alluded to by Asôka in the second Bairat rock-inscription (see General Cunningham's *Corpus Inscriptorum Indicarum*, i. 132). Some discourses of Buddha were commonly known in India as early as Asôka at least, who, in B.C. 250, or 29 years before the destruction of Chinese books, is said to have sent the first Buddhist missionaries to China and to Ceylon.

To Ceylon Asôka's son Mahinda, according to tradition, took the Vinaya Pitaka or 'treasure-box,' the most ancient of the three Pitakas. The Northern or Chinese edition harmonises in all essential points with the Southern or Ceylon canon, though the connection between the two schools was broken. The first canon is wrongly said to have been drawn up immediately after Buddha's death, 79 years after B.C. 473, or B.C. 394, 'a few years later than B.C. 400,' as Mr. Rhys Davids corrects the Ceylon date. It follows, that between B.C. 280 and 150 the authors of the Septuagint, initiated in Essenic and Buddhistic tradition, as we here assume, reckoned backwards from B.C. 473, known as the date of Buddha's birth, the 440 years of the Greek text for the period from the third of Solomon to the Exodus, thence the 430 years to Abraham's leaving Haran, and thus 1017 years were left for the period to the year of the flood, B.C. 2360. The chronology of the Septuagint implies, that

Buddha, ('a greater than Solomon') Moses, Abraham, and Adam were precursors of Christ as incarnations of the Angel-Messiah. Had Philo and Josephus believed this, they would have recognised Jesus as the Christ.

The object of the first attempt to connect Paul with the Essenes, and these with the expectation of an Angel-Messiah, is to explain the striking similarity between the Buddhistic and Christian Scriptures by a fusion of both traditions, as consciously effected by the Essenes. Thus the opinion of Eusebius will be confirmed, who considered it 'highly probable' that the writings of the Therapeuts, which they had received from the founders of their society, have been utilised in the composition of the four Gospels, of Paul's Epistles, and especially of the Epistle to the Hebrews.

The principal result of this argument would be that Paul, not Jesus, was the cause of the separation between Judaism and Christianity.

The germs of this separation can be traced back to the different symbolism, represented on one side by the Hebrews, on the other by the strangers in Israel, to whom the Rechabites and Essenes belonged. The ancestors of both had once lived under one roof in the East. Already the reformation of Brahmanism by Buddhism had shown, that the moral principle in man may lead to different symbols and rites, but that what Humanity has in common is sufficient for 'brethren to dwell together in unity.'

Several centuries before the birth of Jesus Christ some figures of constellations had become symbols of moral doctrines. Sooner or later these were connected with transmitted words of Gautama-Buddha. The Cosmical had become to that extent the symbol of the

Ethical, that the son of the virgin Mâya, on whom, according to Chinese tradition, 'the Holy Ghost' had descended, was said to have been born on Christmas-day, on the sun's birthday, at the commencement of the sun's apparent annual evolution round the earth. On that day, the sun having fully entered the winter-solstice, the sign of Virgo was rising on the Eastern horizon (pp. 23, 24). The woman's symbol of this stellar sign was represented first with ears of corn, then with a newborn child in her arms. Buddha was described as a superhuman organ of light, to whom a superhuman organ of darkness, Mâra or Naga the evil serpent, was opposed (p. 39). Thus also Ormuzd, Osiris, Dionysos, and Apollos were described as divinities of light, opposed by serpent-deities (p. 65). Finally, the Virgin-born Jesus Christ, 'the Sun of Righteousness' (p. 307, note 1), was described as opposed by 'the old serpent,' the Satan, hinderer, or adversary.

This symbolism was connected with the signs of the spring-equinox and of the autumn-equinox. The latter was once marked by the sign of Scorpio and by the constellation of the Serpent, which was represented as aiming at, and almost touching the heel of the Virgin-representation on the sphere. These constellations and signs, especially the mystical sign of Virgo, have led man to compare with the cosmical fight between light and darkness the moral fight between good and evil.

Whether the nature-symbol or the ethical idea be regarded as the first, the fact of a universal revelation, of a continuity of Divine influences everywhere and at all times, remains as the anchor of the soul, as the Rock of Ages, on which Christ's Church will be built.

CONTENTS.

———◦◦◦———

CHAPTER IV.

THE ESSENES AND THE EAST.

CHAPTER V.

THE ANGEL-MESSIAH.

CHAPTER VI.

JESUS AND THE ESSENES.

CHAPTER VII.

PAUL AND THE ESSENES.

CHAPTER VIII.

APOLLOS AND THE ESSENES.

CHAPTER IX.

JAMES AND THE ESSENES.

CHAPTER X.

THE GNOSIS.

APPENDIX.

THE ANGEL-MESSIAH.

CHAPTER I.

Priestcraft and Magic Art—Brahm, Maya, and Bodhi—The Eastern Pâramita and the Western Tradition—Jainism and Buddhism—The Sakas
and Sâkya-Muni—Records of Buddhistic Tradition.

Priestcraft and Magic Art.

BUDDHISTIC TRADITION is a comparatively late deposit of
ancestorial wisdom, written or unwritten. It can be
rendered probable, though it cannot be proved, that
such deeper knowledge was confined to a select number
of initiated, among whom the mysteries were transmitted from one generation to another. Such an organisation for the transmission of knowledge withheld from
the people, presupposes firmly established priestly institutions and a secluded mode of life, regulated by severe
customs. Of an ascetic system like this there is no trace
among the East-Iranians, who were the representatives
of Zoroastrian doctrines, a source from which Buddhism
certainly has drawn. It is exceedingly strange, that
although India is the country where such institutions
and customs seem to have originated, yet that they
were not established there at the indefinite time when
the most ancient Indian records, the Veda, were composed in the Indus valley, and before the Aryan conquerors had established themselves on the Ganges. A
comparison of the Veda with the book of Manu,

B

containing the sacred law of the Brahmans on the Ganges, marks a peculiar development among the Indians; and we arrive at a similar result by a comparison of the Zendavesta with the books and rites of the Magi or priests of the Medes in Mesopotamia, whereby a contrast is established between the Iranians of the East and those of the West.

These two hotbeds of priestcraft, cradles of hierarchical institutions and of asceticism in East and West, offer some important points of analogy, which render it at the outset not improbable that there was some kind of connection between the institutions on the banks of the Euphrates and Tigris, and those which prevailed in the valley of the Ganges. Both Indian communities, that on the Indus and that on the Ganges, worshipped Indra, as both the eastern and the western community of Iranians worshipped Ormuzd. Yet the Aryans on the Indus must have despised their brethren on the Ganges, as the East-Iranians certainly despised their brethren, the Magi or priests of the Medes, in the west of the Caspian. This was the country of wicked doubt; where the bodies of the dead, instead of being burnt in accordance with East-Iranian custom, were buried in the earth, thus desecrating it. Such separate development and antagonism is all the more significant, since the Medes were once all Aryans, and since they continued in the West to venerate the symbolism of the East-Iranians. Thus a system of dualism had sprung up, which in its popular form and interpretation militated against the monotheism of the Ormuzd religion, although the Magi recognised the same. The consideration of this parallel development among the Eastern Indians and among the Western Iranians is a necessary introduction to the history of the origin and propagation of Buddhism.

'The highest development of the Brahmanic system is based on the diametrical contrast of body and soul, of matter and spirit. Considering the body as impure by itself, Brahmanism was forced to set up, not only the demand of a continuous taming and subjecting of sensuality by the spirit, but to declare, in the last instance, the destruction of the body as the only true purity. From this theory, followed, practically, the injuring of the body by ascetic impossibilities. The Zendavesta does not know these premises. The Zendavesta likewise separates body and soul, the spiritual from the material world; also it is not wanting in abstraction, and those hosts of spirits who people heaven are, if taken by themselves, in part very deep-meaning conceptions of spiritual powers, although from the standpoint of a natural and poetical religious spirit they are pale allegories. But the Indian antagonism between the spiritual and the bodily world is unknown to the Zendavesta. The pure and holy spirits have created the world of the senses, not in order to entangle man in darkness and evil, but in order to give him life and prosperity. Here the evil is limited to only one side of this world of senses, to darkness, drought, desert, and death; whilst in India the evil spreads over the whole matter, and this bad side of nature has not emanated from the pure but from the impure spirits. Since, according to the Zendavesta, only a part of nature is separated as evil, man has not to put off his entire nature, but to rejoice in the good side of it, to strengthen the same in and around himself, and to observe a defensive, guarding, and fighting attitude against the evil side of nature only. Thus self-preservation, instead of self-destruction, is set up for man as his aim and end: thus practical and obtainable objects are held out to man; thus are given the conditions of a healthy and active human existence, which have led to other results, than those to which Indians have been led by the contemplation, the quietism, the monkish asceticism, and the relapses into sensuous excesses which are inseparably connected with the former.

In Iran no supernatural purity at the cost of life was aimed at, as in India; in Iran purity was practised in order to live, in order not to be harmed and killed by the Daeva (or evil spirit), but not in order to die as in India.'[1]

Among the Brahmans as among the Magi the intervention and mediation of priests was held to be necessary, and even in the law-book of Manu, still more in the later Sûtras or theological heirlooms, with their higher development of the ceremonial, the laity was absolutely excluded from every active participation in the sacred rites. In Hymns of the Rig-Veda are already mentioned priests on whose prayers victory was considered to depend. Contrariwise, the hymns attributed to Zoroaster know only of holy rites performed by pure men, and even the East-Iranian later tradition, which was recorded in the Zendavesta after the recognition of an order of priests, admits by the side of the Atharva, or fire-priests, all ' pure men ' to the performance of holy rites. The name Magi, by which the West-Iranian priests were called, is unknown to the ancient parts of the Zendavesta. We know of no Medes without Magi, and it is probable though not provable, that the Median conquerors of Mesopotamia, the Casdîm or Chaldeans, in the year B.C. 2458, already had Magi as priests. For already in the time of Dejokes, since B.C. 711, the Magi are connected with an old-established institution; whilst in the Book of Daniel the Magi are identified with the Chaldeans. Cyrus introduced or recognised the Magi among the Persians; yet these always regarded the Medes and Magi as their enemies, and the rule of Pseudo-Smerdis is represented as an attempt of the Magi to set up Median instead of Persian rule.

The Brahmanic and the Magian systems of religion both required the mediation of priests as organs of the supernatural power Maya or Maga; and these institu-

[1] Duncker, *Geschichte des Alterthums* ii., 387–388.

tions on the Ganges and Euphrates were based on the most ancient ancestorial rite of invoking the aid of good spirits against evil spirits. This would naturally lead to the offering of bloody sacrifices as a means of reconciling the offended deity. Human sacrifices and animal sacrifices for the purpose of atonement had prevailed in the earliest historical times among the Hamitic or non-Aryan races in East and West. By an ethnological and geographical explanation of the 10th chapter of Genesis, the Hamites, probably once an unmixed black-skinned race, can be shown to have spread from India, by Arabia, Egypt, Nubia, and Canaan, to Mesopotamia, as the earliest historical inhabitants of the West, an indefinite time before that country was conquered, according to Berosus in B.C. 2458, by the Medo-Chaldeans. It is provable that the mixed race of Iranian conquerors of Babylon and non-Iranian, probably Indian, builders of Babylon, that the first so-called Semitic nation of the West which rose to political power [1] did not abolish the bloody sacrifices, especially those at the time of the spring-equinox. Gradually animals were substituted for human beings. It is important to bear in mind, that these West-Iranian worshippers of Ormuzd, the Median conquerors or Chaldeans of Mesopotamia in the third pre-Christian millennium, did not teach, like their Zoroastrian brethren in the East, that bloody sacrifices are an abomination to the God of light and truth.

The Egyptian Book of the Dead and the Mesopotamian books on magic prove that in both countries magic art existed in remote ages. Copies of the Chal-

---

[1] Shem's birth, which we explain ethnically, was by Israelites held to have taken place in the year of this Median conquest, in B.C. 2458; for, according to Genesis, Shem was an hundred years old 'two years after the flood' (xi. 10), and the year of the Noachian flood was by the Hebrews, according to Censorinus and Varro, computed to have been B.C. 2360 (E. de Bunsen, *The Chronology of the Bible*, p. 11), Japhet + Ham = Shem. In fact, Japhet did dwell 'in the tents of Shem,' and Canaan the Hamite was his servant or slave. The Casdim were Medes and became Shemites.

dean work on magic were placed in the library of the famous school for priests at Erech (Huruk?) near Ur, the present Mugheir, in the low country near the Persian Gulf. Magic rites and the worship of elements can be proved to have preceded in Mesopotamia the connection of deities with stars, and therefore to have preceded the solar symbolism for a longer time. Yet sidereal religion prevailed in this country before the invention of writing, since the earliest symbol of a deity known to us was a star. Thus the deity Sibut, probably connected with the Pleiades, is determined by a star with the number seven by its side. Already, about B.C. 2000, Sargon I. compiled his astrological work, which began with collections of liturgical hymns and magical formulæ.[1] The sacrifice of children in Mesopotamia is by Inscriptions proved to have taken place before the time of Abraham,[2] and the belief in the atoning virtue of such offerings for sin must have been preceded by a belief in the virtue of magic rites. We are thus enabled to assert, that magic rites were introduced into Mesopotamia an indefinite time before Abraham.

Even in much later times, the Mesopotamian magician Balaam commenced his rite by sacrifice. The Mosaic law forbids practisers of divinations, workers of hidden arts, augurers, enchanters, fabricators of charms, inquirers by a familiar spirit, wizards or consulters of the dead, and the law couples with these ancient magic rites the condemnation of sons and daughters being offered by fire. Abraham himself, the son of Terah, was by Arabian tradition said to have been a maker of idols or teraphim, such as existed in the family of Laban, who even called them his gods, as Micah, the Levite, did later. It has been pointed out that the Egyptians connected their magic figure or mummy,

---

[1] Lenormant, *Chaldean Magic* (Cooper's edition), pp. 333, 369, Note 1.
[2] Sayce, *Trans. Bibl. Arch.* iv. 1.

their Shebtee, with the word 'Ter,' which in the pre-Semitic language of Egypt seems to have denoted an idol, what the Hebrews called a *tera*. This probability is almost raised to a certainty by the Arabian tradition just mentioned, which connects the son of Terah, a worshipper of strange gods, according to a Mosaic scripture, with teraphim or idols of his making. For the origin of such tradition would be inexplicable if the word 'ter' had not at some early time designated an idol in Arabian. This it certainly did in Egyptian, and also in Hebrew, as the word 'teraphim' denotes. The Egyptian word 'ter' signifies a shape, type, transformation, and has for its determinative a mummy; it is used in the Ritual, where the various transformations of the deceased in Hades are described. The small mummy-shaped figure, Shebtee, usually made of baked clay covered with a blue vitreous varnish, representing the Egyptian as deceased, is of a nature connecting it with magic, since it was made with the idea that it secured benefits in Hades. It is connected with the word 'ter,' for it represents a mummy, the determinative of that word, and was considered to be of use in the state in which the deceased passed through transformations, 'teru.'[1]

The belief in one God was probably imported into the West by the Medo-Chaldean conquerors who lived in Ur-Casdîm in the time of Terah and his ancestors. This belief would by the Hebrew of later times be opposed to the worship of 'other gods,' symbolised by teraphim or idols. Joshua declared Terah to have been such a worshipper of other gods, and the name Terah points to the teraphim or idols, which also his son Abram is said to have made according to the Arabian tradition already referred to. 'Thus saith the Lord God of Israel, Your fathers dwelt on the other side of the

---

[1] R. S. Poole, *Smith's Dictionary of the Bible*, 'Magic.'

flood in old time, even Terah, the father of Abraham, and the father of Nachor: and they served other gods.' This statement of Joshua confirms that of Moses, whose mother's name, Jokhebed, is a compound of the Jehovistic form 'Jo,' and to whom God revealed his name Jehovah, saying that by this name he 'was not known' to Abraham, Isaac, and Jacob, to whom he appeared by the name of El-Shaddai—God Almighty—literally, 'God Powerful.' Another passage shows that Abram 'lifted up his hand,' and swore, or literally 'did seven,' by Eljun or El-On, God the Highest.[1]

It may, therefore, be now asserted, that magic art was established in Mesopotamia an indefinite time before Terah, who lived, if the transmitted year B.C. 2360 was the year of the Flood, from B.C. 2138–1933. We may go further and safely assume that the invocation of spirits, perhaps originally the worship of ancestors, was connected with the worship of elements and of stars, and that what sooner or later was called 'magic art' had preceded the capture of Babylon, in B.C. 2458, by the Medes. For the purpose here in view it is enough to have pointed out that magic art existed in Mesopotamia before the time of Terah, who 'served other gods.'

Many centuries before the Vedic Hymns are supposed to have been written, in which there is no trace of priestcraft or magic art, the latter, whether under that name or not, was established in the West, possibly seventeen centuries earlier than the generally assumed date when the Vedic Hymns were recorded. The Aryans on the Indus neither imported any magic art

---

[1] Josh. xxiv. 2; Ex. vi. 2; Gen. xiv. 19–22; comp. Deut. xxxii. 6; Prov. viii. 22; Ps. cxix. 13. The name Osiris, derived from Wasar, means the elevated one or 'the Highest,' like the name Zeus of Homer and Hyperion of Hesiodus. All these names of divinities can be connected, like Sibut-Sebaot, with the Pleiades, so that the 'sevening' of Abram may be referred to the god dwelling in this constellation of seven stars (See our *Die Plejaden und der Thierkreis*, 80–81 &c.)

from the North-west, nor acknowledged the same among the subjugated non-Aryan population on the Indus. The aborigines of India may, however, be assumed to have long before the Aryan conquest worshipped elements, stars, and constellations, if not ancestors, and to have invoked good spirits against evil ones. What was sooner or later in the West called 'magic art' was probably on the Ganges in after-Vedic and Brahmanic times connected with the Brahm, or spiritual power, which was only another name for the Maya of the Buddhists.

Brahm, Maya, and Bodhi.

It remains quite uncertain at what time previous to the publication of the Law-book of Manu (about B.C. 700?) the Indian asceticism arose which was connected with the name of Brahma. The higher being who represents this divine power, or the Brahm, that is, the divine mediator, the Brahma, who hears man praying by this divine guide, was called Brâhmanaspati, or 'lord of prayer.' Even the highest God was regarded as an organ of this holy and eternal Brahm, and man can, though the same, secure the answer to his prayer, even immortality, for the spiritual power connects him with higher organs of the same.[1] The conception of this Brahm as the holy spirit of both worlds is essentially identical with the conception of the Maya or spiritual power. It can now be shown, as we shall see, that this supernatural or spiritual power is recorded to have descended as 'Holy Ghost' upon Maya, the virgin-mother of Gautama-Buddha. It may be safely assumed that the Magi in the West were aboriginally so called after the Maga or Maya; and it is quite possible that the Median tribe of the Budii

---

[1] Comp. Duncker, l. c. ii. 65, 66 ; Spiegel, *Zendavesta, Yaçna,* xix. 16-29; 32, 35.

were so called after the Bodhi or Wisdom taught on the Ganges.

The Bodhi, Wisdom from above, or Tradition from beyond, must be connected if not identified with the spiritual power or Maya, and thus with the universal spirit or Brahm. It has been well said, that 'Gautama's whole training was Brahmanism : he probably deemed himself to be the most correct exponent of the spirit, as distinct from the letter, of ancient faith ; and it can only be claimed for him that he was the greatest and wisest and best of the Hindus.'[1] Yet we shall point out, that there is sufficient reason to regard him as a non-Indian by descent. His probable connection with the East-Iranians is confirmed by the presumable fact, that the doctrines of Zoroaster were as well known by Gautama as by the initiated Hindus, though they hid this knowledge more or less from the people. As the incarnation of the celestial Buddha was effected by the Holy Ghost, so it was this spiritual power, Maya or Brahm, which enlightened Gautama, and made him the human organ of the celestial Bodhi or Wisdom. The meaning of the word 'Buddh,' or 'Bodh,' corresponds with that of the Sanscrit Vid, from which the name Veda is derived. 'Veda' means knowledge, and 'Bodhi' means wisdom. It seems that Gautama-Buddha was initiated in the secret tradition of this Bodhi; but there are only few traces in Buddhistic writings of such a hidden wisdom, and they leave it uncertain whether the novitiate of the later disciples dates from the time of Gautama. We know, however, that not all his self-chosen disciples were beggars or Bhikshus, though Sramans, or tamers of the senses. Their instruction varied probably in kind and quantity, according to their individual capabilities. Gautama was only accompanied by five disciples, when he underwent a severe probation of six years.

[1] Rhys Davids, *Buddhism*, 85.

The Eastern Pâramita and the Western Tradition.

The Buddhists distinguish two classes of tradition. They divide their theological heirlooms, in a restricted sense the transmitted sayings of Buddha, into Sûtras of the great and of the small chariot, thus distinguishing the Mahâyana from the Hinayana.[1] Possibly the chariot of tradition, or conveyance of enlightenment, referred to the sun, which is already in the Veda and Zendavesta connected with horses, whilst before the Babylonian captivity, chariots and horses of the sun were regarded as symbols of the Deity by some of the Israelites in Jerusalem. From indeterminable times the chariot of the sun-god Apollos was represented as drawn by four horses.

The Hebrew word for chariot, Rechab, from which the name of the Rechabites (Essenes?) is derived, is of Iranian origin, and it forms part of the word Merkabah, by which the unwritten tradition or gnosis of the Israelites was designated. The first part of the holy Merkabah was called ' The History of Creation,' and the second part, ' The History of the Chariot.' This twofold division in the record of Hebrew tradition may be compared with the twofold division in the records of Buddhistic tradition, that is, with the Sûtras of the great and of the small chariot. The Buddhists who belong to the higher grades of initiation in the mysteries of tradition, know and revere the Prashna Pâramita, literally the science, wisdom, or tradition ' from beyond.' Whilst Prashna means knowledge, wisdom, or Bodhi, Pâramita means brought ' from beyond.' The word is derived from 'para' and 'ita,' the former meaning 'across, over, or beyond,' and the latter word is formed after

[1] In course of time the Northern Buddhists called their developed tradition the Mahâyana, inasmuch as it differed from the shorter tradition of the Southern Buddhists, which their rivals called the Hinayana. The Lamaism of Thibet is the very opposite of original Buddhism, and may be connected with the schism created by Gautama's cousin Devadatta.

'emi,' to go.[1] The Latin word *traditio* has absolutely
the same meaning, being a composite of *trans*, across,
over, beyond, and *ire*, to go.

Thus a connection is established between the meaning of the Western word ' tradition ' and the meaning of
the Eastern word ' pâramita,' as also between the Hebrew
word ' merkabah ' for the unwritten tradition, and the
Sûtras, the once unwritten tradition of the Buddhists,
and of the Jainists, who preceded them. But as it is
non-proven that the new elements of tradition introduced by Jews after the return from Babylon, had been
already by Moses transmitted to the elders, and by
them to future generations, so it is not provable that
the followers of Buddha were in possession of a hidden
wisdom, verbally transmitted by Buddha, and even by
those who preceded him, in promulgating a Zoroastrian
tradition. The Buddhistic Pâramita or tradition was
designated as ' from beyond,' no doubt in order to
point to the super-terrestrial and supernatural origin of
its contents. It was, as we shall see, the wisdom from
above, brought down by the Angel-Messiah, the bringer
of the Spirit of God.

Jainism and Buddhism.

It is certain that the Buddhism which was connected with Gautama, constitutes a late development of
Jainism.[2] According to Jainas and Buddhists, the
words Jina and Buddha have the same meaning ; and
the last of the twenty-four Jaina Tîrthankaras or
Buddhas, called Mahâvîra, who died 527 B.C., is stated
to have been the teacher of the Gautama of the
Jainists, who is also the Gautama of the Buddhists.
But Gautama, who seems by some of his followers to
have been raised to the rank of a deified saint, was not
recognised by the Jainas as a Buddha. One and the

---

[1] Beal, *Buddhist Pilgrims*, 59.
[2] Thomas, *Jainism, or the Early Faith of Asôka*.

same person was by some in India regarded as an anointed man, by others as an anointed angel.

The five duties of Jainism are : mercy to all animated beings, almsgiving, venerating the sages while living and worshipping their images when deceased, confession of faults, and religious fasting. The five sins are : killing, lying, stealing, adultery, worldly-mindedness. Only the first five of the ten commandments of the Buddhists are by the text referred back to Gautama himself, and they forbid to kill that which has life, to steal, to lie, to drink intoxicating liquors, and to commit unchaste acts.[1] The nude statues of Jaina saints or Arhats have been connected with the Buddhist ascetics, whom the Chinese pilgrim, Hiouen Thsang, in the seventh century of our era, designated as a Buddhist sect in India. They did not entirely shave their heads, and walked naked, except when they wore a white covering, perhaps only during the performance of certain rites. So also the nude representations of Vittal or Vithoba, who in the Dekkan is held to be an avatar of Siva, have been compared with the normal ideals of the Jaina statues, as preserved by the sculptured monuments of Mathurá, with their appropriate devotional dedications by the votaries of the Jaina faith, ' at or about the commencement of our era.'[2]

The Sakas and Sâkya-Muni.

The Vittal or Viddhal to whom Buddhistic Scriptures refer, are supposed to have been connected with the Ephthalites, or White Huns of the Byzantines.[3] The Huns had still in late times white and black tribes, and the Ephthalites came from the Oxus and Indus. The

[1] The number five is provably a more ancient nature-symbol than the number ten.

[2] Thomas, l. c. 79–82.

[3] Mr. Wylie, cited in Beal's *Buddhist Tripitaka of China and Japan*, p. 117.

Hindus referred the name Huns to Thibetan tribes, and they were perhaps called Huns after Thibet. This name the Mahomedans have introduced, and the country of Thibet is still called Hundès, the word being probably derived from Hyun-dès, which means snow-land, like Himalaya, Imaus, and Emaus.[1] The white or Aryan Huns were always distinguished from the barbarous so-called Scythian or Sarmatian Huns.[2] The Aryan Huns were probably a cognate race with the Royal tribe (Amyrgian Scythians?) whom Herodotus distinguishes among the so-called Scythians or Sacæ, the Haka of the Chinese, and the Saka of Persian Inscriptions, whose principal seats seem to have been near the Oxus.

Like the Saka, the Parthians were, in part, perhaps chiefly Iranian Aryans. But the Parthians, the Parthwa in Inscriptions of Persian kings, when first mentioned by the Greeks, lived nearer to the Medes, to the east of them. Where the Parthians originally came from is uncertain, but it is not improbable that they had crossed the Indian frontier and lived in Iran as strangers. For Justin states that their name was derived from the Sanscrit Pardès, which means ' of another country,' or ' the country from beyond,' whilst in Iranian (Zend) Parda, like the Sanscrit Pârada, means a person who has come across the border.[3]

---

[1] Markham on 'Bogle in Thibet,' and the article 'Tibet,' in the *Times*, May 15, 1876.

[2] With 'Hun' the name Hun(g)ari may have been connected, as in like manner the name of the Gipsies, the Zigäuner, Zingari, or Singari, seems to have been a compound of Scind-Ari, which is still a local name in India. For their national name Sintè (also Roma) points to Scindia, Hindia, or India. It is certain from their language that the Gipsies are descended from Indian Aryans, that they are, as their name Singari implies, Scind-Ari; and the dispersion of the Gipsies has been identified with the chastisement of the Jat-tribes on the Indus by the Sultan of Ghazni, in the year A.D. 1025. (*Edinburgh Review*, July, 1878). Also the name Ar-Sakes probably points to the Aryans among the Saka.

[3] Benfey, in *Berliner Jahrbücher*, 1842 ; Spiegel's *Erân*, 105. The name

About the year 600 B.C. the so-called Scythians, or rather Sakas, made their inroads into India from the North, and gradually advanced to Mesopotamia and Asia Minor. 'King of the Sakas' was still in the first pre-Christian century a title in Northern India.[1] From these Iranian Sakas was most probably descended Sâkya- or Gautama-Buddha. Had the Sakas been natives of India it would be difficult to explain the fact that no Indian documents, except Buddhistic writings, ever mention them. The Sâkya-prince is described as an Aryan by Buddhistic tradition. His face was reddish, his hair of light colour and curly, his general appearance of great beauty. He married a wife from his own kin; and in harmony with the rites of Northern tribes, he was interred under a mound surrounded by stones.[2]

Records of Buddhistic Tradition.

Which were the fundamental principles of the 'Tradition from beyond,' said to have been promulgated by Gautama, according to the most ancient records known to us of the life of Buddha? We now possess a Chinese translation of a Sanscrit work on the life of Buddha, which is remarkable for brevity and completion. It is probably—in some of its essential parts at least—a translation of the original work or copy from which the expanded version was made, known in Thibet and China under the title 'Lalita-Vistara,' or Ta-Chwang-yen, 'great magnificence.' This primitive work, known under two forms of the same title, was translated into Chinese from Sanscrit, by a priest called Chu-fa-lan, as

Hebrews, or people from beyond (like 'Saracens'?), has the same meaning as Parthians. The Aryan word Pardès occurs in the Song of Solomon, in Ecclesiasticus, and Nehemiah. The authors of the Septuagint, who like Ezekiel (xxviii. 13, 14) connected Eden with the East, have formed from Pardès, or from the Sanscrit Paradeça, 'highland,' the word Paradise.

[1] Beal, On Buddhism, Orient, v. 47 f.
[2] Percy Gardner, Numismatic Chronicle, vol. xiv. 161–167.

early as the eleventh year of the reign of Wing-ping (Ming-ti) of the Han dynasty, that is, 69 or 70 A.D. 'We may, therefore,' says Professor Beal, 'safely suppose that the original work was in circulation in India for some time previous to this date.'

He adds, 'The (Buddhistic) books found in China afford us a consecutive catena of writings dating from at least B.C. 100 to A.D. 600.' In the Chinese copy of the Dhammapada or 'Parables illustrating scriptural extracts or verses,' composed by Ârya Dharmatrâta, that is Vasamîtra, about B.C. 40,[1] is the Sûtra alluded to by Asôka in the stone-cut Bhabra edict, and known as Gautama's exhortation to his son Râhula against falsehood.[2] It is therefore now proved that we possess a Chinese Buddhistic writing, part of which points back to the time of Asôka, who ascended the throne B.C. 268, and convoked the general council at Patna in B.C. 250.

This newly ascertained fact gains in importance when we consider that the stone-cut Bhabra edict refers to then existing records of well authenticated words of Buddha, and that the first Buddhist missionaries whom Asôka sent to China, where they are still reverenced as saints, can now be asserted to have introduced into this country these records of the divine Buddha's sayings to which Asôka's stone-cut edict refers. It becomes therefore increasingly probable that the stone-cut representations on the gateway of the Buddhist monument called the Sanchi Tope, probably copied from earlier wooden representations, and

---

[1] According to Eitel, Vasamîtra 'took a principal part in the last revision of the Canon, as the President of the Synod under Kanishka.' If the latter's date is about B.C. 40, that of Dharmatrâta would be about B.C. 70.

[2] Beal, *The Romantic History of Buddha*, p. vi.; *The Dhammapada*, p. xi. The reference to the Bhabra edict was first announced by Mr. Beal, in a lecture delivered by him since the publication of the *Dhammapada* (1878).

which refer to subjects treated by Buddhist legends, date from a pre-Christian time.[1]

A considerable part of the Buddhist legends transmitted to us by the most ancient Buddhist literature may be safely asserted to date back to pre-Christian times. This will become a certainty if we succeed in proving that the foreign elements represented by Jewish Essenes in pre-Christian times are in part, if not chiefly, Buddhistic. What was known in Judæa more than a century before the birth of Jesus Christ cannot have been introduced among Buddhists by Christian missionaries. It will become equally certain that the bishop and church-historian Eusebius was right when he wrote, that he considered it 'highly probable' that the writings of the Essenic Therapeuts in Egypt had been incorporated into our Gospels and into some Pauline Epistles.

---

[1] As asserted by General Cunningham, an opinion shared by the author of the *Guide Book to the Kensington Museum*, where a representation of this monument can be seen. The brick tope is traced to the years B.C. 500–443, the surrounding structure to B.C. 260, and the gates to A.D. 19–37.

CHAPTER II.

THE LEGENDS OF BUDDHA.

Buddha's birthday on Christmas-day—The Messianic Star—'He that should come'—Karma—Nirvâna is the Sun—Salvation by Faith—Incarnation of the Virgin-son by 'the Holy Ghost'—Krishna—'Birth in an inn' —Heavenly host proclaim joy and peace—Asita, the Simeon of Buddhists—Presentation in the Temple when twelve, and public teaching when thirty years old—Temptation by Satan in the wilderness—Buddha, 'full of grace,' his body surrounded by a 'glory,' 'fiery tongues,' two men represented by his side—The Lamb (Aries)—Trees of life and of knowledge—Baptism in the holy stream—Transfiguration, or 'baptism of fire' on a mount—No bloody sacrifices, &c.—Parable of the sower and the tares—The woman at the well—Promise of another Buddha—Miracles at Buddha's death—The tears of a weeping woman had wetted his feet before his death—How to explain the parallels between Buddhistic and Christian records—Continuity of Divine influences.

Buddha's Birthday on Christmas-day.

ACCORDING to Sanscrit and Chinese scriptures, to the stone-cut edicts of Aṣôka and the Sanchi Tope, certain legends about Buddha circulated in India and in China, not only before the close of the Apostolic age, but more than three centuries earlier. Among these legends the most ancient are those which refer to the incarnation of Buddha as Angel-Messiah.

Prophecies have directed the attention of men to the Tathâgatha, literally to 'Him that should come,' to 'the Anointed,' the Messiah or Kung-teng of the Chinese. The expectation of this Messiah and of the kingdom which he should set up is a general one. He will come from heaven, be born in the flesh, attested by miracles, bring to earth the highest wisdom from above, the Bodhi from beyond; he will establish a kingdom of heavenly truth and justice, live as a man, then die and return to heaven. Like his mother, he will be of royal, not of priestly descent, and genealogies will prove this. The Messiah inhabits the fourth or Tûsita-heaven, a certain locality described as a circle, and which is distinguished from 'the worlds above Tûsita,' thus also from the highest material heavens. Apart from all these, a non-material locality seems to be implied where the highest God dwells, to whom Buddha is said to have prayed, as to the self-dependent and creating God, Isvâra-Deva. So long as Buddha is in the Tûsita-heaven, he is not yet at the height of his development, and he looks forward to the time after his last birth, the birth on earth, when the ways will be open to him which lead to what is called Nirvâña, or destruction, but at the same time to the 'final resting-place of the spirit,' the locality to which men long to come, where 'the harvest' takes place.

We leave the question for the present as an open one, whether the Nirvâña was held to be or not the dwelling-place of the god to whom Buddha prayed, the man who as an Iraniah could not have beeñ an Atheist. But what is said about the non-material nature of the Nirvâna is also said about Isvâra-Deva, 'the universal spirit,' later called 'all the Buddhas,' about the absolutely immaterial spirit, who is so uñlike Buddha before his incarnation—absolutely independent of all influences of matter, being the Mahâ-Brahma, to whose 'bright body' Buddha will resemble. Buddha is yet exposed to these material influeñces even in the fourth heaven, which comparative 'glory' he is resolved to give up for a time in order to attaiñ his final birth, that in the flesh.[1]

In accordance with recorded Zoroastrian doctrines, Gautama seems to have believed and taught, that 'the good and most holy Father of all truth' is the source of the supernatural light, of the spiritual power, wisdom,

---

[1] *Romantic History of Buddha*, pp. 24, 77, 113.

or Bodhi, and thus of the moral element in man. Gautama was considered by his followers to have been a chosen instrument of that Divine power, as Angel and as Man. The Divine Wisdom, personified by the heavenly Buddha, becomes man, according to Iranian tradition, and it had a pre-mundane personal existence according to Zoroastrian and to Buddhistic records. It is owing to this Divine power which is in the incarnate Buddha, that with uplifted eyes, and turned to the East, he can pray to the highest Spirit, and be at one with him. It is only as the highest organ of the spiritual power, proceeding from the highest Spirit, that Gautama could be by some conceived as the source of the world. He was called its developer, and was in this sense identified with Isvâra-Deva, the Creator, to whom he prayed.

At a certain time, which is not clearly defined, Gautama was established 'in the condition of a Buddha, free for ever from the possibility of sorrow and pain, and was therefore named Djina (the vanquisher), possessed of all wisdom, versed in the practice of it, perfectly acquainted with it, firmly grounded in the ways of heaven and in the ways of purity and holiness, possessed of independent being, like all the lords of the world (all Buddhas), ready to accommodate himself to all possible circumstances.'[1] As a spirit in the fourth heaven, he resolves to give up 'all that glory, in order to be born in the world,' for the purpose 'to rescue all men from their misery and every future consequence of it'; he vows 'to deliver all men, who are left as it were without a saviour.' He is called 'the great Physician,' Healer or Saviour, the Bhagavat or 'Blessed One,' the Saviour of the World, the 'God among gods.'[2]

The time of this heavenly Buddha's incarnation is marked by various statements. It is asserted to have

---

[1] *Rom. Hist.*, 278, 2, 53, 76, 130, 133.

[2] Thus also Serosh was identified with Ormuzd and the Divine Word, Memra of the Targumim with Jehovah.

taken place on the eighth day of the second month of spring : we hope to prove conclusively that this is our Christmas-day.

In his treatise on the Vedic Calendar Jyotisham, Weber justly complains that all former works on Indian astronomy are based on such documents as were composed after that the last development of astronomy in India had been reached. The comparison of the most ancient calendars known to us has led Mr. R. G. Haliburton, of Nova Scotia, to prove, that a New Year's festival connected with and determined by the Pleiades was, by almost universal custom, and partly in times called pre-historic, connected with a three days' festival of the dead. It corresponded with the Christian festivals of All Saints and All Souls, at the beginning of November, and was preceded in some countries by a holy evening or Halloween.[1] At first it was the appearance of the Pleiades at sunset, later their culmination at midnight, which determined the commencement of the year. According to the calendar of the Brahmans of Tirvalore the year began in November, and the first month was called after the Pleiades Cartiguey or Krittikâs. The latter name Weber has shown to mean ' the associates,' those who are bound together, the heap, whilst the Hebrew word for the Pleiades, Kimâh, has exactly the same meaning. Also, the first of the Naxâtras, of the stellar houses or stations of the moon, was marked by the Pleiades.

This Indian year, determined by the Pleiades, began with the 17th of November, approximatively at the time of the Pleiades culminating at midnight, and this commencement of the year was celebrated by the Hindû Durga, a festival of the dead. Mr. Haliburton has

---

[1] Haliburton, *New Materials for the History of Man*, partly quoted by Professor Piazzi Smyth, and more fully examined and explained in *Astronomical Myths*, pp. 111–137, by the Rev. T. F. Blake. Comp. E. v. Bunsen, *Die Plejaden und der Thierkreis, oder das Geheimniss der Symbole,*

shown that on the 17th of November, or Athyr—the
Athyr of the Egyptians and Atauria of the Arabs—the
three days' feast of the Isia took place, which culminated
in the finding of Osiris, the lord of tombs, evidently
contemporaneously with the culmination of the Pleiades,
at midnight.   It was on that same day, in the second
month of the Jewish year, which corresponds with our
November, that Noah shut himself up in the ark,
according to Genesis; that is, on the same day when
the image of Osiris was by the priests shut up in a
sacred coffer or ark.   According to Greswell, this new
year's commemoration on the 17th of November obtained among the Indians in the earliest times to which
Indian calendars can be traced back.   It is sufficient for
our argument, that its commencement can be proved
long before the birth of Gautama-Buddha.

If the 17th of November was New Year's-day, the
second month commenced on the 17th of December,
and 'the eighth day,' Buddha's birthday, was the 25th
of December, the sun's annual birthday, when the
power of the sun ceases to decrease and again begins to
increase.[1]   The text in Buddhistic writings we are considering presupposes the commencement of the year on
the 17th of November, and thus points to the 25th of
December.   This is confirmed by another statement
in the same scripture.   At the time of Buddha's birth,
'the asterism Chin was passing and the asterism Koh
was coming on.'   Evidently this refers to the contemporaneous rising and setting of certain stars on opposite
sides of the horizon.   In the assumed but uncertain

---

[1] According to the Christian calendar the birthday of John the Baptist
is on the day of the summer solstice, when the sun begins to decrease. The
words attributed to him in the Fourth Gospel, that he must decrease and
Jesus increase, may be referred to this connection of the respective birth-
days of John and of Jesus with the summer and the winter solstice. As there
are six months between this change in the sun's position, so, according to
the Gospel after Luke, the Baptist was exactly six months younger than
Jesus.   (Luke i. 24.)

year of Buddha's birth, 625 B.C., in the latitude of
Benares, on the 25th of December, and at midnight,
when according to prophecies the birth of the Anointed
One was expected, 'the point of the ecliptic rising
above the horizon was very close to the star λ Virginis,
whilst the stars α and ξ of this sign had already risen
some distance. At this time the point of the ecliptic
setting was in Aries, nearly in the same longitude as
Hamal, α Arietis, the nearest visible star being μ Ceti.'
The whole of Shin (Chin) had set at that hour in latitude 25°. Pisces had also entirely set; and the lunar
mansion immediately above the western horizon was the
one numbered 16 in Williams's list (Sen or Sin ?).[1] It
would seem, therefore, that this asterism Sen was the
one meant in one Buddhist record, where it is called
Chin. On this supposition the two asterisms mentioned
as coming and going at the time of Buddha's birth
would both be correctly referred to. But it is enough
for our argument that an asterism in Virgo is clearly
stated as coming on or rising on the horizon at that
time, for the sign of Virgo was certainly rising on the
eastern horizon at midnight on the 25th of December in
the year 625 B.C., as seen in the latitude of Buddha's
birthplace. The position of the sphere would not be
materially altered in any of the possible other dates of
Buddha's birth.

Thus it is not proved that Gautama-Buddha was
really born on the 25th of December, or rather at midnight on the 24th, at the dawn (Maya) of the first day
of the new solar year; but it is proved, that the birth
of the Angel-Messiah, whose symbol was the Sun, was
expected and asserted to have actually taken place at
this time, that is, on the eighth day of the second
month of the year which was computed to begin on the
17th of November.

---

[1] Kindly communicated by Mr. Proctor. See Williams's *Map of Chinese
Asterisms.*

Buddhistic records imply that Buddha was born at the time of the sun's annual birthday, of its entry into the sign of the winter solstice, when its apparent evolution round the earth re-commences. The Cosmical was regarded as the symbol of the Ethical, the sun as the symbol of divine light, of which Gautama the enlightened was believed to be a chosen instrument. The solar Messianic symbol is thus proved to be more ancient than the time of Buddha's birth. The sun was the symbol of Gautama-Buddha and of Jesus Christ, who is described as ' the sun of righteousness' and as ' the day-spring from on high.' This common symbolism may help to explain several parallels in Buddhistic and in Christian records. Here we have only to point out, that as on the transmitted day of Buddha's birth, so on Christmas-day the constellation of the sphere rising on the Eastern horizon is that of the Virgin, represented as holding the new-born Sun-God in her arms, and followed by the Serpent, who aims at her heel and almost touches it with its open mouth. The symbolism of the sphere on Christmas-day points to Isis with her infant Horus ; to the virgin Maya with her infant Buddha ; and to the Virgin Mary with her infant Jesus, described in the Apocalypse of John as persecuted by the old serpent, the Devil.

Are these and other similar coincidences a mere chance, or have the respective traditions originated in a common source, and is that source a Divine Revelation ?

The Angel who is to become Buddha.

We have shown that among a certain circle of Indians, prophecies were accredited which announced the incarnation of an Angel, called the Anointed or Messiah, who should bring to earth the Wisdom or Bodhi from above and establish the kingdom of heavenly truth and justice. He would be of royal descent, and genealogies would connect him with his ancestors. ' The Blessed One,' the ' God among Gods,' and the ' Saviour of the World,' was, according to Buddhistic records, incarnate by the Holy Ghost of the royal virgin Maya, and he was born on Christmas-day, the birthday of the sun, for which reason the sun became the symbol of Gautama-Buddha.

The angel, whose time of incarnation is astronomically fixed, knows by the position of the stars, that his time is come to descend to earth, as organ of Divine enlightenment, of the Wisdom from above, of the Tradition from beyond the Prashna Pâramita. The Bodhisatva, or next candidate for the Buddha dignity, the Tathâgatha, He that should come, has fulfilled his years in the heavenly dwelling-place as Deva or Spirit, the Kung-teng, the Anointed or Messiah, is about to be born in the flesh. Sadness prevails among his fellow-spirits, because of his approaching departure. One of his companions is consoled by the consideration, that they can attain the privilege of descending to the earth, in order to see the place where Buddha is to be born. Another expresses his wish that his years in the place he inhabits were passed, so that he might be born with him on earth. Again another spirit says: ' Let not your heart be afraid, he will come again.' Finally, one of Buddha's associates addresses the departing one in these words : ' Mahâ Parusha,' great soul, or great Lord, ' do not forget us.' In his parting address the heavenly Buddha says, that birth and death are the cause of all parting, that his fellow-spirits need not be sad about him. For in course of time he had become possessed of a certain condition or Karma, in consequence of his having ' always prepared his heart for the possession of the highest wisdom, by constant vows and prayers,' and that this Karma guards him from a long sojourn in the world.

On the real meaning of ' Karma,' different opinions

among the interpreters of Buddhism prevail. It has been defined as ' a connecting link, a bridge between one life and another,' and yet not as the soul, which Buddhism is held not to acknowledge. Karma is explained to be the doctrine, that as soon as a sentient being dies, whether angel, man, or animal, a new being is produced in a more or less painful and material state of existence, according to the Karma, desert or merit, of the being who had died. Karma is a moral cause, and never dies. From one point of view Karma ' has much analogy with soul ; and from another it is a name given to the moral power working in the universe.[1] We submit that this moral power must be identified with ' the spiritual power ' or Maya, which is also called ' Holy Spirit.' It is this power in heaven and earth which is said to have guarded Buddha from a long sojourn in the world, and which enabled him to fix his heart on what is not material, and finally to enter Nirvâna. Whether Karma be regarded as conscience, or as instinct, in either case it might be connected, more or less directly, with the ' Holy Spirit ' or ' Word,' through which, according to Iranian tradition, the highest God communicates his mysteries to reasonable beings in heaven and earth.

' This, his body,' which Buddha has ' not yet been able to cast off,' though in heaven, would be born in the world, but soon he would receive perfect liberation from all matter in the Nirvâna. ' I now am about to assume a body (Shan-yeou), not for the pleasure of gaining wealth or enjoying the pleasures of sense, but I am about to descend and be born among men (to take " this one birth ") simply to give peace and rest to all flesh, and to remove all sorrow and grief from the world.' The body which Buddha possessed in heaven before his incarnation he was then about ' to quit for

---

[1] Rhys Davids, *Buddhism*, 101-103, 150.

ever.' But later recorded tradition implies, that after the incarnation Buddha would assume another body, the 'spotless and pure,' Dharmakâya, which, in 'the final resting-place of the spirit,' in the Nirvâna he would possess under different circumstances, and 'long after' the human body has passed away. In one of the ancient Gâthâs or hymns, 'the deliverance' (in Nirvâna) is connected with the obtaining of 'a body free from contamination,' that is, free from all material influences, a spiritual body.[1]

Nirvâna is the Sun.

Buddha is described as leaving the fourth heaven, Tûsita, but from this locality, as from all material heavens or Rupa, the highest of which is called Akanishta, is distinguished the Nirvâna. We submit that the mysterious Nirvâna or 'annihilation,' refers to the place where 'all matter' is supposed to be annihilated, that is, to the Sun.

According to Buddhist conception, within the circle of the soul's migrations from one material body to another, one and the same law rules, that is, the deeds of the past life of the soul in a material prison act upon another existence of the soul in the veil of matter. From this never-varying law of rewards and punishments, no escape for reasonable beings is possible; except by continually fixing the mind and the heart on the final destruction of all material influences. These prevent the liberation of the soul from successive births and deaths, and hinder the entrance of the soul into Nirvâna. The soul is the breath or spirit from the spiritual world, which is separated from the material world by a great gulf. The light from the spiritual world, from its centre, shines in a dark place, as the

[1] *Rom. History*, 26, 33, 34, 130, and Beal's *Buddhist Pilgrims*, 400 A.D. and 518 A.D.

glory or Shechina, symbolised by the sun, shone in the darkness of the Holiest of the Holy.

The Buddhists seem originally to have conceived the locality of Nirvâna in a manner similar to the Christian's conception of God's abode, as a place where, as in the sun, there is 'neither variableness nor shadow of turning.' The Nirvâna seems to have been regarded as a locality which, like the sun, does not appear to revolve around other bodies. The Buddhists may be assumed to have regarded Nirvâna as the non-material centre of the universe, and source of light. Since the orbit of bodies in space forms the basis of the doctrine of transmigrations of souls, the sun, as the supposed immaterial centre of these bodies which appear to rotate round this luminary, could be regarded as the appropriate symbol of the Nirvâna, 'the last resting-place of the spirit,' which has then been freed from the ever-returning cycles of birth and death, and returns to its home.

Thus the idea would suggest itself to regard the sun as the purely spiritual and immaterial dwelling-place of the self-dependent, world-creating spirit, Isvâra-Deva, to whom Buddha prayed with uplifted eyes. His system of morality, which he could not connect with the gods of the Brahmans, must have acknowledged a non-terrestrial, spiritual source of moral Providence, unknown to Brahmanism, at least as publically proclaimed. Gautama is recorded to have regarded the origin of the soul, which Brahmanism vaguely connected with Brahma, as beyond human comprehension. But he cannot have separated the soul from the highest spirit, to whom he prayed. The spiritual body of the Arhats, of the righteous, or saints, is to be like the shining body of Brahma ; they shall shine like the sun when they have entered Nirvâna.

In the most ancient Buddhistic writings two essentially different explanations of the Nirvâna are given. On the one side it is described as the end of all existence, even as the extinguishing of a flame, as a cessation of thought. But in other passages it is described as the place of peace, of an existence without births and deaths, as 'a place of repose,' to be enjoyed by the conquerors in the material world—that is, as we may assume, by the souls who have conquered over matter, and who are to enjoy a non-material, a spiritual body. The Nirvâna can only be reached by inward growth, by 'the path of wisdom'; to which way of everlasting life is opposed the way which leads to 'the power and dominion' which the evil spirit, the god of the material world, exercises, and which is to be destroyed. From this it may be concluded, that Nirvâna was connected with the kingdom of the good and bright spirit, with the abode of the self-dependent god, Isvâra-Deva.

Nirvâna is the highest aim, the highest reward of the wandering soul, the place from whence it came and whither it returns, the place of the heavenly harvest, according to a simile of Gautama, to which we shall presently refer. In some of the most ancient Buddhist records, in the Jâtakas or stories, in the Gâthâs or songs which Sâkya is said to have recited, and which show some relations to the Gâthâs of Zoroaster in the Zendavesta, the Nirvâna is described, though not exclusively of other views, as the final resting-place of spiritual beings. Buddha is recorded to have said that he saw individuals in Nirvâna, and many holy men are mentioned by name 'who entered into the brightness of the sun, and attained the straight path.' Their desire is fulfilled, and they 'abide for ever in the true eternal law'; they dwell in 'the only truly great one of the three worlds.' The 'condition of Nirvâna,' to be desired above all things, is contrasted to 'all earthly things,' which are 'perishable.' The narrow path leads to 'the shore of Nirvâna,' to 'the ever constant condition,' to 'the nectar of true religion,' to immortality. Nirvâna is identified with 'the opening of the pure ways of heaven,' of the 'gates of eternal life,' and is actually called the sun, and 'the centre of the supernatural light.'[1]   Thus the immortality of the soul in Nirvâna is clearly acknowledged.   Nirvâna is the place of the in-gathering, the heavenly garner for the ripened fruit sown in the material world : it is the sun as the region of eternal life.

The explanation of Nirvâna as the sun is confirmed by the presumable identity of the sun-god Abidha with the highest spirit, Isvâra-Deva, who thrones in Nirvâna, and also by the direct connection of Buddha with Nirvâna as well as with the sun.   The sun is the symbol of Buddha, who is represented as a ram or lamb—that is, as the stellar symbol of the spring-equinox in his time, as the Sun in Aries.   This interpretation is all the more ad-missible, as we have proved that, according to Buddhistic records, Gautama-Buddha's birth was expected, and had taken place, on the sun's annual birthday.   Again, the connection of the locality of Nirvâna with the sun is confirmed by what seems to have been the aboriginal meaning of the ' four paths ' which lead to Nirvâna, and which we may now connect with the 'four kings ' and the four cardinal points of the Zodiac, with 'the four quarters of the world,' towards each of which the new-born Gautama-Buddha is said to have advanced seven steps.   Buddhists describe Abidha as the god of light (of the sun), as surrounded by four mysterious beings, which form a striking analogy to the four cherubim and four beasts of the Hebrew and Christian Scriptures.

The enemy of the sun-god Abidha is the ' king of death ' and the dwelling-place of Abidha, the king of life, is Nirvâna, from which it follows that the sun was by Buddhists identified with Nirvâna.   In this locality there is neither darkness nor death : ' To be

[1] *Romantic History*, 9, 121, 130, 251. 253, 199, 200, 208, 212, 215, 217; comp. 175, 219, 225.

and not to be, how can this be united in One, how can this be Nirvâna? These two conditions have nothing in common; can darkness and light be united?' As in the sun, so in Nirvâna there is no darkness, no death. As the sun was regarded to be the source of the vital and enlightening spiritual power and of the highest wisdom, as throne of the god of light, so it is the longing of all sons of the Wisdom from above, of the Bodhi or spiritual power, of the Maya or Brahm, whose chief organ Gautáma was, to reach 'the way and the place' into which 'all Buddhas' have entered.[1]

At the same time the word 'Nirvâna' is used to describe a spiritual condition, a 'condition of moral rest,' of which Gautama had received a foretaste whilst on earth, since he possessed the Prashna Pâramita, the Wisdom or Bodhi, the Tradition 'from beyond.' For this reason he was 'in possession of complete spiritual life,' being 'perfected,' and having, in a spiritual sense, 'reached Nirvâna.' His flesh was, therefore, not at enmity with the spirit within the same; and because the opposing principle in himself had been overcome by the required free determination of his will, therefore his liberation from the circle of birth and death took place, and 'through eternity' he was to receive no more 'migratory existence,' but the enduring existence, eternal life in Nirvâna. It follows from these and similar passages that even the personal existence in the flesh did not prevent Gautama entering, during his sojourn on earth, into that spiritual condition which in the highest and abiding sense was connected with Nirvâna as the 'centre of supernatural light' and the 'brightness of the sun.' If therefore in isolated passages Gautama is recorded to have said that after the

[1] Comp. Beal, *Congress of Orientalists*, 1874, p. 155; *Rom. Hist.* 251. Abidha seems to be only another name for Amithâba, the god of boundless light, said by Northern Buddhists to inhabit the Paradise of the West, and for Adi-Buddha of the Nepaulese (Eitel, *Buddhism*, second edition, 98 f., 116 f.

birth of Bodhi in him he at once obtained deliverance, and that hereafter there would be ' no more individual existence,' no more ' bhava,' this expression, the exact meaning of which is doubtful, can only be referred to his body in the flesh, as the last of material bodies. From the ' bhava' must be distinguished the spotless and pure ' dharmakâya,' the spiritual body, in ' the final resting-place of the spirit,' in Nirvâna. This celestial body the Buddhist expects to possess under different circumstances, long after ' the human body' has passed away, after the end of the soul's transmigrations, which only in the exceptional cases of incarnate angels like Buddha were regarded as having come to an end with the life on earth. The body in the flesh was regarded by Gautama, according to the texts, as one of five finite existences, the five Skhandha, of which he is recorded to have said: ' It is impossible to say that either of these is " I," that is âttâ or âtmâ, the " self," which being in its germ of heavenly origin, cannot be identified with any one of the soul's material embodiments. The soul of man is intended finally to be in a body like that of Gautama, which is described as resembling " the bright body" of Brahma, " a body free from contamination," and which alone can " cross over to the shore" of Nirvâna, which body alone can reach the " heavenly land of the Arhats," and the " lake of Ambrosia which washes away all sin." ' [1]

To be like Gautama is to reach the ideal which has been set to humanity, and to be like God. Salvation does not depend on any outward act; but on a change or renewal of the mind, on a reform of the inner nature, on faith in the innate guiding power of God, of which the celestial Buddha incarnated in Gautama was held to be the highest organ. The saving faith, therefore, was brought by and centred in the incarnate Angel-Messiah, the Saviour of the world. Thus also the Hindus held,

---

[1] *Romantic History*, 253–256, 234, 138, 77; Rhys Davids, *l.c.*, 148.

certainly those of later times, that their ancient belief in the doctrine of ' salvation by faith ' or 'bhakti' centred in the God-man, Krishna, one of the incarnations of the Deity. Salvation is by faith, and faith comes by the Maya, the Spirit or Word of God, of which Buddha, the Angel-Messiah, was regarded as the divinely chosen and incarnate messenger, the vicar of God, and God himself on earth.[1]

Conceived by the Holy Ghost, born of the Virgin Maya.

The incarnation of the Angel destined to become Buddha took place in a spiritual manner. The elephant is the symbol, as of the sun, so of power and wisdom ; and Buddha, symbolised by the sun, was considered the organ of divine ' power and wisdom,' as he is called in the ' Tikas.' For these reasons Buddha is described by Buddhistic legends as having descended from heaven in the form of an elephant to the place where the virgin Maya was. But according to Chinese-Buddhistic writings, it was the ' Holy Ghost,' or ' Shing-Shin,' which descended on the virgin Maya. The effect produced by this miracle is thus summed up in the most ancient Chinese life of Buddha which we at present possess ; translated between A.D. 25 and 190 : ' If the child born from this conception be induced to lead a secular life, he shall become a universal monarch ; but if he leave his home and become a religious person, then he shall become Buddha, and shall save the world.'[2]

Gautama had himself chosen Maya for his mother among the daughters of men, when in the fourth heaven he had seen, guided by astronomical signs,

---

[1] Monier Williams, *Hinduism*, 115, 136, 216–209. The Maya, or Holy Ghost of the Buddhists may be safely identified as with the Brahm, so with the original eternal element or Prâkriti, from which the world proceeded according to the system of Sânkhya, well known to Gautama.

[2] Communicated by Prof. Beal ; comp. Beal, *Tripitaka*, 160.

by a Messianic star, that the time for his incarnation had come. Having seen the Messianic constellation, the Angel-Messiah at once chose his parents in the flesh. His choice fell on the King of Kapilavastu and his virgin-bride Maya or Mayadevi. She was so called after Maya, the spiritual, creative and enlightening power of Indian tradition, after the Bodhi or Wisdom from above, the power, word, or spirit, the Brahm of the highest God. This power of the Highest, 'the Holy Ghost,' was to surround her, and thus 'the holy mother' was to give birth to 'the holy son.'

The virgin Queen of Kapilavastu, in the tenth month after her heavenly conception, was on a journey to her father, called Supra-Buddha-Grihapati, living in the city of Devadaho, and she had reached the Lumbini Garden, but according to other accounts she was only halfway in a forest, where she had alighted in an inn, when Buddha was born. The birth took place under 'two golden trees'—under the Bodhi-tree, Palasa, the acacia, originally the fig-tree, symbol of knowledge, and under the Aṣôka-tree, the tree of life. Among the thirty-two signs which were to be fulfilled by the mother of the expected Messiah, the fifth sign was recorded to be, that she would be on a journey at the time of her childbirth.[1] Resting under the Palasa-tree, Maya was thus addressed by 'the heavenly women' who surrounded her : 'The Queen now brings forth the child, able to divide the wheel of life and death;[2] in

---

[1] The thirty-two signs refer to thirty-two deities, headed by Indra, who is the thirty-third, that is eight Vasas, eleven Rudras, twelve Adityas, and two Aswins. There were also eighty signs of secondary importance. The number thirty-two represents the half of the number sixty-four, which, together with the holy number eight, constituted the holy numbers of Chinese tradition before the time of Confucius and Buddha. These numbers added together represented the ancient astronomical cycle of seventy-two, based on the observation, which was not quite correct till much later, that in seventy-two solar years the precession amounts to one day. (Comp. E. v. Bunsen, *Die Plejaden und der Thierkreis*.)

[2] That is, able by a miracle to interrupt the continuous cycle of births and deaths, to enter Nirvâna, the sun, which seems to pass by the twelve zodiacal Nidânas.

heaven and earth no teacher can equal him; able to
deliver both Devas and men from every kind of sorrow:
let not the Queen be distressed, we are here to support
her.' Thereupon Bodhisatwa, perceiving his mother
Maya standing on the ground, with a branch of the
tree in her hand, 'with conscious mind, arose from his
seat and was born.' The attending spirits exclaimed:
'All joy be to you, Queen Maya, rejoice and be glad,
for this child you have borne is holy.' He forthwith
'walked seven steps towards each quarter of the
horizon, and, looking first to the East, he pronounced
the words of the Gâthâ: 'In all the world I am the
very chief, from this day forth my births are finished.'

The 'Saviour of the world,' or 'the Blessed One of
the world,' the Bhagavat, the 'only begotten' Bodhisatwa, is born in the presence of the highest God, of
Indra, the King of kings, and of Brahma. This event
is attested by miracles. Whilst 'the sun and moon are
darkened and deprived of their light,' there is 'a divine
light diffused round his person,' so that the Queen's son
was 'heralded into the world by a supernatural light.'
Then 'the Rishis and Devas who dwelt on earth
exclaimed with great joy: This day Buddha is born
for the good of men, to dispel the darkness of their
ignorance. Then the four heavenly kings took up the
strain and said: Now because Bodhisatwa is born, to
give joy and bring peace to the world, therefore is
there this brightness. Then the gods of the thirty-
three heavens took up the burthen of the strain, and
the Yama Devas and the Tûsita Devas, and so forth,
through all the heavens of the Kama, Rupa, and Arupa
worlds, even up to the Akanishta heavens, all the
Devas joined in this song and said: To-day Bodhisatwa
is born on earth, to give joy and peace to men and
Devas, to shed light in the dark places, and to give
sight to the blind.'[1]

[1] *Romantic History*, 43–56.

D 2

A holy One, a Rishi, called Asïta or Kâla, the ' Black One,' dwelling at peace above the thirty-three heavens,' seeing celestial signs, and hearing the celestial song, descended to the grove, ' where he usually dwelt on earth.' But, according to other accounts, he was a Tapaso or ascetic, from the Himalaya, called Kâla-devalo, which name corresponds with that of Asïta. He gets to Kapilavastu, where Maya tries to make the child bow its head in reverence towards the feet of Asïta. But the child, ' by his spiritual power, turned himself round in his mother's arms, and presented his feet towards the Rishi, who begged to worship his feet.' Then Asïta, unbearing his right shoulder and bending his right knee to the ground, took the child in his arms, and, returning to his seat, rested on his knees. He declared, that ' with the deepest reverence of body and mind,' he took refuge in and submitted to the child. ' Doubtless this child by his Divine wisdom, is completely acquainted with all events, past and future, and will therefore be able to preach the law,' after having become ' completely inspired,' that is, after thirty-five years. Asïta, being of an advanced age, deplores that he is too old to hear himself the Messianic proclamation of the pure law. He returns, rejoicing, to his mountain-home, for his eyes have seen the promised and expected ' Saviour.' [1]

Maya's death took place on the seventh day after the child's birth, when she was ' translated at once ' to heaven, whence she occasionally descends to comfort men. The holy son is placed under the care of a chosen stepmother, Mahâ-Prajâpati, the virgin's son having neither brothers nor sisters. ' The royal prince's

---

[1] *Romantic History*, 54-62. The paintings in the Cave of Ajunta repre-sent Asita with the child in his arms. It is curious, that whilst this Simeon of the Buddhists is called the Black, a Simon-Niger is mentioned in the Acts among the prophets of the Antiochian Church, which we shall connect with Essenes, as these with Buddhists.

foster-mother sedulously attended him without inter-
mission, as the sun attends on the moon during the first
portion of each month, till the moon arrives at its
fulness. So the child gradually waxed and increased
in strength; as the shoot of the Nyagrodha-tree gradually
increases in size, well planted in the earth, till itself
becomes a great tree, thus did the child day by day
increase, and lacked nothing.' This tradition seems to
be very old, as Buddha is compared to the growing
moon,[1] not to the sun growing in strength, the birthday
of which is described, perhaps by relatively later
tradition, as the birthday of Buddha. When the sun
had become Buddha's symbol, and when the tradition
about his life on earth referred to him as ' the glory of
the newly risen sun,' the mother's symbol must have
been changed from the moon to the sun.[2]

Presentation in the Temple and Temptation in the Wilderness.

Up to his eighth year the prince lives in the royal
palace, without receiving any tuition, but from the
eighth to the twelfth year masters are given him. When
twelve years old, the child is presented in the temple,
on which occasion forthwith all statues rise and throw
themselves at his feet, even the statues of Indra and
Brahma.[3] ' He explains and asks learned questions ;
he excels all those who enter into competition with
him.' Yet he waits till he has reached his thirtieth
year before teaching in public surrounded by disciples.

---

[1] According to one of the sacred histories, or Itihâsas, in the Mahâbhârata,
a certain Buddha is called Son of the Moon, and his son was Parûravas, who
introduced the three fires of sacrifice, according to the Rig-Veda, (Duncker,
ii. 35). The holy seventh days of the Buddhists, the Uposatha, refer to
the moon, and are the four days in the lunar month when the moon is full,
or new, or halfway between the two. (Rhys Davids, l.c. 140.)

[2] Comp. the connection of the moon with the child's mother in the Apocalypse of John.

[3] This latter feature is not recorded in the Lalita-Vistara.

'Seeing all flesh weighed down by sorrow, oppressed by the weight of false teaching and heretical beliefs, he thought, how difficult to release them by declaring this inscrutable law of mine! thinking thus, he desired to remain as a solitary hermit (âranya).' According to another account, he left the palace when twenty-eight years old, spent seven years in the wilderness, and not till his thirty-fifth year, having then learnt perfect wisdom, as Asīta predicted, did he become a public teacher. 'The child of heavenly birth is thoroughly acquainted with the human heart,' he has 'arrived at perfect righteousness,' and can now fulfil his 'destiny,' which is 'to establish the kingdom of the highest truth upon earth,' that is, 'the kingdom of righteousness.' Buddha has come 'to deliver man from doubt and fear,' and he is recorded to have said: 'My heart enlightened, I desire to enlighten others.'[1]

It was at Rajagraha, near Patna, and at Savastu that Gautama began publicly to teach. During the rainy season he withdrew with his disciples to the Gardens of Kalanda and of Jeta, and he seems generally to have avoided the cities. The number of his disciples had soon risen to sixty, and he sent them in different directions to preach. Before Gautama can fulfil his desire 'to open the gates of everlasting life,' to prepare men for immortality, he must destroy death by conquering over the God of death. Gautama is now able to withstand, in the wilderness among beasts of prey, the attack and 'temptation' of Mâra, 'the god of death.' He is also called 'king of the world of sin,' the ruler in 'hell.' Gautama's antagonist or Satan, Mâra, 'transformed' himself (appeared in the air), and promised Buddha the rule of the world (in seven days), but 'the Holy One' said to the devil: 'Thou, although supreme in the world of desire, hast no authority or power in the spiritual world; thou art acquainted only with the

---

[1] *Romantic History*, 63, 64, 67, 71, 72, 242, 142, 154, 212, 215.

wretched beings in hell: but I belong not to either of the three material worlds. It is I who hereafter will destroy thine abode, oh Mâra, and wrest from you your power and your dominion. . . . Not long hence I shall attain the highest wisdom, I shall soon become Buddha, . . . my helpers are the Devas of the pure abodes, my sword is Wisdom . . . I scorn the lie.' Having 'defeated and overpowered all the evil influences and devices of Mâra and his companions,' eight guardian-angels 'encouraged and comforted' the Blessed One in various ways. Hereupon supernatural effects were witnessed in heaven and earth. 'There was no ill feeling or hatred in the hearts of men, but whatever want there was, whether of food or drink or raiment, was at once supplied; the blind received their sight, the deaf heard, and the dumb spake; those who were bound in hell were released, and every kind of being— beasts, demons, and all created things—found peace and rest.'[1]

This wicked Mâra who opposes Gautama is by Buddhist legends distinguished from the good serpent Nâga, probably the fire-spirit, symbolised by the serpent-formed lightning, a spirit who does Buddha no harm, and who is present at his baptism. But we may safely assume that the Initiated did connect Mâra, the devil, with the symbol of an evil serpent, with an evil Nâga. For mention is made of a Nâga or serpent with seven heads; and a 'poisonous serpent' or dragon, whom nothing but 'the fire-spirit' could subdue, threatens 'with his flames' Gautama's life. The latter is reported to have said: 'If the place were full of fiery serpents, they could not hurt one hair of my body, how much less this one evil creature.' Again, Gautama is represented, like Siva, sitting on a serpent, as if its conqueror. Among his followers Mâra desig-nates some as 'my army of warriors,' and literally as

---

[1] *Romantic History*, 99-227.

'the Nâgas (serpents), each riding on a pitch-black cloud and launching forth the fiery lightnings.' Like as the sun gains the victory over the dark cloud with its serpent-formed lightning, so Gautama-Buddha, whose symbol is the sun, gains the victory over his antagonist Mâra, who is followed by fiery serpents, and who is himself described as a poisonous serpent. It is implied that Gautama is the organ of the fire-spirit, who can conquer this serpent. Buddha is sometimes represented as a ram or lamb, and since the constellation of the Serpent is placed on the sphere opposite to Aries, the spring-equinoctial sign, at the rising of which Buddha was born, we may assert, that Mâra, the devil, is identified, at least connected with the evil Nâga, the poisonous serpent.[1] It may now be regarded as highly probable, that the Buddhists, like the Egyptians and the tradition in the Apocrypha of the Septuagint, distinguished a good serpent from an evil one. The good serpent was on the Nile connected with the solar disc; but the fire, which had been the earlier symbol of this serpent, was referred to lightning.

The Messiah.

The appearance of Gautama is described as 'full of grace,' his body as surrounded with a 'glory' similar to the sun; and in the representations of this glory fiery tongues are discernible, whilst two men are placed near him, one to his right hand, the other to his left. Before Ananda's conversion, the disciples of Gautama are described as sitting on his right hand and on his left. Buddha is represented as a ram or lamb, which symbol as we have seen, refers to the sun in the sign of Aries. Buddha is never represented as a bull, like Mithras and

---

[1] *Romantic History*, 219, 220. The Hebrew word Nâchash, 'serpent,' is connected with Nâga. All heroes of light were opposed by heroes of darkness, symbolised by serpents (see following Chapter).

the more ancient solar heroes of the time when Taurus was the spring-equinoctial sign. He is also called 'the lion from the tribe of Sâkya,' and 'un-equalled among those born of women.' The 'heaven-descended mortal,' full of grace, brings 'truth' to the earth, 'the incomparable truth,' that is, 'the way of life' and of 'immortality.' At no time Buddha received this knowledge 'from a human source,' that is, from flesh and blood. His source was 'the power of his Divine wisdom,' the spiritual power or Maya, which he already possessed before his incarnation. It was by this divine power, which is also called 'the Holy Ghost,' that he became 'the Saviour,' the 'Kung-teng,' the Anointed or Messiah, to whom prophecies had pointed. Buddha was regarded as the supernatural light of the world; and this world to which he came was his own, his possession, for he is styled: 'the Lord of the world.'[1]

As Gautama was born under the two trees which symbolise knowledge and life, so, according to Bud-dhistic legends, the evil and the good in man are symbolised by trees. The object of man's life ought to be to destroy 'the tree of evil' in himself, so that his 'tree of good' may grow up and bear fruit. This can only be accomplished by prayer and humility, which raise man to the height of 'the unknown'—of the 'san-sarum dalain,' to the knowledge of the 'sansara.' Man must take an active part in the redemption of his soul, yet 'the redemption comes not from ourselves, but from causes which are independent of us.'[2] Although the actions in previous existences of the soul were held to accelerate or retard this redemption, the latter must have been believed to be also dependent on the influences of higher but cognate spirits, and, above all, on the highest, the self-dependent Spirit. This is proved by the transmitted story of Gautama's water-baptism.

[1] *Romantic History*, 169, 16, 34, 49, 53, 197, 248, 241, 243, 249, 296.
[2] Bastian, *Reisen in China*, 'Anhang;' *Romantic History*, 167.

Immediately after his birth, spirits descend and bring water to wash the holy child, a transmitted occurrence, which seems by Buddhists to have been regarded as a supernatural act of purification. But the real symbol of the sanctity which Gautama was to attain, the outward sign of the inward grace, was his water-baptism. We shall see that the latter preceded, and was probably regarded as a symbol of, his 'fire-baptism.' The water-baptism of Gautama has not been sufficiently established hitherto. The Buddhists in Thibet have a water-baptism, Tuisol, preceded by confession of sins; but this rite might not have been sanctioned by Buddha. In a Chinese life of Buddha we read that, 'living at Vaisali, Buddha delivered the baptism which rescues from life and death, and confers salvation.' This statement may have been connected with the account of Gautama's crossing the river Nairañyana. Before stepping into the water, he expressed his resolution to follow in the footsteps of all the Buddhas, to reach 'the other shore,' to 'procure salvation for all men and conduct them to the other shore,'[1] that is, to the locality of Nirvâna, to 'the heavenly country,' where all the Buddhas are, to the sun. A striking parallel must here be pointed out. Israel's crossing of the Red Sea was by Paul regarded as the baptism of Israel's fathers; and, in harmony with Paulinic allegories, Israel's crossing of Jordan to reach the promised land has by Bunyan been described as a type of entering the heavenly land, Jerusalem which is above, with its twelve gates,[2] and the tree of life, where the light shines as the sun. Even in the terrestrial type of the heavenly Jerusalem, that is, in Zion, which the Babylonian Isaiah had called Beulah, Bunyan describes the sun as shining day and night. 'Christian' attempts, with much hesitation, to proceed to

---

[1] Beal, *Rom. Hist.*, 194–198; Schlagintweit, *Buddhism in Thibet*; *Asiatic Journ.*, xx. 172.

[2] Twelve solar mansions, or signs of the Zodiac; comp. Ernst von Bunsen, *Das Symbol des Kreuzes bei allen Nationen.*

the other shore, but he is unable to cross the river unaided. As in Isaiah the Lord is recorded to have said, ' When thou passest through the waters I will be with thee,' and as Christ, the Angel of God, was with the Israelites when they crossed the Red Sea, so Jesus Christ, the Wisdom of God, assists ' Christian ' in crossing the river.[1]

Gautama is described as crossing a certain stream in order.to reach the land beyond, Nirvâna with the Bôdhi-tree, the tree of knowledge or tree of life. Having entered the river- and bathed, whilst spirits ' showered down upon him every kind of flower and perfume, he attempted to proceed to the other shore of the river,' but from want of strength after his six years' penance, ' he was unable to reach the opposite bank.' Then the spirit of a ' certain great tree,' of the Bôdhi-tree or tree of knowledge, which is also the tree of life, and which was in the land beyond, or heavenly land, in Nirvâna, the sun, this Divine spirit, with outstretched arms, assisted Gautama, and enabled him ' to reach the shore in safety.' Hereupon Gautama, as all Buddhas before him had done after crossing the holy stream, advanced to the Bôdhi-tree, and thus reached ' supreme wisdom '; he became ' a perfect Buddha,' and entered life immortal.[2]

[1] Bunyan's *Pilgrim's Progress*; comp. 1 Cor. x. 1-4; Is. xliii. 2; lxii. 4.

[2] The basis of this symbolism about crossing a stream which leads to the tree of life and immortality, seems to have been the Egyptian tradition, of Eastern origin, about Osiris, who is represented with the tree of life before him, and whose body had been cut up into fourteen parts. The Lord of the tombs was symbolized by the setting sun, but previously by the mysterious Pleiades, passing through the stream of the lower world. Thus he passed by the fourteen invisible lunar asterisms in order to rise again in the East, at the end of the supposed stream of death, or the Lethe-river of later traditions, the waters of which are drunk by the souls of the departed before entering Elysium. Mr. R. Haliburton, of Nova Scotia, is prepared to prove that Paradise was supposed to be in the ' land of the Pleiades,' in which was supposed to grow ' the tree of life.' Since the solar symbolism took the place of that of the Pleiades, our interpretation of Nirvâna with its tree of life, as the sun, is thus confirmed. The most ancient (Egyptian) representa-

The Spirit of the tree of knowledge, or Wisdom, who, with Indra, the highest God, is present at the water-baptism of Gautama, is the third person of the Buddhistic trias.[1] That spirit is identified by Buddhists with the fire-spirit, the good Nâga or serpent of Buddhistic tradition, as likewise with the Wisdom or Word of God, ' the Saviour,' of whom the Book of Wisdom (by Philo?) states that it was symbolised by the brazen or rather fiery serpent which Moses set up in the wilderness as a sign of salvation, and with which, in the Fourth Gospel, Jesus Christ, ' the Wisdom of God,' is identified.[2] As at the recorded water-baptism of Gautama-Buddha, so at the recorded water-baptism of Jesus Christ, that is, of the personified Wisdom of God, of the spiritual Rock which followed the Israelites when they passed through the sea and were ' baptised unto Moses,' the highest God (Indra, Jehovah) and the Spirit of God were present,[3] that is, not only the highest God, but also ' the Holy Ghost,' through whom the incarnation of Gautama-Buddha and of Jesus Christ is recorded to have been brought about, by the descent of that Divine power upon the two virgins, Maya and Mary.

tion of the tree of life (about B.C. 1400), is a palm, in Greek phoinix (Job xxix. 18; Ps. xcii. 13), and Herodotus called the Egyptian pi-enech, which means æon, the phœnix, which he described as like an eagle. It is, we suggest, the eagle on the back of the apis, that is, of Taurus with the Pleiades, from whence, that is from the Matarii, the Mâtarisvan or messenger of Agni brought down the fire, according to Mr. Haliburton's discovery. (Ernst von Bunsen, *Die Plejaden und der Thierkreis*, 43–47, 95–100.)

[1] In the Buddhistic Trinity-symbol the tree represents the third link, the Holy Spirit or Wisdom of God, the Sophia Achamoth of the Gnostics. Pointed out by Mr. A. Lillie.

[2] Wisd. ix. 17 ; vii. 27 ; xvi. 6, 7, 12 ; xviii. 15 : comp. Ecclus. xxiv. ; Prov. viii. 22, 31, and *Essenic Doctrines in the Septuagint*, chapter iv.

[3] The symbol of the Spirit of God was the dove, in Greek, peleia (Pleiades?), and the Samaritans had a brazen fiery dove, instead of the brazen fiery serpent. Both referred to fire, the symbol of the Holy Ghost, and the latter is referred to Christ. Birds are connected with the Egyptian representations of the tree of life, and thus with fire, a very ancient symbolism. (Kuhn, *Die Herabkunft des Feuers*.)

Gautama, 'the completely enlightened One,' the 'Omniscient,' is recorded to have said that he possessed 'perfect inspiration,' that he had reached that point of development which enabled him to 'see clearly immortality, the way which leads to immortality,' that is, 'the opened gates of Nom.'[1] These we may identify with 'the straight path' which leads to Nirvâna, to the tree of life, and thus to immortality. By entering these gates man enters into the world of miracles, and is transformed into a higher being.

On one occasion, towards the end of his life on earth, Gautama is reported to have been transfigured or 'baptized with fire.' When on a mountain in Ceylon, suddenly a flame of light descended upon him and encircled the crown of his head with a circle of light. The mount is called Pândava, or yellow-white colour. It is said that 'the glory of his person shone forth with double power,' that his body was 'glorious as a bright golden image,' that he 'shone as the brightness of the sun and moon,' that bystanders expressed their opinion, that he could not be an 'every-day person,' nor 'a mortal man,' and that his body was divided into three parts, from each of which a ray of light issued forth.[2]

Gautama-Buddha taught that all men are brothers, that charity ought to be extended to all, even to enemies, that men ought to love truth and hate the lie, that good works must not be done openly, but rather in secret, that the dangers of riches are to be avoided, that man's highest aim ought to be purity in thought, word and deed, since the higher beings are pure, whose nature is akin to that of man.[3] All sacrifices

[1] Bastian, *Reisen in China*, 'Anhang.'
[2] Eitel, *Buddhism*, 121 ; Beal, *Romantic History of Buddha*, 177 ; Rhys Davids, *Buddhism*, 189 ; Köppen, *Das Leben Buddhas.*
[3] In the *Dhammapada*, Scriptural texts or parables of Buddha, as brought

are to be abolished, as there can be no merit in them. If it were right to sacrifice a sheep, it would be right also to sacrifice a child, a relative or dear friend, ' and so do better.' Sâkya-Muni healed the sick, performed miracles, and taught his doctrines to the poor. He selected his first disciples among laymen, and even two women, the mother and the wife of his first convert, the sick Yasa, became his followers. He subjected himself to the religious obligations imposed by the recognised authorities, avoided strife, and illustrated his doctrines by his life. He preached only in his own Mâgadhî, or Pâli language, but it is recorded that even strangers understood him, everyone of his hearers thinking himself addressed in his own language. Those who belonged to the lowest class or caste, the Sûdra or slaves, were especially the objects of his care, since the Law-book of Manu had expressly excluded them from the knowledge and the rewards of the life to come. We may assume from what we know, that to the poor and uneducated he only spoke in proverbs, whilst he gave to know to the disciples the mysteries of the Wisdom from above. The 'holy Prince' and 'the Prince of Mortals' is recorded to have said : 'You may remove from their base the snowy mountains, you may exhaust the waters of the ocean, the firmament may fall to earth, but my words in the end will be accomplished.'[1]

To a Brahman, who was presiding over a 'plough-feast,' and who compared his labour with the mendicancy of Buddha, the latter replied by a parable, of which various versions have been transmitted to us. 'Brahman, I plough and sow, and of my ploughing and sowing I reap imperishable fruit. . . . My field is the Dharma (truth) ; the weeds which I pluck up

to Birmah by Buddaghosa, occurs the following : 'Buddha's third commandment, Commit no adultery, this law is broken by even looking at the wife of another with a lustful mind.' (Rogers, *Buddaghosa Parables*, 153.)

[1] *Romantic History*, 158, 52, 138.

(are) the cleaving to existence; the plough which I use (is) wisdom; the seed which I sow, the seeking of purity; the work which I perform, attention to precepts; the harvest which I reap is Nirvâna.' 'Having explained these matters at greater length, he exhorted the Brahman to sow in the same field, unfolding before him the advantage of obtaining an entrance to the paths which lead to the destruction of sorrow.'[1] This took place in a village near Rajagrihu, when the Brahman, named Bhâradwâja, was converted by Gautama. Another parable teaches that tares grow up with the wheat.

'Dharma' means truth or religion; Wisdom is identical with the Zoroastrian Divine Word, or 'honover,' through which God reveals his mysteries to man; the 'cleaving to existence,' or 'upadâna,' which is one of the key-notes of Buddhism, ever means the character of the man about to die, the final shape of a man's personal longings or dislikes. If this character be centred on Nirvâna, then to Nirvâna, to the place where God and all the Buddhas live, to the sun, man will go; he will have a spiritual body like to the shining body of Brahma, he will shine as the Arhats, as the righteous shine (like the sun) in the heavenly country, in Nirvâna, the sun. But if there is the least remnant of a desire after further material existence, he will then be born again to die again in some material condition or other, whether as the lowest reptile or as the highest of reasonable beings in the universe who has not yet entered Nirvâna, the sun, where matter is annihilated, and where the harvest of the seed of Divine Wisdom, of the Word, takes place.

Gautama's cousin and favourite disciple, Ananda, once stood at a fountain, with one of the despised Chândala women, called Prâkriti, and said to her:

---

[1] Spence Hardy, *Christianity and Buddhism compared*, 96; comp. Rhys Davids, *l. c.* 134, 135, and 72.

'Give me to drink.' She pointed out her low caste, which forbad her to accost him ; but Gautama's disciple said : ' My sister, I do not ask after your family, I ask you for water,' whereupon she became a disciple, and was saved for the spiritual life. A similar spirit breathes through the legend, according to which the gift of a poor man filled Buddha's eleemosynary pot with flowers, whilst rich men were not able to fill it with 10,000 measures. There is a treasure laid up by man, said Gautama, which is ' hid secure and passes not away,' which ' no thief can steal,' and which man ' takes with him.' The lamp of a poor woman was the only one which burnt during the whole night at a festivity in honour of Buddha.[1]

Gautama-Buddha is said to have announced to his disciples that the time of his departure had come : ' Arise, let us go hence, my time is come.' Turned towards the East, and with folded hands, he prayed to the highest Spirit who inhabits the region of purest light, to Mahâ-Brahma, to the ' king in heaven, to Devarâja, who from his throne looked down on Gautama, and appeared to him in a self-chosen personality. This highest God to whom Buddha prayed, is Isvâra-Deva, (or Abîdha), ' the architect of the world ' ; and the place of his throne is ' the centre of supernatural light,' where there is no darkness, sin, birth or death, the Nirvâna, the sun.

The doctrines of Gautama-Buddha centred in the belief of a personal God, and in man's continued personal existence after death. Buddhism resolves itself into a religion of humanity. The goal is the same as that of the Hebrew Psalmist : ' Unto Thee shall all flesh come.' It is recorded, how Gautama announced to his disciples, that another Buddha, and therefore another Angel in human form, another organ or advocate of the Wisdom from above, would descend from heaven to

[1] Köppen, *Das Leben Buddhas*, i.

earth, and that he would be called Maitreya, or 'Son of love.' It is thus implied, that also the future Tathâgata or 'He that should come,' that the Messiah, whom the Buddhists still expect, will descend as 'Holy Ghost,' like Gautama-Buddha. So do the Hindus expect Kalki, the originator of a new age. The other advocate or Paraclete promised by Gautama, will likewise be a chosen instrument of the Spirit from above, a Spirit of truth, a heavenly messenger full of grace, who reveals the truth.

It was at Allahabad, three months after having announced his departure, that Gautama died, and Buddha returned to heaven, entered Nirvâna, the sun. The miracles which attended his death have been transmitted in various forms by probably later legends. The coverings of the body unrolled themselves, the lid of his coffin was opened by supernatural power, and Gautama-Buddha's feet appeared to his disciples in the form which they knew so well. This was an answer to Kasyapa's prayer. The latter asked Ananda why the departed master's feet were soiled with wet; he was told that a weeping woman had embraced Gautama's feet shortly before his death, and that her tears had fallen on his feet and left the marks on them.[1]

Gautama-Buddha constantly taught the great truth conveyed in the phrase 'vicarious suffering,' or suffering borne for the good of another. The commonest story about him is, that in a former birth he gave his body and blood to a hawk to save the life of a dove (did he know it as the symbol of the Spirit of God?). All the Jâtakas are full of this idea. But Buddhism knows absolutely nothing of the idea of an offended God, who requires reconciliation by vicarious suffering.

---

[1] From the *Vinaya-Pitaka as known in China* (Beal).

Retrospect.

With the remarkable exception of the death of Jesus on the cross,[1] and of the doctrine of atonement by vicarious suffering, which is absolutely excluded by Buddhism, the most ancient of the Buddhistic records known to us contain statements about the life and the doctrines of Gautama-Buddha which correspond in a remarkable manner, and impossibly by mere chance, with the traditions recorded in the Gospels about the life and doctrines of Jesus Christ. It is still more strange that these Buddhistic legends about Gautama as the Angel-Messiah refer to a doctrine which we find only in the Epistles of Paul and in the fourth Gospel.

This can be explained by the assumption of a common source of revelation; but then the serious question must be considered, why the doctrine of the Angel-Messiah, supposing it to have been revealed, and which we find in the East and in the West, is not contained in any of the Scriptures of the Old Testament which can possibly have been written before the Babylonian Captivity, nor in the first three Gospels. Can the systematic keeping back of essential truth be attributed to God or to man? Had we only to consider the statements of Paul, we should be led to believe in the gradual revelation or publication of the mystery kept in secret. For he declares that he preached ' the hidden wisdom,' after that he had ' renounced the hidden things of dishonesty,' or, rather, ' the shameful hiding,' which Moses had first introduced, and which had led to a ' deceitful handling,' or, rather, to a falsifying, of God's Word. According to the theory we are considering, it would have been Paul who, not doing like Moses, had first ' commended himself to every man's conscience in the sight of God ' by ' manifestation,' or, rather, ' revelation of the truth.'

---

[1] Among the prophecies respecting Buddha's coming is the assertion that ' his death shall be a quiet and painless one.' (*Rom. Hist.* 51.)

In this case it might not have been before the second century that, by the publication of the Gospel after John, the preaching of Jesus Christ was revealed in its absolute fulness and purity. The first Evangelists, according to this theory, had to consider the opposition of the Jewish authorities, who had forbidden the public preaching of this secret doctrine, whilst Jesus is implied to have forbidden the Apostles forthwith to preach from the roofs the mysteries which—so we are told— he had made known to them alone, whilst speaking only in parables to the people. According to this explanation of the problem presented to us, Jesus must have been an Essene.

The theory of an essentially similar revelation in East and West would harmonise with the conceptions of Paul. He writes that God had never left himself without witness, that man's conscience is the witness of God, and that a 'mystery' was hid in God from the beginning of the world, which 'eternal purpose' was in his time made known as it had in former times not been made known.[1] According to this universalist conception, held by Origen and Augustine, Christian revelation is directly connected with Divine revelations at all times and in all places, with a continuity of Divine influences.

The doctrine of an Angel-Messiah might, therefore, have been first revealed in the East, and there applied to Gautama-Buddha. On this hypothesis, the latter would have been the forerunner of Jesus Christ, and for this reason Buddhistic tradition would have been applied to Jesus Christ, and introduced into the New Testament Scriptures, which Eusebius considered 'highly probable.' The object would have been to make clear to the Initiated of tradition the connection between Divine revelations in East and West. On this theory it would be an open question : whether Jesus has sanc-

[1] Rom. ii. 14, 15; Eph. iii. 9–11.

tioned the application to himself of the doctrine about the Angel-Messiah ; or whether it was not till after his death that this application and, therefore, enlargement of doctrine, took place.

Did such connections between East and West exist before and during the Apostolic age, that we may assume as possible in the West a knowledge of Oriental tradition ?

CHAPTER III

Introduction.

Is the East the direct or the indirect source of the
doctrines of Pythagoras? The accounts of Pliny,
Apuleius and others about the travels of Pythagoras
to the East, as well as to Egypt and Mesopotamia, may
be dismissed as insufficient evidence. And yet, since
already a century before his time Psammetick (B.C. 666
–612) had opened to the world the ports of Egypt,
these countries can have been visited by Pythagoras
of Samos, the contemporary of Tarquinius Superbus
(B.C. 540–510), and possibly descended from Pythagoras,
king of Kidrusi in Cyprus, who paid tribute to Assur-
banipal in B.C. 684. But the earliest authority for his
journey to Egypt does not reach further back than 150
years after his death. Even without having been in the
East, the founder of the mystic, ascetic, and apparently
aristocratic confederation at Crotona, established on the
basis of secrecy, may have been initiated by Greek
hierophants into the mysteries of a hidden wisdom
which was not unconnected with the East. The
Eastern origin of European languages is proved; and it
is generally admitted, that the aboriginal inhabitants of
Greece imported from the East, together with their
language, 'the general foundations of their religion and
customs,' also that they continued to live under in-

fluences which reached them from the East, partly by way of Thrace and the Bosphorus, partly by the Ægean Sea and its islands. In the face of these general admissions, it is held on the one side, that Greek philosophy was essentially the product of the Greek brain, on the other, that the entire circle of Greek conceptions was imported ready made from without.[1] We submit that some new light can be thrown on this question by comparative mythology.

The Origin of the Gods.

We must here assume, what we tried to prove elsewhere, that the Cosmical was the symbol of the Ethical in earliest historical times, and that the numbers, by which, according to Jamblichus (before A.D. 333), the Egyptians designated their divisions in the heavens, that is, the numbers 2, 4, 12, 36, and 72, can be all referred to astronomical observations, some of which preceded the invention of the Zodiac.[2] According to the contrary argument, as elaborately worked out by von Thimus, the starting-point of symbolism with all nations is 'the revealed doctrine of aboriginal times, as transmitted by the second ancestor of mankind (Noah), to all his nearest descendants in aboriginal, full and untarnished purity.'[3]

Since the Pythagoræans maintained that 'the number rules the Cosmos,' we may at the outset suppose, that the first Greek philosopher who used the word 'cosmos' in our sense, designating thereby the order in the

---

[1] Zeller, *Die Philosophie der Griechen*; Röth, *Geschichte der Abendländischen Philosophie,* i. 74, 241.

[2] *Die Plejaden und der Thierkreis.*

[3] Von Thimus, *Harmonikale Symbolik des Alterthums,* ii. 347. The theory about the harmony of the spheres was symbolised by the Mishkol or balance of the Kabbala, with which was connected 'the little tongue of the balance' in the mystic book Jezirah. These two expressions can be shown to relate, like the Egyptian balance of good and evil, to the equinoctial and the solstitial balance. The earliest symbol of the harmony of the spheres was Apollo's lyre of seven strings, which certainly had nothing to do with the Zodiac.

universe, connected the numbers with that order, that he regarded them as figurative expressions of those forces in nature which under the harmonising influence of a Supreme Will, brought about the regular movements of bodies in space, and thus the order in the universe. From this point of view the Cosmos might be called a revelation in numbers.

It would seem that the Pythagoræan symbolism of numbers referred originally, and perhaps long before Thales and Pythagoras, neither to arithmetic nor to geometry as such, but to a mechanical system of nature, to the relative relations of cosmical bodies, to the order of their revolutions, and to the presumable Divine cause of such order. This is not the place to inquire, whether and to what extent the atomistic science of nature, as taught by the two Grecian philosophers, Leucippus and Democritus (about B.C. 461–361), was also acknowledged, or whether it was opposed by Pythagoras. Nor do we now ask whether he, like the Ionians Anaximenes (about 544), and Heraklitos (about 513), taught a periodic origin and passing away of the earth and other bodies in space. But the views of Pythagoras about the origin of the Gods cannot be doubted, since the theogony, according to the views of his tutor Pherecydes, has been transmitted to us. Next to the theogony of Hesiodus, it is the most ancient we possess, and its substratum can be shown to have been Eastern astronomy. Although it may have possibly been Greece where the first attempt was made to explain the Cosmos by a theory on its origin, it was Eastern science which gave the materials for such speculations.

According to Pherecydes (about B.C. 544), or rather according to the 'Phœnician' tradition to which he referred, the fundamental cause of all phenomena in nature is Zeus or Chronos, whom he also calls, but distinguishes in a certain sense from Chthon, that is, the material substances of the earth, including the sea. He designates Chronos as a deity, dwelling in that part of heaven which is nearest to the earth. We know that Chronos is the Seb of the Egyptians, and with Rhea-Netpe he gave birth to the five planets, in honour of which, five additional days were added to the calendar of 360 days, after that Thot, the God of history and astronomy, who is represented as riding on the moon, and whose mystical number was 72, had played at dice with the moon, and gained for each planet the 72nd part of 360 days. This Egyptian legend seems to have been framed after the Phœnician legend or myth of the seven children of Chronos and Rhea, of which the youngest had been translated to the Gods. Movers has explained these seven children of Zeus-Chronos by the Pleiades, one of which seven stars had disappeared in course of time. Since Pherecydes admits to have drawn from a Phœnician source, he must have known this Phœnician legend, and he may be assumed to have connected with the seven sons of Zeus-Chronos the seven Patæci of the Phœnicians, and the Cabiri of Egyptians and Greeks, whom some identified with the sons of Rhea.

Zeus-Chronos thus seems to have been by Phere-eydes connected with the Pleiades in Taurus, as the divinity dwelling in these seven stars, like the Sibut of the ancient Babylonians, the Sebaot or Zabaot of the Hebrews, and other deities. This hypothesis is confirmed by other details about the theogony of the tutor of Pythagoras. The first creation of Zeus-Chronos was fire. According to the Indian myth on the descent of fire, the same was brought to earth from heaven by a messenger of Indra, by Agni, called the Mâtarisvan. This name, Mr. Haliburton, of Nova Scotia, has conuected with the Matarii, as the Pleiades are still called by islanders in the Pacific. We have pointed out in another place,[1] that the fire-sticks or Arani of the Indians, which were a sacred symbol to the ancient Babylonians, point to the origin of the Cross as con-

---

[1] *Das Symbol des Kreuzes bei allen Nationen; Die Plejaden und der Thierkreis.*

nected with the symbolism of fire. It can be shown
that Bel's flaming sword which turned every way, and
the flaming sword of the Cherub, that is, Kirub or bull,
according to the language of Cuneiform Inscriptions,
originally referred to the Pleiades in Taurus, from whence
fire was supposed to have first descended upon the earth.

The connection of the Cross with fire receives a
remarkable confirmation by the Chinese symbol of the
headless cross or Tau. It becomes increasingly probable that the Chinese interpretation of the cross-
symbol is more ancient than the provable introduction
of the same into other countries. For ' it is now
asserted by one of our best Sinologists (Dr. Edkins),
that the phonetic roots of the Chinese language are the
same as those of Europe ; in other words, that the
Chinese phonetic roots are those from which the languages of Europe, and therefore of India, were originally
developed.'[1]

Among the earliest and simplest ideographic symbols
in the Chinese language is one which resembles precisely
our capital letter T, without the final strokes, signifying
that which is ' above,' and the converse of this, the T
resting on its base (⊥), signifies that which is ' below.'
In both cases a point or a comma, as if a tongue of fire,
is added, as similarly in Europe a dot or tongue of fire
is placed occasionally over an angel or divine messenger,
to signify his more than human character. This dot,
as signifying fire, is clearly pointed out in the symbol
for fire itself in the Chinese language, and it is this : a
piece of wood boring into another piece, and on the
opposite side a spark issuing, indicating the generation
of fire by friction, thus ·K. Now, the dot as signifying
fire was placed, as Agni was placed by the Indians, in a
place of pre-eminence over the visible world. Hence,
connecting this idea with that of the former, with the

[1] Professor Beal in the ' President's Address,' *Journal of the Plymouth
Institution*, vol. vi., part i., pp. 21, 22, from whence the following extract is
derived.

symbol for height or heaven, we have the complete idea represented symbolically of the supreme power pictured as fire or a spark presiding over the lower world, and so placed above it. This symbolism is visible everywhere. In Egypt we find the well-known 'key of the Nile' in the hand of Isis, denoting simply the supreme power exercised by that divinity. The same symbol in China denotes the supreme Lord or Ruler of the Universe, and is, in fact, a part of the expression used to signify 'God.' We have here, then, one of the earliest inventions of man by which is denoted something 'above,' that which is visible to the eye, or 'heaven.'

Hence the symbol 𝕋 means to come down from above, where the dot or fiery tongue denotes a spark or flame descending from the upper world, which is signified by 𝖳. Hence again, ⏊ means the lower world, and the symbol 𝟈 means to go up from below, or to ascend. The Chinese imagine that there are three worlds or spheres, corresponding to the Sanskrit vhû, vhûvar, and svar, and the Chinese symbolise these three heavens by three lines, ☰. When they wish to symbolise the idea of Lord or Ruler of the three spheres, they cross the three horizontal lines by a perpendicular line, 王.[1] The Chinese add to this symbol the dot for a 'flame' or 'fire' above it, thus 主.[2]

When solar-symbolism took the place of fire-symbolism, the sun's disc took the place of the fiery tongue, and thus originated the so-called handle-cross of the Egyptians, the symbol of life. As symbol of life it is represented without the circle under the nostrils of a Pharaoh, whilst a line connects the Tau-cross with the sun or solar disc. Thus was expressed in an Egyptian figure or symbol, similar to one of the Chinese, how the God whose symbol was held to be the sun, breathed into the nostrils of man 'the breath of life.'

[1] The Papal crozier has exactly the same form.
[2] Professor Beal in a letter to the author.

Not only the Tau-cross of the Egyptians, but also the symbolism represented by the candlestick of Moses, astronomically explained by Philo and Josephus, may be connected with the Chinese symbol for the ruler of the three worlds or of the universe. But Moses did not only represent a flame over the central candlestick, following the analogy of the fiery tongue over the vertical line of the divine Chinese symbol, he also represented a flame at the six ends of the three horizontal lines of this Eastern symbol. As the sun's disc over the Egyptian Tau-cross had taken the place of the fiery tongue above the similar Chinese Tau, so, according to the explanation of Philo, the central lamp of the candlestick referred to the sun, although the Initiated in the deeper knowledge or gnosis knew that the central lamp symbolised the Word of God, which, in the Book of Wisdom, possibly composed by Philo, is said to have been symbolised by the fiery serpent in the desert.[1]

The reversed Tau-cross, symbol of the lower world, with the Chinese perhaps the most ancient of the two, may be regarded as having referred in the first place to the horizontal balance of aboriginal times, which connected the two determining single stars on the horizon, like Aldebaran and Antares, by Indians called 'rohin' or red, no doubt because the rising and the setting sun made them appear red.[2] According to this hypothesis, the vertical line of this symbol would date from a later time, and would point to the vertical balance, formed by the culminations of these determining stars. These three points in the sphere formed the very ancient holy triangle, which in the Holiest of the Holy in the Jewish Temple was represented by the Shechina in the midst and above the two Cherubim, and which later was connected with the Divine Trinity in Unity.[3]

---

[1] Nâchash means in Hebrew 'brass' and 'serpent.'
[2] According to Mr. Lockyer's explanation.
[3] *Die Plejaden und der Thierkreis.*

If the astronomical origin of this Oriental symbolism is proved, as also its introduction in the West in pre-Mosaic times, it may be unhesitatingly asserted that the connection of Zeus-Chronos by Pherecydes with that part of the earth which was nearest to 'heaven,' points to the above astronomical symbolism. We may at the outset assume, that what the tutor of Pythagoras conceived as 'heaven' was the exclusively spiritual or non-material world, which notion we find in the Zendavesta and in Ionic tradition, but which was distinguished, uncompromisingly by non-East-Iranian and non-Ionic traditions, from the material world. This system of two worlds may be assumed to have originated in the important discovery of the horizontal, later equinoctial Balance, formed by the two determining stars on the horizon, reddened by the sun, and which seemed to divide the Cosmos into two parts. The light hemisphere seems to have been originally regarded as the spiritual world; but special constellations, later the sun, were regarded as the dwelling-place of the God who causes the order in the universe, and as centre of the spiritual world.

This symbolism enables us to suggest that Pherecydes may have regarded as dwelling-place of Zeus-Chronos the Eastern determining star of aboriginal times, Aldebaran in Taurus, or the Pleiades in the same constellation. Since the seven sons of Zeus-Chronos and of Rhea, according to Phœnician legend were, as we showed, connected with the Pleiades, this constellation, inhabited according to Old-Babylonian and to Hebrew tradition, by the God Sibut-Sebaot, appears indeed to have designated the part of the earth which was conceived to be nearest to heaven and the dwelling-place of Zeus. For the Pleiades stood once nearest to the most ancient equinoctial points observed, and the parts of the sphere determined by the latter mark those points on the horizon where the path of the sun appears to touch the path of the fixed stars, and at the same time the equator, and thus the earth. This explanation is finally confirmed by the fact to which Pherecydes refers, that Zeus-Chronos was the creator of fire and then of the earth, as if the creator of heaven and earth, whilst the Pleiades, as already said, were regarded as the locality where fire originates.

In order to frame the world, Zeus transforms himself into Eros, the god of love, not mentioned in the Homeric Poems, but whom the Orphics before Pherecydes explain to have been the son of Chronos, and the first who issued forth from the mundane egg. Eros was thus connected with Castor, the first-born of the Dioscuri, who were called sons of Zeus and Leda. Since the Dioscuri can be connected with the Aswin, or two Bulls of Indian tradition, with the rising and setting Taurus, to which also Osiris and the Cherubim and Seraphim were referred, the argument gains in force, that Zeus, who was called the highest, like Osiris-Wasar, according to the most ancient Greek theogony known to us, was supposed to be the God inhabiting the Pleiades in Taurus.

Eros became the vicar of Zeus and the framer of the world, and so Serosh took the place of Ormuzd as first of the seven Amshaspands, which referred to the Pleiades. Like Eros, Serosh was considered as the framer of the world. Again, as Serosh-Sraosha was connected with the celestial watchers, and thus with the Pleiades, being therefore opposed by the ideal hero in the opposite constellations of Scorpio or the Serpent, the adversary of Eros is the serpent-deity Ophioneus. Eros must therefore be regarded as one of the ideal heroes of light, who were connected with the constellation of the spring-equinox, originally with Taurus and the Pleiades, and opposed by serpent-deities. Eros was contrasted to Ophioneus as Ormuzd was to Ahriman, Indra to Ahi, Osiris to Typhon,

Dionysos to the serpent-footed Titans, Apollos to Python, Buddha to Mâra (Nâga), Christ to Antichrist, the satan, devil, or old serpent.

The localisation of these Eastern and Western symbols enables us to assert that the theogony of Pherecydes, and therefore also of Pythagoras, was inseparably connected with astronomical observations of the East. It is certainly not only the myth of Demeter and of Dionysos, the Indian Bacchus, which can be proved to have been introduced into Greece from without.

The Orphic cosmogony, which is more ancient than Pythagoras and his tutor, confirms our explanation of the Greek theogony as based on astronomical observations of the East, and on the symbolism connected with it. Chronos, the fundamental principle, creates the opposing principles of light and darkness, the æther and the chaos, from which Chronos forms a silver egg, from which again issues forth the enlightening Phanes, who is also called Eros and Metis, that is, Wisdom, the Greek Sophia and the Indian Bodhi. The Sophia was later designated as daughter of Okeanos and Thetis. The latter already Hesiodus mentions as the first consort of Zeus, who devoured her, at the suggestion of Gæa and Uranos, in order to prevent the birth of a Divine being. Zeus caused Athene, symbol of the morning dawn, to issue forth from his head. The statue and temple of Athene were turned towards the middle dawn of the equinoxes,[1] a trait of the myth which confirms the astronomical character of the earliest known nature-symbols, and the connection of Greek philosophy with Eastern astronomy and symbolism.

We are now in a position to assume that already centuries before Pythagoras, the Initiated among the Greeks, the epopts, were taught in and through the

---

[1] Emile Burnouf, *La Légende Athénienne.*

mysteries a more speculative theology, a deeper knowledge or gnosis, to which the so-called Gnomons referred by dark sentences, riddles, or proverbs. From
this it would follow that, through the Mysteries, secret
doctrines of Oriental priests could be transmitted to
Greek philosophers, which through them reached the
public. All Greeks were admitted to the representation of the mystic symbols, but these were not intended
for the education of the people, and not explained to
them. Moreover, there were certain ceremonies to
which only the Initiated were admitted.

Even without having travelled to the East, Pythagoras, the contemporary of Buddha, could have, and it
will become more and more probable that he had, a
knowledge of Eastern wisdom.

The Transmigration of Souls.

The connection of the Pythagoræan doctrine about
the transmigration of souls with the Dionysian Myth
confirms in the most absolute manner the direct connection between Greek philosophy and Eastern astronomical symbolism. Pythagoras is said to have been
the first who taught this doctrine in Greece, the first
traces of which occur among the Brahmans and Buddhists. According to the Buddhistic 'Tradition from
beyond,' the Bodhi, or Wisdom from above, was personified by angels and by men, and the spiritual power
or Maya, the Brahm, was also called the Word, or the
Holy Spirit. From time to time an Angel is designated
in his turn to be born in the flesh, and to teach as the
enlightened man, as Buddha and as Saviour of the
World, the wisdom which he has brought from the
upper and spiritual to the lower and material world.
This incarnate Angel-Messiah, after having fulfilled his
mission, returns to the upper spheres, his transformations, his deaths and births, his change of body, what

the Greeks called 'meteusomatosis,' have come to an end for him, and he enters the locality, the characteristic feature of which is Nirvâna or destruction, that is, the annihilation of matter. This last resting-place of the spirit, where the harvest takes place, is the abode of the spirits perfected before him, and also the dwelling-place of the self-existent deity, Isvâra-Deva. Nirvâna is the sun.

The doctrine of the incarnation of the Angel-Messiah or Buddha, his birth in the flesh as the last of a series of births, was connected with the doctrine of the soul's transmigrations, and thus with a concatenation of bodily existences. Each of these formed a new prison for the soul, which was held to be of heavenly, of immaterial, of spiritual origin. According to Egyptian conception the soul had to migrate from the lowest animal to the highest, and thus had to become embodied by men as well as by higher beings of other stars. The graduated scale of the soul's transformations was by the Egyptians connected with the Phœnixperiod. The Phœnix-bird or Phenno is by Herodotus described as most like an eagle, and every 500 years, as he was told, the young bird buried the old bird at Heliopolis. At Heliopolis was the Mnevis or black Bull with the white sign of an eagle (Phenno) on its back. This Bull with the mark of the Phœnix can be proved to have referred to the celestial Bull, to the constellation of Taurus, which in the East rises on the horizon as ' the living Apis,' and sets in the West as 'dead Apis' or ' Bull of the West.' The places on the horizon which are marked by the rising and setting Taurus, like those marked by the new moon and the full moon, and which were called ' the two eyes' of the moon-god Thot, were held to be ' the two heavenly gates,' between which the migrations of the soul were conceived to take place according to the Book of the Dead. So also Osiris, originally the God in the Pleiades, had to migrate through the fourteen moon-stations of the lower sphere before he could rise again in the East with the Pleiades in Taurus as the God in the Pleiades, in order to re-commence his rule in the fourteen moon-stations of the upper hemisphere.

The connection of the Pythagoræan doctrine about the transmigrations of the soul with Dionysian or Bacchic rites is generally acknowledged, and is as certain as the connection of the Dionysos Myth with that of Osiris. These myths must be connected with the East and astronomically interpreted, if the locali-sation of these and similar nature-symbols has been established. Assuming this, it follows that the con-nection of Pythagoræan conceptions with provable astronomical observations and symbols of the East can no longer be doubted.

Among the ideal heroes of light which, like Osiris and Dionysos, were connected with the spring-equinoc-tial constellation, and were opposed by ideal heroes of darkness inhabiting the constellation of the autumn-equinox, was also Buddha, the contemporary of Pytha-goras. Because Buddha was symbolised by the sun, he was represented as Lamb, referring to the spring-equinoctial sign of Aries in his time, which rose on the horizon at his birth. Even the expectation of the coming Buddha was connected with this Eastern astro-nomical symbolism. The expectation of his birth on Christmas-day, and at midnight, is connected with a symbolism which is much more ancient than the time of Gautama-Buddha.

The Goddess Hestia.

We saw that the creator of fire, as later of sun, moon, and earth, that Zeus-Chronos throned in the Pleiades according to the theogony of the tutor of Pythagoras, and that according to Indian tradition the Mâtarisvan, the messenger of Indra, sent from the

Matarü or Pleiades to the earth, that Agni, whose secret name was Mâtarisvan, was held to have brought the fire and the fire-sticks to the earth. With these Oriental conceptions of Pherecydes the statement may be connected, that the Pythagoræans placed the fire-goddess Hestia in the centre of the universe. We may assume that Pythagoras knew for what reason the sun had taken the place of fire as symbol of the Divinity. Pythagoras could regard the sun as the centre, though not of the universe, yet of the solar system, with which he seems to have been acquainted. This hypothesis is confirmed indirectly by the place which the Pythagoræans seem to have assigned to the earth as to the second moon, perhaps because the moon accompanies the earth in its rotation round the sun, both receiving their light from the latter.

Pythagoras could assign to the sun the central position in the solar system, without giving up the Oriental connection of the fire with the Pleiades, the latter as the throne of the God by whom fire had been sent. From this the conception would arise of the Pleiades, or a star in this constellation, as the throne of Hestia and as centre of the universe. It is remarkable that, according to the calculations of the astronomer Maedler, the earth's sun appears to rotate round a star in the Pleiades. More important still is it for our purpose, that according to statements made by Cicero and Plutarch about astronomical conceptions of some Pythagoræans, especially of Aristarchos from Samos, who flourished from about B.C. 280 to 264, Copernicus, led by these ideas, as he himself seems to imply, separated the equinoctial points from the solar path, and thus may be said to have re-established the most ancient and absolutely exact year of the East, which was regulated by fixed stars.[1]

[1] *Die Plejaden und der Thierkreis*; comp. *Foerster, wissenschaftliche Vorlesungen.*

Pythagoras and the Dorians.

A connection can be rendered probable between the ethnic dualism of Iranians and Indians on the one side and that of the Sumir and Akkad in Mesopotamia, as well as with the still much disputed dualism of Ionians and Dorians in Greece. Here it must suffice to point out that the Iranians, as well as the Akkad and the Ionians, wrote from right to left, like all 'Semitic' people, and that the Vedic Indians, probably also the ancient Egyptians before they became 'semitised,' and certainly the Dorians, wrote from left to right. From this it becomes probable that the combination of these two modes of writing in alternate lines, the so-called Boustrophedon-form, points to a transition period.[1]

We purpose to substantiate the hypothesis that the Ionians and Dorians, come from the East at different times, introduced two independent philosophical systems, a double Oriental tradition.

According to Clement of Alexandria, the Italic school of philosophy founded by Pythagoras had been entirely different from the Ionic school of Thales. Yet he states that both doctrinal systems originated in Phœnicia. According to our interpretation of what is called Semitic, this can be explained by the assumption that both traditions had once been introduced into Phœnicia, into the land of Canaan, which before the Japhetic immigration was inhabited chiefly if not exclusively by Hamites.

By a geographic and an ethnic interpretation of the genealogical names in the 10th chapter of Genesis, the Hamites can be traced from the lowlands of the Oxus and Indus to the Nile, the Jordan, and the Euphrates and Tigris. So likewise the Japhetites can be traced by the highland of Iran to the south of the Caspian,

[1] *Die Plejaden und der Thierkreis*, 396–400.

from whence they conquered Mesopotamia, according to Berosus in B.C. 2458. This year is implied in Genesis to have been that of the birth of Shem, which took place 98 years after the Flood, the era of which commenced in B.C. 2360 according to Censorinus. These Japhetites or Iranians were called, in their own or a cognate language, Casdîm, or conquerors, as proved by the language of Cuneiform Inscriptions. In Ur-Casdîm the ancestors of Abraham were born. Like all the Hamites who inhabited Mesopotamia and other countries of the West, the Hebrews were subjugated by the Japhetic conquerors, and these combinations of Japhetites and Hamites, ever since the year of Shem's birth, is in Genesis narrated as a family history and referred to in the genealogies of Shem.[1]

Clement further states, that according to the opinion of most people Pythagoras was a barbarian, a word which seems to have been formed after the Indian 'varvâra,' and thus would designate a black-skinned man with woolly hair.[2] If a barbarian or non-Aryan, Pythagoras was a Hamite, a word formed after 'cham' or 'kem,' which in Egyptian means 'black.' The Hamites of Genesis are cognate with the Homeric 'Ethiopians from the East,' and these have migrated from India to the West according to the ethnic scheme just referred to. Accordingly, the barbarian descent of Pythagoras would connect him with India, and his acquaintance with the Indian Bodhi or Wisdom would become increasingly probable, whether he met his contemporary Gautama-Buddha or not. The probability has been pointed out, that the ancestors of Pythagoras, of Tyrrhenian descent, migrated from Phlius in the Peloponnese to the Ionic Samos.[3] In so far the Hamitic

---

[1] Gen. xi. 28; comp. *The Chronology of the Bible*, and T. G. Müller, *Die Semiten in ihrem Verhältniss zu Japhetiten und Hamiten.*

[2] Contrasted to the varvâra was the pulakita, the white-skinned man with smooth and reddish hair. 'Varna' means 'caste' and 'colour' in Sanscrit.

[3] Zeller, *l.c.*

descent of Pythagoras would thus be confirmed, as the Tyrrhenians or Tursi were a cognate race with the Etruscans, the majority of which was certainly non-Aryan, Turian, or Hamitic.[1]

From the early combination of Ionic and Doric elements, which we distinguish as Japhetic-Iranic and Hamitic-Indian, it does not follow that the undeniable tribal distinctions in Greece were at all times of secondary importance, and that they were not influential in moulding the forms of Greek thought and the Greek institutions. All critics agree that in the tendency of the life of Pythagoras the non-Homeric or Doric spirit is clearly distinguishable. The influence of the Ionic conceptions about nature, and of the Ionic language on Pythagoras can be sufficiently explained by the connection of both tribes. It cannot be a mere chance, and it may be designated as a logical consequence of the presumable ethnic dualism in Greece, that Homer represented the Ionic, Pythagoras the Doric tradition, and that the oracle at Dodona was the organ of the one, that of Delphi, with its consecrations, of the other.

' The belief in oracles commences before Homer, is mighty before Solon, and especially in the Delphic sanctuary of Apollos it united the one with the other, even with barbarians. It survives Socrates and Demosthenes, and dies out at the end of the Roman republic, in order to gain an artificial and unreal life under Hadrian and the Antonines; it is only then that the oracles become silent for ever. The consecrations and purifications form the connecting link between Delphi and the Orphics. Orpheus, Musæus, Linus, as already Aristotle clearly says, are mythical names, but names for a real old Thrakian doctrine about the Gods, the oracles and hymns of which Demokritos, the contemporary and instrument of Pisistratos, collected and falsi-

---

[1] *Die Plejaden und der Thierkreis,* 394.

fied by insertions. At that time the Orphics were a kind of fakirs, wandering jugglers and enchanters. But it belonged to the political system of the ancient ruling houses to bring back to their accustomed value everything that was priestly and ritualistic—consecrations, oracles, and ceremonies. To this tendency Homer's consciousness of God is directly opposed.'[1]

According to statements made by Herodotus, who first transmits the names of the Ilias and the Odyssey, Homer the Ionian is said to have flourished about B.C. 850, therefore perhaps not more than two centuries before the birth of Pythagoras. A much earlier date of Homer, or of the authors of the Homeric Poems transmitted to us, is rendered improbable above all by the circumstance that in these poems so little notice is taken of Ionic Athens. This is easily explained if we assume that in the form transmitted to us they were composed after the Doric conquest of the Peloponnese, which may have taken place long before the traditional date B.C. 1104, an hypothesis which seems to be confirmed by the excavations of Schliemann. In this supposition the insertions in favour of the Athenians would be explained, which may have originated in the addresses of the Rhapsodi held at Athens. They were even attributed to Solon and to Pisistratos, and they have certainly not been eradicated in the first written records of the songs which the latter caused to be made. That Lycurgus brought them from Ionia to Sparta is a non-proven assertion.

The more the Ionian Homer can be connected with the Japhetic-Iranian tradition, the more certain will become the descent of Pythagoras from the Dorians, and the connection of the latter with Hamitic-Indian tradition.

Like the Iranian hero Thraêtôna, like the Iranian

---

[1] Bunsen, *God in History*, German edition, ii. 281, 286, 287; comp. Gerland, *Homerische Sagen*.

Sethite Lamech, and like Noah the Hebrew, Hellen the son of Deucalion has three sons :—

Thraêtôna :	Airya,	Tuirya,	Sairma ;
Lamech :	Jabal,	Jubal,	Thubal-Cain ;
Noah :	Japhet,	Ham,	Shem ;
Hellen :	Æolus,	Dorus,	Xuthus.

In the 10th chapter of Genesis the descendants of Japhet, called 'the elder' in the text, are first mentioned, those of Shem last ; a circumstance which indirectly confirms our interpretation of the Shemites as a combination of Japhetites and Hamites. In the order enumerated above, the Æolians, that is the original Ionians, are shown to be identical with the Japhetites, as the Dorians with the Hamites.

This is confirmed in the first place by the fact that the name Ionian, or 'Iaôn, cannot be separated from the name Javan, by which name the Hebrews have at all times until now designated the Greeks. Also in Cuneiform Inscriptions of the eighth century, the name Javnan or Junan occurs as designation of the inhabitants of Cyprus. According to the 10th chapter of Genesis, Javan is a son of Japhet, and therefore belongs to the Iranian tribe, like Madai or the Medes, who as Casdîm, later Chaldæans, belonging to the family of the Akkad, conquered Mesopotamia. The transition of the name Javan to that of Ionians, stands in connection with the worship of Io the moon, which was gradually set aside by the Dorians. The original name of Ionia was Achæa, or Achaia, the land of the Achaians or Akkaians, the Akkaiusha of Egyptian monuments of the thirteenth century. This is to be explained by the cognate relations between the Javan and the Akkad of Mesopotamia. We may therefore connect the name of the Greek Achæans, or Akkaians, with the name of the Akkadians, or Akkad, of Mesopotamia. The name given to the Greeks in the Homeric Poems is thus traced to the Iranian and Median Casdîm, later Chaldæans, who were cognate with the Akkad of Cuneiform Inscriptions, and who subjugated in the year B.C. 2458 the Sumir, the descendants of the builders of Babylon.[1]

Similar to the three tribes of Cretian Dorians, there were three tribes among the Spartans, it is said since Lycurgus, which, however, seem to have existed earlier, at least after the conquest of the Peloponnese, since we meet them everywhere among the Dorians. Probably the first tribe among the Spartans consisted exclusively of Dorians, even though at first some Achæans may have been reckoned to them for the sake of peace. It is said that Lycurgus granted to some Achæans the full rights of citizens, but that later they lost the political privileges. The second tribe, of the Periœki, was formed probably by subjugated but free Achæans or Ionians, and the Helotes consisted of serfs, which class was added by the Doric conquests. The Thetes of earlier times, who for wages performed agricultural labours, were probably reckoned to the Helotes. The statement transmitted to us, may therefore be regarded as

---

[1] We have tried to render probable that the Casdîm of the family of the Akkad were a cognate race with the Hyksos, and also with the Keta, Ket, Seth (Ishita-Isâtu). The same people ruled in Mesopotamia as Medes from 2458 to 2334, then over part of Egypt as the twelfth dynasty, and 511 years as Hyksos over the whole of Egypt, from 2074 to 1563; finally, after a sojourn of twenty-nine years in Arabia, they again ruled in Mesopotamia as the 'Arabian' dynasty of Berosus, or the Canaanite dynasty of the Nabathæans, from 1534 to 1289. (*The Chronology of the Bible.*) Probably, already during the Median dynasty, the Japhetic Casdîm or Cheta, according to the 10th chapter of Genesis, migrated from Mesopotamia to Asia Minor, the Black Sea, and the Lower Danube, to Thrace. Here dwelt, as aborigines, the Geta (Keta), who, according to statements of Herodotus, claimed to be descended from the Medes, thus from the Median Casdîm, or Cheta, according to our ethnic scheme. Accordingly, the first immigrants of Greece, the Pelasgians (the P'lishti, or Whites, as Hitzig suggests), but in combination with non-Aryans, or Hamites, may have come from Thrace, and they may have been a cognate tribe with the Celts, who in divers ramifications spread over Europe and Northern Africa as mixed white and black tribes. The Celts in Britain were certainly a mixed race. According to this theory, the Casdîm may have received the name Chaldæans because, as Medes, they formed a mixed race. In Sanscrit 'kâla' means 'black,' and Herodotus mentions Indian Callatians who ate their fathers (III. 38).

historical, that the earliest quarrels took place between Doric conquerors and subjugated Ionians.

The hypothesis that in the Trojan war the Dorians, though not unmixed, as Hellenes were opposed to the Ionians, is also confirmed by a few personal names which can be ethnically explained. The name Dardanos, of the founder of the royal house of Troy, from whom the legend regards the Romans as descended, is formed after the Aryan ' tartan' or commander. Dardanos is first named as chief of the people in the north-east of the Troas, and then is connected with the island Samothrake, the Samos of Homer, opposite Troy, and of Pelasgian (Ionic?) origin. The island was the principal seat of the Kabirian mysteries, which were almost certainly connected with those of the Ionic Dodona. The name Dodona cannot be separated from the name Dodanim, of the son of Javan, according to Genesis, and brother of Elisha, which name Josephus uses for the designation of the Æolians or Ionians. According to the explanation of the Targumim and the Talmud, the Dodanim were identical with the Dardanians, whereby the connection of the Trojans with the Ionians is confirmed, which latter were the allies of the former according to Herodotus.

Again, the name Erechtheus or Erechthonius, is also the name of the first Athenian king, and points to Erech in Mesopotamia, which city was even more ancient than Babylon. The name of the Troic Assarakos corresponds with the Assyrian Assarak or Serak, a name for kings and gods. The name Ilos must be connected with the divinity Illinos, and the latter with Bel-Hea-Aos, and thus with the third name of the Assyrian Trias, whom Damascius calls Aos. Finally, the name Laomedon literally means ' people of the Medes,' and thus seems to point to the Medes of Berosus, whose capture of Babylon in the year of Shem's birth, B.C. 2458, brought about the ethnical combination of

Japhetites and Hamites, of the probable ancestors of Ionians and Dorians, which combination we call Semitism.

That the Trojans were a cognate race with the Ionians, and thus with the Japhetites of Genesis, the Iranians, is also confirmed by the fact that the Phrygians whom Attic poets and Roman historians identify with the Trojans, are pointed out by Herodotus as a people essentially different from the Indians, and next to the latter as the more numerous. As with the Trojans, the Phrygians were cognate with the Thrakians, whom the Ionians called Thraékoi, with which the names Troas, Trôs, and Teucri might have been connected. The Trojans and Phrygians, as Ionians or Javan, were Japhetites, and this is also confirmed by the connection of the Japhetic Tiras of Genesis with Thrace, according to the Targumim, Josephus, and Jerome, whilst Strabo actually designates the Thracians as Trojans and Pelasgians. It has thus become probable at least, that in the Trojan war Indian Dorians, as Hellenes, opposed Iranic Ionians as Trojans.

If the Ionian Homer cannot be separated from the Japhetites or Iranians, it follows that the name Homer must be connected with the Japhetic Javan (Ion), who in the 10th chapter of Genesis is designated as fourth son of Gomer, the eldest son of Japhet. Accordingly, not only the name Homer, but also that of the Homerides of Greece and of the family of singers in Arabia, the Gomeridæ, would point to Gomer, the tribal father of the Japhetites. Apollos communicated to the tribes of seers the mysteries of Zeus about the past and the future. The families of seers were probably also the families of singers. The family of singers, or more probably the corporation or caste of Initiated in the mysteries of Ionic tradition and life, the guardians of the old and of the new treasure from the East, the Homeridæ of Chios, will have to be connected with

Homeric songs, as with the Ionic-Iranian tradition on which they are founded. Also in Bactria and India there were generations of singers ; and according to the most ancient tradition of the East-Iranians recorded in the Zendavesta, the God of light communicates his mysteries to some men through his Word, later through the mediation of Serosh, the Angel-Messiah.

Homeric singers probably existed long before the Trojan war, and still in the sixty-ninth Olympiad, at the commencement of the Persian wars, Kynaethos is said to have sung Homeric poems in Syracuse and other places, the written record of which, in the form transmitted to us, might possibly not have taken place much before this time. The Homeridæ are said to have been proud of their descent from Homer, and they may have connected, though not publicly, the poet's name with the representative name of Gomer. They could do this even without giving up the personality of the one poet. The name Homer has in Greek the meaning of one who rivets or unites what was separate, and it corresponds with the meaning of the name of the Rhapsodi.

If the Ionic Homer can be regarded as representative of Ionic and therefore Iranian traditions of which the Zendavesta is the most ancient record, the connection is thereby confirmed of the Dorian Pythagoras with the essentially different Indian, though mixed Iranian tradition, with the Wisdom or Bodhi, which his contemporary Gautama-Buddha promulgated. Indeed, the name Pythagoras appears to be a combination of Put, Bud, Bod or Bodhi, and of 'guru,' which word in India was used for a teacher of the Veda; so that the name Pythagoras may be interpreted ' teacher of the religion of Buddha.' This derivation must be preferred to the combination of an Indian and a Greek word, of Put and agoraios, one belonging to the market—an epithet of several gods. The market and Wisdom have been strangely connected in the partly late composed Book of

Proverbs : ' Wisdom crieth without, she uttereth her voice in the streets, she crieth in the chief place of concourse,' or, rather, ' in the market place.' [1]

The connection of Pythagoras with the East, and with the Indian-Iranian Wisdom or Bodhi, which his contemporary Buddha promulgated, if proved, is of great importance, because Josephus compares the Essenic Therapeuts of Alexandria with the Pythagoræans, and because Essenic as also Pythagoræan doctrines and rites can be proved to point back to Parsism and Buddhism.

[1] Prov. i. 20.

CHAPTER IV.

THE ESSENES AND THE EAST.

Alexander, Asóka, and the Parthians, as pioneers of the Essenes—The three classes of the Magi and of the Rabbis—Daniel and the Magi or Chaldæans —Probable Essenic origin of the Massora or Gnosis in Israel, and its introduction into the Septuagint.

The Bridge between East and West.

IN a remarkable passage Philo connects the Essenic mode of life with that of the ascetics among the Magi and among the Indians. He states that in the land of the barbarians wise men are 'authorities, both as to words and actions,' and that there are 'very numerous companies of the Magi, who investigating the works of nature for the purpose of becoming acquainted with the truth, do at their leisure become initiated themselves, and initiate others, in the divine virtues by very clear explanations. And among the Indians there is the class of the gymnosophists (or 'naked wise men') who, in addition to natural philosophy, take great pains in the study of moral science likewise, and thus make their whole existence a sort of lesson in virtue.'[1] These naked wise men were by the Indians called Vanaprasthas, or 'inhabitants of woods,' and they formed the third class of the Brahmans, the members of which had to give themselves up to the contemplation of the Deity, till purified from all terrestrial influences they

---

[1] Philo, *Quod omnis probus*, 11; comp. Clem. Al., *Strom.* i. 15; some of them 'neither inhabit cities, nor have roofs over them, but are clothed in the bark of trees, feed on nuts, and drink water in their hands. Like the Encratites, they know not marriage nor begetting of children.'

can as Sanyasi return to the aboriginal source of existence, the condition of release from matter, to the place
where matter is annihilated, to the Nirvâna of the
Buddhists, which we tried to identify with the sun.
This passage immediately precedes the account which
Philo gives of the Essenes in Palestine and Syria, which
countries, he says, 'are also not barren of exemplary
wisdom and virtue,' and where lives that portion of the
Jews whom he calls Essai, the Essenes of Josephus, whom
he mentions by the side of Sadducees and Pharisees as
forming the third party in Israel.   Thus Philo connects
indirectly the Essenes with East-Asiatic religions.

This connection is confirmed by the austere life of
the Essenes, resembling the asceticism of Brahmans,
Jains, and Buddhists, as also that of the Magi.   It becomes probable that the Essenes introduced Oriental
doctrines and customs into Judaism, since Pythagoræan
asceticism and doctrines can likewise be connected with
the East, and especially with the Indian Wisdom or
Bodhi.   Ever since Alexander's conquest of India,
Eastern science could easily be imported into the West,
and already three centuries earlier, Psammetick had
opened the ports of Egypt to the world. The 'Tradition
from beyond,' or the Wisdom from above which Gautama-
Buddha promulgated, became patronised by the great
king Asôka, after his conversion, probably from Jainism,
in the tenth year of his reign.   In the eighteenth year,
about B.C. 258, he assembled a Buddhist council at
Patna, and settled the Southern Canon.   He sent a
message to the general assembly of Magadha, preserved
in the Bhabra edict, in which he expresses his 'respect
and favour in Buddha, in the law, and in the assembly.'
A distinction is then made in favour of the binding,
because provable, authority of the words spoken by
Buddha. 'Whatsoever (words) have been spoken by
the Divine Buddha, they have all been well said, and in
them verily I declare that capability of proof is to be

discerned; so that the pure law (which they teach) will be of long duration. These things, as declared by the Divine Buddha, I proclaim, and I desire them to be regarded as the precepts of the law.'[1] It would have been impossible for Asôka to have addressed the representatives of Buddhism in such terms, transmitted to us by his stone-cut edicts, if authorised records of Buddha's words had not existed in his time.

In the same year, B.C. 250, and under his auspices, the first eighteen Buddhist missionaries reached China, 'where they are held in remembrance to the present day, their images occupying a conspicuous place in every large temple.' The board for foreign missions, established by Asôka, the Dharma-Mahâmâtra, 'sent forth to all surrounding countries enthusiastic preachers . . . supported by the whole weight of Asôka's political and diplomatic influence.'[2] Asôka's son, Mahinda, with others, went to Ceylon during Tissa's reign in that island (250–230). The Society for the propagation of Buddhism in foreign lands must have imported written records of the words of Buddha. This assertion, based on the fact that the Bhabra edict of Asôka refers to existing records of words of Buddha, is confirmed by the reference in Chinese-Buddhist writings to Buddha's exhortation to his son against falsehood, to which Sûtra Asôka's edict referred, in B.C. 250.

The board for foreign missions in India must have directed its special attention to the independent Parthian kingdom. The same was established by Arsakes in the same year that Asôka established his foreign missions, and sent the first missionaries to China. The Parthian kingdom soon connected the Indus with the Euphrates, and thus formed an uninterrupted bridge from East to

---

[1] Professor Wilson's translation; see Thomas, *l. c.* 53; comp. Rhys Davids, 224.

[2] Eitel, *Buddhism*, second edition, pp. 19, 20. According to Rhys Davids, the Dharma-Mahâmâtra was the office of the chief minister of religion; *l.c.* 228.

West for nearly 500 years. Asôka's missionary board had special reasons for sending its emissaries to the Parthians, if Gautama or Sâkya-Buddha was a desceudant from the kings of the Sakas. Like the name Asôka, or Chasôka, the name Arsakes, which is Asak without the liquid *r*, may be translated 'the strong one,' the holder, possessor, ruler, or conqueror, like the Hebrew Chasad and the title Darius, which, according to Hesychius, meant with the Persians 'the wise,' and with the Phrygians 'the holder.' The name Saka was still known as a royal title in India 200 years after Asôka. It is highly probable, if not certain, that, like the cognate Sakas, the Parthians were in part Aryans and Iranians. This is important, since the Buddhistic reform was based on Zoroastrian doctrines.

The independent Parthian kingdom included the land on the lower Euphrates, or Chaldæa proper, of which the Median Casdîm or conquerors had become possessed in the year B.C. 2458. Here, in the land of Abraham's birth, and where Daniel had been set over the Magi, Cyrus the servant of Ormuzd, and whom a prophet in Israel called the Anointed or the Messiah of God, permitted the Israelites to return to the land promised to their fathers, and which was originally bordered by the Euphrates and the Nile. In this land of the Medes and Magi, whom Cyrus acknowledged in their position, Arsakes and his successors were surrounded by a senate of Magi. The Parthians were, therefore, in a more or less direct connection with India and with Syria about a hundred years before the rise of the Maccabees and the organised body of Assidæans, or Chassidim, the pious ones or saints. With these the Essenes have by many authorities been identified, whose existence as an order is first testified in the year B.C. 148. The Chassidim, or saints, are already mentioned in a Psalm written before the Captivity, and the passage is cited by the Maccabees, whose name has been lately derived˙ from Chabah, 'to extinguish,' a very appro‿ priate title for the destroyers of idolatry.[1]

It seems to have been the introduction of an Indian element among the Medes or West-Iranians, whose priests were called Magi, which caused the separation of them from their Eastern brethren. Though the Magi were worshippers of Ormuzd, the god of light, and though they preserved the ancient dualistic sym‿ bolism of light and darkness, they introduced an austere life among the Iranians of the West which was quite contrary to the doctrines and customs of the Eastern Iranians. This asceticism, so similar to that of the Brahmans and Buddhists, led to the separation of nu‿ merous individuals, if not of a whole tribe, from the rest of the community; they became ascetics for life. The similar and pre-Mosaic institution of the Nazarite or Nazirite for life among the Israelites, probably came to them through the Magi, who may have existed among the Medes or Chaldæans already when they con‿ quered Mesopotamia, centuries before the birth of Abraham.

The spirit in which Asôka, the Constantine of Buddhism, desired his religious faith to be disseminated in India and in foreign countries is akin to the spirit of Him who, about 250 years later, instituted an apostolic propagation-society in Zion. The edicts of Asôka, cut in stones, are the earliest records of that universal or catholic religion of humanity which is wrongly as‿ sumed to have sprung up so suddenly and unconnect‿ edly in the West. Unlike other primitive religions, even that of Moses, Buddhism propagated in pre-

[1] Ps. lxxix. 2, 3; comp. cxxxii. 9; Dan. viii. 13; Mal. iii. 13; 1 Macc. vii. 17. Talm. Berach. i. by the Wassîkim or the pious ones probably refers to the Chassidim as the Essenes. Dr. Curtiss, of Leipzig, derives the Machabee of Jerome from Chabah. The probable connection of Mahomed as Hanyf or Sabean with the disciples of John, and thus with the Essenes, sug‿ gests a possible original reference of the Chaâba at Mekka to the extinguish‿ ing of idolatry by Mahomed.

Christian times more than a tribal morality connected with ritualism and a national deity. Buddhism was, certainly in the time of Asôka, not a religion of race, but a religion appealing to the conscience, a religion of 'self-evidencing authority,' the religion of humanity. The enthusiasm with which it was propagated was tempered by a sincere regard for the religions of other nations. One of the rock-cut edicts dated the twelfth year of Asôka's reign has been deciphered as follows:[1] 'The beloved of the gods, King Ryadasi, honours all forms of religious faith, and no reviling or injury of that of others. Let the reverence be shown in such and such a manner as is suited to the difference of belief ; . . . for he who in some way honours his own religion and reviles that of others, saying : having extended to all our own belief, let us make it famous, he who does this, his conduct cannot be right.' The edict goes on to say : ' and as this is the object of all religions, with a view to its dissemination, superintendents of moral duty ' . . . are appointed.

Although Asôka's grandfather, the adventurer of low birth, Tchandragupta, the Greek Sandracottos, who met Alexander on the banks of the Hyphasis in B.C. 325, had about ten years later driven the Greeks out of India, defeating Seleukos, the ruler of the Indus provinces,[2] yet Alexander's religious policy was quite in harmony with the enlightened spirit of Asôka. It is well known that the founder of Alexandria, of the intended metropolis of the Greek western empire, met the appeal of Aristotle, to treat the Greeks as freemen and the Orientalists as slaves, by the declaration, that he regarded it as his 'divine mission, to unite and reconcile the world.' It has been well said, that Alexander was not simply a Greek, and that he must not be judged by a Greek standard. 'The Orientalism

[1] Edward Thomas, *Jainism, or the Early Faith of Asôka*, p. 45.
[2] Rhys-Davids, *Buddhism*, 220.

which was to his followers a scandal, formed an essential part of his principles, and not the result of caprice or vanity. He approached the idea of a universal monarchy from the side of Greece, but his final object was to establish something higher than the paramount supremacy of one people. His purpose was to combine and equalise, not to annihilate ; to wed the East and the West in a just union.'[1]

Alexander found in Greek literature a deposit of Eastern science. We have no reason to doubt the early record of the doctrines which Pythagoras taught but probably did not record himself, nor is it possible to reject the well-attested tradition, that Philolaus, a Pythagoræan philosopher in the time of Socrates (B.C. 469–399), composed a work in three books containing doctrines of Pythagoras. This work Plato is said to have either bought himself from relatives of the philosopher in Sicily, or through Dion of Syracuse, who bought it from Philolaus. The contents of the greater part of Plato's 'Timæus' are said to have been derived from this Pythagoræan source, and the composition of the former probably took place within 60 to 80 years after the death of Pythagoras. Little more than 200 years later, about B.C. 300, Megasthenes composed a work on India after his stay in that country, occasioned by Seleucus-Nicator having sent him as ambassador to Asôka's grandfather, Sandracottos. Although the original Pythagoræan schools cannot be traced beyond the commencement of the fourth century B.C., it cannot be asserted that the Pythagoræan tradition had at any time died out. Soon after the beginning of the last pre-Christian century a revival of it took place, in a probably enlarged and certainly more Eastern garb, under the name of Neo-Pythagoræanism, the first traces of which seem to point to Alexandria, though Cicero strove to connect Roman with Pytha-

[1] Westcott, in Smith's *Dict. of the Bible*: 'Alexander.'

goræan science.   In and near the city where the new
Pythagoræanism probably originated, and about half a
century earlier, the settlement of Therapeuts near
Alexandria is attested.   Again, it is Clement of Alexandria, who first mentions Buddha by name, whose
doctrines have provably influenced those of the Therapeuts.   It was not Hellenism, but Orientalism, which
assimilated the Neo-Pythagoræan doctrines with those
earlier established ones of the Therapeuts.   Both drew
from an Eastern, probably from a Buddhistic source, and
this explains why the Therapeuts are by Josephus
compared with the Pythagoræans.

Daniel, the Magi, and the Rabbi.

The foreign doctrines and rites which the Essenes
have acknowledgedly introduced into Judaism can be
shown to have stood in some connection with those of
the Magi and with those of the Rabbinical schools.
Thus may be explained the remarkable parallel between the three classes of the Magi and the three
classes of the Rabbi, which has been strangely overlooked.   The Herbed or scholar corresponds as exactly
with the Rab, as the Maubed or master with the
Rabbi, and the Destur-Maubed or perfect master with
the Rabbân or Rabbôni.   Daniel, the prophet, was set
over all the Magi, and he may be identified with
Daniel, the priest of the line of Ithamar, as is done in
the addenda to the Book of Daniel in the Septuagint.
This priest Daniel returned with Ezra in 515, if Artaxerxes, or 'King of the Aryans,' is only another title
for Darius, or the 'King' Hystaspes.   Also Mahomedan
tradition makes Daniel the prophet die in Palestine,
and, according to Rabbinical tradition, he was one of
the members of the Great Synagogue under Ezra.
Nebuchadnezzar can hardly have besieged Jerusalem
and exported this Daniel in the third year of Jehoia-

kim, B.C. 609–608, even as vice-regent.[1] If this Daniel, whom we may distinguish from the one mentioned by Ezechiel, was not exported till 588 as a youth, he may well have returned 73 years later under Ezra, or the priest Daniel was a relative of the prophet. This is not unimportant as regards the connection between Rabbinical and Magian tradition, to which the parallel between the three classes of the Magi and those of the Rabbi unmistakably point. Even if the exported Daniel did not survive the time of the return, the tradition of his Chaldæan and Magian knowledge must have been transported to the Land of Promise.

Daniel was of noble and probably of royal and Davidic descent, like Zerubbabel. If so, he was a descendant from Caleb the Kenesite, and his ancestors were non-Hebrews and strangers in Israel, like the Rechabites or Kenites, who inhabited the land before Abraham entered it, and who continued to live with the Israelites as strangers. By a possible ethnological scheme these naturalised strangers can be connected with the Chaldæans, Casdîm or conquerors, with whom the forefathers of Abraham had lived in Ur of the Chaldees or Casdîm. The pre-Abrahamitic Chaldæans or conquerors of Mesopotamia cannot be distinguished without reason from the Medes who captured Babylon, according to Berosus, in B.C. 2458. These Medes may already at that time have called their priests Magi, and as in the Book of Daniel the Magi are identified with the Chaldæans, Daniel may be said to have been set over the descendants of those Medes who conquered Babylon about 500 years before the birth of Abraham in Ur of the Chaldees. Although Daniel had in Babylon to be taught the learning and the language of the Chaldæans, yet this Aramæan language was known in the eighth century to such men as Eliakim, perhaps a high priest, and Shebna, the Scribe, and they may also

---

[1] Comp. Jer. xxxvi. 1, 9, 29; xxv. 1; xlvi. 2.

have known the wisdom or tradition of the Chaldæans, Medes, or Magi. The non-Hebrew tradition, if not the language of the Medo-Chaldæan strangers in Israel, may therefore have been represented by the latter in every period of Hebrew history. Already 182 years after Abraham had left Ur for Haran, or in the year B.C. 1811, Laban, grandson of Nahor, who had remained in Ur, called the heap of stones by an Aramæan or Chaldæan name, whilst Jacob, Abraham's grandson, gave it a Hebrew name.

It must here suffice to state, that to the presence of two races in Israel, the Hebrew and the non-Hebrew or Chaldæan, may be referred the Elohistic and the Jehovistic records in Mosaic writings, and also the two rival high-priestly lines of Eleazar and Ithamar. The latter of these was in the time of Saul connected with the tribe of Judah, whilst its name points to Thamar, whom Philo calls a stranger. To this ethnic dualism in Israel may also be referred the two political parties of later times, the Sadducees and the Pharisees, the name of the latter having possibly been derived from Pharis (Faris), the Arabian name for the Persians.[1] Finally, with the two races in Israel may have stood in some possible connection the two chiefs of the Scribes, Sugoth or Ishkolin, later Katholikoi. These chiefs of the secret association of the Chaberîm are, according to pre-Christian Jewish tradition, designated as recog-

---

[1] Comp. Phares and Pharesites, or Pherisites (Perizzites). Phares was the son of a mixed marriage, which, by a figurative interpretation, may have been referred to the union of Hebrews and Kenites in Arad. As in the land of Faris the faras or horse of the Arabians was indigenous, which the ancient Babylonians called the 'animal of the East,' it is but natural to explain with Pott, the Hebrew words for the horse—sûs, the driving horse, and pârâsh, the riding horse, respectively with Susa and faras, though in Assyrian faras does not mean the horse, and its etymology is doubtful. In Egypt no reference to a horse was made before the Hyksos-rule. One of the Egyptian words for 'horse' is sûs, the other means 'tribute.' Both point to the importation of the horse by the Hyksos, the Median conquerors, who, after their expulsion from Egypt, returned to Mesopotamia as the 'Arabian' dynasty of Berosus. (*Chronology of the Bible.*)

nised organs of that verbal tradition, the Holy Merkabah, which Moses is said to have entrusted to 70
elders, who transmitted it to the prophets and these to
the members of the Great Synagogue. With the last
surviving member of the latter, with Simon the Just
(B.C. 348?), has been connected the transmitted list of
pairs of Scribes down to Gamaliel.[1]

After the Captivity, not provably before the time
of Herod, three classes of Rabbi were introduced, which
form so remarkable a parallel with those of the Magi,
that we are more and more entitled to assume, if not a
connection, a common Oriental source for the Rabbinical or Synagogal and the Magian institution. It is
remarkable that the introduction of the title Rabbân or
Rabboni, which presupposes the lower titles of Rabbi
and of Rab, is by tradition connected with the contest
between the pair of Scribes represented by Hillel 'the
Babylonian,' or Chaldee, and Shammai, and that it was
Simeon, the son of Hillel, and possibly the Simeon of
the Gospel, who first received the title Rabbân. The
corresponding title of Destur-Maubed must have been
given to Daniel as chief of the Magi, to which office the
title Rab-Mag probably stood in some relation, which
we find already in the Book of Jeremiah. The Rab-
Mag was however a lower title than the Rab-Chartumîm
or Rabbân, though it was a higher title than the Rab-
signîn. Rab was known to the Babylonians as Rabu,
which, like the Hebrew Rab, meant 'great.' The word
is as certainly Semitic or Median as Mag is Japhetic,
Aryan, or pre-Semitic. The three years' noviciate which
Daniel had to pass among the Magi can be compared
to the four classes of initiation among the Brahmans
and the Essenes, since the latter, like the Magi, had
a double noviciate. A similar institution were the
four Rabbinical stages of purity, and the secret association of the Chaberîm or Scribes may have also been so

---

[1] Neh. viii. 13; Zohar iii. 157; Ecclus. l. 1; Pirke-Aboth, 1.

classed. A more direct confirmation of the Oriental
and West-Iranian or Magian source of the Synagogue may be derived from the implied fact, that only
the Scribes and Pharisees visited the Temple as well as
the synagogues, where they strove to occupy the first
seats, whilst the Sadducees are never mentioned as
attending them. This fact is all the more significant
since the Sadducees forbad the Pharisees the open promulgation of the tradition of 'their ancestors,' and
since the former originated the persecution of Stephen
and of those of his followers who called themselves
Christians.

The principles of the Synagogue : universal priesthood, self-responsibility, absence of bloody sacrifices, are
of Iranian origin. Opposed to them are the principles of
the Temple : hereditary priests as trustees of religious
mysteries, as sole proprietors of the key of knowledge,
as a conscience-guiding authority, connected with ceremonial observances and bloody sacrifices, all of which
are provably of Indian origin. The figurative or allegorical interpretation of the letter, the most fruitful of
the principles of the Synagogue, was a necessary couse-
quence of the Sadducean prohibition to promulgate
openly the ancestorial tradition of the Pharisees. Yet
these and the Scribes, not the Sadducees, were said by
Jesus to be, and thus to have continued, in the seat of
Moses, as guides whose directions were to be followed.

The Massora, the Targumim, and the Essenes.

We have no right to discard as pure invention the
tradition of the Pirke-Aboth or words of the Fathers,
about the verbal tradition or Massora, transmitted since
Moses. It helps us to throw light on the Hebrew and
the non-Hebrew or Kenite tradition, of both of which
we may regard Moses the Hebrew to have been the
depositor, since he was acquainted with all the know-

ledge of the Egyptians. The Kenite tradition was that of his father-in-law, but in Israel it was the tradition of the stranger and thus of the minority. Yet Moses seems to have interwoven the Jehovistic records of the Iranian Kenites with the Elohistic records of the Indian Hebrews. Later revisions certainly took place, and made the legal distinctions between the Hebrew and the stranger more severe. If we were to assume, that Moses himself did forbid the marriage of Hebrews and Moabites, Boaz could never have married Ruth, and thus the ancestry of David would be connected with an illegal practice.

It is the theory of a verbal tradition among the Jews since Mosaic times, which alone seems fully to explain the origin and the character of the Targumists or Massoretes, and the relation of these interpreters of Scripture with the Scribes, who are in the New Testament designated as trustees of the tradition, and who certainly cannot have been mere copyists or counters of letters, or inventors of vowel-points. Although the vowel-points hitherto known are of post-Christian origin, a new set of vowel-points, differing from the former, has been lately discovered, and it is held as probable that they are more ancient.[1] Long before Ezra, vowel-points may have been known to the Scribes and elders as guardians of tradition. By the theory of a hidden wisdom the entire Rabbinical literature, which ended in the Talmud, can be better explained than by the assumption that, some time after the Return from Babylon, interpretations of Scripture had become necessary merely because of the Hebrew-Chaldæan or Aramaic dialect, which was not generally understood. In this uniformly degraded language, in which only one verse in the Book of Jeremiah has been written, all the Scriptures from and after the time of Haggai, the Book of Daniel included, have been composed. Not so much

---

[1] This is Mr. Ginsburg's opinion.

the Chaldæan language as the Chaldæan wisdom required
interpretation. The latter enabled the Targumists to
harmonise the Hebrew and the Chaldæan meaning of
the word, and thus also the two traditions. It is quite
possible, that the Targumists were bound by a traditional canon of interpretation, transmitted since the
time of Moses, if not from earlier times, and representing essentially the tradition of the strangers in Israel,
particularly of the Medo-Chaldæans or Chasdîm.

We shall connect the foreign or non-Hebrew doctrinal element, which was provably represented by the
Essenes, with the mixed tradition of the Magi or
priests of the Chaldæans, and especially with Buddhism,
the asceticism of which was so similar to that of the
Magi. The Medo-Chaldæans, like the Scribes and like
the Assidæans and Essenes, formed a corporation, the
members of which, we may assume, were initiated in
the mysteries of ancestorial tradition. With the Assidæans or Chassîdim, the pious ones or the saints, who
were established as an order before the Maccabean
rising, the Essenes have been very generally identified.[1]
Even the name Essenes, like that of the Assidæans, can
have been derived from the Hebrew Chassîn, and Philo
connects their name with their holy life. It is certain
that the name Essenes was connected with the Magi,
since the Megabyzi among the Magi, that is, the circumcised Curetæ or Corybanthians, the priests of Artemis
(Cybele, Ishtar, Diana), which successors of Corybas
represented Cabirian mysteries, are by Pausanias called
Essenænes.[2] The Essenes, and no doubt also the Rabbis
with their three classes, stood in connection with the
Medo-Chaldæan or Magian institution, and formed a
link between Babylon and Jerusalem. The provable
connection of the Jewish books of the Captivity and
Return, as also of the most ancient paraphrases or Tar-

[1] Thus by Rappaport, Frankel, Jost, Ewald, and Ginsburg.
[2] Paus. viii. 3, 1; Clem. Alex. *Exort.* 2.

gumim with Iranian tradition, obliges us to assume either the importation of entirely new doctrinal elements into the Israelitic community, or a verbal tradition or Massoret, transmitted possibly since the times of Moses, if not of Abraham, as the tradition of the Medo-Chaldæan stranger in Israel, developed and partly published after the Return from Babylon. The promulgation of more or less new doctrines in Israel after the Return from Babylon is a fact, and it is probable at the outset, that with this doctrinal development, the provable introduction of non-Hebrew doctrines and customs into Israel by the Essenes, stood in some connection.

The Mosaic Scriptures, said to have been lost during the Captivity, were recomposed in the Aramaic language on the Return from Babylon, or about a thousand years after Moses. Even then the Hebrew Scriptures could not have conveyed to the people a fixed meaning, unless we assume, that already Ezra introduced vowel-points. Not until the time of the Captivity and the Return, can the introduction of the words Shemeh, or name, formed by transposition after the mysterious Chaldæan Sehem, and Memra, Word of God, be proved in Hebrew writings, where they are substituted for Jehova. Yet we find both these words in the Mosaic writings as transmitted to us.[1] This is all the more remarkable, since in the Book of Exodus the ' Name ' of God is connected with the Angel of God, as the ' Word ' of God is connected with man. The most ancient Targumim, perhaps composed soon after the Return, and partly edited in Babylon, not only constantly change the name of Jehova into Memra or Word, or into Shechina or glory, but Memra was the designation of the Angel of God in whom, according to Exodus, is the Name of God.[2] Thus the two new expressions for

---

[1] Ex. xxiii. 21; Deut. xxx. 14; comp. Rom. x. 8.
[2] Lenormant, *Chaldean Magic* (Cooper's edition), p. 42, where Shemeh ought to stand for Memra.

Jehova, whether or not they had been transmitted as
Mosaic verbal tradition, and which were exceptionally
inserted in the Scriptures bearing the name of Moses,
have been some time after the Return from Babylon
connected with the Messiah as the Angel of God. It
was easier to do so, since the Messiah was by Malachi
designated as a messenger or Maleach, which word has
also the meaning of angel.

The promulgation of new names for the Deity after
the Return from Babylon, and through Hebrew Scriptures, must be connected with the first introduction of
the doctrine of angels among the people of Israel.
Although the party of the Sadducees cannot be traced
till after the Captivity, yet they must have represented .
a very ancient tradition, which seems to have been connected with that Elohistic stream which the ethnic
dualism in Israel perhaps enables us to connect with
India. The Sadducees did not believe in angels or
spirits, according to Josephus. They must have therefore either known nothing of an early insertion of the
doctrine of angels into Mosaic Scriptures, or they must
have disbelieved a doctrine which the lawgiver himself
had promulgated by what he wrote. In either case
the Sadducees would make use of their power to forbid
the Pharisees to promulgate the tradition of their forefathers, as Josephus asserts they did. This tradition of
the Pharisees must have included the belief in angels,
for otherwise the Sadducean unbelief in this doctrine,
with which that of the resurrection and future judgment was closely connected, would not have been mentioned as a peculiarity of their religious system. The
ancestral tradition of the Pharisees, including the doctrine of angels, may be with increasing certainty connected with Persia, the Pharis of the Arabians, and
from which name that of the Pharisees may have been
derived. For the doctrine of angels was first introduced and developed by the Iranians, and their tradition

was represented by the Magi in Mesopotamia, by the Buddhists in India, and probably by the Essenes in Palestine and Egypt.

The secret tradition, Massora or Gnosis of the Jews, later called Kabbala, was certainly not derived from Greek philosophy; but it can be connected with the secret tradition of the Essenes, and thus with the Medes and Chaldæans of pre-Abrahamitic times, as also with Parsism and Buddhism. A connection can be established between the Book of Daniel, the Targumim, the Apocrypha of the Septuagint and the whole Apocalyptic literature. The doctrinal development represented by these Scriptures is essentially Essenic.

Essenic Doctrines in the Septuagint.

Whilst the Essenic dogma in many respects can be compared with that of the Sadducees, it certainly differed from the latter as regards angels, the names of which the Essene had to swear to keep secret. At the time when the Essenic corporation can be proved to have existed, about the middle of the second century before the commencement of the Christian era, the introduction of the doctrine of angels, and even of a hierarchy of angels, imported from Babylon, together with the Essenic doctrine of the eternal punishment of wicked souls, had taken place. We find it in the canonical Hebrew and Greek Scriptures of the Jews, in neither of which there is a trace of doctrinal Greek influence, and also in the most ancient Targumim. In the earlier books of the Septuagint, published from and after B.C. 280, the word 'angel' or 'angels' is substituted for Jehova, just as, in the pre-Christian Targumim, Memra, the 'Word,' Shechina, the 'glory,' 'and the Angel of the Lord' are substituted for Jehova, and referred to the Messiah.

The connection of the Septuagint and its Apocrypha

not known to the Hebrew canon, with the most ancient Targumim, partly edited in Babylon, perhaps soon after the return of some Jews to Jerusalem, is of the utmost importance, because the time of publication of the Septuagint is settled beyond doubt. Therefore a review of the doctrines in the latter must precede a consideration of the Messianic passages in the Targumim. The Greek canon was composed in all its parts a few years before the actual attestation of the Essenic order, which was preceded by the similar order of the Assidæans or Cassîdim, even assuming that both were not identical. The more the Essenes, with whom we may safely connect the Rechabites, can be connected with the Magian and Buddhistic doctrines and rites, the more certain will it become that this third and independent party among the Jews introduced Eastern elements, some of them pre-Buddhistic, and among these the doctrine of the Angel-Messiah. With such pre-Christian mysticism, deeper knowledge or Gnosis, the composition of the Septuagint must be connected. This can be proved to demonstration from the Essenic point of view, by a brief analysis of the new and characteristic features of the Greek-Jewish Scriptures, which are about a thousand years more ancient than the first manuscript of the Hebrew Scriptures transmitted to us.

The account given by Philo about the composition of the Septuagint is all the more important for the critical but impartial inquirer, because its conclusion did not take place till his lifetime, if the learned Jerome was right in believing that one of the Apocrypha, called the Wisdom of Solomon, had Philo for its author.[1] Philo's near relation to, if not connec-

---

[1] Jer. *Praef. in lib. Sal.* 'Nonnulli scriptorum veterum hunc esse Judaei Philonis affirmant.' Luther accepted this view. If we can connect Philo with the Therapeuts living near the town of his birth, the view of Eichhorn, Zeller, and Jost about the author being a Therapeut coincides with the tradition transmitted by Jerome. The same would be the case if Apollos were regarded as its author (Noack, Plumptre, and others), as also of the Epistle

tion with, the Essenic Therapeuts of Egypt, especially of Alexandria, is certain. The Essenes are by Philo stated to have asserted the principle of a continued and gradually revealing Divine inspiration, and thus of a higher stage of revelation than that conveyed by the letter of the revered Mosaic Scriptures. Philo believed that the Hebrew Scriptures 'had been divinely given by direct inspiration,' and that they who composed them ' prophesied like men inspired.' The Essenes studied, according to Philo's statement, ' the sacred oracles of God enunciated by the holy prophets.' But the Essenes held, that the prophets of the past had written in such a manner that prophets of the future might find out ' the invisible meaning concealed under and lying beneath the plain words.' The light of the secret meaning thus revealed, was not only assumed to come from the same Divine source which inspires the prophets of all ages, but Philo designates it as a higher stage of inspiration, so much higher as the soul is with regard to the body, with which he compares the law. In connection with the views thus enunciated by Philo with regard to the inspired and prophetic character of the Hebrew Scriptures, he declares, that he considers the composers of the Septuagint version ' not mere interpreters but hierophants (the word taken from the first priest of the Eleusinian mysteries) and prophets, to whom it had been granted, with their honest and guileless minds, to go along with the most pure spirit of Moses.'

The question whether the Septuagint is faithful in substance cannot be better answered than by the light which Paul throws on the inspiration of the Scriptures, especially of the Greek text, which he almost invariably prefers to quote, as Jesus is likewise reported to have done in his sayings. The Septuagint is as faithful to

to the Hebrews, which we shall explain by a development of Paulinic Essenianism.

'the letter that killeth,' as it is possible with due regard to the spirit which 'giveth light' and which inspired its writers, according to Philo's testimony. Nor does Philo stand alone in this view of the higher standard of inspiration as conveyed by the Septuagint. For Jerome, the Father who cites the ancient tradition which attributes the Book of Wisdom to Philo, clearly implies, that the translators were divinely moved to add to the original and thus to perform the office of prophets, giving a new revelation by every addition as well as by all their deviations from the Hebrew text. By so doing they acted in harmony, not with the letter, but with 'the most pure spirit of Moses,' according to Philo's words.[1] If it were argued that he had no authority for saying so, there would remain unexplained the confirmation of this view by the learned Jerome, and the more general testimony of Irenæus and Augustine as to the Divine inspiration of the Septuagint, confirmed as it was by the citations in the New Testament.

The Essenic and Philonian, the Targumistic and Paulinian doctrine of inspiration, according to which fiery sparks of the spirit were to be produced from the letter as from the flint, is indirectly confirmed by the deeper and spiritual sense which the transmitted parables of Jesus convey. He taught the mysteries of the spiritual kingdom to a few only when he was alone with them, not within hearing of the spies who were watching him, and of those whose predecessors in office had 'taken away the key of knowledge.' The preaching of Jesus and the Gospel which Paul preached are by the Apostle declared to centre in the revelation of a mystery kept 'in silence,' in the revelation of 'the hidden wisdom.' Origen writes: 'If we were obliged

---

[1] Philo, *De Vita Mosis*, ii. 6, 7; August. *Praef. in Paral.* i. col. 1419; *Prolog. in Genesin*, i. Canon and Professor Selwyn denies this conclusion, in Smith's *Dict. of the Bible*, 'Septuagint.' He says: 'The Septuagint is the image of the original seen through a glass not adjusted to its proper focus.'

to keep to the letters, and to understand what is written in the law according to the manner of the Jews or of the people, I would blush to proclaim loudly my belief, that it is God who has given these laws; in that case the laws of men, as, for instance, those of the Romans, Athenians, and Lacedemonians, would appear better and more reasonable.' In another passage Origen says: 'I believe that everybody must regard these things as figures, under which a secret meaning lies hidden.' Paul accuses Moses of having hidden.[1]

It may be said against this scheme of a hidden wisdom, which cannot be proved to have existed till after the return from Captivity, that its connection with a verbal tradition entrusted by Moses to the elders is non-proven. Yet Philo, the Essenes, the Targumists, and probably the early Christians, explained the doctrinal development in the Scriptures by the gradual proclamation of mysteries which the Initiated handed down since the time of Moses. They all believed in a new inspiration, and seem to imply, that it took cognisance of the capabilities and of the exigencies of advanced times, and particularly of the contact of Israel with other nations, with the East. The more that the connection of Essenic doctrines and rites with the Magi and Buddhists can be established, the more certain will it become, that the deeper knowledge or gnosis of pre-Christian times, which the Essenes and Rabbis represented, can only then lay claim to revelation, if Zoroaster, Moses, and Buddha are regarded as organs of the same revealing Spirit of God. This is done by men like Clement of Alexandria, Origen, and Augustine; the latter saying, that what is called Christian doctrine was earlier known under different names. On this assumption it could be asserted, that those who composed the Septuagint, writing as divinely inspired prophets, acted in harmony

---

[1] Orig. *Homil.* 7, in Levit.; Huet, *Origeniana*, 167; 2 Cor. iii. 12–18; iv. 1–3.

with the pure spirit of Moses.   The Essenic theory of
inspiration is, in fact, of the same nature as the Rabbinical theory, possibly of later origin, that from the
time of Moses to that of Ezra elders and prophets had
been in possession of a verbal tradition which was
not promulgated in Israel till after the Return from
Babylon.   The belief in a continuous inspiration suffices
to account for the claim of Divine authority for books
showing studied and systematic deviations from those
transmitted as Mosaic.   If Moses could not put an end
to the generally prevailing system of hiding, he could
hardly have deviated from the universal custom of
initiation in mysteries.   Some of the new productions in
the Greek Canon were called Apocrypha or ' hidden,' and
are published under fictitious names, apparently with a
view to invest them with a Divine authority.

The Book of Wisdom, falsely and intentionally
attributed to Solomon, must be regarded, with Basil
and Jerome, as the work of Philo, the only person to
whom the authorship is assigned.   Jerome was the contemporary of the church-historian Eusebius ; and they
both attest, the one in direct connection with the first
stay of Peter at Rome, that in this city, where Jerome
received his earliest education, and where he was later
appointed as teacher, Peter met Philo of Alexandria.
They imply, that this happened A.D. 42, which is also
the year mentioned in the Pseudo-Clementines as the year
when the Apostle first reached Rome.   This information is strikingly confirmed by the fact, that Philo
describes his being in Rome in 41, and gives reasons for
assuming that he was there the next year also.[1]   Philo
and Peter are said to have had ' familiar conversation '
in Rome.   Eusebius regards this as ' not at all improbable,' since in his writings Philo not only ' describes
with the greatest accuracy the lives of our ascetics, that
is, of the Therapeutæ,' but also ' extolled and revered

---

[1] E. de Bunsen, *The Chronology of the Bible,* 81.

the apostolic men of his day.' It is in direct connection with this statement, that Eusebius refers to the 'highly probable' utilisation of Therapeutic Scriptures in our Gospels and Pauline Epistles, especially in the Epistle to the Hebrews.[1] And yet Philo, with whom Peter had familiar intercourse, is said, on the most ancient authority, to have composed the Book of Wisdom, with which the Epistle to the Hebrews (by Apollos) is unquestionably connected, although the Philonian work, by the general tenour of its teaching, excludes the cardinal doctrines of 'Christianity,' the incarnation, atonement, and the resurrection of the body.

The counter-argument, that the doctrinal character of the Book of Wisdom is 'foreign to the pure Hebrew mode of thought,'[2] may be at once dismissed, if a pre-Christian gnosticism can be proved, which Philo adopted. As this Essenic and Eastern gnosis was based on the doctrine of two worlds with its respective rulers, of which there is no trace in Israel before the Captivity, it is a striking confirmation of the Philonic authorship, that in the Book of Wisdom the personal devil, or Satan, the serpent, is mentioned, whilst the Wisdom of God, though identified with the Spirit of God, is personified in the other Apocrypha, in Ecclesiasticus or the Book of Sirach, and in the Book of Proverbs closed at an indefinite time. The identity of personified Wisdom with the Spirit of God, of the supermundane creation of God with the Spirit brooding over the waters, renders futile all subtle arguments about a possible distinction between the personified Word of God and the personified Wisdom of God, as respectively representing 'the mediative element in the action of God' and that 'of his omnipresence.' Fire was the symbol of the Spirit of God, and thus of Wisdom; and as in the Book of Wisdom the Almighty Word of God is compared to

---

[1] Eus. *H.E.*, ii. 17.
[2] Canon Westcott, in Smith's *Dict. of the Bible.*

lightning, so in the same Scripture the fiery and brazen serpent is explained as the symbol of the word of God, ' which healeth all things,' as ' the Saviour of all,' who had already preserved Adam and brought him out of his fall.[1]

The Wisdom of God is only another name for the Word of God; and the personification of this premundane Saviour may be identified with the Angel of God, whom Philo designates in other writings as the companion of the human soul, and at the same time as God's Firstborn and God himself.

Yet in the Book of Wisdom no incarnation of this Angel-Messiah is announced. This may be explained by the secret tradition of the Therapeuts. No more is said, than that through the Wisdom of God pious souls in all ages are made ' sons of God and prophets.' These are the expressed Messianic views of Philo, who personifies the Word of God or Messiah, though he never refers even to an expected Messiah, and no more than John the Baptist (the Essene) regarded his contemporary Jesus as the fulfilment of such expectations. This cannot be a mere chance, since even Josephus, probably for three years an Essene, avoids the Messianic doctrine, perhaps because as an Essene he had promised not to divulge it. The combination of the Philonic, and, as we shall see, Essenic conception of an Angelic Messiah and Son of God with the Hebrew conception of a human Messiah and son of David, a combination which meets us in the Septuagint, seems at the outset to have been effected by the Essenes or Therapeuts of Alexandria. In order to have some ground to claim the authority of Moses for their new theory of an Angel-Messiah, they would so render those passages which Hebrews might possibly regard as prophecies of an anointed Man, that such interpretation should by the

---

[1] Prov. viii. 22, 31 ; Ecclus. xxiv.; Wisd. ix. 17 ; vii. 27 ; xvi. 6, 7, 12 ; xviii. 15.

new text be excluded, and that the more perfect or gnostic text should point to the Oriental and Essenic conception of an anointed Angel.

The personified Wisdom or Word of God, as described in the Apocrypha of the Septuagint, is by the most ancient Targumim identified with the Angel of God who followed Israel in the wilderness, which Angel is by Stephen and by Paul, almost in the same words, applied to Jesus Christ, the Angel-Messiah. According to the Targum called after Onkelos, it was 'the thought or Word of God' who 'created man in his own image, in an image which was (stood or sat) before God.' Again, it was the personified thought or Word of God who said to Adam : 'The world which I have created lies before me, darkness and light lie before me.' The Word of God said : 'Adam whom I have created is now alone in this world, as I am (alone) in the highest heaven.' Thus it was the Word or Memra, the Angel of God, who created Adam.[1]

According to the pre-Christian Targumim, called after Jonathan, it was not God who was with the lad Ishmael, but the Word of God was aiding him ; the 'voice of the Word' was heard by Adam and Eve in Eden ; the glory of God went up from Abraham ; the personified Word came to Abimelech, to Jacob in Bethel, to Moses on Sinai ; the Divine presence, or Shechina, is in heaven and reigns below, and it is by the Targumist identified with the Angel of God who went before and followed Israel in the wilderness. Again, the passages about Shiloh, about Judah's sceptre, and the star of Jacob, are Messianically interpreted.[2] In the Targum after Jonathan the Maleach, or messenger, in the Book of Malachi is described as an Angel, as a celestial and premundane being, hidden from the eyes of men till born at Bethlehem. The two natures of the

---

[1] *Targ. Onk.* Gen. ii. 27 ; iii. 9 ; iv. 22, &c.
[2] Gen. xlix. 10 ; Num. xxiv. 17.

celestial and the terrestrial Messiah are kept distinct.
'My Word' rejoiced over 'my servant the Messiah.'
Among the seventeen passages which in this Targum
are explained Messianically, is also the one about the
serpent-bruiser. The Bereshith-Rabba, a record of
ancient tradition published in the sixth century A.D.,
explains the Spirit over the waters as the Messiah of
the future world, who sits at the right hand of God.
It is stated there that the Messiah has been 'with the
Church in the wilderness,' as 'Rock of the Church of
Zion.' [1]

Conclusion.

The argument which runs through this Chapter is
the following. Philo, the earliest and highest authority
for all we know about the Essenes, connects them, at
least indirectly, with East-Asiatic religions. Like the
Pythagoræans, the Essenes may have derived their
peculiar doctrines directly from the East. Psammetick,
Alexander, and Asôka had paved the way for such
direct transmission, and the Parthian kingdom had ever
since B.C. 250 established a bridge between East and
West. The remarkable parallel between the three
classes of the Magi and the three classes of Rabbi shows,
that after the Return from Babylon close relations were
established between the land of the Jews and the land
of the Magi. The connection of Daniel with the Magi,
their identification with the Chaldæans, the prophet's
probable return under Ezra, and the almost certain
foreign origin of the synagogues, throw some light on
the important period of Jewish captivity in Babylon.
If the naturalised stranger in Israel, to whom the
Rechabite and Essene belonged, at least since the time
of Moses, was descended from the Medo-Chaldæans, who
lived in Abraham's native city of Ur, the verbal tradi-

---

[1] *Targ. Jon.* to Isaiah xlii. 11, 1, and xv. 1; comp. Acts vii. 37, 38;
1 Cor. x. 1–4.

tion of the Jews, the Massora, said to have been transmitted ever since Moses, and perhaps identical with the ancestral tradition of the Essenes, which they kept secret, and of the Pharisees, to whom the Sadducees did not permit its promulgation among the people, this verbal tradition among Israelites may be connected directly or indirectly with the East. The non-Hebrew doctrinal element which the Essenes represented can clearly be traced to Parsism and Buddhism ; and the new words and doctrines introduced into Hebrew Scriptures after the Return from Babylon, as also the doctrinal development in the Targumim, in the Septuagint, and in the canonical and non-canonical Apocalypses, is best explained by the spread of Essenic influence in Palestine and Egypt.

The Essenes believed in Angels, and they also may have believed in an Angel-Messiah. If so, they were bound not to reveal anything with regard to their Messianic expectations, of which, in fact, nothing has been transmitted to us before the time of Elkesai, about 100 A.D. This leads us to assume, at the outset, that the Essenes, according to their secret tradition, and thus before the time of Elkesai, member of their sect, expected as Messiah an incarnate Angel.

CHAPTER V.

THE ANGEL-MESSIAH.

Messianic conceptions in East and West—The anointed Angel and the anointed Man—Essenic expectation of an Angel-Messiah—The Eastern source of that and similar doctrines explains the parallels between the earliest Buddhistic and the earliest Christian records—When was the doctrine of the Angel-Messiah applied to Jesus Christ, as it had been applied to Gautama-Buddha?

Messianic Conceptions in East and West.

IN the most ancient parts of the Zendavesta the one God Ahura Mazda or Ormuzd is designated as the first of seven angels or watchers, in conjunction with whom he created the world by his word.[1] But by later passages in the holy book of the Iranians the honour of the first of seven angels is attributed to a vicar of God, to a mediator, to a divine messenger or angel, to Sraosha. This ideal hero and Messiah of Iranian tradition was originally connected with fire, and thus, with the seven stars of the Pleiades, from which a divine messenger, the Mâtarisvan, according to Indian tradition, brought down the fire, as already pointed out. Fire was the symbol of the spiritual power, the Megh or Meh of the Zendavesta, the Mah or Maha in Sanscrit, and the Maya of Buddhism. This divine messenger and importer of fire, and of the spirit symbolised by fire, was called Agni, whose secret name was Mâtarisvan, the heavenly man from the Pleiades in Taurus, the throne

---

[1] In Genesis Jehovah is recorded to have said, as is implied, to some angels surrounding him: 'Let us make man in our image, after our likeness.' According to the Targum, this was said to the Word.

of the God of seven stars, of Indra, the celestial bull, as of Osiris, of Zeus-Chronos, of the Sibut of the ancient Babylonians, the Sebaot or Sabaoth of the Hebrews, and so also of other deities. We pointed out that Zeus-Chronos, the creator of fire, and whose seven sons may be connected with the Pleiades, in order to frame the world, according to Greek theogony, transformed himself into Eros, the god of love, who became the vicar of Zeus and the framer of the world. Eros stands in the same relation to Zeus that Serosh stands to Ormuzd; and the Eros of the Greeks may safely be identified with the Serosh or Sraosha of the Zendavesta.

It thus becomes probable that the West-Iranians, the Chaldæans, Casdîm, or conquerors of Mesopotamia, in B.C. 2458, the year of Shem's birth, that those whom Berosus calls Medes—and who may already then have had Magi—introduced into the West the doctrine of the Angel-Messiah. At all events not long after, if not ever since this Median conquest by the Casdîm or Chaldæans, whom we regard as the Shemites of Genesis, the ancient Babylonians knew of such a celestial being who distributed good among men, as his name, Silik-mulu-dug (khi ?) implies.[1] He is said to walk before or to be the forerunner, the messenger, of Hea, who is provably the God in the Pleiades, like the Sibut of the Babylonians.[2] As was done by the Agni of the Indians, this Angel-Messiah of Mesopotamia was connected with the Arani or fire-sticks.

A mediatorial position similar to that assigned to Serosh was held by Mithras, who was first connected with fire and then with the sun. Like Ormuzd, Mithras is represented riding on the bull, and Jehovah is described as riding on the Cherub, Kirub or bull. This bull is certainly the constellation of Taurus; and the same Mithraic representation connects with the bull a scor-

[1] *Die Plejaden*, 176.
[2] Lenormant, *Magic*, translated and edited by B. Cooper.

pion, evidently the opposite constellation. Also the
Hebrews knew traditions according to which the Memra
or Word of God, the Messiah, was symbolised first by
fire, that is, by the fiery or brazen serpent, which
probably pointed to lightning, and later the Hebrews
symbolised the Word by the sun.

The transition from fire-symbolism to sun-symbolism
took place in early historical times. The seven stages
of the tower of Babel or Bab-Il were probably commenced by the first king of the Median dynasty, who
ascended the throne in the implied year of Shem's birth,
when the mixed race of conquerors and conquered, of
Japhetites and Hamites, had risen to political importance. This first king of the first historical monarchy is
called Zoroaster, by Berosus, the Chaldæan historian,
after the great Eastern reformer, born in the Aryan
home. Reasons can be given for identifying with this
potentate the Nimrod-Merodach of the Bible and the
Takmo-Urûpis (Urûpa) of Iranian tradition, the possessor
of the same cities which are enumerated in Genesis as
forming the beginning of Nimrod's empire. These
seven stages of the Median tower of Babel, with which
the seven walls may be compared which the Medes
built for Dejokes, were by the finishers and restorers of
this tower, if not by Urukh, certainly by Nebukad-
nezar, dedicated to the seven planets, or rather to sun,
moon, and five planets. Excavations on the Birs-
Nimrud have shown that the sun was symbolised by
the middle or highest stage, the moon and the five
planets by the other stages, which were ranged in
accordance with the Chaldæan reckonings respecting
the distances of these bodies from the earth. Exactly
the same order has been observed in the distribution of
the seven gates of Thebes; and also, excepting one transposition, in the symbolical interpretation given by Philo
and Josephus to the candlestick of Moses. Philo states
that the central lamp symbolised the sun; but that ac-

cording to the deeper knowledge or gnosis it symbolised the Word of God, which the Seer at Patmos describes in the Apocalypse as the Messiah appearing in the midst of the candlesticks, and being the first of seven angels.[1]

The link thus established between Eastern and Western symbolism is confirmed by a remarkable parallel between the seven priests of the Soma-sacrifice in the Rig-Veda, and Zechariah's vision of the candlestick. The central priest of the former invoked the Deity. This may be compared with Ezechiel's vision of the man clothed with linen, as priest, who was surrounded by six other men, and who performed the office of sealing the foreheads of the chosen, a symbolism which in the Apocalypse of John is directly connected with the Messiah. Already in the Book of Proverbs Divine Wisdom is personified and apparently placed above the angels. With this Messianic symbolism of an Angel-Messiah connected with six other angels we shall with ever increasing probability connect the vision of the nameless angel, the Angel of the Lord, as one like a son of man. This vision is recorded in the Book of Daniel, a book certainly not closed till after the foundation of the Essenic corporation, of which we try to prove that its higher members transmitted the doctrine of the Angel-Messiah.

The Messianic conceptions of the East, which were connected with the symbolism of the number Seven, and referred to an ideal celestial hero and Messiah, sooner or later had to make way for the new conception of a celestial Messiah in the flesh, of an incarnate Angel-Messiah. It cannot be even approximatively determined at what time this change in the Messianic conceptions took place in the East, but Gautama-Buddha was not the first to whom this Messianic

---

[1] Ernst von Bunsen, *Das Symbol des Kreuzes bei allen Nationen*, 92–104; *Die Plejaden*, 231–239.

doctrine was applied. Also the ancient Babylonians
knew of an Angel-Messiah among men, probably before
the time of Abraham. The naturalised strangers among
the Israelites, probably descendants of the Chaldæans
among whom Abraham lived, and who in the Book
of Daniel are identified with the Magi, may have transmitted this Eastern doctrine of the Angel-Messiah. Since
Daniel was instructed in the science of the Chaldæans or
Magi, and since the three classes of the Rabbi must be
associated with the three classes of the Magi, we expect
to find that in the Hebrew Scriptures composed after
the deportation to Babylon there will be traces of this
Eastern doctrine about the Angel-Messiah.

We must distinguish in the Old Testament the
earlier prophecies and expectations of an anointed Man
from the later prophecies and expectations of an
anointed Angel.

Already Isaiah the son of Amos had prophesied,
probably in connection with Nathan's announcement to
David, that on a Davidic descendant, 'a Branch,' the
Spirit of the Lord would rest, thus implying that God
would anoint the son of David with the Holy Ghost.
This future Anointed or Messiah would confer on Israel
a Messianic mission. The Babylonian Isaiah, the unknown prophet, the so-called evangelist and precursor
of the Gospel-dispensation, the author of the Second
Part of the Book of Isaiah, had pointed to the people
of Israel to whom the Messiah was to be sent, as the
people to whom the mission of the Servant of God was
to be confided, as the nation through which the Kingdom of God was to be set up on earth. A representative of this Messianic people, Haggai, had called himself the messenger, as if pointing to a man like Moses,
chosen from among his brethren, whose coming Israel
expected, as 'the messenger of the covenant.' This
divinely inspired human messenger, or 'Maleach,' was
by Zechariah again called 'the man whose name is the

Branch.' In another of his visions Zerubbabel and
Joshua are probably referred to as the two Anointed
Ones or Messiahs. It is possible that the Prophet
intended thereby to point to the temporal and to the
spiritual ruler in Israel as the most enlightened organs
of Messianic power among the Messianic nation.

In all these passages the Messiah is described as a
descendant of David who would be anointed by the
Spirit of God and become a messenger of God. But
the word ' maleach ' has the double meaning of messenger and of angel ; and since the introduction of the
doctrine of angels into Israel, probably coupled with
the new definitions for the Deity, Shemeh, or Name,
and Memra, or Word of God, a passage in Isaiah was
Messianically interpreted which originally was understood to refer either to young Hezekiah or to a son
born to Isaiah by his wife. Although the Hebrew
word for virgin, ' bethulah,' is not used in this passage, it
became interpreted as if it were in the text. By such
means the doctrine of a virgin-born Messiah was introduced into the Scriptures, which doctrine Clement of
Alexandria designates as a false doctrine.[1]

A scriptural basis was thus created for the new
doctrine of the Angel-Messiah, of which there is no trace
in any of those Scriptures of which it can be asserted
that they were composed, in the form transmitted to
us, before the deportation to Babylon. The erroneous
passage in Isaiah was connected with the passage in
Genesis about the enmity between the seed of Eve and
the seed of the Serpent, which enmity should lead to
the destruction of the latter by the former. This
passage in Genesis, whether it existed or not in the

[1] *Strom.* vii. 16: 'Many even down to our time regard Mary, on account
of the birth of her child, as having been in the puerpural state, although she
was not.' He makes no mention of the account in Matthew, transmitted to
us, about Mary's virginity ; this he must have done if, in the second century, this passage had already been inserted into the Gospel after Matthew.

time of Isaiah, contains an unmistakable reference to
the Eastern symbolism of successive ideal heroes of
light, who conquer the ideal heroes of darkness, and
who are all symbolised by the serpent, as the Satan or
adversary. This symbolism refers, as we showed, to
the figures on the sphere, where the constellation of
the Serpent and the adjoining one of the Scorpion are
placed near the autumn-equinoctial point, whilst the
heroes of light are connected with the constellations of
the spring-equinox. The position of the sphere on
Christmas-day, on the birthday of the sun, shows the
serpent all but touching and certainly aiming at the
heel of the woman, that is, the figure of the constellation Virgo.[1] This pre-Christian symbolism would
still be historical even if the existence of Gautama
could be doubted, whose symbol was the sun, and who
is reported to have been born on our Christmas-day,
like Jesus, the Sun of Righteousness.

We are thus led to assume, that some time after
the deportation to Babylon the expectation of an anointed Man was by some Jews changed into the expectation of an anointed Angel. Since after the Return
from Babylon, as we have seen, new definitions of the
Messiah were introduced into Jewish Scriptures, and
since at that time the existence of the Essenic corporation, a secret society of Jewish dissenters, can be
proved, by whom some non-Hebrew doctrines and
customs have been introduced into the Israelitic community, the Essenic origin of the new doctrine in
Israel of an Angel-Messiah becomes probable. We
shall now try to prove that the Essenes were the first
historical organs of such an expectation in Israel.

---

[1] In the text of the Itala and in that of Jerome, the woman, that is the
Virgin, is said to be the bruiser of the serpent, and this entirely harmonises
with the position of the sphere on the birthday of the virgin-born, which is
also the birthday of the sun.

Essenic Expectation of an Angel-Messiah.

Epiphanius, Bishop of Constantia and Metropolitan of Cyprus (A.D. 403) states,[1] that 'the Essenes continue in their first position and have not altered at all.' Speaking of the Ossenes, who were closely connected with the former 'sect,' he records the tradition that they had originated in the regions of Nabatæa, meaning not Mesopotamia, but Arabia-Petræa; and among other places he mentions the surrounding neighbourhood of the Dead Sea, on the Eastern shores of the lake, not on the Western, where, according to Pliny, were in his time the settlements of the Essenes. 'A certain person named Elxai joined them at the time of the Emperor Trajan.' The Bishop says, that he was a false prophet, and that he wrote 'a so-called prophetical book, which he propounded to be according to divine wisdom.' . . . 'A Jew by birth, and professing the Jewish doctrines, he did not live according to the Mosaic law, but introduced quite different things, and misled his own sect . . . He joined the sect of the Ossenes, of which some remnants are still to be found in the same regions of Nabatæa and Peræa. towards Moabitis; and these people are now called Simseans,' that is Sampseans, after the sun. Epiphanius finally refers to their rejection of 'the sacrificial and altar-services as repulsive to the Deity,' also to their rejecting 'the eating of animal flesh which is common among the Jews,' and finally of their rejecting 'the sacrificial altar and the sacrificial fire,' though commending 'purifying water.'

According to other traditions, the same Elxai, Elkasai or Elkesai, before he went to Palestine, arose in the year 97 A.D. as a religious teacher in the Northeast of Arabia in the regions of Wâsith and Bassrah. The Christian-Gnostic sect of the Mendæans or Man-

---

[1] *Adv. Hær.* I. x. 28; ed. Col. 1682, and *Adv. Ossenes*, I. xix. 39; comp. Ginsburg, *The Essenes.*

dæans regarded him as its originator. The latest investigations have proved, that Elkesai is identical with an individual whom the Arabian writer En-Nedim calls Scythianus, and whose disciple had been Therebinthus-Buddha.[1] He seems to have come from that part of Scythia to which the independent Parthia belonged, since Scythia in the time of the Roman empire bordered in the south on India, as did the Parthian kingdom of the Arsakides. According to Hippolytus, Elkesai was said to have received the book which was called after him[2] from the Parthians in the city of Sera, the capital of Serica, according to Ptolemy the country in the North-western part of China and the adjacent districts of Thibet and Chinese Tartary. Sera is supposed to have been Singan on the Hoang-ho, by others Peking. Already the Babylonian Isaiah connected the Chinese with Israel by referring to the Sinim, the Persians of the Septuagint, which former word the highest authorities connect with Southern China, the classical Sinæ. The connection of the Book of Elkesai with Parthia is very important, as the Parthians formed a bridge between the asceticism in Mesopotamia and that in India. We may safely connect Elkesai, the Jew, with the Cassîdim or Assidæans of Palestine, and thus indirectly with the Median and Magian Casdîm, the conquerors of Mesopotamia before the time of Abraham, with the Chaldæans, with the strangers in Israel.[3]

The 'name' Elkesai in Hebrew means 'the hidden power,' and thus referred to the invisible 'spiritual power,' the Maga of the Magi and the Maya of the Buddhists. With the name Elkesai may be connected the name of the village Al-kush, near Mosul on the

---

[1] Chwohlson, *Die Sabier und der Sabismus.*

[2] *Refut.* ix. 8–12; x. 25; comp. Eus. *H. E.,* vi. 38; Epiph. *Hær.* xix.; Theodoret. *Hær. fab.* ii. 7.

[3] For the transmitted extracts from the Book of Elkesai, see Appendix to Hilgenfeld's *Greek Hermas.*

Tigris, to which Nahum the Elkoshite is said by modern tradition to have been transported, and where Josephus states that Nahum wrote his prophecy about the fall of Nineveh. Sargon may have transported him in the year 720, and he may well have lived to see the fall of Nineveh. Nahum would hardly have been called by Hebrews the Elkoshite after the presumable place of his captivity where his grave continued to be shown to Jewish pilgrims in the middle ages. Unless this tradition be regarded as fictitious, invented for the convenience of Babylonian Jews, there must have been two Elkosh, for a village of that name in Galilee was pointed out to Jerome, then in ruins. Hitzig has identified this Elkosh with the original name of Capernaum, Kaphar-Nahum, or village of Nahum. Whether we assume the existence of the two places or not, the name of Elkesai, of the Jew who rose as a prophet in Mesopotamia, and who was also accepted as such by the Nazarenes and the Essenes in Palestine, may be connected with the name of the birth-place, if not also of the burial-place, of the prophet Nahum.

Like the secret books of the Essenic Therapeuts, to which reference will presently be made, the Book of Elkesai was a hidden book, an Apocrypha, which was only entrusted to the Initiated and on oath, no doubt on the oath of secrecy, like that of the initiated Essenes, with whom Epiphanius directly connects him. The Mendæans or Christian-Gnostics of Mesopotamia derived their name from Manda de hajje, 'the word of life.' This is their secret name, whilst they give to others Sobba, Saba, Sheba as their name. Their 'great book,' Sidra Rabba, is also called Ginsa, 'the treasure.' They possess a scripture on John the Baptist, who was by Marco Polo found to be highly revered among the Sabeans of Central Asia. The Mendæans were also called 'disciples of John;' and 'the Sabeans of the marshes' between the Arabian desert and the lower

Euphrates and Tigris are, by El-Ulum, the composer of the Fihrist, called Mogtasilah, or ' those who wash (bathe) themselves.' The principal rite of the Mendæans was water-baptism, and the same can be proved to have been the case among the Essenes whom Elkesai joined. Philo calls them Essai ; and as 'As'chai, from s'châ with an aleph prefixed, means in Syriac ' the bathers,' those who are immersed or baptised, so John ' the Baptist' may be regarded as a transliteration of John ' the Essene.' We then understand why the Essenes or disciples of John acknowledged Elkesai as their prophet, who is said to have been the originator of the Mendæans, Sabeans, or disciples of John in Mesopotamia, whose name Mogtasilah has the same meaning as the As'chai of the Essenes.

Even if it could be proved that any of the Fathers ever suspected that Elkesai-Scythianus-Buddha was not an historical individual, but that his was a representative name, the historical germ of the tradition transmitted by Hippolytus, Epiphanius, and others, might be presumed to have been the following. A Buddhistic tradition, contained in a book imported from China, was promulgated by him in the first place among the initiated Mendæans of Mesopotamia, who called themselves disciples of John and also Samans or Buddhists, and in the second place among the Essenes of Palestine. The connection of Elkesai-Buddha's doctrines with the East is proved beyond dispute by the recorded fact, that the Mendæans, before being received into the Christian sect, had solemnly to denounce Zoroaster, whose doctrines were by Buddha more generally introduced into India. The connection of this early Christian Gnosticism with the East, and especially with Buddhism, is confirmed by what we know of the contents of the book called after Elkesai. It was imported from China, presumably having been introduced there by such Buddhists as had been converted to this faith through the instrumentality, direct or indirect, of some of the 18 Buddhist missionaries, who in the year B.C. 250 were sent to China from India by Asôka and by the board for foreign missions which he established. The Book of Elkesai was said to have been revealed by an angel, called 'the Son of God,' that is, by the Angel-Messiah, as whose incarnation, we may now assume, the Essenes or disciples of John regarded Jesus, at least in the year 100 A.D.

This Angel-Messiah, proclaimed by Elkesai, was by him and by the Mendæans mysteriously connected with a female angel, called 'the Holy Spirit,' or Rucha in the language of these Mesopotamian Sabeans, or disciples of John. In Hebrew the word Ruach, signifying the Holy Ghost, is of feminine gender; and in the Korân, that is, in the tradition of the Hanyfs or Sabeans, to whom Abraham and Mahomed are said to have belonged, the Holy Ghost is called Ruh. The connection with the Holy Ghost of Elkesai-Buddha's doctrine about the Angel-Messiah, contained in the book which he is said to have brought from China to Mesopotamia and to Palestine, is all the more remarkable, since the Angel-Messiah or Buddha in Chinese-Buddhist writings, translated from the Sanscrit about the time of Elkesai, is therein recorded to have been incarnated by 'the Holy Ghost.' Thus is confirmed the connection of Elkesai's book with China, and of his Angel-Messiah with Buddha. Since Elkesai was a prophet among the Essenes, these seem to have believed in an Angel-Messiah, and this Essenic tradition may have been of Chinese-Buddhistic origin.

The Elkesaitans, like Philo and like the tradition in the Pseudo-Clementines, regarded the Angel-Messiah in whom they believed, as one of the continuous incarnations of Christ, just as the Buddha of the Buddhists formed a link in the chain of incarnations of the spiritual power or Maya, which is in angels and men. Again, like the Buddhists, they believed the Messiah to be born of a virgin, although the Ebionites, who stood in some connection with the Elkesaitans, denied this doctrine, of which Clement of Alexandria states, as we saw, that it was not founded on fact.

In a probably not correctly transmitted, because contradictory passage, Hippolytus states, that according to Elkesai's assertion, 'Christ was born a man in the same way as common to all (human beings), and that (Christ) was not for the first time (on earth when) born of a virgin, but that both previously and that frequently again he had been born and would be born. (Christ) would thus appear and exist (among us from time to time) undergoing alterations of birth, and having his soul transferred from body to body.' In another passage Hippolytus writes that the Elkesites 'acknowledge that the principles of the universe were originated by the Deity. They do not, however, confess that there is but one Christ, but that there is one that is superior (to the rest), and that he is transformed into many bodies frequently, and was now in Jesus. And, in like manner, that at one time (Christ) was begotten of God, and at another time became the Spirit, and at another time (was born) of a virgin, and at another time not so. And (they affirm) that likewise this Jesus afterwards was continually being transfused into bodies, and was manifested in many (different bodies) at (different) times. And they resort to incantations and baptisms in their confessions of elements. And they occupy themselves with bustling activity in regard of astronomical and mathematical science, and of the arts of sorcery. But (also) they allege themselves to have powers of prescience.' [1]

Like John the Baptist or Essene, Elkesai connected forgiveness of sins with a new kind of baptism, evidently with the repeated baptisms of the Essenes. These

---

[1] Translation by Rev. Alex. Roberts, in *Antenicene Christian Library*, vol. vi. p. 389. On Mendæans, see Petermann, Herzog, *l.c.*

baptisms seem to have taken place daily, since in Rabbinical writings the Essenes or Chassîdim forming 'the holy congregation in Jerusalem' are called, among other names, 'hemerobaptists.' The baptism of the Elkesites was solemnised in the Name of the Father and of the Son, and under invocation of seven witnesses. Similarly to the Essenes, the Elkesites rejected not only the sacrifices and the partaking of meat, but also the Pauline Epistles. It may be presumed that the latter were rejected because of their universality, which principle was upheld by the Essenic Therapeuts in Egypt, with whom we shall connect Paul; but was opposed by the separatist Essenes of Palestine, to which Barnabas belonged. As the Therapeuts are by Josephus directly connected with the Pythagoræans, so Hippolytus states that some of the tenets of Elkesai were adopted from those of Pythagoras. Finally, as the Essenes are in Rabbinical writings identified with the Assidæans, Chas sîdim, or the Pious, so Elkesai is by Hippolytus stated to have called his disciples the Pious Ones. This bishop of Portus, opposite Ostia, near Rome, born soon after A.D. 250, testifies to the presence of Elkesaitans in Rome in his own days. This is not unimportant, since the Christology of the Pseudo-Clementines, published there, and parts of which reach back to the first century, entirely corresponds with Elkesai's doctrine on the continued incarnations of Christ.

It is not necessary to point out what constituted the distinguishing elements of discipline among the 'four parties' of the Essenes mentioned by Hippolytus, and which we shall identify with the four classes of Buddhists and Essenes, and with the four stages of purity distinguished by the Rabbis.[1] Epiphanius states that the Essenes continued 'in their first position, and have not altered at all.' No mention is made by any writer of the Messianic conceptions of the Essenes. As Elkesai

---

[1] *Chagiga*, 18 *a*; Frankel, *l.c.* 451.

became a member of their corporation, and was revered by them as a prophet, the Essenes, who never altered their creed, may be assumed to have held before Elkesai and John the Baptist the Buddhistic doctrine of the Angel-Messiah. This is indirectly confirmed by the silence observed with regard to their Christology; which silence is at once explained, if they believed in an Angel-Messiah, for they were by oath bound not to reveal anything connected with angels.

Philo's writings prove, as we have seen, the probability, almost rising to certainty, that already in his time the Essenes did expect an Angel-Messiah as one of a series of Divine incarnations. Within about fifty years after Philo's death, Elkesai the Essene provably applied this doctrine to Jesus, and it was promulgated in Rome about the same time, if not earlier, by the Pseudo-Clementines. We need not press the point that Philo was, by Clement of Alexandria, called a Pythagoræan,[1] and that Josephus connects the Pythagoræans with the Therapeuts, from which it would follow that Philo was an Essenic Therapeut. In harmony with the doctrine of Brahmans and Buddhists, and with later Essenic conceptions of the Elkesaitans, Philo indicates that Moses was an organ of the Messianic power or Word of God. Moses was neither God nor man, but a supernatural being, who had temporarily taken his abode in a mortal nature. Philo implies that Moses had the power to shake off at will the terrestrial element of his nature, with all its exigencies, and that by fastings of forty days he prepared himself for Divine revelations, so that he was at once priest and prophet.

According to Philo, Moses was finally an incorporeal phantom, similar to Marcion's description of the Messiah. Philo states that Moses was raised to the highest of all beings, that is, 'to the heavenly man, born after the image of God.' This man from heaven had 'no part in

---

[1] Clem. Alex. *Strom.*, i. 15.

any transitory or earthlike essence.' Not as man, but
as spirit, after the death of the body, Moses was perfected. The Word of God, which is in the Angel of
God according to Exodus, comes to man as 'his angel.'
This Word of God, or Angel-Messiah, is by Philo also
called 'the Name' of God. We have seen that the expressions Memra and Adonai were not introduced into
Hebrew Scriptures before the Captivity or the Return.
Philo identifies the Angel-Messiah with the Shechina
above the Cherubim. The Angelic Word is the external
image of God, the pre-mundane type of mankind. The
Angel-Messiah is, according to Philo, the companion of
the human soul, the Divine light shining in the same,
the bread of heaven, the inseparable link of the universe,
the Angel of God and God himself, his Firstborn, the
Mediator between the living and the dead, the Shepherd,
High Priest, and Advocate, the Paraclete or Comforter.[1]

It becomes probable that the Essenes represented, if
they did not introduce, among the Jews, that new Messianic conception of the Angel-Messiah, of which there
is no trace in the Old Testament, but which doctrine
was known to Parsism, and especially to Buddhism.

Parallel Doctrines and Rites of Essenes, Parsists, Buddhists, and Pythagorœans.

The Essenes form the connecting link between
Magian, Rabbinical, and Gnostic Judaism on the one
side, and Parsism and Buddhism on the other. The
place which can thus be assigned to the Essenes in universal history is confirmed by the following points of
contact between the doctrines and customs of the Essenes
and those of the Parsists, Buddhists, and Pythagorœans.

1. The so-called Dualism of the Essenes, their system

---

[1] Comp. *Vita Mos.* iii. 2; *De Somn.* i. 6; *De Incor. Man.* 1; *De Inst.* ii.
8; *De Sacrif.* 2; *De Leg. Alleg.* i. 12; iii. 73; *De Profugis; De Mund. Opif.*;
Quod a Deo; De Plant. Noæ; De Agricul.; Quis Rer. Div. Hær. &c.

of two worlds, the distinction of an immaterial from a material world, is directly connected with the most ancient astronomical symbolism of the East, with the division of the universe into two parts by the ideal line connecting the two determining single stars, later constellations, contemporaneously rising and setting on opposite points of the horizon. The Essenic principle of separation of body and soul, coupled with the assumed antagonism between spirit and flesh, is entirely Buddhistic, and was more rigidly maintained by the Therapeuts than by the Essenes.

2. Similar to the four castes of the Indians, of which that of the Brahmans was the first, and corresponding absolutely with the four grades of Buddhists, the Essenes, like the Pharisees, were divided into 'four different classes.' Josephus adds, 'the juniors are so much inferior to the seniors that the latter must wash themselves when they happen to touch the former, as if they had been defiled by a stranger.' These four orders of the Essenes seem to have originated in the three classes of the Essenes, that of the candidate, approacher, and the associate, which correspond with the three classes of the Rabbis, the scholar, master, and perfect master. The lowest Essenic class—that of the scholar—was subdivided into a double noviciate, of one and of two years, during which time he was an outsider, and was not admitted to the common meals or to any office. This connection is confirmed by the parallel between the Rabbinical and the Magian three classes, for among the Magi there was also a double noviciate. The organisation of the Magi forms a link between the corresponding organisations of Essenes and of Buddhists. The four classes of Aryas or Reverends among the Buddhists are the following :—(a) The Srolaâpanna, or 'he who has reached the stream' which leads to Nirvâna ; (b) the Sakrida-gâmin, or 'he who returns once,' who will be

---

[1] *Babyl. Talmud, Tract Chagiga,* 18 b.

born again but once ; (c) the Anâgâmin, ' he who does
not return,' but is born again in the heaven of the Gods
and of Brahma ; (d) the perfectly pure and sinless
Arhat.[1]   These four classes are directly connected with
the cardinal doctrines of Buddhism.[2]   They correspond
with the four classes of the Essenes and the four classes
of purity among the Pharisees, ' which were so marked,
that one who lived according to the higher degree of
purity became impure by touching one who practised a
lower degree.'[3]

  These four classes of Essenes were perhaps subdivided,
certainly connected with the Essenic eight stages of
spiritual progress, leading up to the mystic state called
' Elijahhood,' a name which confirms the view that Elijah
the ' tishbite ' or stranger belonged, like the Rechabites
or Essenes, to the naturalised strangers in Israel.   The
Buddhists have the ' eightfold holy path ' (Dhammapada),
eight spiritual states leading up to Buddhahood.   The
first state of the Essenes resulted from baptism, and it
seems to correspond with the first Buddhistic state,
' those who have entered the (mystic) stream.'   Patience,
purity, and the mastery of passion were aimed at by
both devotees in the other stages.   In the last, magical
powers, healing the sick, casting out evil spirits, etc.,
were supposed to be gained.[4]   Buddhists and Essenes
seem to have doubled up this eightfold path into four,
for some reason or other.   Buddhists and Essenes had
three orders of ascetics or monks, but this classification
is distinct from the spiritual classification.

  3. On entering the first stage of the noviciate, the

---

[1] Köppen, *Das Leben Buddhas*, i. 398 *f*.

[2] If, according to the monastic system of the Buddhists, a man could
attain at once the position of the Perfected, even as a layman (Hardy's
Eastern Monachism, 280 *f*.) this can only have been a comparatively late
innovation.   (Against Lightfoot, Epistles of Paul, Colossians).

[3] Ginsburg, *l. c.* 21, where the similarity between the doctrines and practices of Essenes and Pharisees is pointed out.

[4] Comp. Burnouf, *Introduction à l'histoire du Buddhisme Indien*, 290 ;
with Ginsburg, *The Essenes*, 13.

candidate for the Essenian order received an axe, an apron, and a white garment. The axe has without sufficient reason been identified with the Levitical spade mentioned in connection with the camp. But the axe could not have been used for the purpose of throwing up the soil; and we know from Pliny, that the axe was with the Magi an instrument of magic, that is, that it symbolised ideas connected with the supposed supernatural world and its spirits, the evil effects of which upon man were to be warded off. The apron of the Essenes may have corresponded with a similar rite of the Magi, for Iranians and Indians had a holy girdle or string, which was a symbol of initiation, and probably was connected with the star-belt of Mithras. Equally probable is the connection between the Essenic 'holy garments,' which had to be laid aside before the bath, according to Josephus, with the Sadere of the Parsees, a short robe of cotton, linen, or silk, which was worn under the girdle. It was without sleeves, and Philo describes the Essenic 'cheap garments without sleeves.'[1] The Magi and Pythagoræans also wore white robes, at least on solemn occasions; and to the Pharisean candidate was also given a kind of garment, according to Talmudian tradition. If the Essene received an apron before he was admitted to higher lustrations, it is not improbable that the Pharisee of higher orders received a white garment for solemn opportunities.

4. The holy baths of the Essenes, to which the noviciates of higher grades were admitted, harmonise well with the holy water-symbol of the Ormuzd religion, especially with the prescribed twenty-nine days of purification in the water which was ordered at the Magian consecration; and they may be identified with the

---

[1] Comp. for this and the following: Hilgenfeld, in *Zeitschrift für wissensch. Theologie*, 1867, 1871, and his *Jüdische Apocalyptic*; Plin. *H. N.*, xxxvi. 19 (34); comp. xxx. 2 (5); Philo, *Apol. Oss.* ii. 633; Eus. *Præp. Ev.* viii. 11; Spiegel's *Avesta* i. 8; ii. xxi.

water-baptism of the Buddhists, who still sprinkle their noviciates with water.[1]

5. The solemn oath which, exceptionally, the Essene had to take on being admitted a full member of the order, gives the same pre-eminence to the duty of always speaking the truth, as this was done with the Iranians, who, like the Essenes, forbad, at all events discouraged, swearing on other occasions.[2]

6. At least since the time of Philo, Pliny, and Josephus, the Essenes had separate settlements, and the same is reported about the Magi.[3]

7. The Essenes abstained from meat and wine, and Eubulos attests the same custom as prevailing among the upper classes of the Magi of later times.[4] Buddhism orders laymen as well as monks, 'Thou shalt not kill what has life, . . and not drink fermented liquors.'[5]

8. Again, in harmony with Buddhistic injunction, and with the Iranian abhorrence of bloody sacrifices, the Essenes abstained from offering the bloody sacrifices ordered in the Mosaic books. In a symbolical sense they regarded, as did the Pharisees, the table spread for their meals, which were accompanied by prayers, as their altar. Josephus reports that they offered spiritual sacrifices 'in themselves,' and Philo reports, that instead of sacrificing any animals, the Essenes endeavoured 'to make their minds fit for holy offering.' The spiritual offering of self to God by prayer and holiness is already enjoined in the Zendavesta or interpreted revelation.[6] Thus also the Septuagint, almost certainly under Essenic influence, makes David say that God 'does' not desire sacrifice and burnt offering. The words ' mine ears hast thou opened ' are

---

[1] See Chapter II., and Schlagintweit, *l. c.*, 95.
[2] Spiegel, *l. c.* ii. lv. f.
[3] Ammianus Marcellinus, xxiii. 6.
[4] Plin. *H. N.,* xi. 42 (97) ; comp. Bernays' *Theophrastos on Piety.*
[5] Köppen, *Das Leben Buddhas,* i. 334, 444.
[6] Spiegel, *Yaçna,* xx. 1 ; xiv. 16.

left out, no doubt because they might be connected with a carnal doctrine of inspiration, according to which it was assumed that man can be made to hear articulated sounds uttered by invisible beings. The spirit of the spiritual and immaterial world could not be supposed to produce articulated sounds audible to man, according to Essenic principles. Instead of the above words of the Psalmist, the text in the Septuagint adds, 'a body hast thou prepared me.' These words may be connected with the essentially Essenic doctrine transmitted by Philo, that the heavenly Messiah takes his abode temporarily in mortal nature, and that the Word of God comes to man as his angel.

9. In East and West the chariot of the sun seems to have been the symbol of tradition, which latter had originated in the East. This may be assumed to have been the case with the Buddhists, who divided their 'Tradition from beyond,' or Wisdom from above, in the great and in the small chariot. The word 'tradition,' or 'merkabah' of the Rabbis, is a compound of 'rechab' the chariot, and the verbal tradition was divided into two classes, the history of creation and that of the chariot. Since the sun was the centre of Essenic symbolism, it is not improbable that Essenic tradition, which was shrouded in mystery, was also symbolised by the solar chariot. The Essenic Cassîdim, the pious, holy ones, or saints, closely resemble the Buddhistic arhats, righteous ones or saints, who were to become like the shining body of Brahma, to 'enter into the brightness of the sun,' the dwelling-place of Abîdha the sun-god, that is, the Nirvâna or destruction of matter, the final resting-place of the soul, and centre of supernatural light.

10. As the Zendavesta recommends watching and praying in the night,[1] so the Essenes, according to Josephus, never spoke about worldly matters before sunrise, but offered up, with their faces towards the

[1] *Vendidâd,* xviii. 15; iv. 122-126.

East, as they did also at sunset, 'some of the prayers transmitted by their forefathers, as if they supplicated it to rise.' It has been pointed out, that the prayer here spoken of seems to have been the national Hymn of Praise, which still constitutes a part of the daily Jewish service. In it the renewal of light is implored from God as the Lord of the Universe, the Creator of the rays of the sun; the (seven?) chiefs of his heavenly hosts are holy beings: 'He exalts himself above the angels, and beams in glory upon his chariot throne,' and the luminaries, 'rejoicing in rising and joyous in setting, perform with awe the will of the Creator.'[1]

11. The three times of daily prayer with the Essenes corresponded with the three times of daily sun adoration prescribed in the Zendavesta.[2] The prayer at noon, which the Jews seem not to have added to the morning and evening prayer till after the Return from the Captivity, coincided with the prayer at the Essenic meal at noon. In accordance with regulations in the Zendavesta, the Essenes bathed before their principal meal; and before as well as after it grace was said by the priest. The daily labour of the Essenes ended in the morning at the fifth hour, when they assembled, girt round with their linen aprons, and had a baptism with cold water before they went to the refectory, 'purified as into a holy temple.' We may therefore assert that the prayer before meal took place exactly at the sixth hour, or at noon.

12. In accordance with Brahmanic,[3] and probably with Buddhistic custom, certainly with that of the Pythagoræans, the Essenic candidate for initiation bound himself by solemn oath not to reveal to such as were not members of this corporation the mysteries which

[1] Comp. *Berachot*, 9; Ginsburg, *l. c.* 69, 70.
[2] *Minokh.* 357 f.; Spiegel, *l. c.* ii. li.
[3] *Laws of Menu*, viii. 110–113; comp. Selden, *De Jur. Nat.* ii. 13; Liv., i. 24.

would be confided to him. But this was only one of
the many obligations laid upon him. Before he touches
the common meal, he swears by most awful oaths, first
to fear God, and next to exercise justice towards all
men, neither to wrong anyone of his own accord, nor
by the command of others; always to detest the wicked
and side with the righteous; ever to keep faith invio-
lable with all men, especially with those in authority,
for no one comes to office without the will of God; not
to be proud of his power, nor to outshine his subor-
dinates, either in his garments or greater finery, if he
himself should attain to office; always to love truth
and strive to reclaim all liars; to keep his hands clear
from stealing and his mind from unholy gain; not to
conceal anything from the brotherhood, nor to disclose
anything belonging to them to those without, though it
were at the hazard of his life. He has, moreover, to
swear not to communicate to anyone their doctrines in
any other way than he has received them; to abstain
from robbing the commonwealth, and equally to preserve the writings of the society, and the names of the
angels.'[1]

Like the Essenes, the Magi formed a secret society.
According to Ammianus Marcellinus,[2] the Magi, whom
Herodotus described as forming a tribe among the
Medes, transmitted only through their descendants their
ancestorial tradition, which had been purified by Darius
Hystaspes, that is, had been more harmonised with the
religion of the East-Iranians or Zoroastrians. The
Magi were a religious caste or order, like the Levites
before the Captivity, after which they ceased to exist as
a body, probably because the Synagogue—which may
be regarded as of Iranian origin—was established without reference to them, and because the Assidæans and
Essenes formed an order for carrying out purity of

[1] Josephus, *De Bell.* ii. 8.
[2] Amm. Marc. xxiii. 6; Spiegel's *Avesta*, ii. vi.

living, for practising holiness. Into this Essenic order many Levites may well have found a place after the Return from Babylon, as guardians of tradition and representatives of the holiness to which the people of Israel was called. On this supposition, it would be explained why Josephus states that the uprightness of the Essenes is 'not of recent date, but has existed among them from times of yore.' Thus alone a meaning can be given to the statement of Philo, that the Essenes, Jews by birth, were a 'fellowship of disciples' formed by Moses. Again, it is only by connecting the Essenes with the Medo-Chaldæans, who lived as 'conquerors' or Casdîm in Mesopotamia about 500 years before Abraham's birth, and by thus connecting the Essenes with the naturalised stranger in Israel, that we can understand how Pliny the Elder (A.D. 23–79) called the Essenes a 'hermitical society,' having existed 'thousands of ages.' We saw that in the time of Nimrod-Merodach, probably the first king of the Median dynasty, whom Berosus calls Zoroaster, the Medes may have had a corporation, if not tribe, of Magi or priests, of whom it can be proved that they formed a senate under Arsakes and his successors since B.C. 250. Thus the 'elders' of Israel formed the 'senate' of the people, according to the meaning given to the presbyters in the Septuagint, in the Books of the Maccabees and of Josephus.

13. The Essenic novice of the first stage, which lasted twelve months, on entering had to cast all his possessions into the common treasury, and this was in harmony with the attested custom of the Magi.[1] The Essenic and Magian and also Buddhistic principle of community of goods, the renouncing even of all personal property by the Therapeuts, is entirely foreign to the Mosaic law and to the cardinal preculiarities of Hebrew character. Yet the ascetic life with which it

---

[1] Diog. Laert. *Prœm.* 6 (7).

is connected is even more ancient than Moses, inasmuch as the Books bearing his name contain regulations for the vow of the Nazarite or Nazirite of days, whilst the institution of Nazarites for life was probably of at least equal antiquity. The great similarity between the Jewish Nazarite and the Indian hermit confirms the foreign origin of this institution among the Jews. It is regarded by Cyril of Alexandria (A.D. 412–444) as introduced from without, and this view is very generally accepted. Although the bishop must have had some reason for connecting the long hair of the Nazarites with an Egyptian custom, yet neither among the Egyptian priests nor generally among male Egyptians such a custom prevailed in the time of Herodotus. The father of history states, that the Egyptians 'from early childhood have the head shaved,' and that the Egyptian priests shave the head. This, as well as the shaving of the beard, was a general custom among the male population. It has been shown, however, that the ancient customs among the Egyptians to anoint the guest's artificial hair with oil, and the priest's touching the king with his finger as a symbol of his having been anointed, point to rites imported from a foreign country. They especially point to India, from whence the original Egyptians seem to have come, and where the rite of cutting off the hair from the entire body never existed.[1] The Brahmanic priest, although wearing the tonsure, was ordered to let his hair grow long on his head, beard, and body, and he was anointed by the holy oil. Contrary to this Brahmanic rite, the Buddhist novice was enjoined 'not to ornament himself with flowers and ribbands, nor to use scents, nor to anoint himself.' Again, the Buddhist Sramana or tamer of the senses, therefore, even the Buddhist of lowest order, was not allowed to possess anything.[2]

[1] Wilkinson, *Ancient Egyptians*, ii. 327 f.
[2] Köppen, *l. c.* i. 334, 366.

The Essenic rule which enjoined community of goods and forbad the use of the anointing oil can only be connected with the corresponding rules among Buddhists and among the Magi. Even the more ancient East-Iranian tradition in the Zendavesta, where the Magi are not mentioned, contains regulations about the cutting of the hair and nails, and removing them from 'the pure men,' which exclude the hairs of the East-Iranians ever having been anointed with oil. Of such practice there is no trace in the Zendavesta. According to Herodotus, and probably according to the monuments, the Assyrians always wore the hair long; and though nothing is said about their ends being cut, it may be assumed that the Zoroastrian order continued to be respected by them. The servants of Ormuzd, and so also the Hebrew priests, were to cut off the ends of their hairs, to poll them. But Xenophon states, that the Medes of the upper classes, and therefore also the Magi, wore wigs.[1] We may therefore assert, that the Magi never anointed themselves, which the Buddhists were forbidden to do. Contrary to the Hebrew practice and order, the Essenes abstained from the use of the anointing oil, which the Jews generally did only as a sign of mourning. This Essenic regulation, like that referring to the anti-Jewish principle of community of goods, cannot possibly be separated from, and must be connected with, the parallel Magian and Buddhistic customs. The Pythagorean use of ointment may be connected with the Brahmanic rite.

14. Love of truth was inculcated by Essaism, as by Parsism and Buddhism, and was promised by an oath.[2] Josephus states of the Essenes, that 'every word with them is of more force than an oath.' He adds: 'They

---

[1] *Vendidad*, xvii. 10 f.; Herod. i. 195; Lev. xxi. 5; Ez. xliv. 20; Xen. *Cyrop.*, i. 3, 2.

[2] Spiegel, *l.c.*, ii. lv. Every member of the royal Kshatriyâ line had to take an oath that he would 'scorn the lie.' (Beal, *Romantic History of Buddha*, 222.)

avoid taking an oath, and regard it as worse than per-
jury; for they say, that he who is not believed without
calling on God to witness, is already condemned of
falsehood.'[1]

15. Prediction of future events was practised by the
Magi, Essenes, and Pythagoræans.

16. Some of the Essenes and all Therapeuts abstained by their own free will from marriage, which
Buddhism forbad for monks only,[2] whilst to all Parsists
celibacy was an abomination. The Pythagoræans must
have allowed matrimony, as Pythagoras was married.

17. The equality of all men was a fundamental
Essenic and Buddhistic principle, which excluded
slavery and made 'all free and mutually serving each
other,' as Philo states about the Essenes. The Buddhistic principle of universality, and of regard for the
religions of others, does not seem to have been implicitly
followed by the Essenes during the rising of the
Maccabees, if we identify the allies of the latter, the
Assidæans, with the Essenes. But they could not in
such trying times have kept their promise to 'detest
the wicked and side with the righteous,' without risking
their lives in the defence of what they regarded as
most holy, the Mosaic law as interpreted by their order.
Yet Philo could attest, that the Essenic body was a
peace society, which discouraged war as much as
possible, and anything which might lead to it.

18. Although the Essenes, according to Josephus,
'did nothing without the injunctions of their overseers,'
and had all things in common, yet they were at liberty
to help the needy, to show mercy, help the deserving
when in want, and to give food to the hungry. With
the Buddhists the first of their six cardinal virtues is to
have compassion.[3]

[1] Clement of Alexandria says the same about the true Gnostic. *Strom.*
vii. 8.
[2] Köppen, *l. c.* i. 352.   [3] Köppen, *l. c.* i. 373.

19. The figurative or allegorical interpretation of symbols is by Philo spoken of as practised by the Essenes, who 'philosophised on most things in symbols, according to the ancient zeal.' They worked out themselves 'the ethical part' of their Scriptures, 'using as their guides the laws which their fathers inherited, and which it would have been impossible for the human mind to devise without Divine inspiration; herein they instruct themselves at all times, but more especially on the seventh day.' As old and young then assembled in the synagogues, the interpreter or Targumist, 'one of those who have most experience,' expounded what the reader had read, and in so doing passed over 'that which is not generally known,' that is, the secret tradition with which the elder members of the society were alone acquainted. From this it follows, that the deeper sense or gnosis, the allegorical meaning of the Scriptures, was entrusted only to the Initiated, that is, to the full members. Writing about the Therapeuts, Philo states, as reported by Eusebius, that 'as they are engaged with the sacred Scriptures, they reason and comment upon them, explaining the philosophy of their country in an allegorical manner; for they consider the verbal interpretation as signs indicative of a secret sense communicated in obscure intimations. They have also commentaries of ancient men, who as the founders of the sect, have left many monuments of their doctrine in allegorical representations, which they use as certain models, imitating the manner of the original institution.'

A similar practice seems to have prevailed among the Magi, inasmuch as, according to Ammianus Marcellinus, they transmitted their ancestorial tradition exclusively through the members of their society, a privilege to which it may safely be assumed the noviciates of both stages were not entitled. Since marriage as a rule was discarded by the Essenes, they could not found their order upon natural descent; and the latter thus differed from the Magian institution. Also the Buddhistic division of their tradition into a great and small conveyance, like the division of the Rabbinical tradition, seems to point to a gradual initiation in the mysteries of transmitted lore.

20. Like the Magi, some of the Essenes were physicians; and the Essenes in Egypt called themselves Therapeutæ, probably not only as healers of the body, but also of the mind and the soul. The Essenes ' investigated medical roots and the property of minerals for the cure of distempers.' According to the Talmud, as well as to Byzantine and Arabian writers, already Solomon was held to have written works on miraculous cures and driving out evil spirits. The physicians among the Essenes may have formed a special class; and, as there were Theosophists among them, these may have formed a class also; and a third class may have been formed by exorcists, or those who drove out evil spirits. Certain it is, that the Magi in the time of Daniel were divided in these three classes, as was also the very ancient Chaldæan book on Magic.

21. From the East, whether through the Magi, or Buddhists, or Pythagoræans, or Egyptians, the Essenes must have derived their doctrine about the immortality of the souls. The Essenes held, that the souls ' come out of the most subtle ether,' that is, from the supposed immaterial world, and that they are enveloped by their bodies as in a prison-house, till, released from servitude, they ' rejoice and mount upwards.' Thus it is implied, that they return to the immaterial world of spirits, where matter is annihilated, that is, to the sun, as to the Nirvâna of Buddhists.

22. The presumable Essenic expectation of an Angel-Messiah is that of the Iranians and Buddhists, and it was kept secret, as were many important Essenic doctrines, especially those connected with angels. Like the Buddhists and Hindus, the Essenes must have believed and taught

their Initiated that salvation is by faith, and that faith comes by the Maya or Brahm, the Spirit or Word of God, of which the Angel-Messiah is the divinely appointed incarnate messenger.

23. As a necessary consequence of the Eastern tradition about the two antagonistic worlds of spirit and matter, the Essenes introduced into Judaism the doctrine of 'everlasting punishment' for the wicked after death. As Buddhists taught that no reasonable being defiled by matter, which is the cause of sin, can enter Nirvâna, that is, as we have suggested, the sun, where matter is annihilated, so the Essenes taught, according to Josephus, the doctrine of rewards for the good, and 'never-ceasing punishments' for the wicked, souls.

24. The Essenic Therapeuts of Egypt, who have been more influenced directly or indirectly by Buddhism than the Essenes of Palestine, had, in common with the latter, the following doctrines and customs :—The distinction of a spiritual and immaterial world from a material world, or the dualism of the East, connected with everlasting rewards and eternal punishments; the corporative system ; a high regard for the transmitted writings of their order, by the side of Mosaic writings ; the highest reverence for Moses, the real and deeper but hidden meaning of whose doctrines they brought to light by a figurative interpretation of the words, ' by mystic expressions in allegories.' Both communities maintained the Jewish-Essenic doctrine of inspiration as regards the Mosaic Scriptures, if not the Prophets; but they recognised a relatively higher stage of revelation or gnosis, of which the books of their own order were the recognised exponents: this Divine revelation they regarded as continuous in mankind, so that their collection of Scriptures was never acknowledged as closed ;[1] Essenes

---

[1] 'The mysteries which were hid till the time of the Apostles, and were delivered by them as they received from the Lord, and, concealed in the Old Testament, were manifested to the Saints, (to the Pious, Saints, or

and Therapeuts had in common the anti-hierarchical character of their organisation; abstention from meat and wine, probably also of animal sacrifices in the Temple, for which reason they were excluded from the Temple-service; their dress; the abolition of slavery; the adoration of the Deity through the symbol of the sun; the strict keeping of the Sabbath, when only the Therapeuts exceptionally anointed their bodies.

The Essenic principle of community of goods is by the Therapeuts heightened to entire absence of property; thus also the self-chosen occasional avoidance of marriage by Essenes is with the Therapeuts a rigidly enforced rule, in harmony with the Buddhistic prohibition of marriage among the priests. The Therapeuts maintained more rigidly than the Essenes the principle of enmity between the spirit and the flesh. Also, they were more severe in their separation than the Essenes, for they lived in huts, like hermits, and thus laid the foundation to the convent-life in the West, which the Buddhists had established in the East. The asceticism of the Therapeuts was extended over the entire day, so that they did not meet for a common meal, which they solemnised with increased solemnity in the night, and which resembled in various points the meal of the Essenes at noon. Every kind of manual labour was abolished by the increased asceticism of the Therapeuts, who led a life of contemplation and prayer without work, closely resembling the hermits among the Brahmans and Buddhists. More rigidly than with the Essenes, it was the aim of the Therapeuts, by the greatest possible separation from what is sensual, to come in contact with the influences of the unseen, spiritual, and immaterial world, above all with the Angel-Messiah, and thus to be pre-

Chassidim, the Essenes).' Clem. Alex. *Strom.* v. 10. He describes the Gnosis as 'the apprehension of things present, future, and past.' *Strom.* vi. 7. The Gnostic receives 'a sort of quality akin to the Lord himself, in order to assimilation to God.' *Strom.* vi. 17.

pared for the setting up of a spiritual kingdom of heaven on earth. The Therapeuts wished, as Philo states, to be 'citizens of heaven and of the world,' to live 'in the soul alone' whilst living in the flesh.

25. The fundamental principle of Essenes and Therapeuts, to strive after purity in thought, word, and deed, though it may be regarded as a development of the Mosaic law, was taught by Zoroaster and acknowledged by the Magi. Like the distinction of a spiritual from a material world, with which the doctrines of angels and spirits, and thus of the Angel-Messiah, were directly connected, the principles of a higher morality as practised by the Essenes, and their submission to an all-governing and predestinating Supreme Will, must be connected with those Iranian and Buddhistic conceptions with which the Israelites during the Captivity had come into contact. Only by the introduction of this foreign or non-Hebrew element, traceable to the Essenes, it is possible to explain the non-Mosaic and anti-Hebraistic community of goods, the abolition of slavery, the prohibition of oaths except the oath of initiation, their all but general preference for the unmarried state, the abstention from meat and wine and from the anointing oil, excepting the Sabbathical rite of the Therapeuts, their abhorrence of bloody sacrifices, and, finally, the doctrine of the Angel-Messiah.

Conclusion.

The conscious incorporation of new or of newly promulgated doctrines, and of new rites, into Judaism by the Essenes can no longer be denied.[1] During centuries before and after the existence of the Essenic order the land of the Medo-Chaldæans or Magi, to whom

---

[1] Canon and Professor Lightfoot admits the introduction of Persian, but not of Buddhistic rites by the Essenes, and denies the conscious incorporation of this foreign element into Judaism.

the Essenes stood in close relationship, was directly connected with India by the independent Parthian kingdom, and nearly five centuries before Abraham these Medo-Chaldæans commenced their rule over Mesopotamia. The similarity between the asceticism on the Euphrates and that on the Ganges confirms the early connection of these countries. The asceticism of the Magi and Essenes is unknown to the Zendavesta and to the Veda, although in the former a material from an immaterial or purely spiritual world is distinguished. The mixed Iranian and non-Iranian character of the Median race explains the strange mixture of Iranian and Indian doctrines among the Medo-Chaldæans with their Magi, and among the Essenes, whom we may ethnically connect with the former.

The connection between Buddhistic and Essenic doctrines and customs is proved, and to the former belonged the doctrine of the Angel-Messiah, of which there is no trace in Hebrew Scriptures which can be asserted to have been written before the deportation to Babylon, nor in the first three Gospels. With the uninterrupted chain of Buddhistic writings in China, translated from the Sanscrit, and dating 'from at least B.C. 100 to A.D. 600,' coupled with the probably pre-Christian representations of subjects treated by Buddhistic legends, we may connect what Buddhistic legends in pre-Christian times taught at least about the birth of the Angel-Messiah. Some of the other recorded traits of the life of Gautama-Buddha as the incarnate Angel-Messiah cannot at present be proved to date from the pre-Christian period.

It is absolutely certain that there is no reliable trace of the doctrine of an Angel-Messiah in Jewish Scriptures till after the deportation to Babylon; that the Essenic order, preceded by the Assidæans and Rechabites or

---

[1] *Exort.* 6; *Strom.* i. 13, 15, 21, 25, 26; ii. 5, 18; v. 5, 10, 11, 14; vii. 2–3.

[2] Beal, *Dhammapada, Intr.* 11.

Kenites, was established not later than B.C. 143; that before this time Buddhistic records about the birth of the Angel-Messiah existed in the East, and that Essenic tradition must be connected with the East. The probability thus shown, that the Essenes believed in and expected an Angel-Messiah, though they were bound not to divulge anything connected with Angels, can be almost raised to the dignity of a fact by what has been transmitted to us about John the Baptist.

The question arises: At what time and under what circumstances was the Eastern and Essenic doctrine of the Angel-Messiah applied to Jesus Christ as it had been applied about 500 years earlier to Gautama-Buddha, who, like Jesus Christ, was said to have been born on Christmas-day? Did John the Baptist, the 'bather' or Ashai, belong to the Assidæans, Essai, or Essenes; and what were the relations between the doctrines of John and those of Jesus?

CHAPTER VI.

JESUS AND THE ESSENES.

The stranger in Israel—Jesus and the Essenes—Jesus and the hidden wisdom—Jesus and the sacrifice—Jesus the Messiah—Conclusion.

The Stranger in Israel.

JESUS is shown by Biblical records to have been a descendant of David, whose ancestor was Caleb the Kenezite
or non-Hebrew.   Who was the stranger in Israel?

The first inhabitants of the West seem to have come
from the East on two main roads.   The earliest historical
stream of Orientalists consisted of black or Hamitic
tribes, who wandered from the land watered by the Gihon-
Oxus, from the land of Cûsh, the later Turan, to India,
and thence, in course of time, by Arabia, Egypt, Libya,
and Canaan, to Mesopotamia, where they built Babylon.
After a long and indefinite time the black inhabitants
of Mesopotamia and adjoining countries were subjugated by a once unmixed white race of Japhetites, by
the Medes of Berosus, whose conquest took place
B.C. 2458, and who had journeyed from the East, originally from the Aryan home, the Eden of Genesis, and
had come across Central Asia by the high table-land of
Iran.   These conquerors called themselves in their own
language Casdîm, later Kaldi or Chaldæans, and they
gave to the conquered plain between the two rivers the
name of Shinar.   This Medo-Chaldæan dynasty in Babylon ruled there from B.C. 2458–2234, and its first king
was called Zoroaster, after the great reformer of the
East-Iranians, but he also received the title Nimrod,

formed after the Iranian deity Merodach. The priests of these Medo-Chaldæans were sooner or later called Magi, and thus is explained the identification of Magi and of Chaldæans in the Book of Daniel.

The subjugation of Hamites by Japhetites in the lowland of the Euphrates and Tigris brought about that ethnic combination with which in Genesis the name of Shem has been connected. Two years after the Flood he was a hundred years old, he was born ninety-eight years before the Flood. For this event Hebrew tradition, according to Censorinus and Varro, designated the year B.C. 2360, so that Shem's birth took place in B.C. 2458, in the year of the Medo-Chaldæan conquest of the country in which the first Semitic settlements were situated, beginning with Elam on the Persian Gulf. It is thus implied, that the birth of Shem must be ethnically explained by the combination of Japhetites and Hamites, who had come from the East and had amalgamated in the land of the so-called settlements of Shem's descendants. Since the conquest of Mesopotamia or the birth of Shem, Japhet did dwell in the tents of Shem, and Canaan, the Hamite, was his servant. From the commencement of this so-called Semitic period, and during all phases of Israel's history, Hebrews lived together with non-Hebrews, principally Chaldæans. The non-Hebrew was ' the stranger ' in Israel, the naturalised foreigner within the gate, who seems to have obtained full rites of citizenship, as is shown by the narratives of Doeg the Edomite, Uriah the Hittite, Araunah the Jebusite, Zelek the Ammonite, and Itmah the Moabite, though the Ammonites and Moabites are in Deuteronomy forbidden to enter the congregation of the Lord.

Abraham bowed before Melchizedec, the non-Hebrew, and Moses did all what Jethro the Kenite, the priest of Jehovah, told him. The sons of Jethro, the Kenites of Midian, were invited by Moses to join, and did join under Hobab, the Hebrews, who left Egypt as a ' mixed

multitude.' They settled with Judah in Arad, and they
were certainly connected with, if not the ancestors of,
the Rechabites, who could say in the time of Jeremiah,
that they had always been strangers in Israel, and whom
the Prophet designated as patterns of obedience. According to the ethnic scheme here followed, the Hebrew
belonged to the Hamitic or Indian stream, he was a
descendant of the builders of Babylon, as was Abraham,
whose fathers had lived, more than 450 years before his
birth, in subjection to the conquerors or Chaldæans,
after whom his native city was called Ur of the Casdîm
or Chaldees. The stranger in Israel was accordingly
the Medo-Chaldæan or Iranian, related to the Magi, with
whom Daniel was connected, and whose overseer he
became.

The Israelites of both races recognised the Mosaic
law, the provisions of which for the stranger, later
called proselyte or convert, were certainly either in
part added later or not carried out. This was the case,
as observed, with regard to his not being allowed to
hold land. Signs are not wanting which seem to imply,
that with the dualism of race in Israel was connected
a dualism of ecclesiastical and of political institutions,
that the two lines of Aaronites and the political parties
of Sadducees and Pharisees originated in the compound
race of Indian Hamites and Iranian Japhetites in Israel.
After the Return from Babylon, the non-Hebrew element
seems for a time to have formed the majority in Israel,
inasmuch as the men of Judah may be assumed to have
been partly descendants of those Kenites who settled with
that tribe in the time of Joshua, and who were also exported to Babylon according to the superscription of the
71st Psalm, as transmitted by the Septuagint. Again,
Zerubbabel was a descendant of David, who was a direct
descendant of Caleb the Kenezite. It certainly was not
till after the Return that the synagogues were generally introduced, the Iranian origin of which is made

highly probable by the parallel between the three classes of Rabbis and those of the Magi or Chaldæans, and by the absence of the Sadducees from the synagogue, which the strangers visited. At the commencement of the Christian era, and probably ever since the time of Ezra and of the Maccabees, a spirit of rigid exclusiveness was established, which would go some way to explain, even if taken by itself, the Sadducean persecution of a teacher in the synagogue, of a stranger in Israel, who was a descendant from David.

The descent of David from Caleb the Kenezite, and thus from non-Hebrews, points to a connection of Jesus with the strangers in Israel. This is confirmed by the significative fact, that the four female ancestors of Jesus who are mentioned in the genealogies of Matthew are all non-Hebrews. Although the descent of Thamar is not specified in the Bible, Philo calls her ' a stranger,'[1] and with this statement the Biblical narrative can be easily harmonised by enlarging the literal sense of it to a figurative one. To do this we have also another reason, inasmuch as the credibility of the account rendered about Thamar will be enhanced by the allegorical interpretation of the text. Already in the history of Abraham, as recorded in Genesis, we find traits which lead us to assume that international relations are sometimes described as family connections. It is probable that Abraham's concubines represented non-Hebrew nationalities, and that the narratives in question refer not to marriages between two individuals, but to relations between the Hebrew and some non-Hebrew nations.

Were we to interpret the story of Thamar and Judah literally, the only possible argument would be, that the most unparalleled immorality was necessary to ensure the descent of Messiah's ancestor from Judah. Of him Jacob is recorded to have prophesied that he

---

[1] *De Nobil.* 5.

would be praised by his brethren, that these should bow before him, that the sceptre should not depart from Judah, and that unto him should be the gathering, or rather the obedience, of the people. This state of things is to endure either until he (his tribe) come to Shiloh, or until Shiloh comes, that is, ' rest.' In order to interpret this passage Messianically, we must accept the latter possible reading, and assume Shiloh to mean, not a locality, but a person, the man of peace or rest. On this supposition the prophecy might be regarded as fulfilled by Solomon, a descendant of Judah, whose name signifies 'rest' or 'peace.' But in order to make this passage refer to a future son of David and Son of God, to the Prince of Peace, to whom the passage in Isaiah was assumed to point, the Shiloh-Messiah must be identified with a man anointed by the Holy Ghost, not with an incarnate angel, of which conception there is no trace in the Old Testament. Taken in its literal sense and Messianically interpreted, the narrative about Judah and Thamar would lead to the revolting conclusion that Pharez, the offspring of that illicit intercourse, was the only link between a Divine promise and its fulfilment.[1]

The only escape from this dilemma is offered by the assumption that, in this passage, as certainly in others,[2] the matrimonial metaphor is used, that the recorded intercourse between Judah and Thamar the stranger, was by the Initiated in the mysteries of Scripture known to refer to the recorded cohabitation of the tribe Judah and of the non-Hebrew Kenites, who settled with them in the wilderness of Arad, and formed an inseparable tie with Judah. These Kenites had previously dwelt in the City of Palms, in Thamar, later called Engedi,

---

[1] It is remarkable that Caleb, descendant of Phares, is excluded from 'the whoredom,' or falling away of the Israelites in the Desert. (Num. xiv. 33.)

[2] Judges ii. 17 ; Ps. cvi. 39.

and before they accompanied Judah to Arad, the king of Arad 'the Kenite' ruled there. The Kenites, like the Rechabites, the strangers, were descendants of Hemath or Hamath; and of the Rechabites, it is provable that they went with the Hebrews to Babylon, whilst after the Return they, like many Levites, seem to have merged into the order of Assidæans and Essenes. Even if we literally interpret the transmitted connection of Judah and Thamar, the name Er or Ger, that is, 'stranger,' given to the first-born of Judah and of the Canaanite Bath-Shuah, indirectly confirms the foreign descent of Thamar, and renders more probable the ethnic interpretation of her so-called marriage with Judah. The same foreign element may be assumed in the compound names of Ger, such as Gershon, Gergasites or Girgashites, and Gerizim.

The second female ancestor of Jesus is Rahab or Rachab, that is, Rechab, and thus refers to the Kenites. Rahab of Jericho, whom Josephus describes only as an innkeeper, was probably connected with the Kenites in Israel before she became the wife of Salmon or Salma, the father of Bethlehem, and Boaz, the husband of Ruth. The Targum of Jerusalem calls the strangers in Israel the Salmaites; and in the Books of Ezra and Nehemiah 'the children of Jericho' and 'the men of Jericho' are mentioned separately, as if representing a non-Hebrew element. Rahab seems to have been called a harlot, because in the time of Ezra, when our Hebrew text was revised and partly re-written, to marry a non-Hebrew woman was regarded as equally abominable as to marry a harlot. It is probable, at least possible, that the matrimonial metaphor was not before this time introduced into such narratives as those of Judah and Thamar, and of Rahab.

The third female ancestor of Jesus, Ruth the Moabite, was a descendant of Caleb the Kenezite, and connected with Rahab the Rechabite or Kenite.

The fourth woman who is mentioned in the genealogies as an ancestor of Jesus was 'the wife of Uriah' the Hittite, that is, Bathsheba, which name in a modified form is Bathshua. She was granddaughter of Ahitophel, who was born in the hill-country of Judah, where the Kenites dwelt, and daughter of Eliam or Ammiel, which was the name of four non-Hebrews. The name Bathshua, or daughter of Shua, connects the wife of the Hittite with the Canaanite or Kenite name Shua, the wife of Judah, whose son was called Er or Ger, the stranger. Also one of the sons of Abraham and of his concubine Keturah (Ket, Cheta, or Hittite of Ur?) was called Shua, which name, with the divine prefix, formed Jeho-Shua, Joshua, or Jesus.

It is absolutely certain that all four female ancestors of Jesus were non-Hebrews, and that, if we interpret their narratives literally, every one of them had become separated from her first love, for one reason or other. Whether these narratives be regarded as not literally true, but as dictated by the Hebrew spirit of exclusiveness which ruled in the time of Ezra and at the time to which the genealogies of the New Testament refer, or whether they be accepted as strictly historical, the non-Hebrew element among the direct ancestors of Jesus is proved. This non-Hebrew element in Israel can be connected principally with the Medo-Chaldæans, with the nation which ruled in Mesopotamia before Abraham was born, and which transmitted that Chaldæan or Magian wisdom in which Daniel was instructed. Speaking broadly, we may say that this was the tradition of the Zendavesta. The connection of Jesus with the Synagogue, and of the latter with Magian tradition, confirms the non-Hebrew descent of Jesus.

Jesus and the Essenes.

It has been rendered highly probable, if not certain, that John the Ashai, the bather or Baptist, has the same meaning as John the Essai, as Philo calls the Essene. If the disciples of John were Essenes, the remarkable fact is explained, that the Essenes, forming the third party in Israel, are never mentioned by that name in the New Testament. On this supposition, we may also explain the still more astounding, though only implied, identification of Essenes and Christians by Josephus, who was for a time himself an Essene if Banus was one. John resembled the Essenes by his life in secluded places—we never hear of him in cities, not even in Jerusalem during the feasts—by his mode of living and his dress, and by his water-baptism. We may assume, that John, in accordance with the recorded announcement of his birth, was a Nazarite for life, which all Essenes were, and that, like these, he never visited the Temple, nor offered bloody sacrifices. In harmony with all we know about the Essenes, John never referred to the Holy Ghost, but pointed to One who should come after him, and who would baptize 'with the Holy Ghost and with fire,' that is, with fire as the symbol of the Holy Ghost. Contrary to the teaching of Jesus, but in harmony with Essenic practice, John made the change of mind dependent on outward acts, on ceremonies; he was a mystic ritualist, as all Essenes were. In the Acts we are told that Paul met disciples of John who had not even heard that there is a Holy Ghost. Also Apollos of Alexandria, a disciple of John, though zealously preaching about Jesus, did not proclaim him as the Christ, as Him whom God had anointed 'with the Holy Ghost and with power,' until Aquila and his wife had instructed the Alexandrian, and possibly the Therapeutic novice, in the more perfect, in the deeper knowledge or gnosis, known only to the initiated Therapeuts near Alexandria and elsewhere.

The doctrine of the Holy Ghost, which John and his disciples connected with the Angel-Messiah whom they expected, must have been unknown to the uninitiated members of the Essenic corporation, as it was unknown to disciples of John the Baptist or the Essene, and it must have formed part of the secret tradition of the Essenes. For in the Mishna there is a passage which can only be referred to the Essenes, and where the gift of the Holy Ghost is connected with the grades of initiation, and with the future Elias, the forerunner of the Messiah. 'The zeal for the law and the Pharisaic purity lead from grade to grade to the Hassi-douth (piety), whence one is led to the gift of the Holy Ghost, who will finally bring the resurrection of the dead through Elias, the forerunner of the Messiah.'[1]   With this Essenic expectation of Elias as organ of the Holy Ghost and as forerunner of the Messiah must be connected the fact, that John the Baptist dressed like Elijah and lived in the region of his chief activity.   John is in the Gospel after Luke designated, on the authority of the angel announcing his birth, as filled with the Holy Ghost, and as going before the Lord 'in the spirit and power of Elias,' whilst he himself pointed to the future Messianic baptism with the Holy Ghost.   This power of God was to be brought from heaven by the Messiah, whom therefore John must have regarded as an incarnate Angel.

John regarded the coming of the Spirit of God to mankind, that is, the kingdom of heaven, as future; Jesus regarded both as 'already come.'   If he and some of his contemporaries among the Jews drove out devils by the Spirit of God, this was a sign that the kingdom of God had already come.   If John knew that, then he believed in Jesus as the Angel-Messiah; but this he certainly did not whilst in prison and shortly before his death.   Sayings of Jesus have been preserved which prove to demonstration, when connected with the above facts, that John did not regard Jesus as the

[1] *Mish. Sotah*, end; *Aboda Sara*, xx. 6, &c.

Messiah, and that Jesus did not regard John as belonging to his kingdom : 'He that is least in the kingdom of heaven is greater than he.' The reason of this is implied by another saying of Jesus, hitherto left in the dark. The doctrine of the Holy Ghost having been in the Old Testament referred to as exceptionally present in few individuals, the coming of this Divine power to mankind was prophesied as something future. In this sense we may interpret the words : 'All the Prophets and the law prophesied until John,' him included, for even if taken to be Elias he would only be announcing the coming of the Messiah with the Holy Spirit from above. But 'from the days of John the Baptist until now the kingdom of heaven' is no longer held by all to be future, for some enter in, though they can only do so 'by force,' since it 'suffereth violence,' that is, it was violently closed by the 'blind leaders of the blind,' by 'the Scribes and Pharisees, hypocrites,' who 'shut up the kingdom of heaven against men,' neither going in themselves, nor 'suffering them that are entering to go in.'[1]

Thus openly and directly did Jesus oppose the teaching of John the Baptist about the Spirit of God not yet being present in man. He would have opposed this his doctrine even in case that John the Ashai or the Essai or Essene, had not expected the Messiah or 'Him that should come,' like the Tathâgata of the Buddhists, to be the incarnation of an Angel, who brought down the Spirit of God. These two doctrines stand in connection with each other ; and the more probable it can be made, that John was an Essene, the more certain will it be, that Jesus opposed also the Messianic expectation of John the Baptist or the Essene. Jesus did not regard himself as the Angel-Messiah ; of which doctrine there is no proof in the Old Testament, or in the first three Gospels, but which was an Essenic

[1] Matt. xi. 11–14 ; xxiii. 13.

tradition, as the preceding arguments seem irresistibly to prove.

Not only John's ascetic life, his rites, as far as we know them, and his doctrines were Essenic, but among the incidents transmitted to us of his early life, there are some which contain corroborative evidence that he was a member of the Essenic body, whose settlements, according to the elder Pliny, were on the west coast of the Dead Sea. Here had been the settlements of the Kenites or Rechabites, who started from Thamar-Engedi for Arad, and whom we have sufficient reason to connect with the later Essenes. It was in this region to the west of the Dead Sea, in the hill country of Judah, and in a city called Juda or Jutta, that the son of Zacharias and Elisabeth was born. Probably this was the city Juta or Jutta, five miles south of Hebron, as first suggested by Reland. It has escaped attention, that, like Hebron, Jutta is mentioned in the Book of Joshua as one of the cities which were given to 'the children of Aaron,' from which Zacharias as well as Elisabeth were descended. Accordingly John was born near the region where the Essenic settlements were. The Essenes were in the habit of adopting children, and a child of double Aaronic descent, whose aged parents may have died before it attained to manhood, would be particularly welcomed by the Jewish ascetics.

Again, it was in this 'wilderness' of Judæa, that 'the word of God' came unto John, whether he began to baptize there or not. But as his progress was from south to north, it is highly probable that he did first baptize in the southern district to the west of the Dead Sea, where the Essenic settlements were. For, instead of 'Bethabara beyond Jordan,' the original reading may have been 'Beth-Arabah beyond Jordan,' that is, 'the house of the desert,'—a locality which may be identified with the city of that name, mentioned by Joshua, as situated 'in the wilderness,' that is, in 'the Arabah' or el-Ghor, in that part of the sunken valley which lies in the northern part of the hill country to the west of the Dead Sea. Any place situated like Betharabah in this part of the sunken valley between the northern end and the cliffs ten miles south of the southern end of the Dead Sea, could be designated as 'beyond Jordan;' whilst the deep sunken valley, called 'the Arabah,' included in its wider sense the entire course of the Jordan from Mount Hermon. It was therefore necessary to give to the place a more restricted meaning; and the designation 'beyond Jordan' is best explained if we assume that Betharabah was meant, whilst it would have no meaning if Bethany had been the name of the place, which Origen found in the oldest manuscripts, although he decided for Bethabarah.[1]

We find, therefore, that John the Baptist was born, received his Divine call, and began to baptize in the region to the west of the Dead Sea, where the Essenes had their settlements; that like these he lived in secluded localities, avoiding the cities, and apparently not even going up to Jerusalem for the feast; that his dress and mode of living resembled that of the Essenes, especially of hermits like Banus, with whom Josephus spent three years, probably the three years of the Essenic noviciate; that, like the Essenes, John was a Nazarite for life, and probably avoided the Temple-services and sacrifices; that he did not refer to the Holy Ghost, like the Essenes, of whom we may assume that they could not do so before the coming of the Angel-Messiah, whom they expected, and of whom John said, that he would baptize with the

---

[1] We cannot accept, with Mr. Conder, for the place intended, the ford or Abârah near Beisân, the ancient Bethshean, called Scythopolis, in the Jordan valley, about twelve miles south of the Sea of Galilee. Near this place was, according to Eusebius and Jerome, the Aenon or Enon, the place of springs, near Salim, where, on the west of the Jordan, the last baptisms of John took place, and where Van de Velde has found a Mussulman tomb, called by the Arabs Sheykh Salim, the city having disappeared, like the town Antipatris, now Kefr-Saba. (Smith's *Dict. of the Bible*, 'Salim.')

Holy Ghost; finally, that John the Baptist is only
another name for John the Ashai or bather, from
which the name of the Essai may now be safely assumed
to have been derived. Considering these many and
either certain or probable proofs of contact, and that
there is absolutely nothing known about John the
Baptist which could be designated as non-Essenic, his
connection with the Essenes can no longer be doubted.

Under the circumstances in which the earliest records
about the life and doctrines of Jesus were composed, it
must be regarded as a difficult if not an impossible task
to distinguish the doctrines which he really taught from
those which to a certain extent, and especially in the
Gospel after John, have been attributed to him under
Essenic influence, as we shall try to prove. The Essenic
Christians must have been as desirous to claim the authority of Jesus for their views, as they had been zealous
in developing their system from the Mosaic Scriptures by
an allegorical interpretation of the same. Yet the principal points in which the doctrine of Jesus was opposed
to that of the Essenes, and those which were common to
both, can be ascertained with sufficient accuracy.

It was not only the Essenic expectation of an Angel-
Messiah, who would baptize with the Holy Ghost and
bring to earth the kingdom of heaven, against which
Jesus protested, whilst excluding John the Baptist from
the kingdom of God which had already come : Jesus
protested also against the extreme rigidness of Sabbath
observance, which was a characteristic custom of the
Essenes. Also, his views about the import of all outward
acts connected with religion were much more free.
Again, the principle of universality, which Jesus enunciated, implied a protest against the Essenic avoidance of
strangers, which was likewise a characteristic feature
among Essenes in Palestine, though not in Egypt. The
asceticism of the Essenes, their strict rules about eating
and drinking, their discouraging marriage, and forbid-

ding the anointing of the head with oil, were not sanctioned by Jesus.[1] Whilst in all these points Jesus did not follow Essenic doctrines or customs, he strongly approved and followed the principle of the Essenes to avoid the Temple-service with its bloody sacrifices, the Essenic simplicity in speech and demeanour, their prohibition of oaths and of slavery, respect of poverty, perhaps community of goods, and certainly the system of initiation in the mysteries of tradition.

The question already here suggests itself, why many Essenes accepted Jesus as the Angel-Messiah whom, as we tried to show, they expected, although he did not belong to their party. Our answer will be, that the death of Jesus at the time of the Passover, and his reported resurrection ' the third day according to the Scriptures,' that is, as the allegorising Essenes explained, both as antitype of the Paschal lamb and of the Paschal omer, removed in their minds all doubt on the subject. It was under the effect of these doubts that John sent the embassy to Jesus, whether he be ' He that should come,' the Tathâgatta of Buddhists, the Angel-Messiah, who would baptize with the Holy Ghost. The answer of Jesus did not confirm such expectations.

Jesus and the Hidden Wisdom.

The Sadducees had forbidden the promulgation of the ancestral tradition of the Pharisees. The name of the latter can be derived from Pharis or Persia, and, if so, would connect the Pharisees, like Jesus, with the non-Hebrews or strangers in Israel, to which dualism of race in Israel the name of Pharez points. From this it would follow, that the ' mysteries of the kingdom of heaven,' which Jesus, as is recorded in the first three Gospels, made known to his disciples when ' alone ' with

[1] Matt. xii. 1–12; John ix. 14, 16; Matt. xix. 12; vi. 17; Luke vii. 46.

them, that his speaking 'in darkness,' his whisperings
in the ear, may have referred to a traditional 'key of
knowledge' which the spiritual rulers of Israel had 'taken
away' from the people.   This connection between the
ancestral tradition of the Pharisees and the secret tradition, deeper knowledge or gnosis, taught by Jesus to his
disciples, and distinguished from his popular form of
teaching by parables only, is confirmed by Jesus recog-
nising publicly the Scribes and Pharisees as sitting in
Moses' seat, as if as organs of a verbal tradition transmitted by elders.   'All therefore whatsoever they bid
you observe, that observe and do; but do not ye after
their works : for they say, and do not.'   Again, Jesus,
the Scribes, and the Pharisees went to the synagogue ;
the Sadducees not.   Jesus has certainly recognised the
authority of a traditional verbal law by the side of the
written law ; and we may assume that he regarded the
fundamental principles of the former as forming canons
or rules of interpretation for the latter.

Jesus believed that God reveals himself in all ages
through his Spirit, that the history of mankind is the
history of a continuity of Divine influences.   The revelations in ages past had been made known to the people
through symbols, which were differently explained by
the Initiated and the Uninitiated.   Jesus knew that the
medium of these revelations was the enlightened conscience of man, as the organ of Divine manifestations.
He regarded it as his mission to point out to every man
'the engrafted Word' which is able to save the soul ; to
convince men 'by their conscience,' at a time when even
Israelites knew not 'the things belonging to their peace,'
because they were 'hid' from their eyes.   After a long
and systematic hiding of the truth, for which Paul made
Moses responsible,[1] Jesus saw no other way for the fulfilment of his Divine mission, than to suggest to the
people by parables as much of the truth as they could

[1] 2 Cor. iii. 12–18 ; iv. 1–4.

then bear, and to prepare a chosen number of disciples, by secret initiation in the mysteries of the kingdom of heaven, for some future time when they or their successors might proclaim in light and upon the housetops what he had told them in darkness and in the ear. Above all, Jesus taught the truth by living it, thus setting an ensample or pattern that his brethren should follow in his footsteps.

Since the doctrine of the Spirit of God in man had been kept in the background by 'the law and the prophets until John,' the people could not understand and profit by what was written about Adam and Eve hearing the voice of God; about Cain's fleeing from God's presence; about the Spirit of God departing from Saul, and urging David to repentance; about the Divine origin of man and his walk with God; about taking in vain or unprofitably bearing God's 'Name' or Spirit, which is also in the Angel of the Lord; about the Word which is near to every man, that he may do it; about the law written in the heart; about 'wickedness condemned by her own witness.'[1] By preaching and living the doctrine of conscience, Jesus opened the way for the gradual revelation of the mystery kept in secret since the world began.

Jesus and the Sacrifice.

David, the ancestor of Jesus, and descendant from the Iranians, to whom every bloody sacrifice was an abomination, had declared that God did not desire sacrifice and offering, neither burnt-offering nor sin-offering; Isaiah had protested against sacrifices, and asked in the Name of the Lord, 'Who hath required this at your hand?' The prayer with the uplifted bloody hand God will not hear; he will forgive sins on the sole condition of man's 'ceasing to do evil, and learning to do well.'

[1] Wisd. xvii. 11.

Jeremiah answers the question raised by Isaiah as to who had required the sacrifices from Israel, by the declaration that God had 'said nothing' unto the fathers 'concerning burnt-offerings or sacrifices,' and that the people had walked backward and not forward, since God brought them out of Egypt, that is, since the time in which the transmitted Scriptures of Moses were held to have originated, and up to the day when Jeremiah spoke to the children of Israel in vain, because they heard not 'the voice of the Lord'; finally, Ezechiel had proclaimed that man's soul is delivered by man's righteousness.[1]

Already from these passages we are led to assume that Jesus cannot possibly have sanctioned the sacrifices ordered by the Scriptures attributed to Moses. His not having ever visited the Temple-services must be regarded as a protest against the bloody sacrifices therein offered; and in the face of such direct opposition to the sacrificial and ceremonial ritual, it requires no explanation why no word of his is recorded, either against the sacrifices or in favour of their being regarded as types of a bloody death of the Messiah, of a sin-removing, an atoning sacrifice. Not even the Targum of Jonathan explains the passage in Isaiah about the servant of God by a reference to the death of the Messiah, of which not a word is contained in the Old Testament. Jesus has not designated his death as a condition of redemption. He never spoke of his death except in direct connection with his life; he never even hinted at a result brought about by his death alone, or by his death unconnected with his life. If he has said that he came to give his life 'a ransom for many,' he has given a figurative expression to the liberation from spiritual bondage, which we owe to him, as to the man who taught men to believe in the power of God's indwelling Spirit. Of a pre-existing Messiah there is no trace in

---

[1] Ps. xl. 6; Is. i. 11 f.; Jer. vii. 22-26; Ez. xiv. 14.

the first three Gospels, which we here alone consider, if we except the passage about the Wisdom of God which has sent prophets in all ages, and to which personified Wisdom words have been referred by Luke, which Matthew had previously recorded as words of Jesus.[1] The doctrine of the sacrificial death of Jesus as the Messiah stands and falls with the doctrine of the Angel-Messiah and slain Lamb of God, who existed before the foundation of the world. The doctrine of the Angel-Messiah can be shown to have been introduced into Judaism by the Essenes, whose connection with the East can be proved. This doctrine seems to have been held by John the Baptist, though he did not apply it to Jesus, certainly not abidingly, and to have been by the latter protested against. If this result can be confirmed by the doctrines of Paul and by those recorded in the fourth Gospel, when investigated in connection with the Essenic doctrine of the Angel-Messiah, then it will be proved, that also the doctrine of an offended God reconciled by vicarious sacrifice was not recognised by Jesus.

Jesus the Messiah.

In the Synagogue of Nazareth, at the commencement of his public teaching, Jesus is by Luke recorded to have designated himself as the servant of God, of whom the Prophet had said, that the Spirit of God should rest on him, because He had anointed him, that is, made him a Messiah, to preach the glad tidings of the kingdom of heaven, not as an angel to the inhabitants of the earth, but as man to men. With a direct reference, it seems, to the 80th Psalm, Jesus called himself 'the son of Man,' because God had made him strong for himself, raising him to ' the man of his right hand.' Like the Finger of God, the Hand of God is a

[1] Matt. xxiii. 34 ; Luke xi. 49 ; about Psalm cx. see further on.

figurative expression for the Spirit of God, so that the passage about 'the son of Man' which God's hand had raised stands in direct connection with the passage in Isaiah which Jesus is recorded to have read at the synagogue and to have referred to himself. It is also to be connected with the passage in Peter's Pentecostal sermon about Jesus raised 'by the right hand of God.'

The passage about the Son of the right hand of God was in the mind of the author of the 110th Psalm, written after the Return from Babylon, perhaps on the consecration of Joshua, who, like Zerubbabel, probably was of Davidic descent. If so, Joshua represented, in a direct manner, the strangers in Israel, especially the Rechabites. To their ancestor Jonadab, Jeremiah had promised, in the Name of God, that he 'shall not want a man to stand before God for ever.' To this the Psalmist refers: 'The Lord hath sworn and will not repent, Thou art a priest for ever, after the order of Melchizedec.' The reference here made to the passage in Jeremiah is all the more certain, as the priestly order of Melchizedec, the non-Hebrew, may be connected with the Rechabites, Kenites or sons of Jethro, the non-Hebrew. The lord of the Rechabites was Jonadab, and to him God the Lord had said that he should 'stand before him' for ever. The promise made to Jonadab would be regarded as fulfilled by Joshua on the day of his consecration, when the Psalmist, possibly Joshua himself, could say: 'The Lord said unto my lord [Jonadab], Sit thou at my right hand.' If the Rechabites merged into the Essenic order, this passage was sure to be allegorically explained with reference to the Angel-Messiah whom the Essenes expected, all the more as in the days of Jesus, the Psalm was, by the people, believed to have been composed by David, who was also a descendant of Jonadab, the lord of the Rechabites or Kenites.[1]

[1] Jer. xxxv. 18, 19; Ps. cx. 1, 4.

We may assume that hopes were entertained that the high priest Joshua or Jesus, whom the prophet Zechariah describes as 'standing before' the Angel of the Lord, would be not only the fulfiller of the prophecy made to Jonadab, and thus to the strangers from whom David was descended, but also of the prophecy made by Nathan to David, that after his death and from his seed God would set up a descendant of his, a son of David. Of him God said : 'I will be his father, and he shall be my son.' Through him David's house and kingdom 'shall be established for ever.' A Psalmist who contrasted with this promise the apparently hopeless times preceding the Captivity, refers to Nathan's promise when he says of the still-expected son of David and Son of God : ' He shall cry unto me, Thou art my father, my God, and the rock of my salvation ; and I will make him my firstborn, higher than the kings of the earth.' And to this son of David and Son of God the author of the 2nd Psalm had referred, probably at an earlier time, or David himself had done so, as stated in the Acts, by saying, ' Thou art my Son, this day have I begotten thee.' It was all the more natural to refer this to the high priest Joshua, since, like the expected descendant of David whom Isaiah had called ' the Branch,' and on whom the Spirit of the Lord should rest, Joshua did fulfil Nathan's prophecy, as Solomon had done before, by building a house of God. Indeed, the prophet Zechariah actually designates Joshua as ' the man whose name is the Branch.'[1]

In the Old Testament there is not one single passage about the promised Son of God which ought to be disconnected from Nathan's promise of a son of David and Son of God. After the introduction, almost certainly by the Essenes, of the new doctrine of the Angel-Messiah, the Messianic attribute, ' the son of God,

---

[1] 2 Sam. vii. 12–14 ; Ps. lxxxix. 26, 27 ; Ps. ii. 7 ; Is. xi. 1–2 ; lxi. 1–2 ; Zech. vi. 11, 12.

received a new interpretation. Although not directly
either in the first three Gospels or the Acts, yet ‘ the
son of God ’ was in Paulinic writings and in the fourth
Gospel referred to a superhuman individual, to a man
not born of human parents, but who had for a time
given up his celestial abode, where he was the first of
seven Angels, and by whom the world had been created.
At first, as by Paul in one passage, the celestial son of
God was identified with the son of David.   The first
recorded assertion that Jesus was the Son of God but
‘ not the son of David,’ as the ‘ wicked ’ Jews maintained,
is found in the Epistle of Barnabas transmitted to us,
which the Alexandrian Clement, Origen, and Eusebius
cite as a writing of the Apostle Barnabas.   The essentially Essenic and anti-Gentile character of this Epistle
confirms the hypothesis that the Essenes introduced
the new doctrine of the Angel-Messiah, and with it the
doctrine of the atoning death of Messiah, into Judaism
and Christianity.   In the sense of Nathan’s prophecy
Jesus called himself the Son of God.   This will be confirmed by a full consideration of the question whether
Essenic influences may not be traced back to the composition of the Gospels and Pauline Epistles, especially
of the Epistle to the Hebrews, as the bishop and church-
historian Eusebius suggests we must do.   We saw that
having identified the Therapeuts of Philo with the Christian ascetics, Eusebius adds : ‘ It is highly probable that
the ancient commentaries which he (Philo) says they
have, are the very Gospels and writings of the Apostles,
and probably some expositions of the ancient Prophets,
such as are contained in the Epistle to the Hebrews
and many others of St. Paul’s Epistles.’ [1]

Jesus was crucified because he himself or others
called him ‘ king of the Jews,’ as the inscription on his
cross announced.   It is possible that he regarded himself as the son of David and Son of God to which the

[1] *Hist. Eccl.* ii. 17.

recorded prophecy of Nathan referred, though it seemed to have been fulfilled by Solomon, and had last been applied to the high priest Joshua. If Jesus really did expect a Messiah, as most Jews seem to have done, and if he regarded himself as Him that should come, he may have thought that the spiritual kingdom which it was his mission to found, could be easier established by his accepting, in harmony with Nathan's prophecy, the dignity of 'king of the Jews,' which multitudes were eager to confer on him. Indeed, what is recorded about the triumphant entry into Jerusalem shows that probably the majority of the people in Jerusalem received him with royal honours as the promised son of David and Messiah-King, who came in the Name of the Lord, that the entire city was in commotion and said, 'This is Jesus, the prophet of Nazareth of Galilee.' The spiritual rulers of Israel spoke of 'all the world' following him; we may therefore assume some of the Essenes to have followed in his train. According to Luke 'many' had joined him from Jericho, near to the Essenic settlements. In the fourth Gospel it is stated, that shortly before his entry into Jerusalem Jesus had gone 'beyond Jordan, into the place where John at first baptized,' and that 'many believed on him there.' It is even possible that these disciples of John who followed Jesus—it is possible that Essenes had helped to bring about, if not to prepare, his triumphant entry into Jerusalem, which Jesus could not have prevented.

The secret society of the Essenes, spread over Palestine, Egypt and other countries, and based on the non-recognition of the Temple-services and of private property, had become a standing danger to the recognised theocratic institutions of Israel. Although not sanctioning, but opposing the Essenic expectations of an Angel-Messiah, Jesus had abstained from any participation in the Temple-services, as the Essenes had always done, and the worship in the synagogues which he eu-

couraged by his teaching was in harmony with some of
the fundamental principles of the Essenes. A public
recognition of Jesus in the streets of Jerusalem, secretly
planned and effectually supported by the multitude to
whom he was so well known, might lead to the abolition of the Temple-services and to their being supplanted
by the Synagogue. This must have paved the way to a
more or less Essenic reformation of Judaism. If he
placed himself at the head of such a movement, Jesus
may have hoped to remove the errors of the Essenian
creed, especially the expectation of an Angel-Messiah.

The prohibition which Jesus is said to have addressed to his disciples, that they should 'tell no man'
that he was the Messiah, could hardly be explained by
the assumption that these words were attributed to
Jesus by those who, like the Essenes, wished to prove
that he had secretly taught the doctrine of the Angel-
Messiah, of which there is no trace in the first three
Gospels. But if Jesus did give this command about
secreting the most important doctrine, that is, his
relation to the Messianic expectations of his time, we
might assume that Jesus took precautions against his
being regarded as the Messiah in a sense contrary to
that which he could approve. He certainly did not
wish to be proclaimed as the Angel-Messiah whom the
disciples of John or the Essenes expected. Even were we
to assume that Jesus thought the setting up of his
spiritual kingdom might have been facilitated by his
accepting the kingship of the Jews, his motives for
doing so would have had to be kept secret by the few
to whom he would naturally have confided and who
would have understood them. All his disciples knew
that he was watched by emissaries from the ruling
Sadducees, who would have gladly espied some words
from him about his relation to the different Messianic
expectations. In the fourth Gospel it is implied by words
of Jesus that he was accused to have taught certain

doctrines 'in secret' only. The Sadducees, who believed not in angels or spirits, as Josephus states, had good reasons to oppose even an indirect spreading of the secretly promulgated Essenic doctrine about the Angel-Messiah.

The mysterious betrayal of Jesus by Judas may have been connected with a breach of trust in this very point, with Judas disobeying his master's injunction, not to tell any man that he was the Christ. At all events, it was not worth even 'thirty pieces of silver '—the price given for the liberation of a slave—to inform the recognised authorities at Jerusalem where Jesus was, who had publicly entered the city, and was daily visited by multitudes on the Mount of Olives. But it was very important for the ruling Sadducees to know what secret instructions, if any, Jesus had given to his disciples about his Messianic views, and what plans the Essenes might have projected to set him up as king of the Jews. The appointed guardians of the Temple had weighty reasons not to underrate the triumphant entry of Jesus into Jerusalem, nor the possible consequences of so unexpected a demonstration, perhaps secretly prepared by Essenes. Even if Jesus should not assume the offered title and dignity of king of the Jews, and even if he should discourage the secret Messianic expectations of the disciples of John, that is, of the Essenes, as Jesus would certainly have done, still he was sure to continue in his hostility against the Temple-services. The Synagogue, which the ruling Sadducees did not visit, might have been raised to the dignity of the Temple ; the latter degraded to a synagogue without priests ; and the Scribes and Pharisees might have been acknowledged by all as sitting in the seat of Moses, as the sole authority with regard to doctrine. If Judas could prove by his evidence that Jesus had spoken in secret to the disciples about his Messiahship, the only possible accusation of the authorities could succeed, that

Jesus, by allowing himself to be proclaimed as king of the Jews, had made himself the enemy of Cæsar. Then it would be easy to bring about a popular riot, a sham trial, the condemnation and crucifixion.

When this had been accomplished, perhaps with the direct assistance of the only non-Galilean disciple of Jesus, by Judas, the man of Kerioth in Judah, who accused himself of having betrayed innocent blood, all fears of the Sadducees seemed to be over. His disciples forsook him and fled. The words which Jesus is recorded to have spoken on the cross: 'My God, why hast thou forsaken me?' can only be referred to the apparent failure of his mission. In the eyes of the world God had forsaken him, by not granting any immediate success.

In the latest revised Gospel Jesus is recorded to have said: 'Behold your house is left (or rather, shall be left) unto you desolate (or deserted), for I say unto you, ye shall not see me henceforth till ye shall say: Blessed is he that cometh in the name of the Lord.' If Jesus has said this, he has confirmed the recorded prophetic visions about a Messiah at Jerusalem, whether himself or not, who shall come in the Name or Spirit of the Lord after the desolation of Israel's house by the Romans, or at a still later desolation of the country. Then Jesus will be seen, in the form of visions or otherwise. In the same Gospel the Messianic time is connected with the rising of nation against nation, with wrong interpretations of Messianic prophecies, especially with Christ's being 'in the desert,' possibly in the wilderness where the Essenes lived. 'The son of man,' or Messiah, is to come suddenly with the clouds of heaven, as lightning does, and his sign shall appear in heaven, and all the tribes of the earth shall see 'the son of man coming in the clouds of heaven with power and great glory.' This fulfilment of the Danielic vision is to come to pass 'immediately after the tribulations of those days,'—probably the Roman conquest. But in Luke the coming of the son of man is deferred to an uncertain time ; and the fourth Gospel is silent on the supposed and expected bodily reappearance of Jesus as Angel-Messiah in glory. And yet we should expect that in this Gospel of types and anti-types the future coming of the Angel-Messiah would be especially referred to as the fulfilment of the Jewish feast of tabernacles, 'the feast of in-gathering,' and ' the latter-day glory,' ushered in by the conversion of all nations.

Only in one sense can Jesus have regarded himself as the promised and generally expected Messiah. We have seen that Messianic conceptions were prevalent in the East before the commencement of Jewish history, and that the last of the expected incarnations of an Angel-Messiah was by many believed to have been Gautama-Buddha, born about 500 years before Jesus. Neither the Scriptures of the Old Testament transmitted to us, although they were not finally revised till after the Return from Babylon, and partly not before the time of Alexander, nor the first three Gospels, contain a clear reference to an Angel-Messiah. But it is evident that the vision recorded in the Book of Daniel about one ' like' a son of man brought before God on the clouds of heaven must be and was referred to a superhuman being. We have not here to consider whether or not this vision had for its source the Eastern expectation of an Angel-Messiah, which prevailed in Mesopotamia in ancient times, and was represented by the Essenes and probably the Rechabites. It is certain that not one of the passages which have been Messianically interpreted and which can possibly have been written before the Return from Babylon, refers to the expected Messiah as an incarnate Angel. In all passages which provably refer to earlier times the Messiah is designated as a descendant from David, on whom the Spirit of God would rest, as an anointed man, and thus Son of God. The first three

Gospels connect Jesus with no other than with this Messianic expectation.

If the tradition recorded in the Gospel after Luke is historical, Jesus has announced himself in his synagogal address at Nazareth as the expected Messiah, seen by the Prophets, as the promised son of David and Son of God, as the fulfiller of the prophecies of Nathan and other seers. It may be urged that even this identification by Jesus is doubtful, inasmuch as Matthew and Mark say nothing about it, whilst in the fourth Gospel, which, like the third, we shall connect with Essenic sources, Jesus is by revelation pointed out to the Baptist as the fulfiller of Messianic prophecies, as he on whom John would see the Spirit of God descend and rest. Whether Jesus did or did not connect himself with this servant of God, with this anointed man, as Joshua had before been connected, Jesus certainly recognised that he was moved to do God's will by the Spirit of God. Jesus declared that he and some of his contemporaries drove out devils or evil spirits by the good spirit, and that it was a sin 'against the Holy Ghost' to say that he and they did so by the evil spirit. To attribute good to evil, or, we may add, to attribute evil to good, Jesus declared to be a sin which would not be forgiven, which would have consequences in this world and in the world to come.

To drive out of man the spirit of evil, to bring him under the direction of the spirit of good, and thus to establish a communion between man and God, who is a Spirit, this is to place man under the conditions which are essential to that development of which his nature is capable in the terrestrial and in the non-terrestrial phases of his existence. Like the magnet, man possesses an attracting and a repelling force; he can attract and repel both good and evil influences, thus placing himself under the guidance of higher or lower, of the highest and of the lowest organs of the Divine Spirit which in a mysterious way proceeds from the personal God, whom no man has seen or can see. It depends on man's will to do or not to do the will of the Father of all spirits, of Him whom Jesus called the only One who is good. It is the gift of God that the Spirit from above has shone in all ages as the light of men, and presumably of all reasonable creatures in other stars. But few knew that there is a Holy Ghost, fewer still were guided by the power of God, and from the people this saving knowledge had been hidden, the 'key of knowledge' had been taken away. 'The law and the Prophets until John,' him included, had prophesied about the future coming of the Holy Ghost, they had 'shut up the kingdom of heaven unto men,' and Jesus declared that John the Baptist did not belong to that spiritual kingdom.

Revealing the presence of the Spirit of God, declaring and proving by word and deed that the kingdom of God has already come, baptizing with the Holy Ghost, Jesus said : Come unto me, take my yoke upon you (the uniting yoke of God's Spirit), learn of me how to obey the Spirit of God, and ye shall find rest unto your souls. Jesus taught and lived this new doctrine of God's anointing Spirit. In the face of erroneous doctrines about the Spirit of God and the Messiah, Jesus regarded it as his mission to preach by word and deed the presence of the Spirit of God in mankind, the universality and all-sufficiency of the Saviour of all ages. In this sense, Jesus came to save that which was lost ; he was the Saviour of mankind who came in the Name or Spirit of the Lord. As a chosen instrument of that saving power by which God had anointed him or made him a Christ, as the man who denounced the law and the Prophets for having prophesied about the future coming, whilst not pointing to the present working of God's Spirit in the flesh—in short, as the anointed Man, not as an anointed Angel, Jesus was and is the Christ.

Conclusion.

The transmitted records of man's history admit of the conclusion that Jesus of Nazareth was the man who reached the ideal of humanity, the One who obtained the prize in the race of the many. By obediently following the dictates of his enlightened conscience, the same had become the hallowed deposit of Divine revelations. Acquainted with the capabilities and wants of the human frame, Jesus fulfilled and delegated to his brethren the highest moral law of which the earth-born son of man is capable. What Jesus has left to mankind is an example which we can follow. We can follow him in the regeneration, in the Divine Sonship, for with our great ancestor we are 'participators of the Divine nature.' God speaks to us through his Spirit, as He spoke to Jesus and to ancestors of his in all ages. For those who have been born again by the greatest of miracles, for those who have been renewed in the spirit of their minds, the miraculous attestations of God never cease, they know that their life is a link in the chain of past and of future developments.

Unless we are prepared to deny the humanity of Jesus, we must accept as a fact that, he also commenced his life in ignorance, that he passed a period of doubt, and finally saw, seized, and lived the truth. Not even in the case of the most perfect man, of One who received the Holy Ghost 'without measure,' and whom God 'anointed with the Holy Ghost and with power,' can we imagine—not even of such a son of God dare we assert—a progress in his spiritual development without error, a progress in his moral evolution without combat. We must distinguish error from sin. The nature of sin is not error; but it is the denial by word and deed of what the responsible being knows to be truth. We cannot assume that the conscience of Jesus was something given him without his co-operation, something which was from the beginning perfect. We must regard his conscience as a gradual and normal development of the moral germ with which he was born, of the moral law written by God on the tables of his heart. Man is a co-operator in the redemption from the evils to which his nature is exposed. Jesus was no exception to this rule, notwithstanding his Messianity and Divinity.

The kingdom of heaven preached by Jesus is not the kingdom of the Angel-Messiah as preached by John the Baptist or Essene. The New Covenant is the covenant of a good conscience with God. Herein lies the efficacy of Christ's redemption, the world-conquering power of Christianity.

CHAPTER VII.

PAUL AND THE ESSENES.

The Hellenists—The person of Christ—Christ and the Spirit of God—The resurrection of Christ—Apparitions of Jesus after death—The day of Pentecost—The Atonement—Conclusion.

The Hellenists.

JESUS had opposed some of the doctrines of John the Baptist or Essene, and so the twelve Apostles opposed some of the doctrines of Paul, at least, during the seventeen years previous to his recognition as an Apostle. Paul was by birth a Pharisee, and the ruling Sadducees had appointed him as chief agent for the persecution which arose 'because of Stephen.' We may assume that Saul of Tarsus in Cilicia was among the men of Cilicia who disputed with Stephen, ' a man full of faith and of the Holy Ghost,' having done 'great wonders and miracles among the people.' Stephen was the first of those ' seven men of honest report, full of the Holy Ghost and wisdom ' whom the Grecians or Hellenists, that is, Greek-speaking Jews at Jerusalem, had elected among themselves to be ' appointed' by the Apostles over the business of daily ministration or assistance to Grecian widows. These Grecians assembled in one or more synagogues of their own at Jerusalem, and among them were Alexandrians. Here it was that those who disputed with Stephen 'were not able to resist the wisdom and the spirit by which he spake.' The 'murmuring' between Grecians and Hebrews, which seems at first not to have been connected with doctrine, made way for the accusation of Stephen before the council, who was charged with having spoken 'blasphemous words against Moses and against God.'

According to Rabbinical tradition there were 480 synagogues at Jerusalem, and yet no Gentile was ever admitted as member of any synagogue. The Alexandrians who disputed with Stephen were therefore certainly Greek-speaking Jews of Alexandria. A few miles from Alexandria was the chief settlement of the Essenian Therapeuts, and it is highly probable that some of them, like the 'Greeks,' had 'come up to worship at the feast.' Such Jewish Therapeuts of Alexandria would be included in the general designation 'Alexandrians.' Stephen himself, the Greek-speaking Jew, who, like his brethren, bore a Greek name, might have been an Essenic Therapeut. It can be proved by two facts that Stephen was an Essene. In his speech he designates Jesus as the Angel who was with the fathers in the wilderness. But the expectation of an Angel-Messiah cannot be shown to have ever prevailed among any orthodox party in Israel; whereas weighty reasons permit us to assume that the doctrine of the Angel-Messiah existed as secret tradition among the Essenes of the pre-Christian and of the Apostolic times. The ruling Sadducees were obliged to oppose this doctrine with all their might, not only because they believed neither in angels or spirits, whilst forbidding the Pharisees to promulgate their ancestral tradition, but because the Scriptures which the Sadducees recognised do not point by a single word to an Angel-Messiah. It would therefore appear as possible that the persecution of Stephen and of his companions in the faith had been chiefly caused by the new doctrine about the Angel-Messiah as applied to Jesus.

The speech of Stephen, as recorded in the Acts, shows that he did apply to Jesus the exclusively Essenic doctrine of the Angel-Messiah. Jesus Christ is by Stephen identified with the 'Angel of the Lord' who

appeared to Moses 'in a flame of fire in a bush,' and
from which 'the voice of the Lord came unto him.'
By the hand of this Angel God had sent Moses as ruler
and deliverer. The Prophet like unto Moses which God
should raise among Israel, was by Stephen identified
with the Angel of God who had spoken to Moses in the
Mount Sinai, and with the fathers, and through whom
Moses had received lively oracles, or living words, to
give unto Israel. But the fathers of Israel would not
obey Moses, and thus they rejected the revelation of
the Angel of God.[1] Stephen implies with sufficient
clearness that if the fathers had obeyed Moses, and thus
the Angel who spoke to him on Sinai, Israel might then
have received the gift of the Divine Spirit through the
Angel. But Israel's fathers and their descendants have
'always resisted the Holy Ghost.' Israel's fathers have
persecuted all the Prophets, and they have slain those
'which showed before of the coming of the Just One,'
of whom the Israelitic contemporaries of Stephen have
been 'the betrayers and murderers.' Stephen, so continues the recorder, ' being full of the Holy Ghost, looked
up stedfastly into heaven, and saw the glory of God,
and Jesus standing on the right hand of God, and said,
Behold, I see the heavens opened, and the Son of man
standing on the right hand of God.' Having prayed to
the 'Lord Jesus' that he would receive his spirit, and
that he would not lay this sin to the charge of them
who stoned him, the first Christian martyr fell asleep.

According to his own statement, Saul of Tarsus was
the young man whose name was Saul, at whose feet,
according to a still prevailing custom, the witnesses had
laid down their clothes, before throwing the first stones
on the man condemned as worthy of death.[2] The man
from Cilicia, who had heard, and probably taken part in
the disputations with Stephen—he who had heard his

---

[1] Comp. Deut. xxxiii. 2–5 in the Septuagint version; Gal. iii. 19.
[2] Deut. xvii. 6, 7.

defence, also heard, as the representative of the Jewish authorities, when he was stoned, his confession of faith in the risen Jesus as the Angel-Messiah promised by Moses, according to Stephen's interpretation. This doctrine, which is contrary to the letter and spirit of the Mosaic Scriptures, we must connect, as with the Essenes, the only Jews who have held it, so at least with some of the Hellenists whom Stephen represented. Stephen is not likely to have been the only one among the Grecians who expected an Angel-Messiah, and who regarded Jesus as the same.

We know not how long before his martyrdom Stephen was elected as the first of the seven deacons, but we are told, that 'the whole multitude' at Jerusalem was pleased with their elections, that 'the word of God increased; and the number of the disciples multiplied in Jerusalem greatly; and a great company of the priests were obedient to the faith.' This account is evidently written with a view to the harmonising objects of the Acts, which are attributed in their present form to Luke. In his earlier written Gospel Luke had not dared openly to assert what he, like Paul, must have believed, that Jesus was the incarnate Angel of God. Yet Luke implied as much when attributing, as he is recorded to have done, words of Jesus to the 'Wisdom of God,' who had sent the Prophets in all ages. 'The faith' of the disciples of Jesus at Jerusalem is in the Acts implied to have been one and the same, that is, the faith in Jesus as the Angel-Messiah. If so, the faith of the twelve Apostles, of Stephen and of Paul, would have been one and the same; and it would be inexplicable that there is no trace of such doctrine in any of the Scriptures composed before the deportation to Babylon, or in the first three Gospels, with the sole exception of the passage just cited, which Luke or a later reviser has freely enlarged after Matthew's record.

It would seem that the Essenic and Hellenistic

teaching about the Angel-Messiah had already become very popular when Herod Agrippa became Roman governor of Judæa. His mother was a Jewess, being descended from the Maccabees, whose allies were the Assidæans or Essenes. Although Herod encouraged the Nazarites, with whom the Essenes were indirectly connected by their austere mode of life, it would be impossible to assume that the zealous defender of the Mosaic law held or favoured the Essenic doctrine about the Angel-Messiah. So popular seems to have been this doctrine, the doctrine of Stephen, that the sudden death of Herod was attributed to the Angel of God with whom Stephen had identified the risen Jesus.

It is probable that Stephen's martyrdom took place in the year of accession of Herod Agrippa, and at the commencement of the first year of his reign of three years. Since Saul was converted in the year of Stephen's death, the three years which Paul spent in Arabia before he returned to Jerusalem are best explained by the supposition that, so long as this despot lived, the man who had been sent from Jerusalem as a persecutor and had become a convert could not have shown himself in that city. Probably, therefore, in the year A.D. 41, the great persecution 'about Stephen' commenced, and, according to the Acts, it was directed against all the members of 'the Church which was at Jerusalem'; these were 'all scattered abroad throughout the regions of Judæa and Samaria, except the Apostles.' It is difficult to explain this remarkable exception, unless on the ground of the supposition that Stephen had been put to death and his followers scattered for spreading doctrines not recognised by the Apostles. The fierce attack of Stephen against the fathers of Israel must have been condemned by the Apostles as much as by the high priest, whose right hand Herod Agrippa seems to have been. The Apostles could become objects of persecution only in so far as they had not up to this time worshipped at the Temple, but in the synagogue only. They could not be made answerable for what Stephen had taught. On the contrary, they must have opposed his doctrine of the Angel-Messiah as one which Jesus had not recognised, as the first three Gospels clearly prove. That James was beheaded and Peter imprisoned by Herod Agrippa may be sufficiently explained by their not having worshipped in the Temple any more than Jesus had done so.

Previous to the death of Stephen, during the seven to nine years after the crucifixion of Jesus, which probably took place at Easter in the year 35, the deacons or overseers of the Hellenists must have had a considerable following at Jerusalem. We may safely assume that already then, if not ever since the death of Jesus, Stephen had proclaimed him at Jerusalem as the Angel-Messiah of the Essenes and Therapeuts. It is even probable that among the very small number of 'about one hundred and twenty' disciples who assembled at Jerusalem a few days after the crucifixion, if not already the next day, on the 16th Nisan, the day of the presentation of the firstling-sheaf, there were some, and perhaps many Essenes, who regarded Jesus as the Angel-Messiah. We may even conjecture that this very limited association consisted chiefly of Essenes, and did not include many who, like the Apostles, as we here assume, regarded Jesus as the promised anointed Man, without believing that ' a new religion was to be set up in the world,' or that ' the professors of that religion were to be distinguished from the rest of mankind.'[1]

After that which the Apostles regarded as idle tales about what women had first declared to have seen at the grave, even after the well attested apparitions of Jesus, many would require additional evidence, such as the recorded miraculous fulfilment of the Jewish Pente-

[1] Paley, *Evidences of Christianity,* ix.

costal type, before they could join those who first
believed in Jesus as the antitype of the Paschal omer.
On that Pentecostal day, the tenth day after the aseen-
sion of Jesus, according to the Acts, 'about three
thousand souls' were added to the first association, and
soon after this 'the number of the men was about
five thousand.'[1]   If the Apostles had been believers in
the Messianic doctrines of Stephen, they could hardly
have remained at Jerusalem whilst the followers of
Stephen were scattered abroad.   Had they regarded
Jesus not as the anointed man, the son of David and
Son of God of Messianically interpreted prophecies,
but had the Apostles regarded him as the anointed
Angel, of whom the Scriptures before the deportation
to Babylon say nothing, they might have been accused,
like Stephen, of having spoken 'blasphemous words'
against the holy place and the law.

The assertion shall now be more minutely confirmed, that there was an essential difference between
the doctrines of the twelve Apostles and those of
Stephen about Jesus as the Messiah.   We have already
seen that if the twelve Apostles did, like Stephen,
believe in Jesus as the Angel-Messiah, it would be
apparently inexplicable why there should be no trace
in the first three Gospels of Jesus having recognised
such a doctrine, on which all Scriptures possibly composed before the deportation to Babylon are silent.

There can be no doubt as to the identity of the
Messianic conceptions of Paul and those of Stephen.
We shall see that when Paul refers to Christ as the
spiritual Rock which followed the Israelites, he points
to the Angel who had been with the fathers in the

---

[1] It is curious that the Essenic corporation is, by Josephus, reported to
have numbered about 4,000 associates, and that the appointment of deacons
is connected with the days when the number of disciples was multiplied, as
if these had been in great part Hellenists, among whom we may assume
Therapeuts.

wilderness, and that he identifies Jesus with that
Angel as Stephen had done. Paul acknowledges that
during the persecution which arose about Stephen
he accepted the faith which once he destroyed. On
his way to Damascus, with the dying words of Stephen
still ringing in his ears, impressed by the martyr's vision
of Jesus, of the Angel-Messiah standing at the right hand
of God, Paul had also a vision. Suddenly a light from
heaven shone about him, he fell to the ground, and
heard a voice saying unto him, ' Saul, Saul, why perse-
cutest thou me?' Using the word of Stephen, he at
once addressed the speaker from heaven as 'Lord,'
whereupon he was told that it was Jesus of Nazareth
who had appeared to him. Not having been prepared,
as Paul was by Stephen, the men that were with him,
though they saw the light, ' heard not the voice' of
him that spake to the conscience-stricken persecutor of
Stephen's Lord. Nor were Paul's companions blinded
by the light which they saw, but they led Paul by the
hand to Damascus, the place appointed him in the
vision. After having been blind for three days, one
Ananias, a ' disciple' of Jesus, came unto him by a
Divine command communicated in a vision, and said,
' Brother Saul, receive thy sight,' and at the same hour
Saul looked up upon him. His sight had returned, and
he was filled with the Holy Ghost, for which reason
Ananias had been sent by Jesus. Ananias announced
to him that the God of the fathers had chosen him
that he should know his will and see ' that Just One,'
that he should hear the voice of his mouth, and be his
witness, being baptized and having his sins washed
away. This water-baptism was regarded by John the
Essene as the symbol of the Holy Ghost which Paul
received through the mediation of Ananias at the bidding of Jesus.

As Paul followed Stephen in calling the speaker
from heaven ' Lord,' so Ananias called him, like Stephen,

'the Just One.' As did John the Baptist and all the
Essenes, Ananias regarded water-baptism as a type of the
washing away of sins, by the Messianic baptism with
the Holy Ghost. We are therefore led to expect, that
Ananias, who is designated as 'a devout man according
to the law, having a good report of all the Jews' at
Damascus, may have represented the Judaism of the
Essenes, who neither accepted circumcision nor the
Temple-ritual with its sacrifices, but who preached
righteousness by faith in the Angel-Messiah. According
to Paul's own narrative, Ananias was instrumental in
God's revealing his 'Son' in the heart of him who had
been the chief instrument in persecuting the believers
in Jesus as the Angel-Messiah.

It can be proved, from a statement transmitted by
Josephus, that soon after the time of Paul's conversion,
a Jew called Ananias, who had come to Adiabene, one
of the Mesopotamian kingdoms, there preached righteousness not by the works of the law but by faith, as
Paul did ; whilst another Jew at Adiabene denied that
this was a purer faith, and insisted on the works of the
law. It was 'upon the death of King Agrippa,' or
about the year A.D. 44, that is, at the utmost three
years after Paul had met Ananias of Damascus, that a
Jewish merchant Ananias said to King Izates of Adiabene, 'that he might worship God without being circumcised, even though he did resolve to follow the
Jewish law entirely, which worship of God was of a
superior nature to circumcision.' Yet another Jew,
Eleazar, 'who was esteemed very skilful in the learning
of his country,' persuaded Izates to be circumcised, by
showing him from the law what great impiety he would
be guilty of by neglecting this Divine command. Josephus, who had probably passed three years as an Essenic
novice with Banus, adds that God preserved Izates from
all dangers, demonstrating thereby, that 'the fruit of
piety (the 'chassidout' of the Essenes or Assidæans)

does not perish, as to those that have regard to him and fix their faith upon him only.'[1]

Ananias may have gone from the commercial city of Damascus to Adiabene; and this merchant-missionary, who reminds us of Mahomed, may have been the same 'disciple' of Jesus who very shortly, at the utmost only a few years before, had been the instrument of Paul's conversion in the street called Straight. This possible identity is confirmed in a remarkable manner by the merchant Ananias at Adiabene having proclaimed the same fundamental truths which the disciple Ananias at Damascus, and afterwards Paul, preached. At all events, it is proved by this narrative, that about the time of Paul's conversion two parties opposed each other among the Jews; and that the one party, represented by one who seems to have been an Essene, whilst being a disciple of Jesus, taught the doctrine, later promulgated by Paul, about righteousness without the deeds of the law, especially without circumcision.

This higher kind of Judaism, this deeper knowledge or gnosis, cannot be asserted to have been recognised and practised by any party in Israel, except by the Essenes. Even of the Apostles at Jerusalem this cannot be proved. Such was the higher Judaism which the Essenes had by allegorical explanations harmonised with Mosaic writings, and it was openly declared in the presence of Paul by Ananias of Damascus. We may with almost certainty assume that Ananias of Damascus was an Essenic disciple of Jesus, for we know that he, like Stephen, regarded him as the Angel-Messiah who was expected by the Essenes only, and to whom, therefore, Ananias, like Stephen, must have belonged. It cannot be shown, nor is it at all probable, that Ananias, as the human instrument in the conversion of Paul, stood in any connection with the Apostles at Jerusalem, with Peter, and 'the other Jews,' as Paul calls them,

[1] Jos. *Antiq.* xx. 2.

who solemnly declares to have been 'independent' of
them, and that they taught him 'nothing new' when,
seventeen years after his conversion, he met them at
Jerusalem.[1]

The scattered Hellenists 'went everywhere preaching the word,' some going as far as Phœnicia, Cyprus,
and Antioch, preaching 'to Jews only,' that is, probably
to such who, like the Essenes of Judæa, excluded the
Gentiles, whilst others in that city 'spake unto the
Grecians,' or Greek-speaking Jews who admitted Gentiles, 'preaching the Lord Jesus.'[2] This statement in
the Acts, which distinguishes Hebrew Jews from Greek
Jews, tends to support the view we wish to establish,
that 'the persecution that arose about Stephen' was
directed chiefly, though not solely, against Grecians
who were Therapeuts, whose doctrine about the Angel-
Messiah Stephen had applied to Jesus, whether he was
the first to do so or not. For, as in Antioch some of
those persecuted preached to Jews only, being particu-
larists like the Essenes of Judæa, so there were others in
that city among those who were persecuted because of
Stephen, who preached like him 'the Lord Jesus' to
Greek-speaking Jews or Hellenists, among whom there
probably were Alexandrians and universalist Therapeuts. The Hand of the Lord—his Spirit was with these
preachers at Antioch, so that a great number believed.
These two parties among the scattered Jews at Antioch,
we distinguish as Essenes of Palestine who admitted
Jews only, and as Therapeuts who also admitted Gentiles. Among them there existed the same difference
as between the two Jewish teachers at Adiabene and
between the two principal prophets of Antioch, Barnabas and Paul. The Church at Antioch, where the
disciples were first called Christians, was founded in
absolute independence of the Apostles at Jerusalem,
and the same was the case with Paul's conversion. The

[1] Gal. i. 16; ii. 6.   [2] Acts xi. 19-26.

Twelve were not scattered when certain (Essenic?) disciples—when followers of Stephen—went to Antioch, and the Apostles were ' all ' afraid of Paul when Barnabas introduced him to them.

In a certain sense Paul declares his Gospel to be another and yet ' not another ' or ' not a second.' The Gospel which Paul announced was certainly and essentially another than that which was preached by the twelve Apostles, if it can be proved that Paul has applied to Jesus the Essenic doctrine of the Angel-Messiah, on which the pre-Babylonian Scriptures and the first three Gospels observe a mysterious silence. From this it follows that Jesus cannot have approved of this doctrine. But if Jesus, who had chosen the Twelve, was the Angel-Messiah who had revealed himself to Paul, this Apostle's Gospel could in a certain sense not be another, though a second, inasmuch as the author of both Gospels was asserted to be the same individual. Only the assumption that the Twelve did not believe in Jesus as the incarnate Angel, and the fact that Paul, like Stephen and Ananias, did so, seems to enable us to explain their fears of Paul when they first came in contact with him. Their fear could not have been caused by a doubt whether he really had become a follower of Stephen, had accepted the faith which once he destroyed. It will become more and more probable, if not certain, that the Apostles feared Paul because he had become an earnest and zealous convert of the new faith in an Angel-Messiah, which Stephen had perhaps first publicly proclaimed.

It was among the Hellenists that Paul preached first, on his return from Antioch to Jerusalem, as if he expected to meet with more sympathy among them than among the Hebrews, and, we may assume, among the disciples of Jesus who looked to the Twelve as their guides. No more weight can be laid on the statement that the Hellenists wished to kill him and

that 'brethren' (the Apostles?) got him away, than on
the statement that Paul went in and out with the
Apostles who were all afraid of him, and that he
'freely' or boldly declared the name of the Lord Jesus,
that is, of the Angel-Messiah.   Both may be attributed
to the compromising tendency of the Acts.

The Essenic element in the Church at Antioch,
which was independent of that at Jerusalem, and to
which Paul was introduced by Barnabas, is confirmed
by the undeniably Essenic character of the Epistle of
Barnabas, which the Fathers attribute unanimously to
the Apostle of this name.   We shall return to this
subject.   Another of the prophets of this Church was
Manaen, who had been brought up with Herod, and
whom we may safely identify with the Essenic prophet
Menahem, who was at school with the tetrarch at
Rome and predicted his future, according to Josephus.
If Paul, another of the prophets of Antioch, can be
proved from his own writings to have attributed to
Jesus, like Stephen, and almost in the same words, the
exclusively Essenic doctrine of the Angel-Messiah, then
the Essenic element in the Antiochian Church will have
been proved as an historical fact.

The names of all Hellenistic deacons are of Greek
origin.   After Stephen the Acts name Philip, who was
also called the Evangelist.   He had prophesying
daughters, and to him, as to Stephen, 'the Angel of
the Lord' appeared, that is, the Angel-Messiah of the
Essenes and Therapeuts.   There are some traits in the
transmitted narrative about Philip which tend to confirm the connection of some Hellenists with Therapeuts.
Of those who had been scattered 'because' of Stephen—
because of the preacher on the Angel-Messiah, some had
gone to Samaria and there preached 'the Word.'   Here
Philip met Simon, a born Samaritan, whose ancestors
seem to have settled there from Citium in Cyprus,
according to statements by Josephus.   He was also

called Magus—a name which may point to the Magi, and thus to the Maga or Maya, the spiritual power of Eastern tradition, especially of the Buddhists, with whose doctrines we have connected the Essenes. The Samaritans are by Josephus designated as Medo-Persian immigrants; and as such their priests, like those of the Medes, may have been called Magi, by others if not by the Samaritans. Simon the Samaritan might therefore as such have been called Magus.

It must here suffice to make the following statements about Simon of Samaria, whom all the Fathers regard as the Father of heresy in the Christian Church, that is, of a false gnosis in the Apostolic age. He was educated at Alexandria, according to the Clementines; the city of Sichem, also called Sychar, and later the city of Antioch, were the centres of his activity; his disciples, like those of Jesus at Antioch, were first called by the name of Christians; the disciples of Simon were baptized; the Initiated among them had to keep certain doctrines secret; their master taught them to believe in Jesus as 'the Word' of all ages, as the Angel-Messiah and aboriginal type of Humanity, who came to the earth 'apparently as man, but not as man,' exactly as it is taught by the Epistle of Barnabas; the Simonians distinguished a spiritual from a material world, and believed in an allegorical meaning of Scripture; Simon in his writings referred to John the Baptist or Essene and to Paul's Epistles; he is reported to have had disputations with Peter in Rome, where a party favourable to him existed before his arrival, as was the case with Paul; the Chrestus- or Christos-party among the Jews in this city, which apparently is mentioned at exactly the same time when Simon is said to have been there, may be regarded as the party of Simon who called himself a Christian, which name originated in Antioch, the centre of his activity.[1]

[1] The name Chrestus, given by Suetonius, is by Clement of Alexandria

All these points connect Simon of Samaria with the Essenes. Simon is in the Clementine 'Recognitions' actually called a disciple of John the Baptist, and thus is directly connected with the Essenes. His reported education in Alexandria would therefore lead us to connect him with the Therapeuts or universalist Essenes of that place, with which we have connected Stephen and Paul. If, nevertheless, the Christian Church separated Simon from Paul by a deep gulph, this can easily be explained by the not far-fetched supposition, that after the Acts had removed every difference between the doctrines of Paul and those of the Twelve, Simon necessarily was made the scapegoat, and the father of all false doctrines which denied the humanity of Jesus. It was necessary to do this, after the recognition by the Church of the Essenic-Paulinic doctrine about the Angel-Messiah, although Simon Magus had also taught that doctrine. It formed the very centre of the disputations between Simon and Peter at Rome, according to the Clementines; and what Peter had openly combated, could not be suffered to appear as that which, like Simon, Paul had taught. This compromise was facilitated, as we shall see, by Paul's considerate open acknowledgment of the human nature of Jesus, and it led to the union of the two parties among the disciples of Jesus, of the aboriginal or Jewish-Christian party, which had regarded Jesus as the anointed Man, and of the Gentile-Christian or Therapeut party, which recognised Jesus as the anointed Angel.

Philip the deacon, though the Acts oppose him to Simon of Samaria, probably preached the Essenic doctrine of the Angel-Messiah as Simon did, for Philip is in the Acts indirectly connected with the Angel-Messiah, because with the Angel of the Lord. According to the Angel's direction, Philip was on his way to Gaza from

given as Christos. It is within the range of possibility that Simon Niger, the prophet at Antioch, was Simon Magus.

Samaria, probably going by Hebron. He had to pass the region to the west of the Dead Sea, where the Kenites or Rechabites, later the Essenes, had their settlements; the country where John the Baptist was born, where he received the Divine call, and probably began to baptize. The servant of the Ethiopian Candace, or Queen, returning from Jerusalem, where he had been worshipping, was told by Philip, before being baptized, that the 53rd chapter in Isaiah refers to Jesus. This explanation had been made easier by the possibly Therapeutic authors of the Septuagint, which text the eunuch was reading. A mystic interpretation had here been given to the passage which refers to the servant of God being taken away 'through tribulation and judgment.' Instead of this, it is said, that 'in his humiliation his judgment was taken away.' Again, whilst the Hebrew text says: 'Who of his contemporaries considers it, that he was taken away from the land of the living?' the Greek version has, 'Who shall declare his generation, for his life is taken from the earth?' Thus already here a hidden reference could be found to Melchizedec, whose generation the Scriptures do not transmit. This passage could be held to suggest that Jesus had neither father nor mother; and that Jesus Christ, as Simon declared, was the Son of God, but not the son of David, as Philip's contemporary the Apostle Barnabas likewise taught in his Epistle. The sudden disappearance of Philip would confirm the Ethiopian in his mystic conceptions.

The connection of Hellenists with Therapeuts can be confirmed by the fact that Paul, after his conversion to the faith of Stephen, like him, preached Jesus as the Angel-Messiah, whom in Israel only the Essenes expected: a doctrine of which there is no trace in the first three Gospels, or in any Scriptures possibly composed before the deportation to Babylon, and therefore before the birth of Gautama-Buddha, the Angel-Messiah of Buddhists.

The Person of Christ.

The doctrinal system of Paul centres in his doctrine of Christ. The undoubtedly genuine Epistles of the Apostle prove, that he regarded Jesus as an incarnate Angel, as the Angel of the Lord who went before and followed the Israelites. Almost in the same words in which Stephen had applied to Jesus the doctrine of the Angel-Messiah, Paul refers to Jesus Christ as the spiritual Rock which followed the Israelites in the wilderness. In the account of the shipwreck recorded in the Acts, Paul describes that ' an Angel of God ' had stood by him in the night, ' whose I am and whom I serve.' If these words refer not to God, but to the Angel, the latter would have been the same Angel who had appeared to him at the time of his conversion to the faith of Stephen, that is, the Angel who had followed the Israelites, the spiritual Rock, or Christ.[1] Since some of the Greek-speaking Jews, like Stephen, believed in Jesus as the Angel-Messiah whom the Essenes expected, we should expect even on this ground only, that the Apostle who says he was to the Jews a Jew and to the Greeks a Greek—that the great Apostle of universal religion would aim at harmonising in his Epistles and addresses the diverging Messianic conceptions.

There was no reason to doubt the human nature of Jesus Christ, at least not for anyone who could say, with Paul, that Jesus was ' made of the seed of David according to the flesh, and declared to be the Son of God with power, according to the spirit of holiness, by the resurrection from the dead.' This might have been said by any disciple, even by one who did not believe, as Paul did, in Jesus as an incarnate Angel. Although this is the only passage in Paul's Epistles where the human nature of Jesus Christ is clearly and directly acknowledged, yet other passages imply it. Paul had especial

---

[1] 1 Cor. x. 4; Acts xxvii. 23; comp. Rom. i. 9.

reasons to be conciliatory at Rome, where the elders of the Jews regarded him as member of a sect 'everywhere spoken against.'

It is more difficult to refer this sect to that of the Christians than to that of the Essenes. For, whilst the Christians at Jerusalem under James had not there been spoken against, since they had exchanged the Synagogue for the Temple, the Essenes were by all the Jews spoken against as dissenters, and their belief in an Angel-Messiah was rejected by every orthodox Jew. We have no right to assert that the Jews in Rome or anywhere could have designated Peter or any of the Apostles at Jerusalem as belonging to a sect 'everywhere spoken against'

Whether the sect in question was the Christian or the Essenian one, of 'this sect,' to which Paul belonged, there were members in Rome before Paul arrived there, for 'brethren' had gone to meet him at the Appian Forum. Signs are not absolutely wanting that these 'brethren' were Essenian Christians. According to the 'Clementines,' Barnabas, whom we regard as a Levite who had become an Essene, taught in Rome and in Alexandria before the crucifixion of Jesus. As already stated, the genuine Epistle of Barnabas, though worked over, shows that he denied the human nature of Jesus, and called those who regarded him as son of David 'wicked Jews.' The 'Clementines,' probably composed in Rome and reaching back to the first century, testify to the existence of an Essenic party in Rome, with which we may connect the party which Simon had in that city. If this Essenic party in Rome, which Barnabas may be assumed to have addressed there, denied the human nature of Jesus, as Barnabas certainly did, Paul had special reasons for clearly stating, what he has done in no other Epistle than in that to the Romans, that Jesus is the son of David as well as the Son of God.

Paul separated from Barnabas on the question of

the admittance of uncircumcised Gentiles; but another reason for his separating from him seems to have been, that Paul, opposing Barnabas and Simon of Samaria, insisted on the recognition of the human nature of Jesus, notwithstanding his Divinity. In the above-cited passage of his Roman Epistle, the Apostle distinguishes the fleshly from the spiritual birth of Jesus Christ in such a manner, that the doctrine of Peter about the man Jesus anointed with the Holy Ghost and with power could be well harmonised with it. It may be assumed that Paul by this Epistle laid a foundation for the 'spiritual gift,' that is, of peace in the Churches, which gift he wished to bring to this divided Church, founded by Peter according to tradition transmitted to us, and in which the Jewish-Christian element predominated. The harmonious co-operation of Peter and Paul in Rome, their common martyrdom in this city, are historical facts; and it may be asserted that the diverging opinions of the Twelve and of Paul on the person of Christ lost their party character by Paul's open acknowledgment of the humanity of Jesus.

Although in a single passage—assuming its correct transmission—Paul clearly insists on the human as well as on the implied angelic nature of Christ, yet his coming in the flesh is explained in a qualified sense, though not altogether drawn in question, by another passage in the same Epistle to the Romans: 'For what the law could not do, in that it was weak through the flesh, God sending his own Son in the likeness of (the) sinful flesh, and for sin, condemned sin in the flesh.' Only in consequence of the sending of God's own Son (the Angel-Messiah), in the likeness of (the) sinful flesh, it became possible to men to fulfil the righteousness of the law, to such 'who walk not after the flesh, but after the spirit.' It is here obviously pointed out, that since the fall of the first Adam humanity has either not possessed the Spirit of God, or possessed it without the possibility of obeying it, because of sin. The Apostle seems to distinguish the sinful flesh from the not-sinful flesh. The Epistles of Paul attest, that he did not believe it possible for even the most perfect of men to walk after the Spirit, to be led by the Spirit of God, to become sons of God, before God's sending his own Son and with him the Spirit of Promise. Paul may therefore be understood to have said, that God sent his own Son, not 'in the sinful flesh,' but 'in the likeness of the sinful flesh,' that is, into a new kind of flesh, into such flesh as had been prepared for the Angel of God, so that the latter might keep his angelic nature after his assumption of a fleshy nature 'like' that of men, 'yet without sin.'[1]

Christ and the Spirit of God.

As the 'Name' or Spirit of God is in the Angel of the Lord, so it is in Jesus, though, according to the flesh, he is the son of David. The flesh of Christ Jesus was by Paul held to be spiritualised flesh, as Tertullian says—'flesh with the Spirit of God.' Not flesh which wars against the spirit, not the flesh of fallen man, which had been un-spiritualised by the withdrawal of the Spirit of God in the time of the flood, not the flesh of 'children of wrath,' to which, the Jews 'even as others,' all men belonged, up to the time of the incarnation of the Son of God, but the flesh of Christ Jesus was by Paul held to be such flesh as would be, and was, directed by the Spirit of God. Without assistance from heaven, without God's unspeakable gift of his Holy Spirit, which was brought down by the anointed Angel of God, man cannot overcome sin, he can only be saved by the grace of God's Spirit, which helps his infirmities, and makes intercession for him.[2]

---

[1] Rom. xii. 3, 4; comp. Tertull. *De Carne Christi*, 3; Ps. xl. 7; Hebr. x. 5; iv. 15; ix. 28; where 'a body' is inserted instead of 'ears.'

[2] Rom. viii. 26, 27, 34; comp. i. 4.

The law could not bring the Spirit of God, and was 'added because of transgression.' Its highest object was to be a schoolmaster, preparing for Christ. Not only till the law, also after it, ' there was sin in the world,' until ' faith came,' till the Angel of God had brought to earth the Holy Ghost, so that those who allow themselves to be led by the Spirit of God are children of God. Sin came by the disobedience of the first Adam, grace came by the obedience of the second Adam. Faith establishes the law, inasmuch as the letter that killeth is interpreted by the quickening or life-giving Spirit, because the ' shameful' system of keeping back, which has existed since Moses, has been laid aside. Because of the withdrawing of God's Spirit, Adam and Eve hid themselves from ' the presence' of God, his ' countenance' shone no more upon them ; the Spirit of God did ' not always strive' or remain with fallen man, he was ' flesh,' only flesh, flesh without the Spirit of God. Even Abraham could not be righteous, but he believed God, who promised the future blessing of mankind in Abraham's seed, the seed to whom the promise was made.

The faith of Abraham was 'accounted to him for righteousness,' and ' faithful Abraham' became the father of those, among Gentiles and Jews, who, ' received the spirit by the hearing of faith,' that is, ' the adoption of sons,' in consequence of which God sent ' the Spirit of his Son' into their hearts, and redeemed their bodies. Abraham rejoiced to see the ' day' when the Angel of God would bring back the Spirit to mankind, would bring the faith which should ' afterwards be revealed,' after the Mosaic law, which has ' nothing to do with faith.' The promised faith and the promised Spirit of God came by the Angel-Messiah, the second Adam, who was a ' quickening spirit.' Henceforth, man has become ' spiritual,' he is ' a new creature,' he belongs to a new generation of men, born under direct celestial influences, he stands in a new relation to God through the mediation of an anointed Angel.

Paul seems to have held that, even after the fall of man, he was possessed of reason and will, but not of conscience. What was to become life and light in man had first to be manifested in the likeness of sinful, because un-spiritualised flesh, by the ' man from heaven,' by the incarnation of the Word from the beginning, the Angel of God in whom that life was. His glory, as of the only one Son of the Father, full of grace and truth, had first to be seen by man in ' the face of Christ,' before the glorified Son, raised by God's right hand, could receive the promise of the Father for mankind, the Spirit to be poured on all flesh. That Divine Spirit was intended to have been restored by the Angel of God who appeared to Moses, and whom Paul identifies with Christ Jesus, as Stephen had done before him. Already then the incarnation of the Angel-Messiah might have taken place. But Israel would not obey Moses, and resisted the Holy Ghost, as it did when Stephen, ' full of the Holy Ghost,' revealed Jesus as the Angel-Messiah. Even John the Baptist or Essene regarded as future the coming into the world of that true light which lighteth all men. The baptism with the Holy Ghost or with fire, typified by water baptism, was to be introduced by the Angel of God, according to John's expectation. The disciples of John had not even heard that there is a Holy Ghost. God had not yet ' introduced his first-born into the world.'

Nevertheless, Paul refers to the passage in the Mosaic Scriptures about the Word which is in man's heart that he may do it. The Apostle states that ' faith,' that is, the faith which should be revealed after the law on Sinai in the fulness of time, ' cometh by hearing, and hearing by the word of God,' that is, as we shall see, by Christ, the spiritual Rock, by the Angel which followed the Israelites, by the Angel-Messiah. Paul is

far from admitting that the Word is an innate faculty or
spiritual power by which, man willing, the sinfulness of
the flesh can be overcome, that the Word or Spirit of
God is a soul-saving power which in measure man has
possessed in all ages, and for the abiding presence of
which in his soul David prayed.

The passage in question, the only one in which Paul
calls Christ the Word of God, is by him explained to be
a prophecy referring to the coming of Christ ' as the
end of the law.'   The ' Word ' of which Moses said that
it need not be brought from heaven nor beyond the sea,
but which was already then in the Israelites that they
might to do it, that Word Paul implies to have been
Christ.   This Word of God, or Christ, is identical with
the Angel-Messiah, or spiritual Rock which followed
the Israelites.   Christ, the Word of God, having come
down ' from heaven ' need not be ' brought down,' and
after his resurrection he need not be ' brought up
(again) from the dead.'   When Moses uttered those
words, he spoke in the spirit about ' the word of faith '
which Paul preached.   The word of which Moses said
that it was then in the ' mouth ' of the Israelite, Paul
explains to be the confession of ' the Lord Jesus ' with
the mouth ; again, the word of which Moses said that
it was then in the ' heart ' of the Israelite, and that it
depended on him whether he followed it and lived, or
did it not and died, this word Paul explains as the belief
in the heart, that God has ' raised Jesus from the dead.'
This new belief the Apostle designates as the condition of salvation.[1]   A real masterpiece of allegorical
interpretation of Scripture in the Essenic spirit, if not
derived from Essenic tradition, as our scheme seems to
suggest.

If Israel's fathers ' always resisted the Holy Ghost,'
as Stephen declared, and if the Holy Ghost had been
withdrawn after the fall, as Paul implies, and as the

---

[1] Rom. x. 4-21; Deut. xxx. 11-20.

narrative about the Flood confirms, then the holiest Israelite could only have resisted an innate germ of good, a moral sensitiveness which, without preparing him for spiritual influences from above, might have prevented his yielding to the germ of evil. What Moses says about the Word in the heart of man, can only be referred to an inborn power of good. In all Scriptures attributed to him there is nothing which points to the future coming of the Holy Ghost, or a future life. The Israelite was placed by Moses under the stern and ritualistic discipline of the written law, which took no cognisance of conscience. For the law treats man as if he had no conscience; and the object of the lawgiver seems to have been the formation of a conscience by moral precepts, and by imposing and suggestive ceremonies. But Paul attributes to Moses the intention, in the passage above quoted, to point to Jesus as by God raised from the dead, and thus determined to be the Son of God, or the Angel-Messiah, ' according to the spirit of holiness.' The Apostle regards Jesus as the restorer of the Holy Ghost, and of the state of things which existed in Paradise.

Between the time of the first and the manifestation of the second Adam man could not be saved. By the first or terrestrial ' man ' came death, by the second or celestial ' Man ' the resurrection of the dead. Thus Paul has paved the way for asserting the absolute necessity of a supernatural Messiah, an Angel-Messiah, as the Saviour of mankind. The Messiah, who was to spiritualise flesh and blood and to save it from corruption, Christ Jesus, is the incarnate Word or Angel of the Lord who was with Moses and the fathers in the wilderness, ' the spiritual Rock which followed the Israelites.'

We saw, that already ancient Rabbinical tradition calls the Angel of God the Rock. This figurative language here used refers to the passages in Exodus, where it is said that ' the Angel of God, which went before the camp of

Israel, removed and went behind them; and the pillar of
the cloud went from before their face, and stood behind
them, . . . it gave light by night to them.' 'Behold, I
send an Angel before thee, to keep thee in the way, and to
bring thee into the place which I have prepared. Be-
ware of him, and obey his voice, provoke him not; for
he will not pardon your transgressions; for my Name is
in him.'[1]   What is said of the fiery pillar is said of the
Angel who followed Israel.   The Angel is described as
the conveyancer of God's 'Name,' which the Aaronites
were ordered to 'put upon' the children of Israel by
pronouncing the blessing. 'Thus' God would 'bless
them.'   In this and in similar passages of the Old and
New Testaments the 'Name' means Spirit or Word.
The symbol of the Spirit or Word was fire, which was on
all altars where God recorded his Name and blessed
Israel.   For this reason the fiery serpent which Moses
made of brass[2] is designated as the Word of God in the
Book of Wisdom, where the Word of God is also compared with lightning, to which the original figurative
meaning of the serpent as fire from heaven referred.
The Angel in whom is the Name of God is therefore
designated as the conveyancer of the Spirit or Word of
God, and for this reason the ministers of God are connected with or symbolised by flaming fire.

We saw that, according to the Targum, it was the
Memra or Word which followed the Israelites, from
which it follows that, according to Jewish pre-Christian
(Essenic ?) tradition, the Angel of God was the Word of
God.   He was called 'the Rock of the Church of Zion.'

Paul has designated the Angel-Messiah as the conveyancer of the Spirit of God.   This interpretation is in
harmony with the cardinal point of Paul's doctrine
about the Spirit of God, asserted to have been absent
from mankind after the fall of the first and before the

---

[1] Ex. xiv. 19, 20; xxiii. 20, 21; xx. 24; Num. vi. 27.
[2] In Hebrew, Nâchash means 'brass' as well as 'serpent.'

coming of the second Adam from heaven. But why
does Paul call the Angel or Word of God, that is, Christ,
the spiritual Rock, as Targumists or authorised interpreters of Holy Writ had probably done before him?

According to Philo, the Word of God was figuratively represented by the sun, which Messianic symbol
took the place of the fire-symbol, and was represented
by the central lamp of the Mosaic candlestick. In the
midst of the same a vision in the Apocalypse of John
describes the Word of God or Christ; and we have
connected, in another place, this symbolism of John
and Philo with visions in the Books of Ezekiel and of
Zechariah, as well as these with the Agni-sacrifice in
the Rig-Veda. The seven lamps of the candlestick, we
are told, referred to sun, moon, and five planets, and
thus we may connect them with the seven pillars of the
House or Church of the Wisdom of God, that is, of
Christ, who is by this symbolism identified with the
Word or Wisdom of God. The seven pillars of the
House of Wisdom were ' hewn out ' from the rock, as
Israel was hewn from its great ancestors Abraham and
Sarah, who are by Isaiah compared to a rock.[1] But the
rock from which mankind has been hewn is the great
celestial progenitor, the aboriginal type of humanity,
the Angel of the Lord, the Angel-Messiah, the Lord
Jesus Christ, ' by ' whom all men are, according to
Paulinic doctrine.

We now understand why Paul attributes the creation
of the world to Jesus Christ as the Word of God. Also
in the Epistle to the Hebrews it is said that the worlds
were framed by the Word of God. Paul writes : ' For
though there be that are called gods, whether in heaven
or in earth (as there be gods many and lords many),
but to us there is but one God, the Father, of whom
are all things, and we in him, and one Lord Jesus

[1] *Das Symbol des Kreuzes bei allen Nationen*, 112–114; Prov. ix. 1;
Is. li. 1.

Christ, by whom are all things, and we by him.' According to Paul's gospel it was by Christ's will and purpose, by his grace, that 'though he was rich' yet for our sakes 'he was (became) poor,' that, through his poverty we might be rich. By coming from heaven to earth, in the likeness of sinful flesh, Christ Jesus gave up the angelic and 'divine form' or 'form of God,' and took upon him the form of a servant.[1]

Paul has accepted, developed, applied, and promulgated the Essenic doctrine of the Angel-Messiah, as bringer of the Spirit of God to mankind. It cannot be proved, or even rendered probable, that an Angel-Messiah, and he as the bringer of the Holy Ghost, was expected by any body of Israelites, except by the Essenes and Therapeuts. With the latter we connected some of the Rabbis, and those Targumists whose doctrines have been transmitted to us by the Targumim. These Essenic doctrines were certainly proclaimed by Stephen, the first of the deacons among the Hellenists, or Greek-speaking Jews, some of whom seem to have belonged to the Therapeuts of Alexandria. If Stephen, the first provable preacher of Jesus as the Angel-Messiah, was a Therapeut, we understand why Paul, having gone over to his faith, promulgated this doctrine almost in the very words of Stephen, and why the Essenes of Judæa, who excluded all Gentiles, regarded Paul as their enemy, after that he represented the doctrines of the universalist Essenes of Egypt, or of the Therapeuts.

Though Jesus had acknowledged the principle of universality, the twelve Apostles did not at once openly recognise it. But the most essential difference between the preaching of Jesus and of his Apostles on one side, and the gospel of Paul on the other, centred in that of the Angel-Messiah, which Jesus had not acknowledged

---

[1] Hebr. xi. 3; 1 Cor. viii. 5, 6; comp. Ps. xxxiii. 6; 2 Cor. viii. 9; Phil. ii. 6.

or applied to himself. If the Apostles at Jerusalem had preached the doctrine of the Angel-Messiah, the first three Gospels would show that Jesus did reveal himself as such. The silence of the first Evangelists about this new Messianic doctrine can no longer be explained by the supposition that this doctrine belonged to a secret doctrine, forbidden by the Jewish authorities. For the Eastern doctrine of the Angel-Messiah, which had in the last instance been applied to Gautama-Buddha, must have belonged to the secret doctrine of the Essenes, since this doctrine cannot possibly be separated from other doctrines and rites which the Essenes have provably derived from the East. If the doctrine of the Angel-Messiah has by the Essenes first been applied to Jesus, and not till after his resurrection on 'the third day according to the Scriptures,' as we shall try to prove, then it will be explained why Paul derives from Christ's resurrection the testimony for his being the Son of God, and therefore for his revelation as the spiritual Rock or Angel of God. It looks as if, until his resurrection, this doctrine of the Angel-Messiah had not been applied to Christ Jesus.

The probable connection of Stephen, and therefore of Paul, with the Essenes, has been confirmed by the equally probable connection of Ananias and others with the Essenes; yet this new standpoint for the critical examination of Paul and of his doctrine requires further support. In the first place, we shall trace back to an Essenian source the doctrine of Christ's resurrection on the third day according to the Scriptures, as taught by Paul, and also his doctrine on the atonement; and we shall then consider whether the 'high probability' expressed by Eusebius can be sufficiently established, that the Scriptures of the Therapeutic order have been used in the composition of Pauline Epistles, especially of the Epistle to the Hebrews, and that they have also been utilised for the composition of the Gospels transmitted to us. Although this statement of the church-historian cannot be asserted to have been a pure invention, yet hitherto nothing has been brought forward in support of it. If the Bishop's opinion can be substantiated, our argument on the Essenic source of Pauline doctrines will stand on firm ground.

The Resurrection of Christ.

In the Old Testament, if literally interpreted, there is no trace either of an expected Angel-Messiah, nor of a Messiah who should visibly rise from the dead and ascend to heaven. We saw that the Essenes, to whom the disciples of John belonged, expected an Angel as Messiah, and that they tried to connect their new Messianic and other doctrines with those of Moses, by a figurative interpretation of the Scriptures attributed to him. Among the Essenic Scriptures, which, according to Eusebius, have been used by the Evangelists and by Paul, there probably were such which referred to the resurrection of the Angel-Messiah whom they expected. Many disciples of John or Essenes are in the fourth Gospel recorded to have believed in Jesus, possibly as the Angel-Messiah, even before his death, although John seems to have died without such belief, according to the first three Gospels. When Paul wrote to the Corinthians that Jesus rose 'the third day according to the Scriptures,' none of the Gospels transmitted to us existed. The Apostle, therefore, must have referred to the Mosaic Scriptures, at least according to their allegorical interpretation. Such figurative interpretation of Scripture can only be proved to have existed among Essenes. From this it already results, that the most ancient historical testimony of Christ's resurrection stands in connection with the Essenic interpretation of Scripture. It can be proved that Paul referred to Moses as his original authority for his belief in the divinely caused resurrection of Christ. We will first show, that the tradition about this reported event, which was later recorded in our Gospels, is so full of contradictions, that it cannot possibly have been the source for that which Paul believed.

It is well known, that in the Gospel after Mark—the end of which, from the 8th verse of the last chapter, has been added later—no appearances of the risen Jesus are recorded. Three women found an open and empty grave, and they saw on the right side a young man, clothed in a white garment, who announced to them the resurrection of the crucified Jesus, and commissioned them to tell his disciples and Peter that they should go to Galilee, where they would see him. But trembling and amazement had possession of them, and they said nothing to any man. According to the account in Matthew, instead of a young man it is an Angel of the Lord who made the same announcement to the women, and gave them the same command, after that, preceded by an earthquake, he had descended from heaven and rolled back the stone from the door and sat upon it. The women departed quickly to bring the disciples word; and on the way Jesus met them, whom they held by the feet and worshipped. This was also done by the eleven disciples when they saw him on the mountain in Galilee, where Jesus had appointed them; but some doubted.

According to Luke the glad tidings were made known to the women at the grave by two men in shining garments, who reminded them how Jesus had foretold his crucifixion and resurrection on the third day. The words of the women seemed to the eleven and all the rest as 'idle tales,' and they believed them not. Nothing is said of their going to Galilee; and in direct opposition to this command, as recorded by Mark and Matthew, it is recorded in the Acts, that the risen Messiah had commanded the Apostles whom he had chosen, that they should not depart from Jerusalem, but wait for the promise of the Father, about which he had spoken to them. 'Not many days hence,' that is, after the forty days, of which the Gospels say nothing, they should be 'baptized with the Holy Ghost.' In accordance with this new version Luke relates how the risen Lord appeared at different times in or near Jerusalem. This Evangelist mentions in one passage as the day of the Messiah's ascension the third day, in another the fortieth day after the burial.

In the place of the young man in Mark, of the Angel in Matthew, and of the two men in Luke, the fourth Evangelist mentions two angels in white, sitting the one at the head and the other at the feet where the body of Jesus had lain. Mary Magdalene having communicated to them the cause of her weeping—her not knowing to what place men had removed her Lord, on her turning round saw Jesus standing, and knew not that it was Jesus, supposing him to be the gardener. But on hearing Jesus call her Mary, she turned herself, and said unto him, Rabboni, which is to say Master. Thereupon the risen Jesus appeared three times to the disciples.

The fourth and the third Gospels contain the valuable information that the twelve Apostles had not looked forward to a visible resurrection of Jesus from the dead. Luke records that the eleven and the rest regarded as 'idle tales' what the women reported to have seen at the grave of Jesus, and therefore did not believe them. The fourth Evangelist relates that Peter and John were not convinced by Mary Magdalene, coming from the open and empty grave, and that only after having run to the grave, and seen the linen clothes lying about, John did then see and believe, but 'as yet they knew not the Scriptures that he must rise again from the dead.' The fact here recorded attests that Jesus had not predicted his resurrection ; and it explains the other fact, attested by all four Gospels, that in the early morning in question none of the Apostles had gone to the grave of Jesus, which they must have done had they expected his bodily resurrection.

The first Apostle who is reported to have believed in the resurrection of Jesus did not connect at once with any passage in the Scriptures the unexpected occurrence. Even John had to learn before he could believe, if he ever did, what Paul believed a few years later, that, ' according to the Scriptures,' Jesus had risen from the dead on ' the third day.' Can John, or any other of the twelve Apostles, ever have believed this ?

Since the Scriptures of the Old Testament, even supposing that they refer to the death of the Messiah, do not fix the day of the year in which it should take place, and since these Scriptures certainly do not refer to the day of his resurrection, Paul's belief presumes that two Mosaic institutions, typically interpreted, could be referred relatively to the former and to the latter, and that the days connected with these types were separated from each other by one day. These two typical institutions can have been no other than the slaying of the Paschal lamb on the 14th Nisan, and the presentation of the firstling-sheaf or Paschal omer on the 16th Nisan. If it is only according to the narrative in the fourth Gospel that Jesus is implied to have been crucified on the 14th, and to have risen on the 16th Nisan. this tradition therein recorded harmonised with the solemn statement made by Paul to the Corinthians : ' For I delivered unto you first of all, what I also (among others) received,' that is, that Jesus died, was buried, and rose again ' the third day according to the Scriptures.'

On the above assumption it would further follow that the tradition about the resurrection of Jesus on the third day after his death, as recorded in the Gospel

after John, was unknown to Peter and John in the
morning of the 16th Nisan, when they as yet knew not
the Scriptures that Christ must rise again from the
dead.   Finally, if in no other Gospel than in the fourth
the types of the Paschal lamb and of the Paschal
omer are represented as having received their anti-
types, the one type by the death of Jesus on the 14th,
and the other by his resurrection on the 16th Nisan, it
follows conclusively either that the composers of the
first three Gospels erred when they narrated the crucifixion of Jesus to have taken place on the 15th Nisan,
or that the tradition about the date of this event, as
recorded in the fourth Gospel, is not historical.   It can
be rendered probable that this tradition in the fourth
Gospel was invented, sooner or later, for the purpose of
letting it appear that Jesus was the antitype of the
Paschal lamb and of the Paschal omer, and that he rose
the third day according to the Scriptures, as Paul declared.   From whence can this tradition have come,
which is testified by Paul, and in the fourth
Gospel?

It is quite certain that, according to the first three
Evangelists, Jesus ate the Paschal lamb with his disciples on the 14th Nisan, before he suffered on the 15th
Nisan ; and it is impossible to assume that Matthew,
Luke, and Mark followed an erroneous tradition as to
these dates.   These Evangelists knew that Jesus was
crucified on the 15th Nisan, the day after the slaying
and eating of the Paschal lamb.   From this it follows
that if they believed in the resurrection of Jesus on
the third day, that day must have been the 17th Nisan.
If, however, we assume that Matthew, Mark and Luke
could have been under an error on this point, and that
the fourth Evangelist is alone right when he clearly
implies that the crucifixion took place already on the
14th Nisan, it would follow with equal force that if
Jesus rose on the third day, he did so, not on the 17th

but on the 16th Nisan. The different statements about the day of the crucifixion must have led to different statements with regard to the day of the resurrection, if the latter event had to be accomplished on the third day after the former. Yet, in the first three Gospels, the resurrection of Jesus is as clearly as in the fourth Gospel described to have taken place on the first day of the week as it began to dawn.

If it can be shown that, according to the fourth Gospel, the day of the resurrection was the third day after the slaying of the Paschal lamb, and was also the third day after the death of Jesus, then it will be proved that the resurrection is in all four Gospels implied to have taken place on the 16th Nisan, and in the very same hours of early morning when the firstling-sheaf or Paschal omer was presented in the Temple. From this it will follow with mathematical certainty, that according to the first three Gospels Jesus rose on the second day after his death, and that according to the fourth Gospel he rose, as Paul declared, 'on the third day according to the Scriptures.' Now, the first day of the week, the Sunday of the Christians, is in all the Gospels mentioned as the day of the resurrection of Jesus, whilst the crucifixion took place according to the fourth Gospel one day earlier than according to the first three. It follows, that according to the latter Jesus was buried on the day previous to his resurrection, that is on the Sabbath, but according to the fourth Gospel on the Friday, so that the resurrection took place on the third day, thus corresponding with the presentation of the first barley-meal, which 'according to the Scriptures' had to take place the third day after the slaying of the Paschal lamb.

Does the fourth Gospel imply that Jesus died on the 14th Nisan contemporaneously with the slaying of the Paschal lamb, and that he rose on the 16th Nisan contemporaneously with the presentation of the Paschal omer?

At the outset it may be observed that unless the day of the resurrection of Jesus was the 16th Nisan, that is the third day after the slaying of the lamb, the Old Testament would contain no possible type, and the New Testament no antitype, to justify Paul's declaration that Jesus rose on the third day ' according to the Scriptures.' If Jesus by his resurrection fulfilled the type of the Paschal omer on the 16th Nisan, he must have fulfilled by his death on the 14th Nisan the type of the Paschal lamb.   Only according to the fourth Gospel, as we shall see, have these two Mosaic types been fulfilled by Jesus, and here only is he designated as the Lamb of God, again in harmony with Paul's preaching.   It is only in the Gospel after John that the Baptist is recorded to have pointed to him as ' the Lamb of God which taketh away the sin of the world '; it is only here that Jesus is recorded to have spoken of the eating of his flesh and the drinking of his blood ; and finally it is here only that Jesus is not recorded to have eaten the Paschal lamb with his disciples on the day before his crucifixion. Jesus could not have done this if the lamb was not yet slain on that day, and if the day after his last supper was the 14th Nisan, when contemporaneously with the slaying, and as antitype of the lamb, he was to be crucified.

These peculiarities in the fourth Gospel would show, even if taken by themselves, that according to the fourth Gospel Jesus was the antitype of the Paschal lamb, and in this sense the Lamb of God.   But other statements in the same Gospel confirm the assertion that, according to the same, Jesus died on the 14th Nisan, contemporaneously with the slaying of the lamb.   The anointing of Jesus before his death is here related to have taken place ' six days ' before the Passover, and yet it is implied that the day of anointing was the 10th Nisan, the same day when the Paschal lamb had to be set apart.   For the Initiated would understand, that the sixth day before the Passover, when Jesus was anointed with oil unto the day of his burying, pointed to the day when the Paschal lamb was slain, to the 14th Nisan, when according to the fourth Gospel, as we shall see, the burial of Jesus took place, of him who was proclaimed as the Paschal Lamb of the new confession.

The 10th Nisan began in the evening of the 9th, and the 14th lasted until the morning of the 15th, so that although only four days were required between the setting apart and the slaying of the Paschal lamb, six days could be reckoned between these events.

Again, the omission of the institution of the Lord's Supper in the fourth Gospel is at once explained if in that record Jesus was to be designated as the antitype of the Paschal lamb.   It is not necessary to assume an unaccountable ' incompleteness in S. John's narrative' with regard to a subject on which we are led ' to expect great fulness of detail,' by the circumstantiality with which the Paschal account in the fourth Gospel begins.[1]   If it was one of the chief objects of this Gospel to establish, at least by implication, the new symbolism and doctrine about the Messianic Paschal Lamb, then no notice could be taken, in this Scripture, of an institution which, in the first three Gospels, is clearly stated to have been ordained after the slaying and the eating of the Paschal lamb.

Thus far we have advanced the following arguments, tending to establish the fact that in the fourth Gospel the date of the crucifixion is implied to have been the 14th Nisan, not the 15th, as in the other Gospels.[2]

---

[1] Dr. Edersheim, *The Temple, its Ministry and Services at the time of Jesus Christ,* published by the Religious Tract Society, 1874.

[2] Canon Farrer admits the discrepancy between the first three Gospels and the fourth Gospel about the day of the death of Jesus, and considers the account in the fourth Gospel as the historical one.   Dr. Edersheim tries to show that according to all four Gospels the crucifixion took place on the 15th Nisan.   He ' tenaciously holds ' the doctrine of ' the plenary inspiration' of the Bible.

The Gospel in which alone Jesus is called the Lamb of
God must connect his death with the slaying of the
Paschal lamb on the 14th Nisan, in order to support
the new Messianic attribute by the fulfilment of a type
from the Old Testament. Again, in this Gospel the
day of anointing can be explained so as to refer to the
14th Nisan as the day of the crucifixion. Finally, if
Jesus instituted a new rite on the day before he suffered, that rite could not by him have been connected
with his eating of the Paschal lamb with the disciples,
as attested by the first three Gospels, if on the following
day he was to be crucified, contemporaneously with the
slaying of the Paschal lamb, as the fourth Gospel
implies.

To these three indirect proofs of the above assertion,
a direct proof has to be added. It is stated in the
fourth Gospel that after the supper, when Judas had
betrayed Jesus, the Jews ' went not into the judgment
hall, lest they should be defiled, but that they might
eat the Passover.' According to this statement, the
supper and the betrayal had taken place on the 13th,
not on the 14th Nisan, on which day the Passover, that
is, the Paschal lamb, was eaten, and had been eaten
by Jesus with his disciples, if the first three Evangelists
can be trusted. But according to the fourth Gospel,
on the day after the supper and betrayal Jesus was to
be crucified contemporaneously with the slaying of the
Paschal lamb.

Since all Evangelists by direct, and Paul by indirect
statements, explain the eating of the Passover as the
eating of the Paschal lamb, no notice need be taken of
the attempt to prove that exceptionally in this passage
of the fourth Gospel, the eating of the Passover is not
to be referred to the lamb, but to the eating of the
chagiga of unleavened bread with bitter herbs. The
same was eaten for the first time after the lamb on the
14th Nisan, but it was also eaten on the 15th Nisan, on

which day Levitical purity was likewise required for so doing.[1]

We are now in a position to assert, that only according to statements made by Paul and in the fourth Gospel, Jesus rose on the third day after his death ' according to the Scriptures.' We repeat the question we have raised : Whence can this tradition have come?

Paul writes to the Corinthians, to whom he had first communicated this tradition, that ' he also' had received it, therefore as others had done before him. Who can these have been ? Certainly not the Apostles, of whom not one expected anything so extraordinary after the burial of Jesus as a visible and corporeal resurrection of the same. The Apostles had not connected the expected resuscitation of the dead on the third day, already mentioned in the Zendavesta, with the offering of the barley-meal on the third day after the slaying of the Paschal lamb, which Moses had ordered. Again, Jesus had not been crucified contemporaneously with the lamb on the 14th, instead of the 15th Nisan. Otherwise the idea might have suggested itself to the Apostles, that the ceremonials ordered by the law for the 14th and the 16th Nisan, according to God's eternal purpose, would be antitypically fulfilled by the death and resurrection of Jesus. After the crucifixion the Apostles might have looked forward with a holy expectation to the 16th Nisan, if this day had been the third instead of the second after his death. Since we must regard this reckoning as correct, it is absolutely clear that those passages in the first three Gospels, according to which Jesus is said to have predicted or confirmed his resurrection on the third day, are unhistorical, and have been inserted for the purpose of misleading the readers.[2]

---

[1] Wieseler, followed by Dr. Edersheim, l. c.
[2] Matt. xvi. 21 ; xvii. 22, 23 ; xx. 17 ; Mark viii. 31 ; ix. 30, 31 ; x. 34; Luke ix. 22, comp. 45 ; xviii. 33 ; xxiv. 7, 21, 44.

Among these statements, the most important are contained in the narrative of the disciples of Emmaus, who 'on the first day in the week,' thus on the 16th Nisan, as we know from the fourth Gospel, are said to have believed this was 'the third day' after the crucifixion. Luke cannot have inserted this narrative, since he knew, as his Gospel testifies, that this day was the second after the crucifixion. For the same reason, the two disciples on their return to Jerusalem cannot have convinced the assembled eleven, that He who had been crucified on the day previous to the 16th Nisan was risen on the 16th Nisan, as on the third day after his crucifixion. The testified apparition of the risen Jesus in their midst could not turn the second day into the third. Thus even the possibility falls to the ground, that Jesus, on his appearing to the eleven and the disciples of Emmaus, could have reminded them of the words which he had spoken to them whilst he was yet with them, 'that all things must be fulfilled which were written in the law of Moses, in the Prophets, and in the Psalms, concerning him, saying unto them: Thus it is written, and thus it behoved Christ to suffer and to rise from the dead the third day.'

This narrative cannot be accepted as a proof that the day of the reported apparition near Emmaus, to which Paul does not refer in his enumeration of the apparitions of Jesus after death, was 'the third day' after his crucifixion. Yet the account shows that those who inserted it at the end of the Gospel after Luke regarded it as an introduction to the narrative published or to be published in the fourth Gospel. They claimed the sanction of Jesus, expressed before and after his crucifixion, for the typical reference of the slaying of the Paschal lamb on the 14th, and of the offering of the omer on the 16th Nisan, respectively, to his death and resurrection, as the Messiah or Christ foretold by the Law, the Prophets, and the Psalms. This intentionally invented narrative was to confirm the fourth Gospel and to rectify the first three Gospels. Accordingly, the twelve Apostles ought to have understood the Scriptures and known that Jesus must rise from the dead. They ought to have watched at the sepulchre 'in the end of the Sabbath as it began to dawn toward the first day of the week.' This their unaccountable ignorance is explained by one of the later inserted passages in Luke, in which we are told that the disciples 'understood not this saying, and it was hid from them, that they perceived it not'; that is, the saying of Jesus, about the Son of Man being betrayed into the hands of men, which is said to have been by Jesus connected with the prophecy of his rising on 'the third day.'[1]

It follows from this, that neither before or at any time after the 16th Nisan any one of the twelve Apostles can have believed in the resurrection of Jesus 'the third day according to the Scriptures.' For the day on which the Apostles, called by women to the sepulchre, are stated to have seen and believed what they did not expect, was not the third day after the burial, but the second. The Twelve may have believed in the resurrection of Jesus oñ the second day, as such is reported in the first three Gospels, but they can never have believed that this occurred 'according to the Scriptures,' in which not a single passage, however figuratively interpreted, can be made to point to Messiah's resurrection on the day after his death. Thus it is proved by evidence drawn from the Old and the New Testament, that the twelve Apostles did not belong to those, of whom Paul clearly implies, that they had before him received this tradition about the resurrection of Christ on 'the third day according to the Scriptures.'

In order to answer the question, who these can have been, who 'also,' like Paul, had received this tradition, unknown to the twelve Apostles, we are led to

[1] Luke ix. 45, comp. 22.

surmise that they may have been Essenes, who alone among the Jews recognised a figurative interpretation of Scripture, such as is demanded by the Paulinic doctrine of the resurrection on 'the third day according to the Scriptures.'

We pointed out, that the forerunner of the Messiah expected by the Essenes would be Elijah the tishbite, or stranger, the chariot or 'rechab' of Israel, probably one of the Rechabites, with whom we have connected the Essenes.[1] This Messiah, who was to come in the spirit of Elijah, was expected to bring about the general resurrection from the dead. The resurrection of departed man was connected by Oriental tradition with the third day after his death.[2] The Essene, who was well acquainted with Oriental tradition, might therefore expect, that the Messiah, whether an incarnate Angel or not, as an introduction and announcement of the general resurrection, would rise on the third day after his death as firstling or 'firstfruit of them that sleep.' Sooner or later, this expectation would begin to take root among the Essenes. At all events, after that Jesus had died at the time of the Passover, the idea must have suggested itself, to connect the three days between the slaying of the lamb and the offering of the flour from the first ripened corn, with the three days which might possibly have elapsed between the death and the resurrection of Jesus as the Messiah. The crucifixion had been accomplished in such a hurried manner that to many, especially to the Essenes, who chiefly lived in the country, it may have been doubtful, whether Jesus had died on the 15th or on the 14th Nisan. Those Essenes who believed in the latter date must have looked to the 16th Nisan with an extreme excitement, with a holy

---

[1] Not only is the personal appearance of Elijah described like that of the Baptist, but the chief events in the lives of both took place in the same wilderness of the Dead Sea, where the Essenes had their settlements.

[2] Comp. Spiegel, *Acad. der Wiss.* VI. § 89 ff.; *Die Plejaden*, 71.

expectation. Those who, like the Baptist, had doubted whether Jesus was He that should come, must have expected to see their doubts set aside or confirmed at morning-dawn on this day. If Jesus should then rise visibly, and on the supposition that he had died on the 14th Nisan, he was powerfully manifested, not only as the firstling of the general resurrection, and as Son of God, as the Essenes expected of the Messiah, but his death and resurrection had been typified by two Mosaic institutions, by the slaying of the Paschal lamb and the offering of the Paschal omer.

Delegates from the Sanhedrim had, already on the 14th Nisan, chosen a spot in a field near Jerusalem, where a few bundles of the first ripened barley were reaped at sunset on the 15th Nisan, and brought into the court of the Temple. The corn having been duly prepared, an omer of barley-flour, the tenth part of an ephah, was, in the earliest morning-hour of the 16th Nisan, offered in the Temple. Since the previous day, the 15th Nisan, the first day of the Paschal Feast was kept holy as a Sabbath, on whatever day of the week it might fall, the time of the presentation of the Paschal omer could not be more accurately referred to than in the words in which, in the Gospel after Matthew, the time of the resurrection of Jesus on that same day is determined : ' In the end of the Sabbath, as it began to dawn towards the first day of the week.' On ' the morrow after the (Paschal) Sabbath,' and the third day after the slaying of the Paschal lamb, when the barley-sheaf, or rather the omer of barley-flour, was waved by the priests before the Lord, and when the Israelites offered ' an he-lamb without blemish ' for a burnt-offering, it was on that day that Jesus was believed to have been visibly raised from the dead, and on the clouds of heaven, as the son of man of the Danielic vision, to have been brought before God.

The following parallel between the offering of the

firstling-sheaf and the reported resurrection of Jesus could not but strike the Essene, who, on the strength of his figurative interpretation of Scripture, expected an Angel-Messiah. After the slaying of the Paschal lamb on the 14th Nisan, on the third day following, in the early morning hours of the 16th Nisan, a measure of flour obtained from the first ripened corn, from the firstling-sheaf, was offered before God, which sheaf of the first ripened barley had been on the 15th Nisan cut off from the land which bore it, from a field outside Jerusalem. Thus the early ripened or early perfected servant of God 'was cut off from the land of the living,' and for the transgression of God's people 'was he stricken.' Jesus was 'brought as a lamb to the slaughter,' as anti-type of the Paschal lamb; his life was made 'an offering for sin' on a hill outside Jerusalem; they gave him 'his grave with the wicked,' and heaped stones upon it, as on graves of malefactors,[1] 'though he had done wrong to no man, neither was deceit in his mouth.' But 'by his wisdom,' he, Jesus, the servant of God, has 'justified many,' he has borne 'their iniquities,' he has borne 'the sins of many,' and 'made intercession for the trans-gressors.' 'Free from the travail of his soul,' he has 'satisfied his eyes;' for 'the third day according to the Scriptures,' God raised him from the dead, as 'the firstfruits of them that sleep'; the 'One like a son of man,' was on the clouds of heaven brought before God. This parallel presupposes the 14th Nisan for Christ's death.

A very different parallel would suggest itself to those who believed that Jesus had died, not on the 14th, but on the 15th Nisan, and who did not expect the Messiah promised by Moses to be an incarnate Angel, or the antitype of the Paschal lamb, the Lamb of God, nor that he would rise from the dead 'the third day according to the Scriptures.'

---

[1] Possible reference to Jeremiah, who was stoned to death in Egypt, ac-cording to Epiphanius. The Hebrew word 'Hamah,' hill or height, often refers to idolatrous heights. Bunsen's *Bibelwerk* to Is. liii.

On the 15th Nisan, according to generally received tradition, the Sinaitic law had been given; and this was the day on which Israel, the firstborn of nations, was liberated from the Egyptian house of bondage, after that on the previous day the Passover had been slain. According to this typical parallel the spiritual liberation which Jesus had brought had been accomplished on the 15th, not on the 14th Nisan, and it stood in no connection with the Mosaic institutions of the 14th and of the 16th Nisan.

Only through the mediation of Essenes can Paul 'also,' as Essenes before him, have received the tradition, that Christ rose 'the third day according to the Scriptures.' Other circumstances likewise point to the Essenic origin of this doctrine, which the Apostles at Jerusalem can be proved not to have recognised. The new doctrine of Christ as the Lamb of God, that is, as antitype of the Paschal lamb, and which cannot be separated from the new doctrine about Messiah's resurrection 'according to the Scriptures,' has been recorded, as by Paul and the fourth Gospel, so in the essentially Essenic Epistle of Barnabas, which we shall later consider.

The disciples of John in the second century, the Essenic Jews, like the Jewish Christians, kept the legal Passover on the 14th Nisan, when Jesus had eaten the Paschal lamb with his disciples according to the first three Gospels. Jews and Jewish Christians formed the anti-Paulinic party of the Quartodecimans, and denied that Jesus died on the 14th Nisan, or that on that day a redeeming sacrifice by Christ could have taken place. But, in harmony with the fourth Gospel, the elders of the Church at Rome maintained in the Paschal dispute the anti-Quartodeciman tradition, which was that of Paul and also, as we may now assume, of the Essenic Christians. The statements in the fourth Gospel are at the end of it attested as true by certain persons, whom we may regard as elders of the Roman Church.

The Roman and Paulinian party, which took its stand on the Gospel after John, was opposed during this dispute by the Asiatic Church, represented by Polycarp, as direct disciple of John, and bishop of Smyrna, who visited Rome in 155. He failed to persuade the bishop (Pope) Anicetus that, in accordance with the Apostle John's practice, the 14th Nisan ought to be kept by fasting, and that the contrary tradition of Roman elders ought not to be opposed to Apostolic tradition.[1] The Paschal dispute confirms the continued existence of two parties in the Christian Church, and their connection respectively with original Apostolic and with Paulinic tradition, as the latter is recorded in the fourth Gospel, in contradiction to the tradition. contained in the first three Gospels.[1] We may also infer, that the Gentile Christians, who kept aloof from the Jewish Christians, and still assembled in separate churches in Rome about the middle of the second century, according to the testimony of Justin Martyr, had then risen in this city to higher influence. It is the time when the leading Gnostics (Essenes?) flocked to Rome, when they addressed the question to the elders of this Church, whether it be expedient to pour new wine, possibly the Essenic-Paulinian doctrine, into old skins? It was by the chiefs of the Jews, probably by the elders of the essentially Jewish-Christian Church in Rome, said to have been founded by Peter, whom Paul called a Jew at Antioch, that Paul was regarded as the member of a sect 'everywhere spoken against.'

In the fourth Gospel, where alone the narratives about the crucifixion and resurrection correspond with the two Mosaic types, as with Paulinian and probably Essenic tradition, the statement is contained, of which there is no trace anywhere else, that several of the

---

[1] Eus. *H.E.* V. 24; comp. IV. 14; III. 36. Hier. *De Vir. ill.* 17; *Chron. Pasch.*, 257. Comp. Hilgenfeld, *Einleitung in das N.T., Erste Ausg.* 403 f., 698, 730, 736.

disciples whom Jesus had chosen, were disciples of John or Essenes, and that many of the Baptist's disciples believed in Jesus before he made his entry into Jerusalem. Again, Paul designates Jesus as the firstfruits or firstling of them that sleep—as if he had in view the type of the firstling-sheaf. Finally, as only in the fourth Gospel the parable of the corn of wheat is contained, which brings not forth fruit unless it die, so Paul writes: 'What thou sowest,' that is, a mere corn or grain, 'is not quickened unless it die.' The writers of both passages may have had in view the first ripened corn offered in the morning of the resurrection-day.

The Essenic origin of the tradition about the resurrection of Jesus on 'the third day according to the Scriptures,' will increase in probability in the same degree as it may become possible to connect the fourth Gospel with Essenian, Paulinic, and Roman tradition. Already now we are enabled to assert, that the narratives about the resurrection, contained in the first three Gospels, have been added to the revised text of the most ancient Gospels, probably not before the publication of the Fourth Gospel in the second century. For we have proved by comparison of the Scriptures, that the resurrection of Jesus, testified by Paul and the fourth Gospel as having taken place 'the third day according to the Scriptures,' was neither expected by the twelve Apostles, nor can at any time have been believed by them.

The Apparitions of Jesus after Death.

Paul asserts that the twelve Apostles, convinced by apparitions, had proclaimed the resurrection of Jesus to believing audiences. But he does not say that any of these apparitions of Jesus took place at the empty grave, or that an empty grave had been attested, nor that these apparitions convinced the Twelve that Jesus

had risen 'the third day according to the Scriptures.'
Paul assures us that all the Apostles preached Christ
risen from the dead : 'Whether it be I or they, so we
preach and so ye believed.' The Apostle does not say
that all the Apostles preached like him, 'that Christ
died for our sins according to the Scriptures,' that is,
as antitype of the Paschal lamb, 'and that he was
buried and that he rose again the third day according
to the Scriptures,' that is, as antitype of the Paschal
omer. The twelve Apostles could not believe in the
resurrection of Jesus on the third day, and therefore,
also not that he was the antitype of the Paschal lamb,
and in this sense the Lamb of God. Nor can it be
asserted that either they or Paul believed that the
body of Jesus in the grave had been saved from
corruption. It is all the more important that the
narratives about apparitions of Jesus after death rest
on better evidence. We have sufficient ground for our
conviction, that by his appearing after death, wherever
and whenever it may have been, Jesus has confirmed
the ancient belief in a life beyond the grave, and he
has raised that traditional belief to an incontrovertible
fact. As such, the resurrection of Jesus has been
asserted by the first teachers of Christianity, although
they could not and did not all agree as to the supposed
typical and supernatural import of this event.[1]

When seventeen years after the conversion of Paul
to the faith of Stephen in the risen Jesus as the Angel-
Messiah of the Essenes, the Apostles at Jerusalem gave
him the hand of fellowship, they did so because they
could not shut their eyes to the fact, that 'he that
wrought for Peter unto the Apostleship among the

---

[1] There is nothing which could justify the disconnection of the evidence
of the apparitions of Jesus after death from the numerous stories that are
extant of apparitions of dead men, and which are some of the undeniable
proofs of superhuman, though not of supernatural, agency. Similar apparitions after death have been attested not less forcibly in recent times with regard to Thomas à Becket and Savonarola.

circumcision,' the same wrought also for Paul 'unto the Gentiles.' He who had chosen the twelve Apostles, was by them believed to be the man whom God anointed or made Christ, 'with the Holy Ghost and with power,' and who as anointed man was 'the Son of the living God.' The same Jesus of Nazareth was regarded by Stephen, by Paul and others, as the anointed Angel of God who had appeared to Moses, and to the Fathers in the wilderness, and had risen the third day after his death, ' according to the Scriptures.' On this latter point the twelve Apostles could agree to differ with Paul, whilst all disciples of Jesus believed and preached that Jesus lives, that he died and rose again, whether he was an anointed man or an anointed angel. Such a conviction, caused and confirmed by apparitions of Jesus after death, even if we assume that they had not in fact originated from a non-human source, would suffice to enable the Apostles to cast off all fear and despondency, and to merge their differences, preaching, at the risk of their lives, Jesus crucified and risen.

With regard to the recorded apparitions of Jesus after death, two more or less probable suppositions have to be considered. Either they originated in man, all or some of them, or they were determined by a non-human will. Possibly for more than a century before the commencement of the Christian era, those who were initiated in the mysteries of Essenic tradition seem to have cherished the hope, that the Angel-Messiah, whom they expected would rise on the third day after the slaying of the Paschal lamb as antitype of the same and of the Paschal omer. It cannot be denied that these expectations, even if we assume them to have been caused by the crucifixion of Jesus about the time of the slaying of the Paschal lamb, might mislead men into regarding what may have been mere phantoms, called forth by the intensity of their feeling, as real apparitions caused from without, such as they believed—we think rightly—to have been the exceptional privilege of individuals in all ages.

On the other side, it can be argued that the devout and mystically trained mind of the Essenes might have prepared them in an exceptional manner for seeing and rightly interpreting real, that is, objectively determined, apparitions. It may be surmised, that thus trained, the spiritual nature of the Essenes might have received a higher development; that the Essenes might thus have been enabled to discern the typical import of the Paschal lamb and of the Paschal omer; and that the Essenes might have been led rightly to expect the resurrection of Jesus on 'the third day according to the Scriptures.' Assuming this, it could be held that. Jesus, the Angel-Messiah, was before Abraham, that he participated in the glory of God before the creation of the world, that the One like a son of man was brought before God on the clouds of heaven.

On either supposition, whether Jesus did or whether he did not really appear to some after his death, the fact would remain, that what some men in bygone times had vainly desired to see and to hear, was seen and heard by contemporaries of Jesus, that is, they saw and heard the life and preaching, and apparitions after death of a man, according to others of an incarnate Angel. Those who believed that Jesus really appeared to them after his death, may have had, and they believed they had, exceptional and direct spiritual communion with a departed spirit, with a human soul raised in power. Nor need we think that this was the exclusive privilege of a few in the Apostolic age.

The Day of Pentecost.

According to the doctrines promulgated by Paul, a visible, local, or limited communication of the Spirit of God was not to be expected, even after the resurrection of Christ. Although the Apostle refers to the annual day of Pentecost, he does not refer to the Pentecostal miracle. It is even more surprising that his unsparing opponents in the Galatian and other Churches do not appear to have raised the objection to Paul's Apostleship, that he had not on the day of Pentecost received the Holy Ghost together with the twelve Apostles. Against such a charge of inferiority Paul must have defended himself in his Epistles, if it had ever been made. Far from admitting such a manifestation of the Spirit as man could have heard and seen, and as if during his lifetime no tradition about the Pentecostal miracle existed, Paul compares the manifestation of God's Spirit with what neither eye has seen nor ear heard or man's mind could conceive. Yet the account of the Pentecostal miracle as transmitted by the Acts is essentially in harmony with the spirit of Paul's clearly implied doctrine about the withdrawal of God's Spirit from mankind after the fall, and on the restoration of this power of God after the death of Christ, when he was made ' a curse for us ' so ' that we might receive the promised Spirit through faith.'

The Acts commence with the command given on the Mount of Olives to the Apostles by the risen Jesus, ' through the Holy Ghost ' and at the end of forty days, that they should wait at Jerusalem ' for the promise of the Father,' which they had heard from him, that is, for the sending of the Spirit of truth, about which, according to the fourth Gospel, Jesus had spoken to his disciples. ' Not many days hence,' or, rather, ' not long after these days,' after these forty days of which neither Paul nor the Gospels give any account, the Apostles would be ' baptized with the Holy Ghost.' This distinction of the future spiritual baptism through the Messiah from the baptism with water had been made by John the Baptist or Essene, again according to the fourth Gospel, when he pointed to that which Jesus,

the Lamb of God, would do.   The spiritual baptism of
the Apostles at Jerusalem on the day of Pentecost, thus
announced, is directly connected with a recorded prophecy of John the Baptist or Essene about the future
coming of the Holy Ghost, of the existence of which
certain disciples of John declared to Paul they had
heard nothing.   'When the day of Pentecost was fully
come,' or ' as the day of Pentecost was approaching its
fulfilment,' that is, when the time had come for the
fulfilment of what the Jewish feast of Pentecost was
held to have prefigured, probably only by the allegorising Essenes, a beginning of the re-established rule of
God's Spirit took place, in harmony with the prophecy
of John the Baptist or Essene as confirmed by the
risen Jesus.

Not long after the forty days, during which Jesus
' showed himself alive after his passion by many infallible
proofs' or demonstrations, when he had been seen of
the Apostles, and had spoken to them about the kingdom
of God, that is, on the fiftieth day after his resurrection,
was a great day in the Jewish calendar.   Fifty days after
the solemnity of the beginning of the harvest, early on
the 16th Nisan, seven weeks after the offering of the
firstling-sheaf or Paschal omer, after the time when
the last wheat had ripened, the end of the harvest was
solemnised.   Of the last ripened wheat two loaves were
made and offered to the Lord in the name of Israel.
Also two lambs were offered as thank-offering, followed
by fire- and sin-offerings and by festive meals.   Jesus
had died on the 14th Nisan, as antitype of the Paschal
lamb, and had been raised again on the 16th Nisan,
as antitype of the firstling-sheaf.   So Paul and the
fourth Gospel testify, and so the allegorising Essenes
seem to have believed.   This Messianic symbolism necessarily suggested, that fifty days after the resurrection of
Christ, thus contemporaneously with the Jewish Pentecost, the disciples who followed him in the spiritual

regeneration, and who might be compared with the later ripened wheat, that these brethren would be added, as it were, to the Lord's offertory. Also of the Jewish day of Pentecost it had to be expected that it would have a typical and Messianic importance. If the risen Christ had promised that in a few days the Apostles would be baptized with the Holy Ghost, as John had predicted, then an extraordinary operation of God's Spirit must have been expected on that fiftieth day.

The Acts presume that the Apostles at Jerusalem did not doubt that Jesus had died on the 14th Nisan, had risen the third day according to the Scriptures, on the 16th Nisan, and that on the fiftieth day after the latter date the fulfilment of the promised spiritual baptism would take place. It is implied that in this expectation ' they were all with one accord in one place,' when on the tenth day after the ascension of Jesus, the day of Pentecost was approaching its fulfilment. The presence of the Holy Ghost, symbolised by fire, was attested by visible ' cloven tongues, like as of fire,' one of which ' sat upon each of them,' whereupon they all were ' filled with the Holy Ghost,' and thus were caused to speak ' with other tongues,' to the astonishment of a large concourse of people of many nations.

According to the preceding disquisitions we assume as proved that it was impossible for the Apostles at Jerusalem to believe in this certainly Paulinic, and probably Essenic, symbolism, which is presupposed by the transmitted Pentecostal miracle. For this symbolic scheme presumes that the day of the crucifixion was the 14th Nisan, whilst the Apostles knew that the death and burial of Jesus had taken place on the 15th Nisan, whereby this scheme was deprived of every possible typical basis. The Apostles also knew, that although the Baptist had described as future the coming of the Holy Ghost and, therefore, of the spiritual kingdom of God, yet that Jesus had attributed to the

operation of the Spirit of God the miraculous works
which he and others performed, thus designating the
kingdom of God as already come, the Spirit of God as
present in mankind before his crucifixion.   The following recorded four facts form the groundwork for the
doctrine of the Holy Ghost which is contained in the
Acts.   The just mentioned conception of the Baptist
or Essene about the Messianic baptism with the Holy
Ghost; the doctrine of Paul, that the Holy Ghost, and
with it faith, had not come till after the resurrection of
Christ ; and, finally, the statements in the fourth Gospel,
that the Holy Ghost had not yet come at the time of
the crucifixion ; and that Jesus before his death promised
to send the Spirit of truth.

Like the doctrine of the resurrection of Christ, ' the
third day according to the Scriptures,' which the dates
in the first three Gospels exclude, the narrative in the
Acts about the Pentecostal miracle cannot have been
composed till about the time of the publication of the
fourth Gospel, as introduction and confirmation of the
same.

The Atonement.

The figurative interpretation of the Scriptures revealed to the Essenes their real intended meaning, as
transmitted by the key of knowledge.   Before others
they have given a typical meaning to the Paschal
lamb slain on the 14th Nisan, the blood of which had
caused the avenging Angel of God to pass by the houses
of the Israelites in Egypt.   Even according to the literal
meaning the blood of the lamb was regarded as a sign
and necessary condition of atonement or reconciliation.
If it has been shown that the Essenes expected as
Messiah that same Angel who had also appeared to Moses
in the burning bush, and gone before and followed
Israel in the wilderness, then it will follow that the
Essenes were led to regard this Angel-Messiah as the

antitype of the Paschal lamb, and to expect that
he must necessarily by his blood make an atonement
for the souls of men, as Aaron had done typically.
Whether or not this can be proved to have been Essenic
doctrine, it was certainly Paulinic doctrine. Paul
is the only one among the authors of the New Testament Scriptures, who has introduced the word ' atonement,' and connected it with the atonement made by
the blood of Christ, as typified by the blood of the
Paschal lamb, which blood had been yearly shed since
the exodus from Egypt.[1]

In order to strengthen the preceding arguments,
which connect Stephen and Paul with the Essenes,
we shall now try to show that the leading doctrines
and rites of the Essenes can best be explained by their
presumable typical explanation of the legal sacrifices.
Sooner or later after the crucifixion the Essenic
disciples of Jesus must have believed that by the bloody
sacrifice of his death, as the incarnate Angel of God, as
the Angel-Messiah and antitype of the Paschal lamb, Jesus
had brought about the fulfilment or end of the law.

Under directly Divine guidance Moses had ordered
the slaying of the Paschal lamb as a sign of the deliverance from Egypt, that is, from the house of bondage. From these premises the Christian Essenes seem
to have arrived at the conclusion, that the deliverance
of the soul from its earthly house of bondage, from
the bondage of sin and death, that the redemption
wrought by the Angel-Messiah, by the crucified Jesus
Christ, must have been typified by the slaying of the
Paschal lamb. Those who believed Jesus to be the
Angel-Messiah could not regard it as a mere chance
coincidence that Jesus had been crucified, as Paul,
and probably many Essenes affirmed, contemporaneously
with the slaying of the annual Paschal lamb. Thus the
14th Nisan was regarded as hallowed by the law, which

---

[1] Rom. v. 8–11 ; 1 Cor. v. 7.

they believed was ' ordained by angels in the hands of a mediator.'

The Essenic Christians seem to have also believed that the crucified Messiah had been likewise typified by the fiery serpent, since fire was the symbol of the Spirit of God, brought by the Angel-Messiah, and since the aboriginal symbol of the serpent connected the same with the serpent-formed lightning. The essentially Essenic Epistle of the Apostle Barnabas proves that the Christian Essenes of the first century regarded the brazen serpent, the cross, and the Paschal lamb as types of the Messiah. The connection between Barnabas and Paul would lead us to expect that Paul followed Essenic tradition when he applied to Jesus Christ the symbol of the Paschal lamb, and consequently gave to the cross a new symbolical and sacrificial interpretation, of which there is not a trace in the Old Testament, or in the first three Gospels, which also do not refer to the brazen serpent.

In this Essenic sense Paul could emphatically say, that he was ' determined not to know anything' among the Corinthians ' save Jesus Christ, and him crucified.' For he regarded Christ as ' the end of the law,' who had become ' a curse for us ' by having been crucified, which is a curse according to the law. The typical sacrifices of the law were now brought to an end. This the Essenes believed to have rightly foreseen during at least a century and a half before the coming of Christ. For this reason they had abstained from all bloody sacrifices, as the Rechabites had probably done before them.

Philo, whose doctrinal principles are chiefly Essenic, and who was probably a Therapeut, explains that the offerings of frankincense on the golden altar within the inner Temple were more holy than the bloody sacrifices on the stone altar outside of it. The former figuratively showed our thankfulness 'for our rational spirit which was fashioned after the archtypal model of the Divine

image ; ' both were ' symbols of things appreciable by
the intellect,' and ' the mystical meaning which is concealed beneath them must be investigated by those who
are eager for truth in accordance with the rules of allegory.' He states, that ' the altar of God is the grateful
soul of the wise man,' and that ' God looks not upon
the victims as forming the real sacrifice, but on the
mind and willingness of him who offers them.' ' Blood
is a libation of life,' so that bloody sacrifices typified the
offering of self. Under the archtypal model of the
Divine image Philo understands the Essenic Angel-
Messiah, whom he designates as ' the true Highpriest '
who ' has no participation in sin.' When men ' bring
themselves ' as an offering to God, ' they are offering the
most perfect of all sacrifices.' [1] Discerning the deeper
and true sense of the letter, the Essenes had regarded
it as their chief mission to prepare mankind for the
coming of the atoning Angel-Messiah, for the Angel of
God, who can ' pardon ' transgressions, because God's
' Name is in him,' for the incarnate Angel's vicarious
and atoning death, and thus for the fulfilment of all,
which was figurative, typical, and prophetic in the
bloody sacrifices of the law. According to the figurative interpretation of the law by the Essenes, it is implied
that the law pointed to the self-sacrifice of the Messianic
Highpriest without sin. This symbolism Paul applies
to Jesus as the Angel of God, and antitype of the Paschal
lamb, as ' our Passover.'

Christ redeemed us, or bought us off from the curse
of the law, by resolving to suffer the death on the cross,
to become ' a curse for us,' so ' that we might receive
the promised Spirit through faith.' This faith came
with Christ, and ' has nothing to do ' with the law.
The promises to Abraham cannot be cancelled by
the law given to Moses on Sinai. As to Moses so to
Abraham, the Angel of the Lord, Christ, the Angel-

[1] ' On those who offer sacrifice,' 3-5.

Messiah, had appeared. That Angel had redeemed Abraham ' from all evil,' had prevented the sacrifice of Isaac, and had, in the Name of the Lord, blessed ' faithful Abraham,' and all nations in his seed. In consequence of this Angel's voice from heaven, Abraham sacrificed a lamb. To the allegorising Essene the Paschal lamb of Moses would seem to have pointed back to the lamb sacrificed, instead of Isaac, at the Angel's command, and to have at the same time pointed forward to a future bloody sacrifice, not of an animal, but of an incarnate Angel, of the same Angel of God who can ' pardon ' transgressions, or make an atonement, and who forbad the human sacrifice in the case of Isaac. This symbolism necessarily implied that the Angel-Messiah, as antitype of the lamb slain by Abraham and by Moses as the true Paschal lamb, would offer himself to God.

Paul's doctrine of the atoning sacrificial death of the Messiah is a simple development of the typically interpreted narrative about the lamb slain by Abraham and by Moses, and its connection with the Angel of God, who appeared in Jesus as Angel-Messiah, in order to be crucified as antitype of the Paschal lamb.

Before Christ ' our passover,' or Paschal lamb, had been slain, before he had become ' a curse for us ' by his crucifixion, we could not receive ' the promise of the Spirit,' or the ' promised Spirit through faith.' When ' we were yet without strength,' that is without the Spirit, which did not come till after the crucifixion, ' in due time Christ died for the ungodly,' and now ' being justified by his blood, we shall be saved from wrath through him ; for, if when we were enemies, we were reconciled to God by the death of his Son, much more, being reconciled, we shall be saved by his life ; and not only so, but we also joy in God through our Lord Jesus Christ, by whom we have now received the atonement.'

The blood of the Messianic Paschal Lamb ' justifies '

and 'atones,' and saves from wrath, as the blood of the Mosaic Paschal lamb saved the Israelites from the avenging Angel, who can forgive transgressions or not do so, according to his will.[1]

This undeniable connection of Paul's doctrine of the atonement with an allegorical interpretation of the Old Testament, such as can only be proved to have prevailed among the Essenic, and thus the Therapeutic Jews, leads us to suppose that Paul may have drawn from an Essenic source. The essentially genuine and Essenic Epistle of Barnabas leaves no doubt that the Paulinic doctrine of the atonement was that of the Christian Essenes. But independently of this testimony, some Essenic rites seem to point to the existence of such a doctrine among the pre-Christian Essenes.

The holy daily meal of the Essenes was preceded by the solemnity of a water baptism. The members of the secret society, who had sworn not to communicate a certain knowledge to the uninitiated, appeared in their 'white garments as if they were sacred,' they went into the refectory ' purified as into a holy temple,' and prayer was offered up before and after the sacred meal. It can only be compared with the Paschal meal of the other Jews. The bread figured in both, whilst among the Essenes water took the place of the wine at their meal on common days. But an especially sacred meal may be presumed to have been held by the Essenes on the 14th Nisan, and on this occasion the partaking of the cup with wine may have been exceptionally ordained. As a similar exception to the rule, the Therapeuts were permitted to anoint themselves exceptionally on the Sabbath-day, to mark its holiness. Since the Essenes felt constrained by their principles not to slay the lamb ordained by the law, they would have especial reason to give a typical and Messianic significance to the bread and to the wine of the Jewish

[1] 1 Cor. ii. 2, v. 7 ; Gal. iii. 13, 14, 23 ; Rom. v. 6–11 ; Ex. xxiii. 21.

Q

Paschal feast, and to transmit this significance to the bread of their daily meal, all the more if they had not a specially solemn meal on the 14th Nisan.

The allegorising Essenes, especially the Therapeuts of Egypt, could not fail to connect the bread on their daily table with the twelve shewbread on 'the Lord's table.' They were placed near the candlestick, the form of which resembled a tree, so that the candlestick could be regarded as a symbol of the tree of life and knowledge, which 'beareth fruit every month.' Thus the twelve shewbread would be regarded as symbols of the yearly fruit of the tree of life. This symbolical meaning of the shewbread would lead the Essenes to regard the daily bread on their table as a symbol of the bread of life, and thus of Christ, the Wisdom of God. This assumption is in so far confirmed by Philo and Josephus, both of whom were probably allied with the Essenes, inasmuch as these writers of the first century connect the twelve shewbread with the twelve months of the year, and thus indirectly with the tree of life bearing fruit every month. To this interpretation seem also to point the other designations of the shewbread in Holy Writ, as 'the perpetual bread' or 'food of God,' or the 'holy bread,' which in the Syriac text is called 'the bread of the table of the Lord.' In the Book of Proverbs the Wisdom of God (Christ) is recorded to say : ' Come, eat of my bread, and drink of the wine which I have mingled.' [1]

The Egyptians represented the tree of life as a palm, or as a mulberry fig-tree, the former of which has fresh shoots every month, whilst there are mulberry figs every month.[2] The stem of the Egyptian

[1] The two rows evidently referred to the six signs of the Zodiac in the upper and to those in the lower hemisphere. Prov. ix. 5.
[2] The parable of the fig-tree, whose time of figs was not yet come, though fruit was expected on it, seems to be best explained by the mulberry fig-tree.

tree of life was in pre-Mosaic times represented as connected with the figure of the goddess Hathor, ' the eye of the sun,' or of Nutpe, the expanse of heaven. In the time of the Ptolemies the tree of life and know-ledge was in Egypt represented by the figure of the Divine Wisdom, or Sophia, which formed the stem of the tree and dispensed to the souls of the departed the water of life and the fruit of the tree of life. At this time the Therapeuts were established near Alexandria; and then were composed in this city, probably under Essenic influence, the Apocrypha of the Septuagint or scriptures of hidden wisdom. In one of them, in the Book Ecclesiasticus, the Wisdom described as palm-tree and vine, that is, as tree of life, is recorded to say: ' Come unto me, all ye that be desirous of me, and fill yourselves with my fruits; for my memorial is sweeter than honey, and mine inheritance than the honeycomb. They that eat of me shall yet be hungry, and they that drink of me shall yet be thirsty.' [1]

In Hebrew, to make an alliance or covenant, or to eat, is expressed by a similar term, for ' bârâ,' to eat, forms the root of ' bĕrith,' or covenant. In this sense, the eating of the shewbread, or perpetual bread, by the priests, is designated as a ' memorial ' and an ' ever-lasting covenant.' Not only was bread and wine brought forth by Melchisedec when he blessed Abraham, but it was offered to God and eaten before him by Jethro and the elders of Israel, and some, at least, of the mourning Israelites broke bread and drunk ' the cup of conso-lation ' in remembrance of the departed, ' to comfort them for the dead.' ' A new covenant ' was announced by Jeremiah for a future day, when God would write his law in the hearts, when all shall know God, and when he will forgive iniquity and no longer remember sin. Looking for allegories, the Essenes would connect

[1] Ecclus. xxiv. 19-21.
[2] Lev. xxiv. 5-9; Hos. ix. 4; Jer.xvi.7; xxxi. 31-34.

this new and atoning covenant with the reign of the Angel-Messiah whom they expected, with the Angel of the Lord who can pardon transgression. To those Essenes who regarded Jesus as the Angel-Messiah, Jesus Christ was the incarnation of the Divine Wisdom who distributes the heavenly manna, the bread of life. If the Essenes, like Paul, identified Christ with 'the Wisdom of God,' it followed that Christ, or the Wisdom of God, must in a figurative sense be eaten and drunk, in accordance with the Books of Proverbs and Ecclesiasticus, and Egyptian representations.

Only in this figurative sense, and in connection with this Hebrew-Egyptian symbolism, Jesus can have said, as according to the fourth Gospel he has said, that his flesh is 'the living bread which came down from heaven,' and that whosoever shall eat thereof shall not die ; but that he that shall not 'eat the flesh of the son of man and drink his blood' has not 'eternal life,' and Jesus will not 'raise him up at the last day.'[1] Whether Jesus really has spoken these words, and why the first Evangelists should have kept them in secret, depends upon the question, whether Jesus regarded himself as antitype of the Paschal Lamb, and his death as the atoning and vicarious sacrifice which would essentially change the relation between God and man. For according to the above narrative, Jesus also said that he would give his flesh as heavenly bread 'for the life of the world.'

Unless we have failed to prove that the Essenes and Therapeuts expected an Angel-Messiah, and that many regarded Jesus as the incarnation of the same, we are now permitted to assume that the Essenes would hold the 'angels' bread' to have become flesh and blood in Jesus Christ, that they would believe, as Paul did, that the Paschal bread broken by Jesus, had become 'the communion of the body of Christ,' the cup blessed had

[1] John vi. 48-58.

become ' the communion of the blood of Christ.' This assumption is confirmed by Clement of Alexandria, to whom the ancient doctrines of the Therapeuts in and near that city must have been well known, and who thus interprets the Passover of the Christians : ' The blood points out to us the Word, for as rich blood the Word (that is, Christ) has been infused into life . . . . the Word Himself, the beloved One, our nourisher, hath shed His own blood for us, to save humanity . . . ; the flesh figuratively represents to us the Holy Spirit,' and thus ' the Lord who is Spirit and Word.' [1]

Without sanctioning the Essenic views about the Angel-Messiah, and his sacrificial death as antitype of the Paschal lamb, which expectations Jesus seems to have opposed, he must have referred to his approaching death, when for the last time, and as he had heartily longed to do, he partook of the Paschal lamb with his disciples. We may presume that the accidental coincidence of the Passover Feast with his death, led Jesus to refer on this, his Last Supper, to the liberation of Israel from the Egyptian house of bondage, of which the Paschal lamb, at that time instituted was the ' memorial.' This connection might have further led him to suggest, that the Mosaic Exodus was a parallel to the liberation of mankind from that spiritual bondage, against which Jesus had protested by word and deed, by an obedience unto death. In this sense Jesus could connect his approaching death, not with the Paschal lamb which he had just eaten, and which on that same 14th Nisan Moses had ordered to be annually slain 1600 years ago, but with the liberation of Israel which followed it on the 15th Nisan, on the day when Jesus was to be crucified.

If the new, the spiritual and atoning covenant announced by Jeremiah was the kingdom of heaven which Jesus had come to establish on earth, he might

[1] 1 Cor. x. 16; *Paed.* i. 6.

have compared it with the 'memorial,' memorial-feast, or covenant instituted by the eternal Wisdom of God, represented in pre-Christian times as distributing celestial food and drink to the souls of men. Regarding the Divine covenant made with Moses as a type of the new covenant, and since the former was symbolised by blood, and thus by the symbol of the soul, by 'the blood of the covenant, which the Lord hath made,' Jesus could not fear to be misunderstood if he called that new covenant which he brought 'the New Testament (or covenant) in my blood.'[1] Jesus could say this without even indirectly suggesting that his death was typified by the slaying of the Paschal lamb, that the blood of the yearly slain lamb points to his blood, which the following day would be shed on the cross, in consequence of a presumable affixing of his body by nails instead of ropes according to Roman custom. What Jesus is said to have commanded was to be done not in remembrance of his death only, but of his life. As bread was eaten at the burial of the dead, and 'the cup of consolation' was partaken by Israelites 'to comfort them for the dead,' so Jesus may have commanded, and we believe that he did so command, his disciples and followers to eat bread and drink wine, as they had just done at the Passover, but to do so henceforth in remembrance of him.

Jesus could not designate himself as 'the Passover' or Paschal lamb, slain for us, as Paul calls him, without admitting the Divine sanction of his death on the cross, nor without thereby implying that his death was to be an event which would essentially change the relations between God and man. Since no possible types in the Old Testament could be referred to an atoning Messianic death, since even the allegorising Targum did not so interpret the isolated passage in the Book of Isaiah

[1] Ex. xxiv. 8; Hebr. ix. 19, 20; Matt. xxvi. 28; Rom. iii. 24, 25; 1 Cor. xi. 25.

about the sufferings of the servant of God, Jesus could not have left his disciples in ignorance or doubt as to the importance of his death. The knowledge of the atoning death of Jesus as antitype of the Paschal lamb, 'according to the Scriptures,' might have prevented Judas Iscariot from betraying innocent blood, and certainly would have prevented his attempt to atone for his crime by suicide. We saw that the first three Gospels are silent with regard to the Messianic antitype of the Paschal lamb, and the recorded prayer of Jesus in Gethsemane, and his words on the cross, seem even to exclude the belief of Jesus that his death on the cross was divinely appointed as means of salvation.

Yet Paul solemnly states, that a new sacrament has been instituted by Jesus, instead of the Paschal rite, and that this fact has been communicated to him in some mysterious manner by 'the Lord.' He asserts that 'the Lord Jesus, in the night when he was betrayed, took bread, and pronounced the thanksgiving, brake it, and said: This is my body, which is given for you, that do in remembrance of me. After the same manner (he took) also the cup after supper and said: And this cup is the new Testament in my blood, that do ye, as often as ye drink it, in remembrance of me. For as often as ye eat this bread, and drink this cup, ye do show the Lord's death till he come.'[1]

Paul accepted and applied to Jesus, as we tried to show, the Essenic doctrines about Christ as the Angel-Messiah, and about his atoning death as Lamb of God, with which doctrines that about the Last Supper is inseparably connected. The earliest account of the Last Supper, as contained in the First Epistle to the Corinthians, is repeated literally in the Gospel after the Paulinic Evangelist Luke, as if no other than Paul's authority could be claimed for it. Luke distinguishes between the Passover and the new sacrament, which

---

[1] 1 Cor. xi. 23–26 ; comp. Luke xxii. 19, 20.

Matthew and Mark do not. The fourth Gospel does not say, but implies that Jesus introduced a new institution. This omission, all the more important because the Gospel after John is the Gospel of the Lamb of God, we have explained by the impossibility to harmonise the different dates about the crucifixion in the first three Gospels and in the fourth Gospel respectively.

Assuming that what Paul had received about the Lord's Supper had been communicated to him by one or more organs of the Essenic secret tradition,[1] he might have designated this communication as come to him from 'the Lord,' because it harmonised with the voice in his heart, with the Father's revelation of his Son in him on his way to Damascus. Paul's narrative about the Last Supper, like that about the resurrection, seems to have been the source of all parallel notices in the Gospels. The Apostle's accounts were certainly written some time before the composition of the earliest Gospels transmitted to us, and probably about eighteen years after his conversion to the faith of Stephen whom we have connected with the Essenic Therapeuts of Alexandria. What we may now call the Essenic interpretation of the reported institution of the Last Supper, whether strictly historical or not, had become firmly established in many Christian Churches before Paul wrote his account of it.

The Apostles could believe his narrative to be based on a historical fact in the sense in which Essenes distinguished a literal and a higher figurative meaning of the Scriptures. It was for the Essenes not enough to know what words Jesus did actually pronounce on this

[1] During the three years spent in Arabia, after his conversion by Ananias (the Essene) to the Christian-Essenic faith, Saul may have passed through the Essenic noviciate of three years, as Josephus seems to have done with Banus. As initiated Essene Paul would have been bound by oath not to speak 'the hidden wisdom' to others than 'the perfect' or initiated. (1 Cor. ii. 6, 7.)

and on other occasions, they also held it necessary to find out what his words were meant to imply to those who had been initiated into the mysteries of allegorical Scripture interpretation, how from the dead letter the quickening spirit has to be developed. These conceptions would necessarily lead those Essenes who believed in Jesus as the representative of their doctrines, to attribute to him words, possibly spoken in secret, which implied what they felt convinced was in his mind, when he spoke to the people in parables only, and when even his disciples were unable to understand all the mysteries, which should afterwards be revealed to them. These recorded words of Jesus, recorded by Essenes, but which they may never have heard him speak, were to be the medium of conveying the method of spiritually discerning the more perfect doctrine of Christ, ' the mysteries of the kingdom of heaven.'

Philo, and probably all the initiated Essenes in pre-Christian times, had enlarged the meaning of the recorded words of Moses, of Psalmists, and of Prophets, in order to make them point, in accordance with their assumed hidden meaning, to the Essenic doctrines of the Angel-Messiah. Sooner or later the Essenes connected with the latter his atoning death as antitype of the Paschal lamb, and his resurrection as antitype of the Paschal omer on the third day after it. These two Mosaic institutions, by what was written about them, certainly did not point typically to the future, the one to Messiah's death, the other to his resurrection. Yet they were probably by Essenes, and certainly by Paul, held to convey the truth by suggesting it to such to whom in future ages it would be given to ' discern the Lord's body,' to regard the death of Jesus as the antitype of the Paschal lamb, and thus the Paschal lamb as a divinely instituted symbol of the Angel-Messiah's sacrificial death as the Lamb of God.

Paul seems to have confidently believed during the

first years after his conversion to the faith of Stephen, that Jesus had recognised the Messianic conceptions of the Essenes, that he did reveal himself as the Angel-Messiah and Lamb of God, although not to the people, yet to those to whom it was given to know 'the mysteries of the kingdom of heaven,' and that he, as antitype of the Paschal lamb, had instituted a new sacrament in the place of the Passover, and in connection with his atonement by 'the blood of his cross.' Paul may also have for a time believed that this was the doctrine of Christ which the Apostles kept in secret, its publication being forbidden by the chiefs of the Jewish Church. But already his mysterious meeting with Peter, and still more, the fear which he inspired in all the Apostles at Jerusalem, notwithstanding the conciliatory conduct of Barnabas, must have convinced Paul that Jesus had not sanctioned the typical reference of the Paschal lamb and of the Paschal omer to himself as to the Angel-Messiah whom only Essenes expected. Paul must have known, that Jesus had not been crucified, contemporaneously with the Paschal lamb, on the 14th, but on the 15th Nisan, so that there was no historical foundation at all for the typical scheme of Paul, which he seems to have received through the Therapeuts, to whom Stephen belonged.

The Essenic doctrine of Christ which Paul promulgated could be developed from the Old Testament by a figurative interpretation of the same, such as the following :

The Angel of the Lord, and therefore Christ, the spiritual Rock which followed the Israelites, can pardon the transgressions of men, for God's 'Name' or Spirit is in him, whilst it had been withdrawn from mankind. Because Jesus is the incarnation of the sin-removing, the atoning Angel, therefore 'the body' and 'the blood' of Jesus Christ, that is, the incarnate 'Wisdom of God,' constitutes the first 'temple of the Holy Ghost' after the fall of Adam. Whosoever believes this, receives the same spirit, Christ dwells in him by faith, and such a believer becomes also a temple of God, for the Spirit of God dwells in him again since Christ has brought it back from heaven. By the quickening or lifegiving spirit which Jesus, as 'the man from heaven,' as the Angel of God, has brought to mankind; by the first manifestation of such flesh and blood as can inherit the kingdom of God ; by Him who, as Son of David and as Son of God, was the first proof that 'mortal can put on immortality'; by 'the firstfruits of them that sleep' a transformation of human nature has taken place. Henceforth mankind forms One mystical body, for God's Spirit is now potentially in every man, since the incarnate and anointed Angel has brought those near who were afar off so long as they had not this spiritual link, which constitutes the real presence of Christ.

The manna in the wilderness was the symbol of the 'angels' food,' of the spiritual sustenance of man, of the power which creates conscience. The fruit from the tree of life and knowledge, the bread and water of life, comes to him from without, whence Christ Jesus, the Angel of God and Bread of Life, has brought it. The mystical breaking of bread, the eating of bread before the Lord, refers to this bread from heaven ; and the bread in the hand of the priest, as once the Paschal bread in the hand of Jesus, symbolises the extraneous source of the soul's sustenance.[1] In a similar sense the incarnate Angel is the tree of life, the vine which God has planted, and the life-giving essence rises from the Divine root through the vine to the branches. In the unity of that mysterious vital force which was believed to have an absolutely non-material origin, root, vine, and branches are one. In all men is Christ Jesus, in the same sense that God the Father is in Him who is

---

[1] In this sense Keble's revised lines convey a true meaning: 'As in the hand, so in the heart.'

the Son of God 'according to the Spirit of Holiness,' whilst according to the flesh he is the Son of David. By his spiritualised flesh, which was only ' like ' sinful flesh, by flesh with God's Spirit, the incarnate Angel of God has brought about a reconciliation of the world with God, the spiritual atonement, the righteousness of God.

At the time of the crucifixion of Jesus the Holy Ghost was not yet come. This was the Paulinic, and we may now venture to say, the Essenic, doctrine of Christ. If the direct connection has been sufficiently proved between the Paulinic doctrine of the atonement and the Old Testament-doctrine of the atoning Angel of God, who was incarnate in Jesus, the Angel-Messiah, then it follows conclusively that Jesus cannot have sanctioned the doctrine of the atonement by his blood, without at the same time revealing himself as the anointed Angel, as Angel-Messiah, of which doctrine there is no trace in the Scriptures before the Captivity, nor in the first three Gospels. Although Jesus regarded himself only as the anointed Man, and in this sense as the Messiah, he may yet probably have been led by the chance-circumstance of his crucifixion taking place during the Passover, to institute a new Paschal or Easter rite. We believe that he did so, and that he connected it with, though he did not substitute it for, the Mosaic Paschal rite. But we may confidently assert that Jesus, if he has instituted a new sacrament, he did not thereby, or by any word or intended inter- pretation of the same, wish to convey that his ap- proaching death was the antitype of the Paschal lamb, a sin-removing, atoning, and vicarious sacrificial death, of which the Paschal lamb was by God intended as a symbol.

The mission of Jesus on earth was not finished on the 14th Nisan, when the Paschal lamb was slain and by him eaten with his disciples ; but on the 15th Nisan, on the same day of the year when Moses led the children of Israel out of the bondage of Egypt. Jesus wished to put an end to the spiritual bondage of Israel and of mankind. He pointed out to man his freedom to become a citizen of the kingdom of heaven, which the Scribes and Pharisees had shut up by taking away the key of knowledge, by their preventing, instead of fostering by word and deed, the conviction that the Spirit of God is in man.

Jesus has indirectly protested against the Essenic doctrine of the Angel-Messiah, by his remark that John the Baptist or Essene did not belong to the kingdom of heaven. This kingdom, the rule of the Spirit of God in and through man, John regarded as future, though near, Jesus as being already come, as being like the Word of God near to man, that is, in his heart that he may do it ; and Paul testified that it had not come till after the atoning sacrificial death of Christ. From this and from other words of Jesus recorded in the first three Gospels, it follows that Jesus must have protested against the Essenic denial of the presence of the Spirit of God in man and in all ages, of which doctrine that of the atonement is the necessary consequence. If it had entered the mind of anyone to conceive, before the crucifixion of Jesus, that the Holy Ghost would not be given to mankind till after the sacrificial death of the Messiah, after the glorification of Jesus, as the fourth Gospel asserts, in harmony with Paul's teaching, then against such a doctrine would Jesus have solemnly protested.

The dogma of Jesus was that which is contained in the Sermon on the Mount. His creed was the deed.

The spiritual union and communion between man and his God : this spiritual at-one-ment is the atonement or reconciliation of which it can be said that we have received it by Jesus Christ, inasmuch as the man Jesus of Nazareth, whom God ' has anointed with the Holy Ghost and with power,' has first clearly and fully

proclaimed this relationship by word and deed. The
atonement of Jesus Christ is the covenant of a good
conscience with God.

Retrospect.

The convert to the faith of Stephen became the
proclaimer of Jesus as the Angel-Messiah whom no
other Jews than the Essenes and Therapeuts expected.
Paul's doctrine about Christ was not that which was
sanctioned by Jesus and by the Apostles whom he had
chosen. John the Baptist or Essene, the Ashai or
bather, and therefore called Assai or Essai, as Philo.
called the Essenes, did not recognise Jesus as Him that
should come, that is, according to Essenic interpretation
of Scripture, as the Angel-Messiah. Yet John paved
the way for the application of that new doctrine to
Jesus by Stephen and Paul. The Baptist believed that
the promised Messiah who should come after him would
be an incarnate Angel and would baptize men with the
Holy Ghost. So little did he think it possible that the
Spirit of God was already in mankind that, years after
his death, disciples of his had not even heard that there
is a Holy Ghost. No disciples of John were by him
prepared to understand how Jesus and contemporaries
of his could by the Spirit of God be enabled to drive
out devils. But some disciples of John or Essenes,
after the death of John and of Jesus, believed in the
latter as the Angel-Messiah, and therefore expected the
baptism with the Holy Ghost. These Essenes were the
forerunners of Paul.

Following in the footsteps of Stephen whom he had
seen stoned to death, Paul taught that Jesus was the
Angel who had been with the Fathers in the wilderness,
the spiritual Rock who had followed them. According
to Paul's Gospel the Holy Ghost was sent by God to
mankind in consequence of the atoning, sacrificial, and

vicarious death of Jesus Christ. Paul does not refer to the Pentecostal miracle, which is narrated in the Acts (of Luke, his fellow-worker?), but he certainly believed in the miracle which he asserts to have happened fifty days before the Pentecost. Paul taught that Jesus was crucified as the antitype of the Paschal Lamb, and that he rose from the dead 'the third day according to the Scriptures,' that is, as antitype of the Paschal omer containing the first ripened barley which was waved before the Lord on the 16th Nisan, fifty days before the day of Pentecost.

Between the doctrines of Jesus and those of Paul there was not the same fundamental difference as between the doctrines of Jesus and those of John the Baptist, although the latter and Paul both represented Essenic doctrines, especially that of the Angel-Messiah, which Jesus had not sanctioned. Because Paul believed that the kingdom of heaven was come, because he recognised the Spirit of God among the Gentiles as among the Jews, therefore the twelve Apostles recognised him as a chosen organ of the Spirit of God, and thus as a follower of Jesus. They believed and taught that Jesus was the Christ, the Son of the living God, because the man Jesus had by God been anointed 'with the Holy Ghost and with power,' had been made Christ. But Paul believed and taught, as Stephen had done before him, that Jesus was for quite another reason the Son of God according to the Spirit of Holiness, because he was the risen incarnate Angel of God, who created the world, the man from heaven, the Angel-Messiah, whom only the Essenes among the Jews expected.

In spite of the essential difference of the doctrine about the person of Christ, Paul could and did agree with the other Apostles in this, that the only foundation of the Kingdom of God is the Spirit of God. Simon Jonah, that is, Simon the dove, the symbol of the Spirit, he who was also called Peter the Rock, the

Apostle whose name referred to the spirit and to the rock, to the spiritual Rock, was moved by that Spirit of God when he made his great confession about Jesus being the Christ, the Son of the Living God, who promised to build his Church on this spiritual foundation, on this spiritual rock. Paul acknowledged that the same 'spiritual rock' is Christ.

The doctrine of the anointed Angel, of the man from heaven, the Creator of the world, the doctrine of the atoning sacrificial death of Jesus by the blood of his cross, the doctrine of the Messianic antitype of the Paschal lamb and of the Paschal omer, and thus of the resurrection of Jesus Christ 'the third day according to the Scriptures,'—these doctrines of Paul, which can with more or less certainty be connected with the Essenes, could not be and were not recognised by the twelve Apostles. It becomes almost a certainty that Eusebius was right in surmising, that Essenic writings have been used by Paul and the Evangelists. Not Jesus, but Paul is the cause of the separation of the Jews from the Christians.

CHAPTER VIII.

APOLLOS AND THE ESSENES.

Introduction—The Christology of the Epistle to the Hebrews—'The High-priest of our confession'—Conclusion.

Introduction.

THE ' Epistle to the Hebrews ' is said to have been like-wise inscribed ' to the Alexandrians,' and it seems to have in view the Church at Alexandria, to which its probable author, Apollos, belonged. In the neighbour-hood of Alexandria the Egyptian Essenes or Therapeuts had their settlements, and with these Greek-speaking Jews, Grecians or Hellenists, we have connected Philo, and Stephen, the forerunner of Paul. The connection of Apollos with Paul renders it probable at the outset that the former, the eloquent and zealous Jew of Alexandria, stood likewise in connection with the Thera-peuts. All we know about Apollos harmonises with the characteristic features of the author of this Epistle, for which reason, ever since Luther, many Biblical inter-preters have regarded Apollos as its composer. This hypothesis receives a new confirmation from two re-ported facts, that Apollos was a disciple of John, or an Essene, and that the Epistle to the Hebrews is by Eusebius especially mentioned among those Scriptures of which he regarded it ' highly probable ' that they stood in direct connection with the written tradition of the Therapeuts.

The Therapeuts distinguished a figurative from a literal interpretation of the Old Testament. Their deeper

knowledge or gnosis we may identify with ' the more
perfect way of God,' in which Aquila and his wife instructed Apollos.   The latter having known only ' the
baptism of John,' like him seems not to have recognised in Jesus the Angel-Messiah, whom all the Initiated
among the Essenes expected.   But the initiation in the
mysteries of tradition, by Aquila and Priscilla, taught
Apollos the disciple of John, that Jesus was the expected
Angel-Messiah.   Being ' fervent in the spirit ' Apollos
had ' taught accurately about Jesus,' except that he
knew only the baptism of John, that is, he had taught
only within the range of the Baptist's teaching, but having been taught ' the way of God more accurately,' or
' the more perfect way of God,'—he knew and preached
' that Jesus is the Christ.'

As in the Acts ' the more perfect ' doctrine, taught
by Aquila to Apollos, is contrasted to the doctrine of
John the Baptist, so in the Epistle to the Hebrews ' the
more perfect ' doctrine is contrasted to the ' elementary
doctrine of Christ.' ' Therefore we will leave the elementary doctrine of Christ and turn to the perfect ' doctrine,
or ' to perfection.' [1]   In this Epistle the writer contrasts
with the ' weak ' and unprofitable law of Moses, which
' has done nothing towards perfection,' the covenant of
Abraham, which according to Paul was confirmed ' of
God in Christ.'   Accordingly Aquila and also his wife
Priscilla must have been initiated in the more perfect
doctrine of Christ, which went beyond ' the baptism of
John,' and referred to the baptism with the Holy Ghost
by the Angel-Messiah.   Since a similar deeper knowledge or gnosis, based on a figurative interpretation of
Scripture, was transmitted by the Therapeuts, we are
led to surmise that Aquila and Priscilla may have belonged to the Therapeuts, who alone admitted women to
the initiation in their mysteries, and whom Eusebius
identifies with the Christians of the Apostolic age.

[1] Acts xviii. 24-26; v. 12; Heb. vi. 1.

A Targumist and Greek translator of the Old Testament, called Onkelos, Ankilas, Akilas, or Aquila, who, like the Aquila of the Acts, was from Pontus, is said to have been brought up by Rabbis in Jerusalem and to have been the contemporary of Gamaliel the elder and of the Apostles. From Pontus also was the Aquila who instructed Apollos in a deeper knowledge or gnosis, which we may connect with the hereditary Targumistic lore. The identity of these two Aquilas is therefore highly probable. The Targum called after Onkelos or Aquila, though he was not the author of it, has been distinctly traced to Babylon, where it was collected, revised and edited, and it is distinguished from that called after Jonathan, composed in Judæa.[1]

Since the doctrine about Christ in the Epistle to the Hebrews can be proved to be the Essenic-Paulinic doctrine about the Angel-Messiah, Apollos, the pupil of Aquila (the Therapeut?) if he wrote this Epistle, must have connected 'the more perfect doctrine of Christ,' to which he refers, with the secret tradition, deeper knowledge or gnosis of the Therapeuts, which Paul had promulgated and Apollos developed. Such a doctrinal development of Paulinic doctrines as is contained in the Epistle to the Hebrews renders it highly probable, if not certain, that Apollos, of whom Paul writes that he watered what the Apostle had planted, is the author of this Epistle. We shall regard him as such. But if the tradition be preferred that Paul himself is its author, our argument would be all the stronger, that the doctrinal system of this Epistle cannot be separated from Essenic tradition, with which we have connected Paul. This Apostle also might have written the passage in this Epistle about the elementary doctrine of Christ and the more perfect doctrine, deeper knowledge or gnosis, since he wrote to the Romans that his Gospel and the preaching of Jesus Christ centred in

[1] Deutsch, in Smith's *Dictionary of the Bible*, ' Versions,' p. 1657.

'the mystery' which had been kept in secret, or in silence, since the world began.

We regard the Church to which the Epistle to the Hebrews is addressed, probably that of Alexandria, unlike that of Antioch, as essentially free from the Gentile-excluding bondage of the law. The majority of its members we hold to have been universalist Therapeuts, who were in danger of falling into the snares of a narrower Judaism, presumably that of the Palestinian Essenes, for these insisted on the exclusion of the Gentiles. Barnabas, who probably belonged to those Levites who had become Essenes, is said to have taught in Alexandria. As Paul opposed his fellow-worker Barnabas in Antioch, so Apollos seems to have opposed Barnabas and his followers in Alexandria for a similar reason. The Epistle is certainly written before the destruction of the Temple, which is described as existing. How early it was composed cannot be determined. The peculiar principles of the Alexandrian Church harmonised with those of the Therapeuts.

The Christology of the Epistle to the Hebrews.

According to Philo's writings, ' the eternal Word ' is the archtype of Humanity. Man is created in the image of the eternal Word, and this Divine Word is more ancient than creation. The Word is not only a spiritual power which God uses as ' a rudder,' but a celestial being, the personal ' Son ' of God, the heavenly Highpriest, the Angel-Messiah of the Essenes and Therapeuts. It is only through the mediation of angels and therefore of the Angel of God, that men can become ' sons of God.' ' The perfect man ' is ' the image and the form ' of the Divine Word, he belongs to ' the better species of men,' to those who can ' claim the Divine nature.' These are created by the first of the angels, by ' the firstborn and ' eldest Son ' of God, by that being who ' in no wise departs from the Divine image,' by the ambassador and advocate of God, who is ' neither God nor man,' neither uncreated like God nor created like man, ' something on the border between uncreated and perishable nature.' This eternal Word or eternal Messiah Philo calls ' the great Highpriest of the confession,' and he is, according to Philo's conception, not a man of the past, present, or future, but the Angel of God who transmits the Holy Ghost.[1] It is evident that Philo's conception of the Messiah is the Essenic one of the Angel-Messiah, with which we have connected the Christology of Paul.

The Epistle to the Hebrews begins by pointing out the connection between the Divine revelations in the old and the new covenant. ' God having in times past spoken unto the fathers by the prophets in sundry forms and in divers measures, hath in these last days spoken unto us by the Son.' Apollos follows Paul by designating Christ, the Angel-Messiah, as participator in God's creation of the world. In direct connection with what is said in the Book of Wisdom about the Wisdom of God, to which in the Gospel of Luke words of Jesus have been attributed, Apollos describes God's Son as ' the refraction of his glory and image of his being,' who, after having accomplished the purification of our sins, ' sat down on the right hand of the majesty on high,' as Stephen had first described him. According to the Philonian and Essenian doctrine of angels, the Angel-Messiah was held to be higher than all angels, and thus the Apocalypse of John had described Christ as the first of seven angels, in harmony with Eastern symbolism. Then Apollos wrote that the risen Jesus was made or became ' so much better than the angels, as he hath by inheritance obtained a more excellent name than they.' The learned Alexandrian and Therapeut instructed by Aquila in the secret tradition of the Thera-

[1] *De Ling. conf.* 1; *De Somn.* 1; see p. 248.

peuts, finds sufficient proof for his assertion in the
Alexandrian version of the 2nd Psalm, which he
refers not to Solomon's or another king's accession to
the throne, but to the Angel-Messiah. So he cites, likewise after the Septuagint, Nathan's promise to David,
that Solomon, his son in the flesh, would build a temple
to God, who will stablish his throne for ever, and who
is recorded to have said, according to the Greek
text : ' I will be to him a father, and he shall be to
me a son.'

Referring to the return of Jesus which by Essenic
Christians was then considered to be near at hand, Apollos
cites words of God, nowhere recorded in our Scriptures,
according to which ' all angels shall worship him,' as
they are recorded to have served Jesus on the occasion
of his victory over Satan's temptation in the wilderness.
Again, whilst God's angels are described as spirits (or
winds) and his ministers flames of fire, Apollos ventures to
assert, on the authority of the Septuagint, that the 45th
Psalm does not refer to the Davidic kingdom as to a
' throne of God,' but to the kingdom of the Son, to
whom the Psalmist is assumed to have given the attribute of ' God ' : ' Thy throne, O God, is for ever and
ever.' If not the earliest, at all events the latest, real
authority for this application of the Divine attribute is
Philo, who calls the Son of God ' the second God,' in
harmony with the late Targumistic tradition, which
identifies the Word or Memra, that is, the Messiah, with
Jehovah. We are, therefore, not astonished that Apollos,
again following the Greek text, changes the Hebrew
Psalmist's words, which probably refer to the king's
being anointed above his fellows by God, even his God.
Instead of this, Apollos writes : ' therefore, oh God, thy
God hath anointed thee with the oil of gladness above
thy fellows.' Finally, the assertion is repeated which is
contrary to the 102nd Psalm, that not God, but the
Angel-Messiah, has laid the foundations of the earth, and

that the heavens are the work of his hands, for which reason, though they perish yet he remains, and is the same, and his years shall have no end. In this case Apollos can connect his new interpretation with the Hebrew text of the 33rd and 119th Psalms, in which it is said that ‘ by the word of the Lord are the heavens made,’ and ‘ for ever, O Lord, thy word is (remains) settled in heaven.’ The latter Psalm is probably from the time of the Maccabees, whose allies were the Assidæans or Essenes, so that the Word of God in this passage may have been referred, at least by the Initiated and possibly by the Psalmist, to a celestial being. As such in the Book of Proverbs and in the Books of Ecclesiasticus and of Wisdom the Word or Wisdom of God is designated. Paul had also implied a similar explanation of the engrafted Word as originating in a wisdom which descends from above.

Apollos, like Stephen and Paul, has applied to Jesus Christ the Essenic doctrine of the Angel-Messiah, and so Apollos, like Paul, connects in the Epistle to the Hebrews with the Divine the human nature of Jesus. Although the expression ‘ the veil of his flesh ’ might be explained in a superhuman sense by those who denied Christ in the flesh, as did the false teachers to which the First Epistle of ‘ John ’ refers, yet Apollos has as clearly defined the human nature of Jesus Christ as Paul has done in one passage of the Roman Epistle. According to Apollos, the author of the 22nd Psalm has in the spirit referred to the incarnation of the Angel-Messiah. He who is above the angels is ‘ not ashamed ’ to call men his ‘ brethren ’ and his children, just as God is declared not to be ashamed to be called the God of Israel’s fathers. Because the Name or Spirit of God is in the Angel of the Lord, in the Angel-Messiah, and through him also in mankind, therefore ‘ he that sancti-fieth,’ that is Christ, ‘ and they who are sanctified,’ his brethren, are ‘ all of one.’ Thus far it is only said that there is a spiritual union between the sons of men and the celestial Son of God. But Apollos, as if not satisfied with Paul's mysterious reference to 'the likeness of sinful flesh,' clearly states that Christ partook of the same flesh and blood as his children, and that he took on him 'not the nature of angels,' but 'the seed of Abraham,' since 'in all things it behoved him to be made like unto his brethren.' He also suffered and was tempted 'in all points like as we are, yet without sin'; and in the days of his flesh he 'offered up prayers and supplications with strong crying and tears unto Him that was able to save him from death.' It was because of his 'piety' that he was heard, and 'though he was (a) son yet learned he obedience by that which he suffered, and being made perfect he became the author of eternal salvation unto all them that obey him.' Christ Jesus could not have 'come to do' the will of God unless he had been an Angel.

The doctrine about Christ in the Epistle to the Hebrews is the Essenic doctrine about the Angel-Messiah which was first promulgated by Stephen and Paul, as applied to Jesus Christ.

The Highpriest of our confession.

'The firstborn,' God's 'Angel-Word' or 'Archangelic Word,' the 'Angel being the Word,' His 'most ancient Word,' Philo calls 'God,' the 'second Deity,' and 'the Highpriest of the confession,' or of the Creed.[1] By applying to Jesus Christ the latter title, and that of the 'Word of God,' Apollos confirms his evident relation to the doctrinal system of his great townsman. The gulf between the spiritual and the material world was bridged over by God's ambassador, who is neither God nor man, by the Angel-Messiah of the Essenes. Those

---

[1] *De Conf. ling.* 14; *De Somn.* i. 38, 39, 41; *Quis est,* 42; *De Mut. Nom.* 13; *De Quest. et Sol.* 62.

who, unlike Philo, believed in the incarnation of the first of seven angels, and that Jesus was the incarnate Angel-Messiah who had brought the Spirit of God to mankind, were compelled to distinguish from the Mosaic covenant the new covenant of Christ as the fulfilment of the covenant promised to Abraham and his seed. Paul had said of this covenant that 430 years before the Sinaitic covenant it had been confirmed ' of God in Christ.' Christ or the Angel of God had been with Abraham as he had been with Moses on Sinai and with the Church in the wilderness. Because of sin the second retrograde ' weak ' and ' unprofitable ' law on Sinai, to which ' perfection ' is impossible, was promulgated through the mediation of angels, probably of lower angels. To these is contrasted the Angel of God who had followed the Israelites, Christ who had been made ' perfect ' in eternity or for ever, and who had become incarnate and brought the perfect covenant promised to Abraham. Hence it had become necessary to ' leave the elementary doctrine of Christ' and ' the first principles of the oracles of God.' Therefore a new Highpriesthood was by Apollos contrasted to the Aaronic Highpriesthood ; and the former, like the new covenant, was traced back to Abraham, who had bowed before the non-Hebrew Highpriest Melchisedec.

We have drawn attention to the distinction between a Hebrew and a non-Hebrew Highpriesthood, which seems to have been recognised before the Babylonian Captivity, if not ever since the time of Moses. We connected with this double Highpriesthood the two lines of the Aaronites ; that of Ithamar represented the priesthood of the naturalised strangers in Israel, to whom the Kenites of Jethro and the Rechabites belonged, with which latter the Essenes may safely be connected. We also showed that the 110th Psalm, probably written for the consecration of Joshua the Highpriest, seems to refer to this Highpriesthood for ever promised to Jonadab, the

ancestor of the Rechabites, and whom the Psalmist calls
his Lord.   The Lord had spoken through the prophet
Jeremiah unto the Psalmist's Lord Jonadab, to whom
the promise had been made about the Highpriesthood
for ever among the sons of Rechab.   This eternal Highpriesthood among the strangers or non-Hebrews in
Israel the Psalmist connects with the Highpriesthood of
the non-Hebrew Melchisedec, with 'the order of Melchisedec.'

Whether the 110th Psalm had originally referred
to and possibly was composed by Joshua, or whether
it was composed by David, a descendant from non-
Hebrews, to whom the superscription refers the same
in the text transmitted to us, in either case the Psalm
may be connected with the Rechabite Highpriesthood
promised by Jeremiah to the sons of Jonadab or of
Rechab, the strangers in Israel.   The Essenes, whom
we cannot disconnect from the Rechabites, would regard this promise as made to their order, and they
would identify this eternal Highpriesthood with the
Angel-Messiah whom they expected, whom Philo had
called, and Apollos after him, 'the great Highpriest of
our confession.'   Apollos fully explains how the celestial Highpriesthood promised by the words of God
recorded in the 110th Psalm, refers to Jesus, who, like
David, was descended from non-Hebrews.

The incarnate Angel-Highpriest and celestial son
of God, 'Jesus, the Son of God,' is 'passed through
the heavens,' both at the beginning and at the end
of his 'days in the flesh,' or as Paul had said, 'he
that descended is the same that ascended.'   Referring
the 110th Psalm to Jesus, Apollos considers himself
authorised to say, that Jesus was 'called' or addressed
by God as 'a Highpriest after the order of Melchisedec.'
Thus a hope is set before us, 'which we have as an
anchor of the soul, both sure and stedfast, and entering
into the part within the veil, whither as forerunner on

our behalf Jesus entered, having become an Highpriest for ever after the order of Melchisedec.' In the Hebrew language, which was that of Canaan, the name Melchisedec means 'King of Righteousness,' and Salem or Shalem means ' peace ' or ' peaceful,' and probably here refers to Jerusalem. Not only the references to Jerusalem, to righteousness and peace, add force to the explanation of Melchisedec as type of Jesus the incarnate Angel-Highpriest, but the omission of Melchisedec's descent, that is, of his genealogy, would suggest the mystery of the incarnation of Christ Jesus. Because neither the father nor the mother nor the genealogy of Melchisedec is referred to in Genesis, Apollos finds it easy to interpret the passage figuratively, in harmony with Essenic custom, to give it a deeper meaning than that conveyed by the literal sense, and to suggest mysteriously that the King of Jerusalem, who, in company with the King of Sodom, went to meet victorious Abraham, had in fact neither father nor mother nor genealogy, 'and neither beginning of days nor end of life, but (being) like unto the Son of God, he abideth a priest for ever.'

Apollos therefore clearly implies that Melchisedec was not only a type, but an earlier incarnation of the Angel of God, of the Word of God whom Philo had designated as ' neither God nor man,' and ' the great Highpriest.' Jesus is the full manifestation of the celestial Highpriest. Unlike the sons of Levi, who are not suffered to continue priests by reason of death, the celestial Highpriest, ' because he continueth for ever, hath his priesthood unchangeable,' or imperishable. Instead of human Highpriests, 'which have infirmity,' Jesus, as ' the Highpriest of our confession,' is ' the Son made perfect in eternity.' Apollos asserts, in accordance with his interpretation of the 110th Psalm, that this has been declared by the Word of God's oath, ' after the law,' or, as thus implied, in the time of

David, to whom the composition of that Psalm is assigned.

'If perfection were (possible) by the Levitical priesthood (for on the ground of it hath the people received the law) what further need was there that a different priest should rise after the order of Melchisedec, and that he should be called not after the order of Aaron? For where the priesthood is changed, there is made of necessity a change of the law also. For he in reference to whom these things are spoken belonged to a different tribe, of which no man hath ever given attendance at the altar. For it is evident that our Lord sprang out of Judah, of (for) which tribe Moses spake nothing concerning the priests,' that is, concern-. ing those priests which might be taken from Judah for the Highpriesthood.

This passage confirms the connection of the High-priesthood of Melchisedec and of Jesus, the non-Hebrews, with the Aaronic line of Ithamar, so called after Thamar, the non-Hebrew. For the line of Ithamar had its possessions exclusively in Judah, where the Kenites or Rechabites had amalgamated with Hebrews, and during the war between Saul of Benjamin and David of Judah the line of Ithamar, represented by Abiathar, sided with David, the line of Eleazar, repre-sented by Zadoc, with Saul. Only in so far could Apollos assert that Moses spoke nothing concerning the priests which might be taken from Judah for the High-priesthood, inasmuch as, in fact, the Scriptures, which twice give the genealogy of the line of Eleazar, do not give the genealogy of the line of Ithamar. But Apollos was wrong in his assertion, for Eli and his successors did give ' attendance at the altar,' though they belonged to the junior Aaronic line, being priests of Judah as High-priests of the line of Ithamar. The promised eternal Highpriesthood of Rechabites in Judah, Ezechiel's uncircumcised Highpriests, to which Joshua or his

antagonist in the sanctuary may have belonged, probably were of the line of Ithamar. That youngest
surviving son of Aaron may by Moses have been set
over the Kenites of Jethro, and Ithamar's successors in
office may have represented the Highpriestly order of
the uncircumcised stranger in Israel.

This Highpriestly order of non-Hebrews in Israel,
of Rechabites and Essenes, we now venture to connect
with the order of Melchisedec. Since the ethnic
dualism in Israel, represented by Hebrews and naturalised strangers within the gate, had probably existed
already in the time of Abraham, it is reasonable to
assume that Moses recognised this dualism when he led
the ' mixed multitude ' out of Egypt. If so, to the fusion
of Hebrews and non-Hebrews, such as was exemplified
by the Kenites settling with the tribe of Judah, the independent Elohistic and Jehovistic narratives in the
Mosaic Scriptures may owe their origin, as also the two
chiefs of tribal tradition. According to this assumption, the lawgiver placed the two sons of Aaron respectively over the Hebrew and the non-Hebrew part of the
community.

From this it would not follow that all the members
of Highpriestly families were descended from the two
sons of Aaron. For, at all events, up to the time of
the Exodus there is no trace in the Mosaic Scriptures of
a priestly tribe or hereditary priesthood, but the eldest
son inherited from his father the priestly office. Thus
the men who offered sacrifices in the time of Moses are
called ' young men from the children of Israel,' and
Israel was ' a kingdom of priests and a holy people.'
The Israelites had not deputed their priestly duty to
representatives, and still less had given it up in favour
of a hereditary caste, such as the Levites are described
in the later Scriptures, called after Moses. Contrary to
these later regulations, the sons of David are called
priests, or Côhenîm, literally, those who approach God,

an expression which first occurs in the Bible in connection with the non-Hebrew priesthood of Melchisedec and Jethro. By the side of a Hebrew Levitical priesthood a non-Levitical one of the strangers in Israel seems to have existed, since the prophets Jeremiah and Ezechiel, and probably also the 110th Psalm, refer to it. Perhaps it is not a chance-coincidence that the name of Levi's eldest son, Gerson, refers to Ger the stranger. It becomes increasingly probable that Melchisedec, Jethro, Eli, and Joshua belonged to the order of the stranger in Israel, and that the same was presided over by the so-called sons of Ithamar since the time of Moses.

Upon such possibly historical basis Apollos has by a free allegorising of the texts built up his theory of the celestial Highpriesthood of Jesus, the Angel-Messiah. If James the brother of Jesus really had the privilege of entering the Holiest of the Holy with the golden plate of the Aaronites on his forehead, the two brothers of Davidic or non-Hebrew descent may have belonged, as we shall suggest, to one of the Highpriestly families of the strangers in Israel, to the so-called sons of Ithamar. John the Baptist or Essene, by his mother of Aaronite descent, may have belonged to the sons of Zadoc, which Highpriest was of the elder Aaronic line of Eleazar, after whom the Sadducees seem to have been called, who with the Essenes defended the rigid maintenance of the law.

Jesus opposed some doctrinal principles of John the Baptist; and the Sadducees, probably allied with the line of Eleazar, persecuted Jesus. His opposition to the Temple-services was all the more dangerous if he and his brother James stood by birth in connection with the rival line of Ithamar. This connection, though not improbable, cannot be insisted upon. Be this as it may, the theory of the celestial and eternal Highpriesthood of Jesus Christ stands and falls with the theory of an

Angel-Messiah. This theory was first applied to Jesus by Stephen the Hellenist, probably of Alexandria, where the Therapeuts had their settlements, and who certainly was an Essene or Therapeut, since no other Jews can be proved to have expected an Angel-Messiah. Paul became a convert to the Essenic doctrines of Stephen, and what Paul planted Apollos has watered.

We are therefore not surprised that Apollos in his Epistle has connected with the celestial Highpriesthood of Jesus the Paulinic doctrine about the atonement, which is the necessary consequence of the Essenic and Paulinic doctrine that God's Spirit was not in fallen humanity until the Angel-Messiah restored it. Apollos also regards the bloody sacrifices as types of the bloody sacrifice of Christ.

'The tabernacle is a parable,' or rather a type or symbol, 'for the time now present, according to which are offered both gifts and sacrifices having no power to perfect in conscience,' or, 'according to conscience, him that attendeth to the service of God.' These ordinances were imposed 'until the time of reformation.' For this reformation the Essenes had been preparing mankind, looking to the coming of the Angel-Messiah who should appear, and now had appeared as 'Highpriest of the good things to come.' As the Highpriest had to enter once every year into the Holiest of the Holy,[1] so Jesus 'entered once for all into the holy place, and obtained eternal redemption for us,' by entering 'through the greater and more perfect tabernacle, not made with hands, that is to say, not of this creation, nor yet through the blood of goats and calves, but through his own blood. For if the blood of goats and bulls, and ashes of an heifer sprinkling the defiled, sanctifieth to the purity of the flesh, how much more shall the blood of

---

[1] Possibly on the shortest or the longest day of the year, when the sun, symbol of Divine presence, may have thrown a ray of light on the tabernacle, as it throws a shadow on the altar at Stonehenge.

Christ, who through the eternal Spirit offered himself without fault to God, purge our consciences from dead works to serve the living God?' . . . 'It was therefore necessary that the symbol of the heavenly (sanctuary) should be purified with such (sacrifices), but the heavenly (sanctuary) itself with better sacrifices than (were) those. For Christ entered not into a holy place made with hands, the counterfeit of the true, but into heaven itself, now to appear before the face of God for us; nor yet that he may offer himself often, as the Highpriest entereth into the holy place every year with blood not his own; for then it would have been necessary for him to have suffered oftentimes since the foundation of the world; but now once at the end of the world hath he appeared for the putting away of sin by his sacrifice. And as it is appointed unto men once to die, but after that the judgment, so also Christ was sacrificed once, to take away the sins of many, and he shall appear a second time without sin to them that wait for him unto salvation.'

Apollos refers to the bloody sacrifices not having 'ceased to be offered' in the still existing Temple, though they had never been offered by the Essenes, and probably by all those who, like Jésus, attended only the service in the Synagogue. The Essenes claimed to have rightly foreseen that the Angel-Messiah would sanction the abolition of the bloody sacrifices, which were ordered by the law, and yet cannot 'take away sins,' as Apollos declares. Apollos interprets the Greek text of the 40th Psalm as containing a prophecy of the promised Messiah's protest against the bloody sacrifices. 'Burnt offering and sin-offering hast thou not required,' said David; instead of such a written commandment, God is said to have given him perforated ears or 'open ears' to hear the spiritual commandments of God. Thus he was enabled to say: 'Lo, I have come,' or 'here I am . . to do Thy will, O God, have I desired, as it is written for me in the volume of the book ; and thy law is within my heart.' These words of David are by Apollos explained, in harmony with the Septuagint, to refer to Messiah's coming ' into the world,' to the incarnation of the Angel, for whom God had 'prepared a body.'

With this altered text Paul's saying may be connected, that flesh and blood cannot inherit the kingdom of heaven. Only as an Angel become incarnate in a body especially prepared by God, as an Angel in whom is the ' Name ' or Spirit of God, could the Messiah come to do the will of God, that is, to take away the bloody sacrifices that he may establish the spiritual or self-sacrifice. It is by this human body exceptionally prepared by God for the Angel-Messiah ; it is ' through the offering of the body of Jesus Christ,' in pursuance of his self-sacrifice, and of God's will done, that ' we have been sanctified once for all.' By this ' one offering he hath perfected for ever them that are being sanctified.' Thus the spiritual covenant promised by Jeremiah has been fulfilled : God's law is written in the hearts and minds of men ; God will no more remember their sins and iniquities, but will abolish all ' offering for sin,' for Christ is ' the fulfilment of the law.'

The basis for this most eloquent and devout scheme of Jesus Christ's celestial Highpriesthood, and his sacrificial, atoning, and vicarious death, as presented to us in the Epistle to the Hebrews, whether written by Apollos, Barnabas, or by Paul, is not the body of the Scriptures or any part of them, but their systematic figurative interpretation. It was invented by the Essenic order at different times, and partly during the hundred and fifty years before the Christian era, when the Essenic order can be proved to have existed. This Essenic interpretation of Scripture had been introduced into non-orthodox Judaism for the purpose of connecting with the Law, the Prophets, and the Psalms the Eastern and Essenic conception of an Angel-Messiah. Of this

doctrine there is not a trace either in any of the
Scriptures possibly composed before the deportation to
Babylon, or in the first three Gospels.   The very ancient
and Eastern doctrine of an Angel-Messiah, (the first of
seven Angels ?) had been applied to Gautama-Buddha,
and so it was applied ·to Jesus Christ by the Essenes
of Egypt and of Palestine, who introduced this new
Messianic doctrine into Essenic Judaism and Essenic
Christianity.   But although the doctrine of the Angel-
Messiah, through the instrumentality of Magi and of
Kenites or Rechabites, of Parthians, Pythagoræans,
and Essenes, has been transplanted from the land of
Buddha and countries to which Buddhism had spread,
to the land promised to the seed of Abraham, yet no
attempt was made in the East to develop from the Veda
a theory of Buddha's sacrificial death.   Nor do Buddhistic Scriptures ever refer to or oppose such a doctrine as prevailing among Christians.   This is all the
more remarkable since vicarious sin-removing and reconciling human sacrifices at the time of the spring-
equinox, when the sun passes over the equinoctial
point, at the Passover, can be traced back in East and
West to pre-Abrahamitic times.

Conclusion.

We regard as proved, what Eusebius considered
'highly probable,' the direct connection of Paulinic
writings, especially of the Epistle to the Hebrews, with
Scriptures of the Therapeutic order.   The same may
be asserted with regard to the Septuagint and the
writings of Philo, although here the new doctrine of the
Angel-Messiah was only gradually revealed, and no expectation of his incarnation was referred to.   Following
in the footsteps of Stephen and Paul, the writer of the
Epistle to the Hebrews or Alexandrians, almost certainly Apollos, applies the Oriental doctrine of the

Angel-Messiah to Jesus Christ, as the end of the law and the bringer of a new dispensation. The non-Palestinian Essenes of Egypt and other countries insisted on their liberty to discard such of the injunctions of the Mosaic law as were derived from its literal interpretation. Apollos had been 'instructed in the way of the Lord' by disciples of John, and, like the latter, he looked forward to Him who should come to baptize with the Holy Ghost, to the Angel-Messiah. Like John the Baptist or Essene, and like Philo, Apollos did not at first believe that Jesus was the Christ. But since Aquila and Priscilla had taught him 'the way of God more accurately' than the disciples of John had done, he confuted in public the Jews and Essenes, 'showing by the Scriptures that Jesus is the Christ.'

In like manner Apollos, by his Epistle to the Jewish-Christian part of the Alexandrian Church, confuted the Jews who were 'dull of understanding' things 'difficult of interpretation.' They ought to have been 'long ago teachers,' but they 'again have need' to be taught 'the first principles of the oracles of God.' They 'have need of milk, not of solid food,' they are 'unskilled' or 'without experience' in the words 'of righteousness'; they are 'babes,' or, as Paul had said, 'babes in Christ,' that is, not spiritual but carnal men. The readers of this Epistle were in the position in which Apollos had been when 'he knew only the baptism of John,' and when he had probably not even heard that there is a Holy Ghost. But having learnt the way of God more perfectly, Apollos urges in this Epistle, the Hebrews of Alexandria to 'leave the elementary doctrines of Christ' and to 'turn to perfection.' He teaches, that for this perfection the law, in its literal interpretation, had done 'nothing,' that with the new faith the law has 'nothing to do,' that it is the faith of which Paul had said that it should be revealed after the law, as the end of the law.

To learn this difficult interpretation of the Scrip-

tures, to see that they point to the eternal and angelic
Word of God, to the eldest Son of God, and Highpriest of our confession, as Philo had already shown,
and, beyond this, to understand and believe that this
celestial Messiah or ' man from heaven,' the Angel who
followed the Israelites, as Paul said, has become incarnate in Jesus Christ, the Hebrews of Alexandria must
be taught the more perfect doctrine of Christ, the
deeper knowledge, the gnosis.   Did the Apostle James
acknowledge this interpretation of the law of Moses ?

CHAPTER IX.

JAMES AND THE ESSENES.

The Problem—The Herodians and the Essenes—The descent of James—
James the Nazarite and Highpriest—The Epistle of James.

The Problem.

THE history of James, 'the brother of the Lord,' is enveloped in darkness. When, and under what circumstances 'James, the servant of God and of the Lord Jesus Christ,' was placed over the Apostles at Jerusalem; in what sense he was called the brother of Jesus; whether it is probable that he was a Nazarite, and that he could enter the Holiest of the Holy; and finally, what causes led to his martyrdom, when a Rechabite priest was standing at his side, these are generally acknowledged problems. New difficulties seem at first sight to arise from the preceding arguments, which tend to show that Jesus opposed the principal doctrines of the Essenes, with whom the Rechabites and the institution of the Nazarite must be connected. Yet it may be possible from the Essenic stand-point to throw some light on the life of the Prince of the Apostles, so as not to increase, but to diminish, the difficulties which surround it.

The Herodians and the Essenes.

The family of the Herods from Idumæa was descended from the Edomites, therefore from those non-Israelites who joined the armies of Nebucadnezar when he besieged Jerusalem, and who, during the Captivity, had spread westwards from the eastern side of the valley of Arabah, and had even got possession of Hebron. Then Edom proper or Mount Seir, of which country, Esau's heritage, the Hebrews never possessed a foot-breadth up to the time of Joshua, was taken possession of by the Nabathæans, descendants from Nabaioth, the first-born of Ishmael, who was connected with Esau, in-habited Edom, and married a daughter of Ishmael. The Nabathæans of Arabia Petræa seem to have been con-nected with the Nabat of Mesopotamia, also called Cuthæans, and to have belonged to the Medo-Chaldæan race, to the Casdîm or conquerors, to the Medes of Berosus, who conquered Babylon in B.C. 2458. These Medes may already then have introduced Magian asceti-cism into Mesopotamia, and the combination of non-Iranian asceticism, and Iranian dualism, which the Essenes or Assidæans introduced into Judaism may be explained by the highly probable ethnic connection of the Essenes with the Casdîm, later Chaldæans (Nabat?) of Mesopotamia.[1] This hypothesis is confirmed by the connection of the Essenic prophet Elkesai with the Mesopotamian Sabians, Mendæans, or 'disciples of John,' of the Baptist or bather, the Ashai, Essai, or Essene.

The Herods came from a country which was alter-nately occupied by Edomites and Nabathæans; the former of whom had become possessed during the Babylonian Captivity of the country to the west of the

[1] The Essenes, Kenites, or Rechabites, who came from, and whose 'father' was Hamath, may be connected with the Jehovistic and Iranian non-Israelites, apparently connected with Hamath by Amos, who wrote, about B.C. 790, that in Juda and Samaria they would burn the bodies of Israelites, as the inhabitants of Jabesh-Gilead had done with the bodies of Saul and his son, whereupon they fasted seven days. (Amos vi. 1-14; 1 Sam. xxxi. 12, 13). Already the name of the city, Rechoboth, which Ashur (Nimrod) built, that is one of the four cities which formed Nineveh, must be connected with Rechab, and an aboriginal Hamath 'the great,' in Mesopotamia, (another name for Nineveh the great?) is possible, after which Hamath on the Orontes was called. (*Einheit der Religionen,* i. 217 f.)

Dead Sea, where the settlements of the Essenes were, where John the Baptist or Essene was born, and where he seems to have first baptized. The Nabathæans who took the place of the Edomites in the country of the Herods to the east of the Dead Sea, came from Mesopotamia, with which country we tried to connect the Essenes. The Nabathæans were in possession of Petra at least 300 years before the commencement of the Christian era, and thus about 150 years before the existence of the Essenic order is by Josephus referred to. Some of the Nabathæan princes bore the name Aretas, and this was the name of the father-in-law of Herod Antipas, who possessed Damascus at the time of Paul's conversion to the Essenic faith.

The probability of a sort of connection of the Herods with the Essenes is strengthened by the latter having been, as Assidæans, the allies of the Maccabees, with whom the Herods were connected by Herod the Great's wife Mariamne. The name Hasmon, ancestor of the Hasmonæans or Maccabees, points to the city of Hashmonah, a station of the Israelites near Mount Hor, which was on the boundary line of Edom. As the Herods were connected with the land of John the Baptist's or the Essene's birth and first activity, so Chasmon, like John's father Zacharias, of the priestly course of Abijah or Abia, belonged to the Aaronic line, since according to Josephus a citizen of Jerusalem and a priest ' of the sons of Joarib.' The Idumæans were conquered and converted to Judaism by the Maccabæan John Hyrcanus in B.C. 130, according to Josephus, who states that since that time they regarded Jerusalem as their mother-city, and claimed for themselves the name of Jews. Considering the probable ethnical connection between Essenes and Maccabees, whose allies the Assidæans were earlier than B.C. 143, it may be assumed that the Essenes and Idumæans were a cognate race.

According to later Jewish tradition, Herod the Great

was successively the servant of the Hasmonæans and the Romans.[1] The probability gains ground that the Herodians were connected with the Essenes or Assidæans, the allies of the Maccabees, for political reasons, if not also for reasons of descent.

The Herods aimed at independence from the Romans as well as from the Jews. To them religion was only a policy, and they furthered the establishment of a universalist religion of the Hellenistic (Therapeutic) type, such as the Maccabees and the Gentile-excluding Essenes of Palestine had tried to prevent by a zealous adherence to the law. But the son of a Maccabæan mother, Herod Agrippa I., forsook the idolatry of his father, and was a strict observer of the law. Thus the Essenes of Judæa could look up to him, and they would support him in his determined policy against those universalist Hellenists, some of whom were Therapeuts, like Stephen and Paul. These particularist Essenes may have formed the party of the Herodians, which is not mentioned by Luke or by Josephus, but which in the Apostolic age was, like the Essenes, distinguished from the Sadducean and Pharisaic party. The Herodians joined the Pharisees in questioning Jesus whether it was right to pay tribute to Cæsar, and Jesus is recorded to have warned his hearers against the leaven of the Pharisees and of Herod.

It may be asserted that the zealot Herod Agrippa I., of half-Maccabæan descent, who encouraged Jews to take the Nazarite vow, was friendly to those Essenes who adhered to the law and who rejected the Gentiles without the law, but that he persecuted the universalist Essenes or Therapeuts, to whom Stephen and Paul belonged. It was during the reign of Herod Agrippa, probably in the first year of his terrorism and of the persecution which arose because of Stephen, that James ' the brother of the Lord ' was placed above the

---

[1] Jost, *Geschichte des Judenthums*, 319.

Apostles at Jerusalem. It is almost certain that this elevation took place in the year 41, on the death of James the brother ?of Zebedee, whom Agrippa had caused to be beheaded, and when Peter was imprisoned. For when the latter, after his miraculous deliverance, left in the night Jerusalem ' for another place' (Rome?), Peter sent a message to ' James and the brethren.'

The Descent of James.

Paul testifies that three years after his conversion he saw at Jerusalem James ' the brother of the Lord.' Only in two passages the word ' brother' is in the Bible used in its wider sense. Abraham the Hebrew and Lot the Moabite are called brothers, and the same is said of Israel and the Edomites. In all other passages the word ' brother' refers to a brother in the flesh. In accordance with this meaning, the Gospel after Matthew refers to the brothers of Jesus and to the sons of his mother Mary by giving their names, James, Joseph, Simon, and Jude, and it is added that Jesus had also sisters. Confirming the only possible inter-pretation of this passage, it is asserted as well in Matthew as in Luke, that Jesus was the ' firstborn' son of Mary, as if she had other children; and in the first three Gospels ' his mother and his brethren' are in such a manner named in conjunction with Jesus, that his brothers must necessarily be regarded as sons of his mother.[1] It is therefore not necessary to dwell on the impossibility of the assumption that two sisters had the same name, which would be without precedent in Israelitic history. According to the Gospel after Matthew it is absolutely certain that Mary was the mother of Jesus and of other children. Yet there is a passage in Mark which is absolutely irreconcilable with the above passages and their evident meaning.

[1] Matt. xiii. 55, 56, i. 25, xii. 46, 47; Mark iii. 31; Luke ii. 7.

Mary the mother of Jesus is distinguished from Mary
the mother of James the Less and of Joses.[1] Two
sisters are here supposed to have been called Mary, and
to have inhabited the same house at Capernaum and
Jerusalem, and yet the names of the two sons of the
one correspond with those of the two elder sons of the
other.   It is needless to consider such absurdity.

Discarding the tradition recorded in Mark as not
possibly historical, and seeing that Mary was the mother
of other children than Jesus her firstborn, it is of but
secondary importance to enquire whether Jesus alone
was held to be the son of Joseph the carpenter, or
whether the brothers and sisters of Jesus had likewise
Joseph for their father.   Whilst Eusebius writes that
James was called the brother of the Lord ' because he
also (like Jesus) was called son of Joseph,' Epiphanius
designates James as the son of Joseph by a previous
marriage.   By the latter statement it is implied that
Jesus cannot have been the only son of Joseph, though
he might possibly have been the only son of Mary.
Both Eusebius and Epiphanius agree that James was
the son of Joseph, and the Gospel after Matthew refers
to a James and Joseph and Simon and Jude, as brothers,
and to sisters of Jesus, as children of Joseph and Mary.
We saw that an attempt was sooner or later made in
the Gospel after Mark to distinguish the mother of
Jesus from the mother of his brothers and sisters.   For
this there was the obvious reason that the supposed
Angel-Messiah, like Gautama-Buddha, must be considered to have been born of a virgin.   In like manner
an attempt was made, no doubt for the same reason, to
undermine the tradition about James and Jesus being
brothers in the flesh.   The earliest Fathers who mystify
the descent of James are Chrysostom (born 347) and
Theodoret (bishop since 420), who designate him as
son of Alphæus (Cleophas). Both originally belonged to

[1] Mark xv. 40; comp. Eus. *H. E.*,ii. 1.

the Antiochian Church, which we have connected with the Essenes. Since they believed that Jesus was the Angel-Messiah, the Essenes probably denied that he had brothers and sisters, as Buddhists did about Gautama.

The third and the fourth Gospels can be shown to be the principal records of Essenian tradition, and in them alone the name of Clopas or Cleophas occurs. The name of one of the two disciples of Emmaus was Cleophas, and the name of his companion is not given. Paul refers to an apparition of the risen Jesus to James the brother of the Lord, and as no reference is made in any Gospel to this apparition, whilst Luke and the later revisor of the third Gospel was the most likely Evangelist to supply this omission, we are at the outset led to the possibility, that James was intended to have been the companion of Cleophas or Alphæus by the composer of the narrative of the disciples of Emmaus. We have seen that this narrative, which Luke cannot have written, is certainly not historical in the form transmitted to us. The question has now become one of secondary interest whether the inventor of the narrative about the disciples of Emmaus intended to suggest that James was the nameless companion of Cleophas. The tradition transmitted by Jerome as recorded in the Gospel of the Hebrews indirectly confirms this narrative by transmitting the legend that James fasted after the crucifixion till the risen Jesus appeared to him and bade him eat. This tradition as well as the probably identical one about the apparition of Jesus to James according to Paul, is not confirmed by any Gospel-record, unless James was the unnamed disciple of Emmaus, and it is possible that the composer of this fictitious narrative intended to suggest this.

Every explanation hitherto attempted of the irreconcilable statements in the Gospels about the descent of James, ' the brother of the Lord,' leads to forced and to improbable, if not impossible, assumptions. If it can be

proved that Eusebius was right in considering it
'highly probable' that our Gospels, like the Pauline
Epistles, were composed under direct Essenic influence
and in harmony with written Essenic tradition, all
passages which refer directly or indirectly to an exclusively supernatural birth of Jesus, whether or not in
the writings in question he is recognised as the Angel-
Messiah, will have to be connected with this source.
Among these passages we reckon the isolated statement in Matthew about the virgin-born, to which
Clement of Alexandria does not refer, as if the text did
not then contain it, when he declares, as already
shown, that the views of some about the virginity of
Mary, the mother of Jesus, were not founded in fact.
With these additions must be connected all the passages in the Gospels which imply that another Mary
than the mother of Jesus was the mother of his
brothers and sisters.

James the Nazarite and Highpriest.

According to the Acts, the leader of the Apostles
was Peter, and he remained in this position for some
time after the crucifixion of Jesus, and probably till he
was imprisoned by Herod Agrippa, we suggest as
early as in the year 41. We saw that there are good
reasons for assuming that in the sixth year after the
death of Jesus, or about a year later, James took the
place of Peter. For when this Apostle, miraculously
liberated, left Jerusalem for another place, he requested
the disciples whom he had found gathered together in
the house of Mark's mother, to inform ' James and the
brethren ' of his escape. Whilst Peter was absent from
Jerusalem, perhaps in Rome,[1] Paul was in Arabia, that
is, in the East Jordan country, and they both met at
Jerusalem after three years, that is, after the death of

[1] See *Chronology of the Bible.*

Herod Agrippa I., who had ruled three years. Thus it becomes probable that the three years which Paul spent in Arabia, and Peter possibly in Rome, coincided with the three years' government of Herod. What happened at Jerusalem during the mysterious fifteen days when Paul abode with Peter, we know not, but Paul says that he also saw James, 'the Lord's brother.' In the same Epistle he mentions James before Cephas and John, when referring to their being regarded as 'pillars.' There can be no doubt that James was placed at the head of the Apostles ever since Peter's imprisonment, and he maintained that position for more than a quarter of a century, up to his martyrdom.

We know not for what reason James the brother of John was beheaded, and why Peter was put into prison. It is quite possible, as we pointed out, that this was owing to their opposition to the Temple-service with its sacrifices, and to their frequenting exclusively the anti-hierarchical synagogues, as Jesus had always done. This example had even been followed by some of the Pharisees, although the rigid maintainers of the law, the Sadducees, never attended the synagogue. Son of a Maccabæan mother, Agrippa would aim at the restoration of the Temple-services as the exclusive form of Jewish devotion. Herod the Great, his father, had been too lax in this respect, and had encouraged idolatry of the grossest kind. Supported by the Sadducees, who had persecuted Jesus and his disciples, we may safely assume that Agrippa I. insisted on the regular attendance of the Apostles at the Temple-services. For it is a recorded fact, that they were regularly in the Temple at the time of prayer. Thus they ceased to follow the example of their Master. Although the Apostles were not scattered during the persecution which arose because of Stephen, they were in fact included in this persecution; but it seems to have been soon stopped for two reasons, because the second

Agrippa was more friendly to them, and because they regularly attended the Temple-services, which Jesus had never done. This is what all Nazarites did ; and as Nazarite James, the brother of Jesus, could offer to Agrippa I., the reported friend of the Nazarites, every guarantee which he must have been desirous to obtain.

The traditions respecting James which have been transmitted by Hegesippus, the first Jewish-Christian, and possibly Essenic-Christian Church-historian, if we could safely regard them all as historical, would be important, because his parents were contemporaries of the Prince of the Apostles, and because, as Eusebius says, Hegesippus stood nearest to the days of the Apostles. According to this tradition James had been called the Just or Zadik 'from the time of the Lord to our own days, . . he was holy from his mother's womb, he drank not wine or strong drink, nor did he eat animal food ; a razor came not upon his head, he did not anoint himself with oil, he did not use the bath; he alone might go into the holy place, for he wore no woollen clothes but linen ; and alone he used to go into the Temple, and there he was commonly found upon his knees, praying for forgiveness for the people, so that his knees grew dry and thin (hard ?) like a camel's, from his constantly bending them in prayer, and entreating forgiveness for the people.' [1] We shall point out why James 'alone' went into the Holiest of the Holy, whilst, contrary to the custom of his brother Jesus, all the Apostles regularly attended the daily services in the Temple. We may regard these statements as equally historical, and as throwing light on the early relations between Judaism and Christianity.

Of the remaining account it is here sufficient to state that the martyrdom of James in the presence of ' one of the priests of the house of Rechab,' (priests of

[1] Eus. *H. E.* ii. 23.

the Essenes), took place in consequence of his having declared in the Temple, that ' Jesus the Son of Man sits in heaven on the right hand of great power, and will come on the clouds of heaven.' By this declaration, if he made it, James proclaimed the Essenic and Paulinic faith in his brother Jesus as the Angel-Messiah. This Essenic Christianity is said to have been proclaimed openly in the Temple by James at the time of the Passover, immediately before the Romans laid siege to Jerusalem. Hegesippus states that ' many were convinced, and gave glory on the testimony of James, crying Hosannah to the Son of David.' Whereupon the Scribes and Pharisees stoned James to death.

Since Hegesippus does not censure the conduct of James in proclaiming the Essenic and Rechabite doctrine of the Angel-Messiah, applied to Jesus, as Stephen and Paul had done, we have sufficient reason to regard Hegesippus as an Essenic or Paulinic Christian, and to doubt his transmitted testimony that James believed his brother Jesus to have been an incarnate Angel. But there is no reason to doubt that some of the Rechabites, Nazarites like James, would sympathise with his death, though he had not proclaimed Jesus as the Angel-Messiah, which Hegesippus says he did, almost in the very words of Stephen. If Hegesippus believed in Jesus as the Angel-Messiah, he would see the importance of attributing that doctrine to James the brother of Jesus, and of describing him as stoned to death, like Stephen, as a supposed blasphemer.

Discarding this tradition of Hegesippus, it may be regarded as not improbable that James was a Nazarite for life, and thus stood in near relation to the Essenes, with whom we must connect the Rechabites. According to their descent both James and Jesus were connected with the naturalised strangers in Israel, with the Rechabites and Kenites, and thus almost certainly with the Essenes, who were probably descendants of the

Medo-Chaldæans. Jesus opposed the principal doctrines
of the Essenes, especially that about the Angel-Messiah.
He was an Essenic reformer, and not a Nazarite. The
Pharisees were Iranians, like the Essenes, Rechabites,
and Kenites, according to our ethnic scheme. If so, the
Pharisees knew the mixed Indian and Iranian or Magian
doctrines which the Essenes propounded, as well as
those purer doctrines of the East-Iranians or of
Zoroaster, which Jesus proclaimed by word and deed.
The condemnation of Jesus, not by the Sadducees but
by the Pharisees, would be thus accounted for.

The connection between Rechabites or Kenites and
Essenes, apart from their probably cognate descent,
enables us to consider as possibly historical the statement of Hegesippus, according to which he could, like
a Highpriest, enter the Holiest of the Holy. This
account is confirmed by Epiphanius, who states, on the
authority of Clement, Eusebius, and others, that James
' the son of Joseph ' was permitted to wear on his forehead the golden plate with the words ' Holiness to the
Lord,' or ' Holy Jehovah.' This statement is again confirmed by the tradition transmitted by Polycrates and
credited by Eusebius, that also the Apostle John, son
of Zebedee, possessed this privilege of the Aaronites.
The same tradition refers to the unnatural death of the
two sons of Zebedee, that of John being also testified by
a recently found fragment of Papias, probably the
bishop of Hierapolis.[1] The two remarkable statements
may therefore be regarded as probably historical, that
James could enter the Holiest of the Holy, like a Highpriest, and that he possessed also the Highpriestly and
Aaronic privilege of wearing the golden plate or Petalon
described by Josephus, who says that the identical one
made in the times of Moses existed at his time. It may
be possible from the Essenic or Rechabite point of view

---

[1] Epiph. *Hær.* xxix. 4, lxxviii. 14 ; Eus. *H. E.* v. 24 ; comp. Scholten,
Der Apostel Johannes ; Holtzmann, *Bibel-Lexikon*, iii. 383.

to throw some new light on the highpriestly character attributed to the Prince of the Apostles.

It is necessary to repeat what we have pointed out about the two Highpriests in Israel and about their probable connection with the two Aaronic lines, if not with the political parties of the Sadducees and the Pharisees, the latter of which was not so ancient as the party of the Essenes or Rechabites.

Jeremiah had in the Name of God promised to the Rechabites or strangers in Israel an uninterrupted standing before the Lord, that is, a succession of Highpriests of the sons of Rechab, who should officiate in the Holiest of the Holy. At the time of the Return from Babylon Ezechiel complains, that Israel has brought into God's sanctuary strangers uncircumcised in heart and in the flesh, to be in God's sanctuary 'to pollute it, even my house when ye offer my bread, the fat and the blood.'[1] This can only refer to a Highpriest representing the uncircumcised stranger in the Holiest of the Holy, in harmony with the prophecy of Jeremiah, the fulfilment of which Ezechiel clearly condemns in the Name of the same God who had commanded Jeremiah to make that solemn promise. Ezechiel seems to imply that the junior Aaronic line of Ithamar had been admitted to represent the Highpriesthood of the naturalised stranger in Israel, of the Gêr, who, as distinguished from the foreigner or Nokhri, was admitted, like the Hebrew, to the Temple-services. For Ezechiel states that the sons of Zadoc only, who belonged to the elder Aaronic line of Eleazar, and who had stood by David during Absalom's rebellion, that they shall 'stand before' God, that is, appear as Highpriests in the Holiest of the Holy. At the time of Zerubbabel, when Ezechiel wrote, the prophet Zechariah approved in the Name of God everything that was done by Zerub-

---

[1] Jer. xxxv. 18, 11 ; Ezek. xliv. 7–31 ; *Einh. der Rel.* i. 288–312.

babel and Joshua.[1] The latter may have belonged to the Aaronic line of Ithamar, which name is a compound of Jah, and Thamar 'the stranger,' according to Philo.

The remarkable omission of the generations of the line of Ithamar in the Book of Chronicles, whilst those of the line of Eleazar are twice mentioned, can hardly be otherwise explained than by the assumption that these two lines of Aaronites represented respectively the ethnic dualism in Israel, the Hebrew and the non-Hebrew or the stranger, who seems to have been uncircumcised from the statement made by Ezechiel about uncircumcised Highpriests in the Holiest of the Holy. This dualism is in so far confirmed by Scripture-accounts, as the Aaronites of the elder line had their possessions exclusively in Benjamin, the junior line exclusively in Juda, with which tribe the Kenites or Recha-bites were united ever since the time of Joshua. The Kenites of Jethro had been invited by Moses to join the 'mixed multitude' which went out of Egypt, and according to the Book of Chronicles both Eleazar and Ithamar 'executed the priest's office.' Again, in the time of Saul, the Benjamite, the elder line sided with him, the younger line with David; and if Abiathar had not escaped from the massacre at Nob, all the members of the line of Ithamar would have been killed. David made peace between the apparently rival Aaronic lines by establishing the double Highpriesthood of Abiathar and Zadok.

Such a double Highpriesthood seems to have been appointed after the Return from Babylon. For at that time Ezechiel complained of the uncircumcised High-priest in the Holiest of the Holy, and Zechariah de-scribes Joshua and Satan or the adversary, as if the second Highpriest, standing before the Lord in the

---

[1] We have already referred to Joshua's having probably composed the 110th Psalm, which seems to refer to Jeremiah's promise to the Rechabites, perhaps first fulfilled by Joshua's Highpriesthood.

Holiest of the Holy. In the time immediately preceding the accession of James to the leadership of the Apostles, the double Highpriesthood is testified by the Gospel-records. Luke mentions Annas and Caiaphas as contemporaneous Highpriests, and he connects Annas as well as Caiaphas with others who were ' of the kindred of the high priest.' It cannot be doubted that among these a second bore the title of Highpriest, since ' the Highpriests ' are said to have demanded the crucifixion of Jesus. Before the deportation to Babylon Zephaniah was joined as ' second priest ' to Seraiah, ' the first priest,' both of whom were slain at Riblah. We are justified in assuming that either Caiaphas or Annas was in a similar sense the second Highpriest, who, according to Rabbinical traditions, was the Sagan. The position of James at the head of the Apostles is described as one similar to that of the Highpriest. As Highpriest James would have the privilege of entering the Holiest of the Holy and of wearing the Aaronic gold plate on his forehead.[1] Assuming that James really had these privileges, we should be driven to the further assumption that the family of Joseph, the father of Jesus and James, was one of those from the members of which the Highpriests were chosen. We should have to assume the same about the family of Zebedee.

If the brother of Jesus and Prince of the Apostles, whose life bridges over almost the entire Apostolic period, not only went with the other Apostles to the Temple at the hour of prayer, contrary to the custom of Jesus, but if James also entered the Holiest of the Holy with the Aaronic mark on his forehead, whether or not he belonged to one of the Highpriestly families, an important connection of the first Christian Bishop with the Jewish Highpriesthood, the amalgamation of both institutions would thereby be confirmed.

[1] Luke iii. 2 ; Acts iv. 6 ; John xviii. 15, 16 ; comp. 2 Kings xv. 18 ; xxiii. 4 ; Acts xxi. 17, 18 ; xxiii. 2, 5.

The Epistle of James.

Two arguments have been raised against the James of this Epistle being the first Christian Bishop. The statement of Hegesippus is not relied upon, that 'immediately' after the martyrdom of James 'Vespasian invaded and took Judæa,' and the year 62 is preferred for his martyrdom on the strength of a passage in Josephus, although it is on good grounds regarded as a late interpolation. Since this Epistle unmistakably refers to the Epistle to the Hebrews and to the Apocalypse of the year 68–69, this Epistle could not have been written by ' the brother of the Lord ' if he died in 62. This conclusion has been supported by the assumption that the statement of the poor being drawn before the judgment seats by the rich refers to a general persecution of Christians by those rich who were outside of Christianity, by the Romans, which cannot be proved to have taken place before Trajan.[1] We do not accept either argument, and regard the Apostle James as the author of this Epistle.

Indirectly connected with the Essenes as a Nazarite, though not an actual member of the Essenic body in Palestine, James defends the strict keeping of the Law, including the exclusion of Gentiles, of whose admission he says nothing, against the figurative interpretation of the Law, as practised by the Essenes or Therapeuts of Egypt, and against their illegal principle of universality. A regard for peace, and for the high position gained by Paul, causes James not to mention Paul by name, but his principal doctrines are unsparingly opposed. Paul having referred to the temptation to commit idolatry, without denouncing the eating of things sacrificed to idols, and having expressed the glory of Christians in ' tribulations,' James also advises the brethren to count it all joy when they fall ' into divers temptations,' yet points not, like Paul, to ' hope,' but to the ' perfect

[1] Hilgenfeld, l.c., 520 542.

work.' The temptations come from within, and they can be resisted. For ' of his own will ' the Father of Lights, the source of every good and perfect gift, has begotten ' us,' the Israel of the twelve tribes, including the Christians as in the Apocalypse, ' with the word of truth, that we should be a kind of firstfruit of his creatures.' [1]

Already Moses had said that ' the Word ' is in the Israelite that he may do it ; and referring to this passage, or to a ' Scripture ' not transmitted to us, James writes : ' The Spirit that he placed in us zealously (urgingly) desireth us,' prompts us, or demands of us. It is the ' Name ' or Spirit, or Word of God, which is in the Israelite as in the Angel of the Lord. Thus Israel, ' the firstborn of nations,' was always destined to be a kind of firstfruit of God's creatures. But Paul had regarded this passage in the Mosaic Scriptures as a prophecy that Jesus would be ' raised from the dead ' as the ' end of the law,' as the Son of God ' according to the spirit of holiness,' as the restorer of the Spirit or Word of God, through whose death came ' the free gift ' of God, ' the promised Spirit through faith'. That faith should be revealed after the law, which latter has nothing to do with faith. The law cannot justify, and enables man to serve only ' in the oldness of the letter,' not ' in the newness of the Spirit,' or in the new created being of the Spirit, ' as a new creature.' The restorer of the Spirit of God, which was not ' always to strive with man,' has been raised from the dead as ' the firstfruits of them that sleep.' This new doctrine, connected by Paul with the type of the firstling sheaf and thus with the resurrection of Jesus as the first fruits on ' the third day according to the Scriptures,' James opposes by his doctrine of ' the firstfruit of God's creatures.' Thus he denies the new dispensation of Paul's Christianity, together with any theory about the visible resurrection of Jesus, on which, as on

[1] James i. 2–17; 1 Cor. x. 13; Rom. v. 3–5; James i. 17, 18.

the atonement, the Epistle observes a mysterious silence.
Not the sacrificial death of a crucified Angel-Messiah,
but the implanted, or ' the engrafted Word,' of which
Moses spoke as then already at work in Israel, if not in
mankind, is able to ' save ' the soul.[1]

' The word of truth,' which God has implanted in
Israel alone, or, at least, of which only Israel is conscious, cannot make man a firstfruit of God's creatures
unless that word is done as well as heard. That inner
voice, coming from without, produces conscience, the ark
in which ' the law of liberty ' has been deposited, which
shall judge the elect. Man is to be ' a doer of work,'
and if he is prompted to do it by the Wisdom from
above, he will be ' blessed in his deed.' No ' faith ' can
save him. ' A man may say: Thou (Paul) hast faith,
and I have works, show me thy faith without works,
and I will show thee faith from my works.' Having
shown that ' faith without works is dead,' and taking
no cognisance of Paul's recommending ' faith which
worketh by love,' James opposes Paul's scriptural authority for his doctrine of justification by faith. Paul
had said that faithful Abraham's belief in God, not any
work of his, ' was reckoned to him for righteousness.'
For the works of the law placed man ' under a curse,'
which continued till ' Christ redeemed us from the curse
of the law, having become a curse for us,' which was
necessary ' that we might receive the promised Spirit
through faith.' Apollos had followed in the same strain,
and designated the offering of Isaac, and Rahab's reception of the spies as a deed prompted by faith. But
James insists that Abraham was ' justified by works
when he offered Isaac,' and so, likewise Rahab, ' when
she received the messengers and thrust them forth
another way.' The Epistle of James is a protest against
the Paulinic doctrine, that it is impossible to be ' under

[1] Deut. xxx. 11-20; Rom. x. 4-21; Gal. iii. 13, 14; vi. 15, 2 Cor.
v. 17; 1 Cor. xv. 4, 20.

the law' and yet to be 'led by the Spirit.' The Prince of the Apostles denies that the Spirit of God has not been in Israel till Christ's death restored it to the faithful in mankind. The great lawgiver had said that the Word is in man that he may do it.[1]

James implies that the implanted 'Word,' the real Saviour, is identical with the 'Wisdom' which 'descends from above,' as also with the 'Spirit' which God made to dwell in us. Thus the Apostle clearly opposes Paul's doctrine that the Word of God, which already Philo designated as a premundane person and second Deity, that 'the man from heaven,' the Angel of God who had followed the Israelites, had become incarnate in Jesus. Yet he calls him 'our Lord Jesus Christ, the Lord of glory.' Standing on the rock of Peter's confession, James regards his brother as the man whom God has anointed or made Christ 'with the Holy Ghost and with power,' and in this sense as 'the Son of the living God.' Not the Lord Jesus Christ, but 'the Lord' and 'the Judge,' God, was expected soon to come.'[2]

The Chrestus-party among the Jews in Rome, to which Simon Magus the 'Christian' seems to have belonged, shows that the name of Christians, which had originated in Antioch, the centre of Simon's activity, was used soon after the accession of James to the Apostleship. Yet it is doubtful whether he acknowledges even indirectly the designation of the disciples of Jesus as Christians, when he refers to that 'beautiful name' by which the scattered Israelites are called, whom he addresses, and among whom he includes the disciples of Jesus Christ. It is customary to connect this passage with the Name of God by which Israel was called.[3] Even if this could be proved, it might be explained by the 'Name' as the Spirit or Word of God, which is in

---

[1] Rom. iv.; Gal. iii.; comp. Hebrews x. 8–10, 17–31; James ii.
[2] James i. 1; ii. 1; v. 7–11.
[3] Deut. xxviii. 10; 2 Chron. vii. 17; Jer. xiv. 9, xv. 16; Am. ix. 12.

the Angel and in the Israelites. But James seems to refer to the name of ' brethren,' as which he regards all Israelites, rich or poor, whether Hebrews or Grecians, whether disciples of Jesus or not. The poor or the Ebionite was an early designation of the followers of Jesus, some of whom continued in the fourth century to call themselves Nazaræans, and did not acknowledge Paul. The rich, wearing gay clothing, were admitted to better seats in the ' synagogue' than the poor ; they were despised, and yet Jesus had preached the Gospel to the poor.

The Epistle which Peter addressed to James from Rome, according to the Clementine Homilies, corresponds with the injunction in the Recognitions, not to accept any teacher who had not brought a testimonial from James. ' The chief of the Jews ' at Rome, who connected Paul with ' a sect everywhere spoken against ' (the Essenes), declared that they had not received ' letters out of Judæa concerning him.' The additional statement, that none of the brethren that came had showed or spoken ' any harm ' of him, is a contradiction to what precedes it, and must be regarded as a later addition, made in harmony with the fundamental principle of the Acts, the non-recognition of two antagonistic parties in the early Church. It is hardly a chance-coincidence that James in his Epistle complains that there were ' many teachers ' in Israel, wise men ' endowed with knowledge,' but not with ' meekness,' who had ' bitter envying and ribaldry ' in their heart, who boasted and lied ' against the truth,' whose wisdom descends not from above, and who did not ' work peace.' These teachers, even if authorised by James, as Paul had been by the Twelve, to preach among the scattered tribes of Israel, had not carried out their mission as James wished. Paul makes a similar charge.[1]

The acknowledged Essenic colouring of this Epistle

[1] James iii. 1, 13–18; Recog. iv. 35; Phil. i. 15–18.

is shown by James's recommendation to be 'swift to hear, slow to speak, slow to wrath,' by his prohibition of swearing, his warning against riches, and against the blemishing influences of 'the world.' Although only connected with the Essenic system as a Nazarite, yet, like the Essenes, James was a stranger in Israel, and must have known the Essenic-Buddhistic tradition. It cannot possibly be a mere chance-coincidence that James refers to 'the wheel of birth,' identical with the Buddhistic expression of 'the wheel of life and death,' that is, the cycle of births and deaths, or the soul's transmigrations.[1] James was by the Initiated understood to say, that the tongue, set on fire by hell, inflames the whole body, even of future generations.

The Epistle of James proves, that up to the time of Judæa's invasion by the Romans, the chief of the Apostles, probably the Jewish Highpriest, and first Christian Bishop, recognised no difference between the Jews and the followers of Jesus, and did not acknowledge the cardinal doctrines of Paul, which we have connected with those of the Essenic, universalist, and law-undermining Therapeuts.

In what connection stood the Essenic tradition to the Gnosis of the Apostolic and of the after-Apostolic age?

---

[1] James iii. 6; comp. p. 34 n. 2; The wheel, Gilgul in Hebrew and in Chaldee, is in the Talmud used: 1) in connection with the resurrection of Jews dying in foreign lands, like Jacob (Gen. xlvii. 30), which is connected with the motion of a subterranean wheel, an evidently Eastern conception; 2) when discussing the question whether the planets rotate round their axis or round the fixed stars; 3) as a figurative expression of the changes of man's destiny. *Kethubot*, 111; *Pesachim*, 94; *Sabbath*, 151. (Communicated by Dr. Leopold Seligmann.)

CHAPTER X.

THE GNOSIS.

Essenic Scriptures—Retrospect.

Essenic Scriptures.

THE deeper knowledge or Gnosis of the Essenes, their secret tradition of Eastern origin, which they connected with the Scriptures of Moses by a figurative interpretation of the latter, has been generally accepted by the Targumim, but rejected in essential points by the Talmud. Applied to Jesus, this gnosis was promulgated by Stephen, Paul, and Apollos, in the universalist or Therapeutic form. Paul opposes in his Epistle to the Colossians the gnosis of the separatist Essenes, with their aristocratic initiation, their asceticism, and their doctrine of more than One Angelic mediator. ' All the fulness ' dwelt by God's pleasure in the incarnate Word of God, the Angel who followed the Israelites, and in whom is the Name, Spirit, or Word of God. He is 'the Christ, even Jesus the Lord,' whom Paul does not connect with other Arch-Angels, as was done a few years later in the Apocalypse of ' John.' It has been sagaciously suggested by a high authority that the above cited words of Paul may point ' to the distinction of the heavenly Christ from the earthly Jesus,' which doctrine was taught by Cerinthus, his junior contemporary.[1]

Paul and Apollos regarded the deeper knowledge or gnosis as eternally existing in heaven, as known to, but hidden by Moses, and as first fully revealed by the preachers of ' the hidden wisdom,' under the especial

[1] Bishop Lightfoot, *Colossians* (ii. 6), p. 112.

guidance of Jesus Christ, the Angel-Messiah or Wisdom of God who had sent all the prophets. If the doctrine of the Angel-Messiah was the starting-point of the gnosis, and if Jesus has not recognised the doctrine of the Angel-Messiah, thån he must be regarded as having opposed the gnosis, which was supposed to have been revealed by the Angel-Messiah. From this it follows, that if Jesus made known mysteries to his disciples, though he spoke to the people only in parables, suggesting but not defining the truth, the 'mysteries of the kingdom of heaven,' made known by him to the Twelve only, cannot have referred to the doctrine of the Angel-Messiah. The silence on this doctrine in all Scriptures of the Old Testament possibly written before the Exile, and in the first three Gospels, leaves no doubt as to the relation of Jesus to the Essenic gnosis, even to that form of it which was preached by Paul and Apollos.

The Book of Daniel.—We regard as proved that this Scripture, as transmitted to us, was not completed before the times of the Maccabees, probably in B.C. 164, whose allies, the Assidæans, we have connected with the Essenes and thus with the Rechabites, who were exported with other Israelites to Babylon. The Scriptures distinguish two Daniels, if not three: the Daniel to whom Ezechiel refers at the time when Jerusalem was besieged (588–584); the prophet Daniel who was exported to Babylon; and Daniel the priest of the line of Ithamar, who in 515 signed the covenant at Jerusalem.[1] But if the mission of Ezra took place in the reign of the 'Artaxerxes' Darius Hystaspes, Daniel the priest can have been identical with Daniel the prophet. This identity is asserted by the Septuagint and by the Mohammedan tradition, according to which Daniel the prophet returned to Judæa, and it is indirectly implied by the Book of Daniel, in which the three companions of Daniel

---

[1] *The Chronology of the Bible,* 61–66.

are mentioned among those who returned to Jerusalem. Indeed, they could be all four alive in 520 if they had been exported to Babylon in 588, or even in the year 608, the third year of Jehoiakim. Then no siege of Jerusalem by Nebucadnezar, whether Crownprince or King, can be proved to have taken place, whilst statements in the Book of Jeremiah seem to exclude the possibility of such a siege.[1]

Daniel the prophet was exported to Babylonia contemporaneously with the Rechabites, who shared the captivity of the Hebrews, according to the superscription of the 71st Psalm in the Septuagint version, where the Psalm is designated as dedicated to David of (by) the sons of Jonadab 'the first of the captives.' The Targum confirms this. These Rechabites or Kenites, who had declared to Jeremiah that they had always been strangers or non-Hebrews in Israel, and to whom a priesthood for ever had been promised, we have tried to connect with the Medo-Chaldæans, the Chasdîm or conquerors, who conquered Mesopotamia about 500 years before Abraham's birth. It is in the language and wisdom of these Iranian Chaldæans, whom the Book of Daniel identifies with the Magi, or priests of the Medes, that young Daniel was brought up. The highly probable connection of Rechabites and Essenes, if not their identity, increases the importance of the probable non-Hebrew and Davidic descent of Daniel the prophet, who bore the name of David's second son, of his initiation, after three years of ascetic discipline, into the mysteries of the Chaldæans or Magi, and of his being set over all the wise men of Babylon. The connection between Daniel and the Magi, and between Essenian and Magian rites renders it highly probable that the Rechabites, Assidæans and Essenes after the Captivity transmitted the Eastern wisdom of which

---

[1] Jer. xxxvi. 1, 9, 29; comp. xxv. 1, 2, and our further remarks.

Daniel had been the principal organ during the Captivity. This connection of Daniel with the Essenes is confirmed by the doctrinal contents of the Book of Daniel.

We saw that the Essenes must at all times have expected an Angel-Messiah, which doctrine, contained in the Book of Daniel, cannot be proved by any ancient Scripture to have prevailed in Israel. As presumably among the Essenes, so in the Book of Daniel we find a fully developed doctrine of Angels, of which there is no trace in Scriptures possibly composed before the Exile. The world of Angels, which the Essenes and all Gnostics separated by a great gulf from the material or terrestrial world, is presided over by a not stated number of watchers or saints, whose decrees are those of God. As there are seven archangels in the Book of Tobiah, so we may assume a similar number in the Book of Daniel, although only Gabriel and Michael are named. Thus we are led to connect the chief angels in the Book of Daniel with the seven watchers or Amshaspands of the Persians. The name Gabriel means 'man of God,' and his office is to be God's representative, just as Serosh was the vicar of Ormuzd, taking his place as the first of the seven Amshaspands, probably because the God of light takes himself no part in the fight against the God of darkness. In the New Testament Gabriel announces the Messiah.[1]

Daniel's recorded vision about the universal rule of a celestial or Angel-Messiah following upon four successive Empires, symbolised by beasts, cannot be entirely separated from the knowledge which Daniel had acquired by his initiation in Chaldæan wisdom. The Medo-Chaldees or Magi over whom Daniel was placed, represented the Iranian tradition as promulgated in the West, in part perhaps ever since the Median conquest of Babylon in pre-Abrahamitic times. We saw that

---

[1] Dan. iv. 14, 21; vii.; Tob. xii. 15; Luke i. 19, 26.

these Medes probably introduced into the West the very ancient Eastern tradition of an Angel-Messiah and vicar of God, since the ancient Babylonians knew about a Divine Messenger who would distribute good among men, as his name Silik-mulu-dug implies. Like the fire-bringer Agni-Mâtarisvan of the ancient Indians, this Mesopotamian Angel-Messiah was connected with the fire-sticks. We may safely assume, that the rule of this Messiah was by the Medo-Chaldæans of Mesopotamia connected, if not identified, with the rule of the Divine Messenger and mediator Sraosha or Serosh, which was expected to follow on Ormuzd's rule of 3,000 years and Ahriman's rule of 3,000 years, as the last 1,000 years, thus concluding the 7,000 years.

The doctrine of this Messianic Millennium expected to be brought about by a celestial messenger, and which would lead to the resurrection of the dead, has been more fully described and possibly developed in the Bundehesh and other writings of the time of the Sassanides, long after B.C. 216. The Iranian traditions were recast under the Sassanides, as this had been done much earlier by Ezra with the Hebrew traditions. In both cases it would be as unreasonable to attempt to draw a line of demarcation between the old and the new, as to deny the probability of a secret tradition as the source of such development. But as regards the Iranian symbolism of the alternate rule of light and darkness, of Ormuzd, Oromasdes or Ahura-Masda, and of Ahriman, Areimanios or Angromainjus, we hope to have proved by an astronomical interpretation, and thus by a localisation of this and of similar myths, that these Eastern conceptions are more ancient than the commencement of Egyptian history.[1]

The parallel between Serosh the vicar of Ormuzd, and Eros the vicar of Zeus, confirms the identity of

[1] See Chapter III, 54 f.; *Die Plejaden*, 48-85,

Zeus and Ormuzd, first observed by Eudoxus, and Aristoteles, born B.C. 384. We may now safely assert, that the Magian tradition transmitted by Theopompus of Chios, born about B.C. 378, is more ancient than the time of Nebucadnezar, according to which a Millennium will precede the resurrection of the dead. Directly connected with the statements of Theopompus are those in the Bundehesh and other writings, according to which the time of the resurrection will be preceded by four cosmical periods, which are also designated as four kingdoms of gold, silver, steel, and iron.

In the Bahman Yesht, first cited by Spiegel, it is written: 'As revealed in the Ctûtgar: Zertusht demanded from Ormuzd immortality; then Ormuzd showed to Zertusht the omniscient wisdom; he then saw a tree with such a root, that four trees had sprung up from it, a golden one, a silver one, one of steel, and one of iron.' Zoroaster is then told by revelation, that the tree with one root, the tree of knowledge, 'is the world,' and that the four trees are 'the four times that shall come.' The golden time is that of Zoroaster (or of king Vistâspa); the silver tree is the kingdom of Artashir; that of steel, the kingdom of the son of Kobat; the iron tree is the wicked dominion of the Dêvs, or evil spirits. Then comes the kingdom of Serosh, Sraosha, Sraoshyank, literally 'the helper,' or Saviour, also called the Holy One and the Victorious. According to later traditions several prophets were to be his forerunners. With this tradition Spiegel has connected, on the strength of remarkable parallels which cannot be casual, the Buddhist expectation, still maintained, of another Buddha, of Maitreya, the son of love (like Eros) who shall take up the lost thread of Buddha's doctrine, who shall take of the words of Buddha and make known the truth.[1] Thus it is indirectly proved

[1] Diog. Laert. procem. 8; Spiegel, *Zeitschrift d. M. G.* iii. 467; vi.

that the Iranian symbolism and prophecy of four
Empires preceding the Messianic Millennium is more
ancient than Gautama-Buddha and his contemporary
Cyrus.[1]

Whether the prophet Daniel returned to Judæa or
not, the evidently parallel organisation of the Rabbis
and their three classes with the Magi and their three
classes, as existing when Daniel was set over them,
renders it almost certain, that the Magian tradition
about a future Angel-Messiah and his rule of a thousand
years was introduced by some of the returning Jews
into Palestine. We have shown in another place that
the Chronology of the Bible has been connected, perhaps by Ezra, with a scheme of 7,000 years, ending with
the Messianic Millennium. The year of the destruction
of the temple by Nebucadnezar's general, in B.C. 586,
was made the starting-point of the second cycle of 70
jubilees or 3,500 years, which two periods made up the
7,000 years, supposed to have been decreed as the limi-
tation of the earth's existence. According to this scheme,
the first 70 jubilees commenced with the creation of
Adam, seventy years after the creation of heaven and
earth, and they ended B.C. 586. The fulfilment of seventy years' exile, recorded as a prophecy of Jeremiah,
had been accurately accomplished in the year 516,
when the Second Temple was consecrated, if they were
reckoned from the destruction of the Temple in 586.
But this fulfilment had been ushered in by the permission to return in 536, in the fiftieth or jubilee year.

---

78 f.; *Acad. der Wissen.* vi. 89 f.; *Avesta,* 32–38, 244; Duncker, *l. c.*
ii. 369 f.; Delitzsch, in Herzog, *l. c.* ' Daniel.'

[1] Professor Beal points out the coincidence in the epithets ' the man
greatly beloved,' or ' much beloved' (literally coveted) in Dan. ix. 23; x. 11,
19, with Piyattissa's (Priyadassi or Priyadosa), ' the beloved.' Mr. Thomas
(*l. c.* 54) dwells on the importance of the Bhabra Inscription rejecting the
title still used in earlier inscriptions of Asóka: Devánampiyo or ' beloved of
the gods.' If Buddha prayed to the highest Spirit, Isvâra Deva, or to
Abîdha, the Sun God, Asóka after his conversion from Jainism to Buddhism
would object to this polytheistic title on that ground.

Seventy years were enlarged to a second set of seventy jubilees, or 3,500 years, from B.C. 586 to 1914 A.D., the last twenty jubilees forming a parallel to the last twenty years of Jeremiah's seventy years. Thus the 20 × 50 years, the Millennium, was placed A.D. 1914–2914.[1] This scheme cannot have been invented before B.C. 516. We shall see that the Revelation of 'John' supplements the Book of Daniel, and refers to the Millennium.

The Book of Daniel follows the oriental tradition about the four monarchies, in placing the kingdom of the celestial Messiah in the position of that of Serosh, the first of seven angels, and vicar of the highest God. This Iranian scheme is reproduced in various forms in the Book of Daniel, where the four eras are applied to that of four successive kingdoms, beginning with that of Nebucadnezar and ending with that of Alexander, upon which the Messianic kingdom was expected to follow. The first form in which the Eastern tradition has been moulded, by revelation or not, is a dream which Nebucadnezar is said to have had, and which Daniel was able to relate as if he himself had dreamt it. The king had seen a great image, the head of which was gold (Nebucadnezar), breast and arms of silver (probably the Mede), belly and thighs of brass (the Persian), legs of iron, but the feet part of iron part of clay. This last, or Greek, kingdom was to be divided, partly strong partly broken, 'and its parts shall not cleave together.' The king had also seen that a stone, cut out of the mountain without hands, smote the image, broke it in pieces, and became a great mountain. This is the kingdom which the God of heaven shall set up, and which shall never be destroyed.

In another form the same events, to which Chaldæan tradition, as well as Nebucadnezar's dream referred,

---

[1] *The Chronology of the Bible*, 4–7.

V

was symbolised by Daniel's dream.   From the sea, the
symbol of the Gentile world, four great beasts came up.
The first, a lion with eagle's wings, known to us by
Mesopotamian representations, is again the kingdom of
Nebucadnezar.   The second beast, like a bear, is the
Median kingdom ; the three ribs in its mouth seem to be
the three cities on the Tigris which the Medes captured.
The beast is described as standing upright on one side
only, for before this kingdom can be firmly set up, a
third beast, a leopard arises, with four wings and four
heads, that is, the Persian kingdom, to which dominion
was given.   The four heads are four kings, enumerated in
the eleventh chapter.   The fourth beast, more terrible
than the others, with iron teeth, devouring, breaking in
pieces and stamping the residue with the feet of it, and
having ten horns, is the Macedonian kingdom, with
the ten Seleucidian kings.

Among the ten horns another little horn came
up, before whom there were three of the first horns
plucked up by the roots, and in this horn were eyes
like the eyes of man, and a mouth speaking great
things.   This little horn is Antiochus Epiphanes ; and
the three horns plucked up by him are his three
brothers: Seleucus, who was murdered; Heliodorus,
who was expelled; and Demetrius, who had to go
to Rome, as hostage, instead of Antiochus.   He spoke
great words against the Most High, and wore out his
saints, and intended to change times and laws.   For
three years and a half the saints were given into his
hand ; but then came the judgment by the Ancient of
Days, the beast was slain, his body destroyed and given
to the burning flame.   His dominion was taken away,
like that of his predecessors, and a universal and everlasting dominion was given to ' One like a son of man,'
who was brought on the clouds of heaven before God,
and who by the interpreting angel is implied to be the
representative of ' the people of the saints of the Most

High,' to whom, as to the Messiah, the kingdom under the whole heaven, an everlasting kingdom, shall be given.

Again, in a third form, the Messianic kingdom is described which was expected to follow upon Antiochus Epiphanes. The eighth chapter describes the Medo-Persian kingdom in the figure of a ram, with two horns, of which one was higher than the other and came up last. The ram, having pushed westward and northward and southward, is attacked by a he-goat, having a notable horn between his eyes, the Macedonian kingdom. This great horn, however, was broken, after Alexander's death, when four notable horns towards the four winds of heaven took its place, that is, the four principal dominions which arose from Alexander's empire. Out of one of these four horns a little horn arose, a king of fierce countenance, who shall destroy many also of the holy people. But after that he shall have prevented the daily morning and evening sacrifice 3,500 times, that is, after 1,150 days, or three and a half years, the sanctuary shall be cleansed and the transgression of desolation ended.[1]

The ninth chapter refers to the same times and circumstances. The novelty lies in this, that the seventy years of Jeremiah, enlarged into seventy weeks, or 490 years, are incorrectly implied to end with Antiochus Epiphanes. 'Seventy weeks are determined upon thy people and upon thy holy city, until the transgression shall be finished, and the measure of sins shall be filled, until iniquity shall be reconciled, and everlasting righteousness shall be brought, until prophecy and prophet shall be sealed, and a Most-Holy be anointed. And thou must know and understand : From the going forth of the commandment to restore and to build Jerusalem unto an Anointed, a Prince, are seven weeks. And during threescore and

---

[1] Bunsen's *Bibelwerk*, iii. 670–673 ; Holtzmann, in *Geschichte des Volkes Israel*, 101–109.

two weeks the city shall be restored and built with street and wall, although in distressed times. And after the threescore and two weeks shall an Anointed be cut off, and have no one. And over the city and the sanctuary shall bring destruction the people of a Prince, who cometh and findeth his end on (the march of) the overflooding host; yet unto the end war continues, judgment and desolation. And he shall make a strong covenant with many for one week; and during the half week he shall cause the sacrifice and oblation to cease; and on the pinnacle are seen abominations, terrible things, but only until destruction and judgment are poured on the horrors.'

If the seventy weeks are considered to be 490 years, the first seven weeks might be calculated as reaching to Cyrus. But every attempt has failed to let the sixty-two weeks, or 434 years, reach to the clearly implied time of Antiochus Epiphanes, who, after the murder of Seleucus IV. Philopator, ascended the throne in 176–170, and reigned seven years, or one week. Curiously enough, these 434 years, if reckoned back from 176–175 reach to 609, or to the third year of Jehoiakim (609-608), when Daniel is said to have been exported.[1] They could be made to reach the fourth year of that king (608–607), when the commandment or Jeremiah's prophecy went forth. But accordingly the first seven weeks would have commenced in 658, or twenty-nine years before the thirteenth of Josiah, when to Jeremiah, then 'young,' came the word of the Lord for the first time. It is not necessary to add, that the 490 years cannot possibly bridge over the time from the commandment to restore and build Jerusalem to any possible year of the birth of Jesus Christ.[2]

[1] For the dates, see *The Chronology of the Bible*. It is not probable that because of the above reckoning of 62 weeks the third year of Jehoiakim, B.C. 608, instead of the probable year 588, is mentioned as the time when Nebucadnezar besieged Jerusalem.

About the late Mr. Bosanquet's scheme of three successive periods of

The same subject, the Messianic kingdom ushered in by political events ending with Antiochus Epiphanes, is once more referred to in the last three chapters of the Book of Daniel. An angel appears to him, unseen by his companions, and reveals to him what shall befall Israel in the latter days. The same or another angel formed 'in the similitude of the sons of men,' refers with much detail to the combats between the Ptolemies and the Seleucidæ. Among the latter great prominence is given to Antiochus Epiphanes, 'a detestable person, not intended for the dignity of the kingdom, and who shall come unexpectedly.' He gains victories over the Egyptians; but ships from Chittim, containing the Roman envoy Popilius Lænas, who demands the restoration of the conquered land, oblige him to return. Now he turns against the holy covenant, pollutes the sanctuary, 'places the desolation that maketh desolate,' he takes away the daily sacrifice, he magnifies himself above every other god. Three years and a half this has to be endured. But 'the people that do know their God' (the Maccabees) will manfully stand up 'and do exploits.' At last Antiochus has to yield to the kings of the South and North, and the Divine judgment follows.[1]

The Book of Daniel helps us to bridge over the time from the exportation to Babylon to the rise of the Maccabees. Their allies, the Assidæans, we have sufficient reason to connect, if not identify, with the Essenes, and these with the Rechabites who were transported by Nebucadnezar to Babylon. The Maccabees and Assidæans (Essenes) may be presumed to have expected the kingdom of the Angel-Messiah after the fall of Antiochus Epiphanes. It is this Essenic expectation which has been recorded in the Book of Daniel.

seventy weeks ending with the birth of Jesus Christ, see *Transactions of Biblical Archæology*, vol. vi.

[1] For a detailed explanation, see Holtzmann, *l. c.*

When it was seen that after the death of Antiochus Epiphanes, that is, after the end to which all 'prophecies' in the Book of Daniel so clearly point, the long expected kingdom of the Angel-Messiah did not come, the expectation was carried on by a prolongation of the Danielic times. Almost fifty years before A.D. 6, when Judæa had become a Roman province, a new interpretation of the four monarchies preceding the Messianic Millennium was set on foot. The four kingdoms were now explained in the oracle of the Jewish Sibyl, then in the Fourth Book of Esdras, and the Epistle of Barnabas as the Babylonian, the Medo-Persian, the Greek, and the Roman kingdoms. Thus the ground was prepared for the new conception of Jesus Christ as the Angel-Messiah of the vision recorded in the Book of Daniel, and first applied to Jesus in the Revelation of 'John' though without direct reference to the four kingdoms preceding his coming.

We come to the following conclusions about the Book of Daniel. Initiated in all the wisdom of the Chaldæans or Magi, Daniel knew of the scheme, recorded to have been revealed to Zoroaster, about four eras and kingdoms, after which should be established on earth the heavenly kingdom of the Saviour Serosh, 'the Holy One,' the Angel-Messiah. If Nebucadnezar really had the dream about the image, and if Daniel explained it to him and had similar visions as recorded, they were both imbued with the sense that the Angel-Messiah must come, but that his Millennium must be preceded by a new cycle of four monarchies, of which that of Nebucadnezar, corresponding to that of Zoroaster and King Vistâspa, was the first. Assuming, for the sake of argument, that the entire Book of Daniel as we possess it, was not completed in the time of the Maccabees, and that it is not a 'prophecy after the event,' we might be led further to assume that Daniel referred the little horn to Antiochus Epiphanes, and that moreover he, like the Maccabees of that time, expected the Angel-Messiah to come after the death of this enemy of 'the saints of the Most High.'

But the connection of the Book of Daniel with the Iranian expectation of four monarchies followed by the celestial kingdom cannot possibly be denied, nor the composition, or at least the completion, of this book in Maccabean times. Yet it may be held, that Daniel did not see Antiochus Epiphanes, that he did not share the expectation of the Maccabees about the then coming Messiah, and that the prophet was enabled to see after the Greek empire, the Roman empire as the fourth, and Jesus of Nazareth as the real Serosh or Angel-Messiah, whose second coming or return in glory, to establish a terrestrial kingdom, a new heaven and a new earth, would be preceded by Nero or by Mohammed as the little horn.

We will only observe here, that on this latter assumption the Essenic expectation of an Angel-Messiah must have been sanctioned by Jesus. If so, the silence of the three first Gospels on this all-important point remains inexplicable, and Paul, as well as the authors of the Revelation of ' John ' and of the fourth Gospel, must be regarded as the first full revealers of ' the truth as it is in Jesus.'

Maccabean Psalms. Some of the Psalms, possibly all after the seventy-fourth, seem to date from the Maccabean time. This is very generally regarded as certain with regard to the seventy-third and seventy-fourth Psalms ; whilst some will see in the second Psalm a hidden reference to the time when, as during the reign of Antiochus Epiphanes, the coming of the Messiah was supposed to be near. The contents, the language, and the form of several Psalms transmitted to us are surprisingly similar to the collection entitled ' Psalms of Solomon,' which were probably composed in the year B.C. 47.

The Book Ecclesiasticus, or Jesus-Sirach, we have in

another place tried to connect, as 'Sirach of Jerusalem,' with the Highpriest Seraiah in the time of Nebucadnezar's siege, as whose son or grandson the author seems to describe himself in the Appendix to the fiftieth chapter. According to the Alexandrian Codex and several of the most ancient manuscripts the Highpriest Seraiah is stated to have been the son of Eleasar of Jerusalem, and in the Talmud the author of this work is called Jehoshua, ben Sira, ben Elieser. Now, Elieser or Eleazar is only another form of Azariah, and this was the name of the father and predecessor of the Highpriest Seraiah who was murdered at Riblah in 588. His son was called Jehozadak, and his grandson was the Highpriest Joshua, who must have known Daniel the prophet, if the latter was identical with Daniel the Priest. As this Joshua called himself son of Seraiah, or ben Sira, though only his grandson, so Ecclesiasticus, originally written in Hebrew, may have been composed and possibly translated by a descendant of the Highpriest, since the author calls himself Jesus or Joshua, ' son of Sirach of Jerusalem.' It is immaterial, whether the translation was made during the reign of an earlier or of a later Ptolemy.[1]

The original title was probably ' the Wisdom of Sirach,' later called ' Proverbs of ben Sira.' The connection of the contents of this book with the last Highpriest before the Captivity, if accepted, would be a proof of the existence of a secret tradition, of which the Highpriests were the highest organs.

The absence in this book of every allusion to an expected Messiah is best explained by the assumption, that according to the secret Jewish tradition, hidden wisdom, or Apocrypha, partially revealed by this book, an Angel-Messiah was expected. Here there is yet no trace of a personification of the Word of God or Wisdom

---

[1] *Einheit der Religionen,* i. 466 f.

of God, the organ of sanctification, but not the organ of immortality. Yet Wisdom, coming from the Lord, and eternally with Him, raises her sons, those who love her as 'the life,' and are loved by the Lord. He created her from 'the beginning,' and promised her a 'possession' in Israel, where she served before him in the tabernacle. A similar notion is expressed in Proverbs.

Essenic-Buddhistic, especially Therapeutic, is the absence of all reference to bloody sacrifices, although the incense-offerings of Moses are mentioned; so are the injunctions referring to meals, to mercantile speculations, to the furthering of strict morality and thus of social progress; the emphasizing of the life of the soul, the immortality of the individual; equality of all men, which is the basis of community of goods; importance of the truth and generally of moral duties, independently of mere outward works, partly instead of the latter; prohibition of slavery, and the recommendation of hopeful submission.

The Book of Wisdom we have already considered as the almost certain work of Philo, and in connection with the introduction of Essenic doctrines into the Septuagint.

The Books of the Sibyl are written at different times in Hebrew. The third book is composed B.C. 140 by an Alexandrian Jew, possibly a Therapeut, and the fourth book by a Jew in A.D. 79, who expects the return of Nero. About B.C. 170 the Jewish Alexandrian Aristobulus had composed a Jewish version of an Orphic Hymn, and so a Jewish Alexandrian work was attributed to the Ionian Phocylides of Miletus (about B.C. 540). These were no actual forgeries, since the Essene stood in connection with Ionic and with Orphic tradition. The prophecies of women, called Sibyls probably after the Ionic word for the will of God, have been traced from Asia Minor to Italy, from Cyme, where they were collected in the seventh century, to Cumæ and thus to

Rome.[1] The third book of the Sibyl occupies the standpoint of the Book of Daniel, and is the earliest Scripture known to us in which the Messianic kingdom is placed after the Roman empire. The Messiah is identified with Simon the Maccabee. From the land of the sun God will send a King, as he once sent Cyrus the Anointed or Messiah. He will promulgate over all the earth peace and the Israelitic covenant, by receiving the Pious or Saints. These may have referred especially to the Pious of the Maccabees and the Saints of the Essenes, possibly 'the Saints of the Most High' in the Book of Daniel. This Messianic kingdom, which is to go forth from Jerusalem, will be preceded by an attack of Gentiles on the city and by signs in heaven. The supposition of a double Messianic personality, a celestial and a terrestrial one, though not excluded, is not in any way suggested.

The Book of Enoch, who is called 'the seer' has been traced to Northern Galilee and to the years B.C. 130–100, although some passages may have been interpolated after the beginning of the Christian era.[2] It was originally written in Hebrew, and several Hebrew fragments have been traced.[3] The Essenic and especially Therapeutic contents of the book are incontestable. No specifically Pharisaic principles are referred to, whilst the Sadducees, the non-universalists, are designated as enemies. Especially Essenic are the injunctions to pray at sun-rise, not to swear, to estimate highly the secret tradition, deeper knowledge, or Gnosis, not to over-estimate the value of Scripture, thus implying that it must be allegorically interpreted; the non-reference to bloody sacrifices, and a fully developed doctrine of angels, headed by the Angel of God or Angel-Messiah. The

[1] Bernays, comp. Hilgenfeld, *l. c.* 167, n. 4; Duncker *l. c.* iii. 190, n. 3.

[2] A later date, as suggested by Volkmar, would not affect our argument.

[3] Jellinek, in *D. Morgenl. Ges.* vii. 249, designates the book as a remainder of Essenian literature, which forms the introductory history of the Cabbala, or secret tradition of the Jews.

Danielic vision of One like a son of man is interpreted
to refer to One who is also similar to Angels, to the
Word of God and Son of God, the Lord from heaven,
the One chosen by the Lord of Spirits. The Messiah is
also called Wisdom, Spirit, Grace, Power of God from
the beginning, Name of God, the never ceasing light
of Sabaoth, the light of the people of God, of the
chosen ones, the Son of God. At the same time Messiah is called 'son of a woman,' probably in reference
to the Book of Isaiah. His name Messiah was named
before God before the foundation of the world, and is
known to the righteous.

In harmony with Buddhistic conceptions, the Angel-
Messiah is described as coming to the earth in order to
dwell among men, but not having found a dwelling
place he returned to the angels. We saw that Buddha's
descent is figuratively described as that of an elephant,
and so here Messiah is described as coming down in
the form of a white bull with large horns. In the Book
of Daniel the two-horned he-goat refers, not to Cyrus
the Messiah, but to Alexander, whom the Korán designates as Dulkarnaim or the two-horned One.[1] According to the Book of Enoch, already Adam had come to
earth as a white bull. We have interpreted the bull-
symbolism as referring to the celestial bull, to the constellation of Taurus with the Pleiades, and have connected with these seven stars the seven Amshaspands
and seven Buddhas. Here Enoch, 'the seventh from
Adam,' as if the seventh Buddha, is identified with the
Angel-Messiah, that is with the One like a son of man
in the Danielic vision. Enoch's terrestial body is described as melting away, and his spirit was transformed
into a heavenly body, 'the second body,' expected after
the coming of Serosh. This is a parallel to Buddha's
transformation on the mount. Enoch, whose translation

[1] Ashteroth-Karnaim (Gen. xiv. 5) refers to the two-horned Astarte,
(Ishtar, Diana), symbolised by the bull; *Die Plejaden*, 91 f., 441.

is referred to in Genesis, was regarded as the seventh incarnation of the Angel of God. No longer after seventy weeks, but after seventy undefined epochs, Judaism will bring about the promised end. Enoch, or the Messiah, will return, the general resurrection of the dead will take place, and then the Messiah will clothe the righteous with 'garments of life.' But Messiah will not take part in the judgment over which God alone presides.

The Ascension of Moses, written about the year of the death of Herod Agrippa I., A.D. 44, by a probably Roman Jew, and is known to us in a later interpolated edition. Its interest lies in the absence of every trace of Essenic doctrine, at the very time when Peter had probably founded the Church at Rome, and when Paul, about two years after his conversion to the (Essenic) faith of Stephen, had not yet been introduced by Barnabas to the Church at Antioch. The book ignores the pre-Christian Jewish expectations which were recorded in the Danielic and Maccabean Scriptures, in the Jewish Sibyl, in the Apocrypha of the Septuagint, in the Book of Enoch, but probably not already then in the Apocalypse of Esdras. This development of doctrine, which we have traced to an Essenic and thus to an oriental source, formed the basis of the Jewish verbal tradition, later called Cabbala.

The Zohar, literally 'splendour' or 'glory,' is a book which we may here consider, although we know it only in the revised form in which it was published in the thirteenth century. By eminent Jewish authorities it is regarded as the universal collection of the Cabbala, of the tradition about the religious philosophy, deeper knowledge, or gnosis within the circle of Judaism.[1] We accept the view that the Zohar is connected with

---

[1] This is the opinion of Franck and Matter; but Grätz seems to prove that the Zohar is not the source of the Cabbala, which Jellinek traced back to the Essenes.

Essenic tradition, which formed the introductory history
of the Cabbala, and also with Parsism and Buddhism.
We connect it with the wisdom of the Chaldæans or
Magi in which Daniel was brought up, and of which
the Book of Daniel purports to be the earliest record.
The parallel between the three classes of the Magi and
those of the Rabbis leads us to assume as probable the
division of Rabbinical books into three parts, according to
the degrees of initiation.   Such divisions we find in the
Zohar, and their respective titles are : ‘ the Book of the
Mystery,’ then ‘the Large Congregation,’ and ‘the Small
Congregation,’ in which latter the dying Simon is said
to have communicated to a limited number of disciples
his last instructions.   This Simon is asserted to have
been the father of Gamaliel, at whose feet Paul and
Aquila are reported to have sat.   It is not impossible
that a genuine scripture from the Apostolic age forms
the groundwork of the Zohar, and that it embodied the
Messianic views of the great Simeon the son of Hillel
‘ the Babylonian,’ and the first who received the title
Rabban.   He is by some authorities identified with the
Simeon of the Gospels.   The connection of the Zohar
with Essenianism, and thus with Buddhism, tends to
render this identity of the Rabboni Simeon with the
Simeon of Luke’s Gospel more probable, since the
Buddhistic legend of Asïta forms such a striking parallel
with the Gospel narrative of Simeon, who ‘waited for
the consolation of Israel.’
    The Zohar contains a full development of the Essenic
doctrine of the Angel-Messiah. The Word or Wisdom of
God, the celestial Messiah, is designated as the Creator
of all things.   By this Messiah Adam was to such a
degree enlightened before his fall, that even angels
became jealous of him. This reminds us of the Book
of Wisdom, where the first father is said to have been
preserved by Divine wisdom. The Zohar relates how
Adam and Eve heard a voice ‘ from above ’ by which

they were instructed in the wisdom from above. So long as they kept the supernatural power which was engrafted on their nature, they were clad, like the angels, in garments of heavenly light. Yet the soul has a different covering in the heavenly and in the terrestrial world. The Angel-Messiah or 'tree of life,' like Serosh called 'the Holy One,' dwells with such men only, in whom the male principle, probably the Word or Memra, is united with the female principle, the spirit or 'ruach,' which word is of female gender. These conceptions correspond closely with the doctrines contained in the writings of Simon of Samaria, whom we have connected with the Essenes.

If the oriental gnosis was introduced into heterodox Judaism and into 'Christianity' chiefly by the Essenic Therapeuts, then it is easy to explain the prevailing mysticism of Essenes and Cabbalists. But between the two there was the essential difference, that the Essenes connected with their doctrinal speculations, which were kept secret, their practical and moral aims. Both Essenes and Cabbalists regarded tradition as the source of a deeper gnostic Scriptural interpretation; but whilst the Essenic doctrines were partly assimilated to Greek culture, especially among the Therapeuts, as also in the Septuagint and in Philo's writings, no such traces can be found in the Talmud or in the Zohar.

The Book Yezira, or Creation, corresponds with the first division of the holy Merkabah or verbal tradition of the Jews, whilst the Zohar seems to have referred to the second division, to that mysticism which was connected with the car or rechab of Ezechiel's vision. The word 'Merkaba,' being a compound of rechab confirms this connection, as also that of the Jewish gnosis with the Essenes and their predecessors, the Rechabites.[1] This remarkable book, possibly composed by the great Rabbi

---

[1] Philo, *Quis est*, 44, 45; *De Somn.* i. 14, 15; *Das Symbol des Kreuzes*, 91–104.

Akiba (135 A.D.), perhaps junior contemporary of the
Apostle James, has been explained to contain an indirect
but sharp attack against a prevailing heretical gnosis, such
as Paul promulgated and which the Apostle James disap-
proved.[1]   Although the book contains striking analogies
and parallels with some of the doctrines of Paul, and also
with the gnostic writings of the second century, yet one
of the principal doctrines is the strict Divine oneness,
coupled with the negation of the dualism which was
more or less implied by the introduction of the new
doctrine of the Angel-Messiah and framer of the world,
which Paul had accepted and applied to Jesus.   This
protest is all the more important since also in the
Talmud the Angel of God, who stands by his throne,
therefore called Metatron, though regarded as the highest
being after God, is neither considered as an object of
worship nor as a mediator.

In a polemical dialogue between a Christian heretic
and Rabbi Idit, the latter admits that the Angel who goes
before and follows Israel, in whom the 'Name' of God
is, and who can pardon transgressions, (therefore, the
Angel whom Paul calls Christ), is the Metatron, and
his importance is allowed to be similar to that of God.
But the heretic having deduced from this that the
Angel of the Lord ought to be worshipped 'like' God,
the Rabbi replies : 'Thou shalt not confound him, the
Metatron, with God ; we have the conviction, that we
may not even accept him as a mediator.'   Again, the
apostacy of Elisa ben Abuya, commonly called Achar, is
in the Talmud attributed to the circumstance that he regarded the Metatron as of about equal rank with God,
from which he drew the conclusion that there are two
Divine powers.[2]

[1] An intimate associate of the Apostle James, Rabbi Eliazar ben
Hyrkanos, narrowly escaped death during Trajan's persecution by his
emphatic 'No' to the question whether he was a Christian (Aboda Sara,
16, 17; Grätz, 24, note).

[2] *Sanhedrim*, 38; *Shagia*, 15; comp. Hirsch Grätz, *Gnostizismus und
Judenthum*, 1846.

The Revelation of John. The key for the opening of
this sealed book is the mysterious symbolism of the tree
of life in Paradise. The tree of life was symbolised by
the tree-shaped candlestick of Moses, the seven lamps
of which, like the seven elevations of the temple of Bel
or tower of Babel, and the seven steps or ' altars ' of
the Great Pyramid, referred to the seven planets, that is,
to sun, moon, and five planets. According to Philo the
central candlestick represented the sun, but according
to the deeper knowledge or gnosis ' the Word of God,'
or ' the Archangelic Word,' the second Deity.' In the
Apocalypse of John a vision is described, in which
Christ, the Word of God, appears in the midst of the
seven candlesticks or lamps. About five hundred years
before Philo this symbolism, applied to the risen Jesus
by the Seer of Patmos, was referred to by Zechariah
the prophet, in his vision of the golden candlestick
with a bowl on the top of it, from which by pipes the
gold or golden oil was conveyed to the seven lamps.
Two olive trees on both sides of the candlestick are
explained to be two Anointed Ones (Moses and Elijah,
not Joshua and Zerubbabel), two vessels of the Holy
Ghost, symbolised by oil, who empty or pour out from
themselves the gold. The tree of life is the symbol of
Divine enlightenment, which comes from above to all
the seven lamps alike, including the central lamp, the
symbol of the Word of God, of Christ.

This Divine enlightenment coming from above, and
of which men are allowed to partake, has for its source
the seven eyes of the Lord of hosts or of Sabaoth,
' which run to and fro through the whole earth.' The
Lord Sabaoth or Sebaot, that is of the seven stars, of
the Pleiades, later of the planets, sent an Angel to
Zerubbabel with the message, that, ' not by might nor
by power,' but by the Spirit of God the things shall
come to pass which were only typified in those times.'
Zerubbabel brought forth, or rather put up, the head-

stone of the temple under shoutings of joy, the stone which God laid before Joshua, and on which are set or engrafted the seven eyes of Sabaoth. But Joshua and those who sit before him are ' men of mark,' or men of prophetic import, types of God's servant, of ' the man whose name is the Branch,' types of the Messiah. The latter may by Zechariah have been connected with the six men or angels, as Ezechiel had done before him. Paul had this symbolism of the candlestick and the planets in view when he described Christ-Jesus as ' the chief corner stone ' of ' the holy temple in the Lord,' in whom the believers are ' builded together for an habitation of God in the Spirit.' [1]

The symbolism of the candlestick, finally applied to Jesus Christ as appearing in the midst of the seven candlesticks, had been applied before Zechariah by Ezechiel to six men, and as a seventh in their midst he described and distinguished from them, ' one clothed with linen and a writer's inkhorn by his side,' such as is represented on Egyptian monuments and still worn in the East by the scribes and men of learning. The linen clothing marks as a Priest the angel of grace in the midst of the six angels of wrath. In a similar clothing an angel, the Angel of the Lord, the Angel-Messiah, the Highpriest of Philo, is described as appearing to Daniel. It is the Angel of God who followed the Israelites in the wilderness and through the Red Sea, and who can ' pardon' transgressions. The Divine presence, Shechina, or glory above the Cherub, called this angel of mercy and said unto him : ' Go through the midst of the city, through the midst of Jerusalem, and set the mark of Tau (T, the headless cross) upon the foreheads of the men that sigh and that cry for all the abominations that are done in the midst thereof.' It is the Angel-

---

[1] Zech. iv. 3; vi. 12; Eph. ii. 19–22. *Das Symbol des Kreuzes*, 184–208 ; comp. 87 about Simon of Samaria connecting with the tree of life ' the man of Judah,' the Messiah, ' the man of the tree.'

X

Messiah 'from the rising of the sun,' and distinguished from other angels, who seals with 'the seal of the living God' (the Tau-Cross) the elect of God in the midst of the Divine judgments.[1]

The cross, the sign of Divine enlightenment, was first connected with fire, as coming from the Pleiades in the most ancient spring-equinoctial sign, then with the sun. When, before the Exodus from Egypt, at the time of the spring-equinox, the sun had passed over the sign of the spring-equinox, Aries, the ram or lamb, then a lamb was slain, with the blood of which the doorposts of the Israelites were marked. These formed a blood-stained Tau-Cross, seeing which, the avenging Angel of God passed by the dwellings of the Israelites. The same sign of the Tau-Cross is to save the faithful (144,000) in the time of the Messiah, the first of the seven angels, who had been with the fathers in the wilderness.

The planetary symbolism of the candlestick, applied to the Messiah by Ezechiel, Zechariah, Philo, and John the seer, can be traced back to the construction of the great Pyramid and of the temple of Belus, or tower of Babel, and it can be connected with the most ancient Indian rite known to us, the Soma-sacrifice of the Rig-Veda. The juice of the Soma-plant, or *Asclepia acida*, symbol of the tree of life, flowed from the Samudra-bowl into the chalices of the seven priests who poured it into the sacred fire, following their leader, or Nestri, who invoked the Deity symbolised by fire.[2] As in the Soma-sacrifice one out of seven priests was distinguished, so Ezechiel distinguished the Angel of God or Messiah from six men or angels, and so Philo distinguishes the central lamp of the candlestick, as the Sun or Word of God, from the six other lamps symbolising the moon and five planets. Finally, John in the Apocalypse follows this

---

[1] Dan. x. 5; xii. 6; Ezech. ix.; Rev. vii.; *Das Symbol des Kreuzes*, 19.

[2] *Das Symbol des Kreuzes*, 113, 114; E. Burnouf, *Essai sur le Veda*, 303.

Oriental symbolism by describing Christ, the Word of God, as appearing in the midst of the seven candlesticks, thus assigning to him the place of the Vedic Nestri, and by connecting the seven angels with the seven vials, similar to the seven chalices of the Soma priests.

The connection of the tree of life in Eden with the four rivers, and with the Messiah, as of the latter with the sun, led to the connection of the tree of life with the four seasons. Thus Christ, whose symbol is the sun,[1] is in the Apocalypse connected with the tree of life and with four angels 'standing on the four corners of the earth,' as also Christ, the lamb, is surrounded by four beasts. We saw that the tree of life and knowledge, of Divine wisdom, was already by ancient Iranian tradition connected with four other trees, representing four monarchies which should precede the Millennial kingdom of heaven, to be established on earth by the Angel-Messiah. We pointed out that the vision of the image of Nebucadnezar and the visions of Daniel about the four monarchies must be connected with the Chaldean or Magian science in which Daniel was brought up.

We need not here point out in full detail how the planetary symbolism of the candlestick of Moses, and thus of the tree of life, has been in the Revelation of John applied to the risen Jesus Christ. This was done between July 68 and June 69, during the reign of Galba, when the return of Nero, or Neron-Kesar, was expected, the letters of which name have the value of 666.[2] Suffice it to say that Christ, the Word of God, who appears over the central lamp of the candlestick, the symbol of the sun and of the Word of God, is also connected,

---

[1] The Alpha and Omega, 'the first and the last,' refers to the first and the last letter of the Zodiacal Alphabet, Aleph and Oin (later Ain), applied to God and to Jesus Christ, and thus to Taurus and Aries, the earliest spring-equinoctial signs (*Die Plejaden*, 409–417).

[2] The word *Lateinos* could never be referred to 'a man.'

as one of seven angels, with the seven spirits of God,
with the seven stars in his hand, with the seven eyes
and horns of the lamb, with seven thunders, and the
opening of the seven seals.

We pointed out that the seven planets took the place
of the Pleiades, with which seven stars the seven archangels of the Iranians seem to have been connected.
The first of these Amshaspands was the God of light
himself, till Serosh, the Holy One, the Messiah, took the
place of Ormuzd, and became his vicar. When the sun
had taken the place of the principal star in the Pleiades,
which must have been regarded as the symbol or dwelling-place of Serosh, when the sun had taken the place
of the fire coming from the Pleiades, then the spring-
equinoctial sign, first Taurus, then Aries, became the first
of the twelve constellations through which the sun
seemed to pass. Thus Aries, the ram or lamb, had
become, perhaps already since the time of Abraham,
connected with the Messiah, whose symbol was the sun,
first having been fire, as represented by the brazen
serpent.[1] The connection of the solar with the stellar
symbolism is indicated in this Apocalypse by the lamb
with seven eyes and seven horns.

The reference of the number seven to the planets is
confirmed by the vision of the book with seven seals,
each of which is connected with one of the planets.
For the planets are here enumerated according to the
days of the week, and the first four seals are evidently
connected respectively with the moon, Mars, Mercury,
and Jupiter. For the colour of the horses corresponds
with that of these planets, being white, fiery red, black,
and pale or green-yellow. The only inaccuracy is that
the colour of Mercury is dark blue, not black. From
this it follows that the fifth seal was connected with
Venus, the sixth with Saturn, the seventh with the sun.

---

[1] *Die Plejaden*, 265–321. In Hebrew Nachash means 'brass' as well a
'serpent.'

The angel described standing at the altar, having a golden censer, is evidently the Angel of God or celestial Messiah, whose symbol is the sun. It is the angel of mercy, the priest of Ezechiel's vision, who there as here seals the foreheads of the servants of God, being here described as an angel having the seal of the living God.[1]

The kingdom of the heavenly Serosh was connected with the seventh thousand of years, and so here the Messianic kingdom and Millennium is connected with the number seven, whilst the connection of this Scripture with Oriental tradition leaves no room to doubt that this kingdom is intended to represent the seventh Millennium, as the Epistle of Barnabas asserts. Not till after the opening of the seventh seal, trumpets were given to the seven angels, and not before the trumpet of the seventh angel had sounded there were great voices in heaven saying : 'The kingdom over the world is become our Lord's and of his Christ, and he shall reign for ever and ever.' According to still more ancient Oriental symbolism, confirmed by the Book of Daniel, the Messianic kingdom was to follow on four monarchies, and so here the first four of the seven seals are in a way separated from the rest. The events connected with the fourth kingdom of the wicked spirits, according to Iranian tradition, and with the fourth kingdom followed by the little horn in the Book of Daniel, are here connected with the opening of the fourth seal. The pale horse with Death as its rider is followed by Hell (Hadés), by famine, pestilence, and war between the beasts, or kings of the earth. The same signs are enumerated in the Gospel after Matthew

[1] Joh. Brandis, *Die Bedeutung der Sieben Thore Thebens; Zeitschr. Hermes,* 1867. He suggests that also the other cycles of seven follow the order of the planets, each cycle apparently beginning with the planet of each following week-day. For the attributes of the sun are referred to in such a manner in x. 1, xiv. 1, xix. 17, 'that each vision corresponds with one of the above-named planets.'

as preceding the coming of Messiah and the final judgment which the Maccabees expected after the death of
Antiochus Epiphanes.

As the fourth monarchy in the Book of Daniel is
followed by Antiochus Epiphanes, so here upon the
fourth seal Nero seems to follow, although his fall is
described after the sounding of the seventh trumpet.
After the return of Nero, which was expected at the
end of 68 or in the beginning of 69,[1] 'John' expected,
at once the fall of 'Babylon,' or Imperial Rome, the descent of the heavenly Messiah and the heavenly Jerusalem, symbolised by the sun.

The opening of the first seal is connected with a
crowned and victorious rider on a white horse, it is
Augustus, during whose reign the Messiah was born.
The second seal, being opened, refers to the time of
Tiberius, who carried his 'great sword' to the Holy
Land. The third rider, on a black horse, 'having a
balance in his hand,' introduces us to the famine
under Claudius, probably in the year 44. The fourth
epoch is characterised as Death riding on a pale
horse, with Hell, famines, pestilences, and war in
his train. When the lamb opens the fifth seal, are
seen the Christian martyrs slain by Nero, the fifth
emperor, 'the souls of them that have been slain for
the Word of God, and for the testimony which they
bore.' They are the Christians slain in 64, after the
burning of Rome. The opening of the sixth seal refers
to the time of Galba's reign, from June 68 to January
69, to the time when the Apocalypse was composed,
when the entire Roman Empire seemed to be shaken. As
Pliny refers to terrible disasters then caused by earth-
quakes in Asia Minor, so in Matthew the beginning of

---

[1] About the historical pseudo-Neros of this time and of later times see
Hilgenfeld, *Einl. N. T. erste Ausg.* 451; *Nero der Antichrist; Zeitschrift f.*
w. T. 1869, iv. 421.

the world's judgment is described with an eye to the prophetic explanation of passages in Isaiah and Ezechiel.[1]

Our object has been to establish the connection of the Revelation of John with the Book of Daniel, and thus with Oriental traditions, especially with the planetary symbolism of the Mosaic candlestick. We have connected the latter with Philo's writings, with the visions of Zechariah and Ezechiel, as also with the great Pyramid and the tower of Babel, and finally with the Soma-sacrifice described in the Rig-Veda. The Messiah of this Apocalypse, as of the Book of Daniel and of the Jewish Scriptures which we have connected with it, is the Angel-Messiah of the Essenes, who introduced that conception into non-authorised Judaism, and applied it to Jesus. As far as we know, this was first publicly done through Stephen and Paul.

We saw that the latter promulgated the universalist doctrines of the Essenic Therapeuts of Egypt, and we shall see that for this reason even Barnabas, a Levite and probably a Palestinian Essene, separated from the great Apostle. Also Barnabas has in so far represented an illegal Judaism, as he, with the Essenes, interpreted the Scriptures allegorically, thus attributing to them an essentially different sense. The hatred against Paul, as the universalist Essene and open condemner of the works of the law, has found its strongest expression in the Revelation of 'John.' Paul is not recognised as an Apostle, possibly even referred to as a false prophet, and the Therapeutic and Paulinic principles of toleration, submission to authority, even to that of Nero,[2] equal recognition of Jews and Gentiles are condemned.

---

[1] Pliny's *Letters*, vi. 16, 20; Is. xxxiv. 4; ii. 18; comp. Rev. vi. 15 with Is. xxiv. 21, 22; verse 16 with Hos. x. 8; see Luke xxiii. 30. This historical interpretation is taken from Holtzmann, in Bunsen's *Bibelwerk*, iv. 644–646; see ff. and Hilgenfeld, *l. c.* 407–452, for the remainder.

[2] Rom. xiii. 1. f.; comp. Rev. xvi. 13, &c. Volkmar identifies Paul and the 'false prophet.'

The Christology of the Apocalypse does not, any more than that in the Book of Daniel, clearly define the Messiah as an incarnate angel come down from heaven. As if wishing to spare those who expected the Messiah to be the anointed man of the Old Testament, Christ is in both Scriptures described as 'One like a son of man,' raised by the clouds of heaven to the throne of God. The seer does not say, but implies, that the Messiah is the Creator of the material world, an opinion which was shared also by Paul. Christ is in the Apocalypse described as ' the beginning of the creation of God,' who is perhaps regarded as the Creator of the immaterial, spiritual, or heavenly world only.

Of the first-created beings, presumably those whom God is in Genesis reported to have addressed as co-Creators of man, Christ is by 'John' regarded to have been the first, the first of seven archangels. He is distinguished from the six other angels, and is alone entrusted with ' the seal of the living God.' A premundane created being like Christ, according to Essenic conception, could be regarded as the Creator of the material world, and yet God could be described as the real Creator of heaven and earth, who had delegated the power over all things to the first of created beings. A similar doctrine was taught by Paul.[1] The conception of Christ as the first of seven angels forms an exact parallel to the Eastern symbolism of Serosh, the vicar of God and first of seven archangels, to whom the rule over the material world was transmitted by the God of light. Paul in his Epistle to the Colossians protests against such a connection of Christ with other angels.

These conceptions of the seer 'John' about the Messiah are inseparably connected, as we pointed out, with the planetary symbolism of the Mosaic candlestick, and with corresponding earlier Egyptian, Mesopotamian, Indian, and Chinese traditions. As the juice from the

---

[1] Rev. x. 6; comp. Rom. xi. 36; 1 Cor. viii. 5, 6; xv. 28; Eph. iii. 9.

Soma-plant and the oil from the olive tree, both symbols
of the tree of life, was represented above the seven Indian
priests, and above the seven candlesticks of Zechariah's
vision, denoting thereby the superhuman source of enlightenment, so the Divine Presence above the Cherubim, seen by Ezechiel, called upon the one of seven men
who was clothed in linen, the Messianic Highpriest,
whether angel or man, to mark the foreheads of the
servants of God by the sign of the Tau-Cross. Again,
as Philo had described the central lamp of the candlestick to be the symbol of the sun and also of the Word
of God, 'the Archangelic Word,' so in the Revelation
Christ is called the Word of God, and described as ' he
that walketh in the midst of the seven candlesticks,'
and also as the first of seven archangels, who seals
with ' the seal of the living God ' (with the Cross) the
servants of God. This is not Paulinic Christology.

Paul had not stated whether or not Jesus was born
like other men, nor whether the Holy Ghost was first
communicated to him on his baptism. ' John ' clearly
distinguishes the celestial from the terrestrial nature
of Christ, yet connects the Word of God with Jesus.
' John ' was in the island ' on account of the Word of
God and the testimony of Jesus.' The revealer announces
himself as Jesus who was dead and now is ' alive for
evermore,' having the keys of death and hell, and being
' the First and the Last, the living One.' Thus the
risen ' Jesus Christ, the faithful witness, the Firstborn
of the dead, and the ruler of the kings of the earth,' is
recorded to have revealed himself under the same title
which is given to ' the Alpha and Omega,' to the ' Lord
God, which is, and which was, and which is to come, the
Almighty.' [1]

It is in harmony with this identification of God and
of Christ, or the first of seven angels, that the angel
who had an opened little book, speaks alternately in

[1] Comp. Rev. i. 5, 7, 8, 9; ii. 17, 18; xxii. 13.

the name of God and of Christ, as whose two witnesses
the reappearing Moses and Elijah seem to be implied.[1]
From this angel and all other angels, thus also from
Christ, is clearly distinguished Jesus, ' the Lion which is
of the tribe of Judah, the Root of David,' the One of all
the inhabitants of heaven or of earth who was ' able to
open the book,' and ' who has conquered,' (so as) 'to open
the book and the seven seals thereof.'   This Jesus, born
like other men, for he genealogically descended from
David, has been raised as ' One like a son of man,' and
has become at one with the first of ' the seven angels
which stand before God.' And yet, as ' Jesus Christ, the
faithful witness,' he is distinguished from any angel.
Having been raised on the clouds of heaven to the
throne of God, having occupied the position of Christ
as the premundane Word of God, as the first of seven
angels, he who on earth was the ' fellow-servant' of
John, now sends his angel to the seer, and forbids him,
as Rabbi Idit forbade later a Christian heretic, to worship any other than God.

The same Angel whom the raised Jesus Christ
designates as ' My Angel,' is in the same chapter explained to be the Angel of the God ' of the spirits of
the prophets.'   For both, God as well as Christ-Jesus,
are the Alpha and Omega, the First and the Last.   Yet
in the Apocalypse of John the eternal Word of God,
the first of seven Angels, is distinguished from and at the
same time identified with the risen Jesus Christ. The Lion
of the tribe of Judah, the Root of David, the faithful
witness who was crucified at Jerusalem, ' like a son of
man ' was carried on the clouds to the throne of God,
and is now the first of the seven Archangels standing
before God, the Angel from whose hands Jesus took the
book of mysteries.

Paul opposed in his Epistle to the Colossians the

[1] Rev. x. 6; xi. 3: comp. xiv. 14, 17 ; v. 1-5; xxii. 7-20.; Hoekstra,
Th. Tijdschr. iii. 373 f; 398 f.

distinction, which is made in this Apocalypse, of a celestial Christ and a terrestrial Messiah, by the doctrine of the fulness or Plenitude of God dwelling bodily in the one person Christ-Jesus.

The Apostle warns the Colossians against an Essenic false teacher, against ' a certain person,' whom he might name, and who threatens to carry them off as plunder ' by philosophy and (which is) vain deceit, in accordance with mere human traditions and earthly rudiments, and not in accordance with Christ.' It has pleased God, that the eternal Christ, ' who is the Image of the Unseen God, the Firstborn of all creation,' in whom, by whom, and unto whom ' all things have been created,' both in heaven and earth, that this ' man from heaven,' as Paul writes to the Corinthians, that He who is the embodiment of ' the whole ' Plentitude of God, not of a Divine plentitude divided among Angels, should, as Jesus, ' in the body of his flesh, by death,' yea ' by the blood of his cross ' make peace, and ' reconcile ' those who were alienated from God and his enemies.[1]

We saw that the same double personality of a celestial and a contemporaneous terrestrial Messiah, which is the characteristic feature of the Christology in the Apocalypse, is assumed in the pre-Christian Targum after Jonathan, where the Messianic Word of God is said to rejoice over God's servant, the Messiah. The same distinction was made by the Christian gnostic Cerinthus, whose Christology, in every essential point, may be regarded as identical with that in the Revelation of ' John.' For even the view of Cerinthus that Christ, because a 'spiritual being,' departed from Jesus before he suffered, is not excluded by the doctrine of Christ in the Apocalypse. According to the earliest statement of Irenæus, Cerinthus did believe in the humanity of Jesus, ' that Jesus suffered and rose again'. This is emphatically declared by ' John,' who refers to the redemption by

[1] Col. ii. 6-9 ; i. 19–22, comp. Gal. i. 7 ; 1 Cor. xv. 47.

the blood of Jesus, to his translation on the clouds of heaven as one 'like' a son of man, and to his appearing as Jesus and as Christ after his death.

Thus according to Cerinthus and according to John at Patmos the man Jesus was after his death united with Christ, whom the one calls a 'spiritual being,' the other, the first of seven Angels from whose hands Jesus took the book. Because Cerinthus distinguished Jesus from Christ whilst on earth, Epiphanius declares, that Cerinthus denied that Jesus was the Christ,[1] that Christ had come in the flesh. Like Paul's Epistle to the Colossians, the First Epistle of the Apostle John protests against this, as we shall consider further on. If so, the Apostle John cannot possibly have written the Apocalypse, containing the Cerinthian doctrine of Christ.

According to a tradition which reaches back to Polycrates, a personal disciple of the Apostle John, the latter designated Cerinthus at Ephesus, where he met him in a bath, as 'the enemy of truth.' Cajus, a Roman presbyter, at the end of the second century, asserts that Cerinthus falsely attributed to the Apostle John—probably by reference to Churches in Asia Minor, where the latter was known—his own record of visions or revelations conveyed to him by angels.

Dionysos of Alexandria (+ 265) referred to the assertion of some of his predecessors among the presbyters of Alexandria, that 'the book has a false title, for it is not of John,' nor 'even a revelation;' and Cerinthus, 'wishing to have reputable authority for his own fiction, prefixed the title.' Dionysos adds: 'It is highly probable that Cerinthus designedly affixed the name (of John) to his own forgery; for one of the doctrines which he taught was, that Christ would have an 'earthly kingdom' of a thousand years' duration, as recorded by 'John' in the Apocalypse. Dionysos regarded as uncertain who the John of the Apocalypse

---

[1] Epiph. *Hær.* xxviii. 1.

was, but he saw no reason for doubting that 'a John' wrote it. He implies that the non-Apostolic author may have had a double name, like John-Marcus who, as he observes, yet is called John in the Acts. His only reason for not venturing to set aside the book is, that 'there are many brethren who value it much.'[1]

Dionysos does not say a word against the presbyterial tradition of Alexandria (as of Rome), that Cerinthus was the John of the Apocalypse, thus almost implying that this gnostic was called John-Cerinthus. If we add to this the supposition that Cerinthus may have been one of the elders of Ephesus, the whole difficulty of the dark passage in the writings of Papias (+ 156 or 162[2]) might be cleared up, who distinguishes a presbyter John from the Apostle John. Papias refers to the tradition that two Johns lived in Asia and were buried at Ephesus, where the monument of the Apostle was not distinguished from that of his namesake. He adds: 'We are bound to take notice of this (the two Johns), for it is natural that the other (the presbyter John) is accepted, when somebody will not (will not accept?) that the former (the Apostle John) has seen (had the visions of) the Apocalypse published under the name of John.'[3]

What we know about the Church at Ephesus can be well harmonised with the assumption of efforts made by Cerinthus in that Church, as almost certainly in that of Colossæ, against Paul and his doctrines. Paul had spent two years at Ephesus, where he left Aquila and Priscilla, and was followed by Apollos. From Ephesus Paul wrote to the Corinthians that a great and effectual door was there opened unto him; but he

---

[1] Eus. *H. E.* iii. 28; vii. 25; Iren. *Hær.* i. 26; Epiph. *Hær.* xxviii. 6; Theod. fab. *Hær.* ii. 3.

[2] Waddington, *Inscr.* xxxi. 2, p. 232 f. (1867).

[3] About the text see Eus. *H. E.* iii. 39; comp. Leimbach, *Das Papias Fragment*, 1875; Weiffenbach, *Das Papias Fragment*; Hilgenfeld, *Zeitschrift f. w. T.*, 1875.

admitted at the same time and place that there were
'many adversaries.' Among these may well have been
such who had before him preached Christianity in a
non-Paulinic form. That the Church at Ephesus was
founded by Paul is a mere assumption, not proved by
the Scriptures. He refers to such, who did not regard
him as an Apostle. When he took leave of the elders
of Ephesus, whom he had summoned from Miletus,
he warned them that after his departing 'grievous
wolves' would 'enter in' the presbytery, 'not sparing
the flock.' 'Also from among yourselves men will
arise who speak perverse things to draw away the
disciples after them.' Among the perverse elders of
Ephesus, who would arise after Paul's departure from
Miletus, and against whom he warned the Ephesian
elders in his farewell address in this city, may have been
Cerinthus, whom at Ephesus the Apostle John called an
enemy of the truth. Paul pointed to him in his Epistle
to the Colossians, all but calling him by name, and he
seems also indirectly to refer to him as a dangerous false
teacher in his address at Miletus.

If Cerinthus had an opportunity in any of his writings, we may safely assume that he would reckon Paul
among 'wicked persons,' and especially as belonging to
those who have been tried by the Church at Ephesus,
by the Church where Paul had met so 'many adversaries,' and which evil persons Ephesus could not 'bear.'
Cerinthus would not have resisted the temptation of
referring to such who 'say they are Apostles, and are
not,' thus pointing to Paul's statement, that to some he
was 'not an Apostle' though he asserted to be one.
Cerinthus may have been led to say that Ephesus has
found such to be 'liars.' Paul having accepted the faith
of Stephen, of the colleague of Nicolas, called proselyte of Antioch, Cerinthus could regard Paul as belonging to the Nicolaitans, who, as we shall see, derived
their name from the former, and who would be hated

by Jewish Christians because of their dealings with Gentiles, which in the received figurative sense would make them chargeable with immorality. Cerinthus might well have lamented, after the death of Paul, that the Church at Ephesus had left her 'first love,' that is, that she had changed her original form of Christianity, probably more akin to the gnosticism of Cerinthus, for another, perhaps for Petrinic Christianity, and this would be designated by Cerinthus as a fall.[1]

These passages in a Scripture which excludes Paul from the Apostolic body, which promulgates Cerinthian Christology, and which was attributed to Cerinthus by presbyterial tradition of the Roman and of the Alexandrian Church, can be easily referred to Paul. For the latter in the Epistle to the Colossians, by the expression 'a certain person,' seems to have pointed to Cerinthus, and likewise in his Epistle to the Galatians, the Apostle uses the same word in the plural, 'certain persons,' when speaking of some who troubled the Galatians, and strove to 'pervert the gospel of Christ,' as preached by Paul.

These anti-Paulinic views of Cerinthus were confirmed by his followers; for, like the anti-Paulinic Ebionites, they continued to use, up to the fourth century, Matthew's Gospel only. There were Ebionites still in the time of Epiphanius (+ 403), who connected Christ with angels and archangels, as this is done by the 'Revelation of John.' It can be proved that Ebionites and Elkesaitans, like Cerinthus and probably all Palestinian Essenes, rejected Paul and his Epistles, as also the canonical Acts.[2] The first Christian Apocalypse, that of 'the twelve Apostles of the Lamb,' and of the ruler of the Gentiles 'with a rod of iron,' represents that anti-Paulinic Jewish-Christianity, with which the Gentile-

[1] Rev. ii. 1–7.
[2] Iren. Hær. i. 20; Orig. c. Cels. v. 61, 65, &c.; Eus. H. E. iii. 27; Theod. Hær. fab. ii. 1; Epiphanius, Hær. xxx. 3, 16; Hilgenfeld, l. c. 39–41.

excluding Essenes of Palestine and Cerinthus may be connected.[1] Cerinthus lived in Asia Minor, and was brought up in Egypt, where were such who taught a narrow Judaism, against which Apollos, like Paul, protested, as the latter did against Cerinthian Christology, which we meet in the Apocalypse. To the Gentile-excluding principle of Cerinthus points also the statement of Epiphanius, that Cerinthus belonged to those who blamed Paul for his relations with Cornelius, the reported first fruit of the Gentile Church.

The connection of a celestial but Gentile-excluding kingdom of thousand years with the reign of an Angel-Messiah was, as we pointed out, an Oriental tradition, only partly, or without the Millennium, developed and applied to Jewish history in the Book of Daniel. Cerinthus is the first of whom we can prove that he thus supplemented the Book of Daniel by the doctrine of the Millennium, whether he wrote the Revelation of John or not. The Book of Daniel, the pre-Christian Targumim and Cerinthus, like the Ebionites and Essenes, made no distinction between Judaism and the kingdom of heaven, or that which was already in the time of Cerinthus called Christianity. But Irenæus informs us that Cerinthus, unlike some Ebionites, regarded the Word of God or Christ as Creator of the world, and taught that the world did not know the true God till he was manifested in Christ. This contrast between the God of Judaism and the God of Christianity, and thus between the Old and New Testament, was the fundamental doctrine of Marcion, who, like Philo and Cerinthus, placed the highest subordinate spirit, the mighty but not almighty framer of the world, between God as the absolute good, and the Devil as the principle

---

[1] Some Ebionites (Essenes?) admitted the human nature of Jesus, and so did Cerinthus and the 'John' of the Apocalypse, but Barnabas denied the descent from David. The distinction of the Angel having power over the fire from the Angel of the waters (Rev. xiv. 18; xvi. 5) may be connected with the Essenic water- and fire-baptism.

of evil. Cerinthus taught that Jesus, the son of Joseph and Mary, was born like other men, ' not of a virgin,' and 'after his baptism Christ descended upon him in the form of a dove from the Supreme Ruler,' when ' he proclaimed the unknown Father, and performed miracles; at last Christ departed from Jesus, and then Jesus suffered and rose again, while Christ remained impassible, inasmuch as he was a spiritual being.' [1]

With these views it is easy to connect those attributed to him by Epiphanius about the continued validity of all the injunctions of the law, and about the Millennium, to which Cajus refers. Cerinthus, like Barnabas and Eleazar at Adiabene, regarded the works of the law as absolutely necessary to salvation, and he must have opposed Paul as violently as Eleazar opposed Ananias at Adiabene, and as, for the contrary reason, Paul opposed Peter at Antioch. We saw that a similar difference existed between the Palestinian Essenes, as strict observers of the law, notwithstanding their allegorical and gnostic Scripture-interpretation, and the Egyptian Essenes or Therapeuts, who insisted on the perfect equality of Gentiles and Jews. We shall connect Barnabas and Cerinthus with the Palestinian Essenes, and we have connected Paul and Apollos with Therapeutic doctrines. If Cerinthus was led to Christianity through Alexandrian Judaism, he cannot have accepted the Therapeutic principle of universality, like Paul and Apollos, but he clung to that narrow Judaism, the spreading of which Paul tried to check in Colossæ, Apollos in Alexandria.

Cerinthus opposed that liberty which regarded itself not bound by the fetters of the law, which liberty Paul had openly confessed and generally promulgated. That ' glorious liberty,' checked only by the Spirit of God, and which relies on conscience as a sufficient guide, had

[1] Iren. *Hær.* i. 26.

led Paul not to condemn the eating of meat sacrificed
to idols. Cerinthus must have hated this liberty, and
what it often led to, as much as the writer of the
Apocalypse hated the Nicolaitans, who ate 'things
sacrificed unto idols' and committed 'fornication.' We
explain this latter charge by that figurative sense in
which alone it could be said that Israel 'went a
whoring after other gods,' or 'with their inventions.'
In this sense we have explained the narratives about
Thamar and about Rahab. Ezra had condemned the
marriage between Hebrews and strangers as an unclean-
ness and abomination, and had ordered the prescribed
atoning sacrifice. Thus also Zechariah's vision about
the woman in the ephah, symbolising 'wickedness,' probably referred to the same illegal concubinages or
whoredoms. So the Nicolaitans may have been charged
with fornication because of their making no distinction
between Gentiles and Jews. By not forbidding the
eating of things sacrificed to idols, a bridge between
Jews and Gentiles had been erected—an illegal affinity
between them. Again, in a figurative sense, those
Christians who are called Nicolaitans are designated as
'children' of Jezebel, and followers of the teaching of
Balaam, which led Israelites 'to commit whoredom with
the daughters of Moab' and to eat and bow before their
gods. The reference to Paul's First Epistle to the Corinthians is confirmed by the hidden reference to the
'deep things' or depths of the knowledge of God,
to the gnosis, which Paul and others preached, and
which led to 'the depths of Satan,' in the opinion of
'John.'[1]

The intention to connect Paul with the Nicolaitans,
admitted by many interpreters, becomes more plausible
when we consider the connection we tried to establish
between Paul and Stephen, whose colleague, as one of the
seven deacons, was Nicolas, 'the proselyte of Antioch,'

[1] See pp. 141-143; Rev. ii. 24; I. Cor. ii. 10.

according to Irenæus, from whom the Nicolaitans derived their name. The unimpeachable testimony as to the identity of this deacon with the founder of the sect of Christians who ate things sacrificed to idols, which Paul did not forbid, and who committed 'fornication,' indirectly confirms our figurative interpretation of this charge. For it is absolutely impossible to assume that Nicolas, one of the 'men of honest report, full of the Holy Ghost,' on whom after prayer the Apostles laid their hands, should have been in the literal sense of the word a fornicator, or the founder of a sect of Christians who could be charged with such offence.

Together with the Apostle Barnabas, the author of the Epistle bearing his name, and which we shall now consider, Cerinthus may be connected with that phase of Oriental and Essenian gnosticism which was represented by the Anti-Paulinic and Gentile-excluding Essenes of Palestine, as distinguished from the universalist Essenes of Egypt. If Cerinthus wrote the Revelation of John about the return of Jesus as Angel-Messiah, he is the most probable individual of whom a conversation with the patriarch Rabban Gamaliel is recorded in the Talmud. The latter asked a Christian philosopher about the continued validity of the law after the future coming of Christ, and was answered in the affirmative, the Christian citing words of Jesus, as probably recorded in the Gospel of the Hebrews, known to us by a later version in Matthew: 'I am not come to diminish or to enlarge the law of Moses.'[1]

We regard Cerinthus as the probable author of the Apocalypse of John. The Apostle John cannot have believed in Jesus Christ as present or future Angel-Messiah, of which doctrine there is no trace in the first three Gospels. Early presbyterian tradition of the Roman and of the Alexandrian Church pointed to Cerinthus as the real author of the Apocalypse of John. Like John-

---

[1] Cited by Grätz, l. c. 23, 24.

Marcus, Cerinthus may also have been known under the name of John, as Dionysos seems to imply. In this case John-Cerinthus may have been 'the presbyter John,' mentioned by Papias (+ 156 or 163) as a living authority, whom he distinguishes from the Apostle John and the other ' disciples of the Lord,' without referring to Paul, as if this Apostle had been one of the repeaters of 'strange precepts,' not ' given by the Lord,' an outsider. The presbyter John was buried at Ephesus by the side of the Apostle John. Paul refers to perverse elders at Ephesus, where he had long ministered, and where were disciples of John or Essenes ; the John of the Apocalypse refers to wicked persons at Ephesus, who wrongly called themselves Apostles, as Paul did, in the opinion of some. Whilst there is nothing in this Scripture which, from what we know of Cerinthus, he could not have written, the Christology of the Apocalypse does not exclude but clearly includes that of Cerinthus, as transmitted by Irenæus. Nor do we know that anybody else preached such a doctrine. Cerinthus (and Papias) expected a Messianic Millennium, the late transmitted details of which probably originated in a carnal explanation of what Cerinthus may have referred to the spiritual marriage feast of the Lamb of God. The connection of the doctrine of Cerinthus and of the Apocalypse of John with the Eastern and Essenic gnosis is undeniable, to which latter also belonged the scheme of a Messianic kingdom of heaven, forming the seventh thousand of years. This scheme was indirectly recognised by Ezra, since the chronology from Adam to Moses has been so arranged as to place five links between them, and thus to make Moses the seventh organ of oral tradition from Adam.[1]

Whoever may have been the author of the Revelation of John, no more than the Book of Daniel

[1] Adam, Methuselah, Shem, Isaac, Levi, Jochebed, Moses; comp. the Millennial scheme, the centre of which is the year B.C. 586, pp. 288, 289.

does it contain any prophecy. The spirit of prophecy has been checked by the misleading influences of dogma.

The Apocalypse of Esdras, or Ezra, first written in Greek, and of Roman origin, cited by the author of the ascension of Moses, was composed before A.D. 44, and probably about B.C. 30. The eagle-vision can only be referred to the Greek empire, to the Seleucidian kings followed by the Roman triumvirate.[1] The Messianic kingdom is not to last a thousand years, but only 400. It will be inaugurated by the descent of the Angel-Messiah (not Jesus), who is higher than all angels, and will descend on Zion with thousands of angels in his train.

The Epistle of Barnabas was composed by the Apostle Barnabas some time after the destruction of Jerusalem, essentially in the form we possess it, according to the unanimous voice of the ancient Church. The text known to us is cited, as written by the Levite of Cyprus, seven times by Clement of Alexandria and thrice by Origen, whilst Eusebius and Jerome regard the Epistle as authentic. Not even a doubt is mentioned about the fellow-worker of Paul having written this Epistle, although it has probably been revised in later times. The arguments brought forward by modern critics against the Apostolic source of this Epistle are a very natural upshot from the artificially prepared soil, on which the dogmatic structure of the Christian Church has been erected. The fundamental principle of the Acts is not to admit the presence of two antagonistic parties at the beginning of the Apostolic age, the one headed by Peter and James, the other by Paul, and to exclude the Essenic element from the Apostolic Church. According to the Acts, Barnabas was chosen and sent by the Holy Spirit, for which reason he received Apostolic rank. The author of the Epistle of

[1] Hilgenfeld, *Zeitschrift f. w. T.* 1878, III., p. 400 f.

Dead Sea Scrolls

Barnabas was evidently an Essene, and denied that Christ was the Son of David as well as the Son of God. The writer, whose Christology seems to have been akin to that of Cerinthus, could not be acknowleged as the twelfth Apostle, and as the Levite of Cyprus and one of the Seventy, although the ancient Church had done so and called him an apostle.[1]

The arguments invented by modern criticism for the purpose of correcting a Clement of Alexandria, an Origen, and the Church-historian Eusebius, are chiefly based on the supposition that a learned Levite could not have had so incorrect notions of the Mosaic law and its institutions as the writer of this scripture betrays.[2] But apart from the impossibility of admitting that the highest authorities of Christian antiquity could have overlooked or not sufficiently weighed these circumstances, the evident Essenic character of the Epistle leads us to regard Barnabas as a Levite who had joined the Essenic association, having been brought up with Paul under Gamaliel, according to late recorded Cyprian tradition. As an Essene, Barnabas would not consider himself bound by the letter of Scripture, and his Epistle proves that, like the Essenes, he regarded not the literal but the figurative sense of the law and its institutions as conveying the full truth.

Here again we have a double name, for Barnabas was called Joseph, and received, from the Apostles, we are told, the surname of Barnabas, or 'son of prophecy' or 'admonition.' He has on sufficient grounds been identified with Joseph Barsabas, who, with Matthias, was set up as a candidate for the twelfth apostleship, between the fortieth and the fiftieth day after the resurrection of Christ, according to the Acts. This Joseph belonged to those men who had 'companied' with

[1] Eus. *H. E.* i. 12; comp. iii. 25; Clem. Alex. *Strom.* ii. 7, 20; v. 10.
[2] Bishop von Hefele, *Das Sendschreiben des Apostels Barnabas*; Heberle, in Herzog's *Cyklopädie.*

the Apostles all the time that the Lord Jesus ' went in
and out' among them, beginning from the baptism of
John, unto the same day that he was taken up from
them. Such a change of letters is not unusual, and
moreover the Codex D and the Ethiopian translation
read, in the passage quoted, Barnabas instead of Barsabas. In the Recognitions the name of Barnabas, not
of Barsabas, is identified with that of Matthias. This
leads to the supposition that the substitution in the
Acts of Matthias for Barnabas the Essene is not historical.[1] Indeed the connection of Essenes with the
aboriginal Church would have undermined the fundamental principle of the Acts, as it would have proved
the existence of Oriental and Gnostic elements in the
Church.

Like the Epistle to the Hebrews, Barnabas aims at
the conversion of his readers, probably the Judaising
party in Alexandria to which Apollos had referred,[2] to
a higher because typical interpretation of the law,
to the new covenant dimly foreshadowed by the old, to
the spiritual fulfilment of all which seemed prophetic in
Judaism. At the same time the Apostle insists on that
particularist Judaism which excluded the Gentiles, as all
Essenes or disciples of John in Palestine seem to have
done, in contradistinction to the fundamental doctrine
of the universalist Therapeuts. Because Paul represented
the doctrines of the latter, Barnabas separated from
him, and so did Mark, the nephew or sister's-son of
Barnabas, and the reported first bishop of the Alexandrian Church. If Barnabas was in Alexandria and in
Rome before the crucifixion of Jesus, as the tradition
in the pseudo-Clementines implies, he and probably

---

[1] Acts 1. 21-25; *Recog.* i. 60; *Strom.* ii. 20; Hipp. (?) ii. App.

[2] Barnabas is said to have been as a direct disciple of Jesus in Alexandria, according to the tradition recorded in the *Homilies* (i. 6-9) and
Recognitions (1. 7). If the latter gives the more correct and the original
tradition, the preacher in Rome, of whom the *Homilies* speak, was Barnabas,
and he pointed out to Clement of Rome the new doctrine.

Mark were teachers in Alexandria before Apollos wrote, if he did, his Epistle to the Hebrews or Alexandrians, attributed to Barnabas by Tertullian;[1] that is, the Epistle to the Jewish Christian part of the Alexandrian Church.

The Christology of the Epistle of Barnabas differs not only in the question about the admission of Gentiles from that of Paul and Apollos. Barnabas, like these, regards Christ as the Angel-Messiah, though, unlike Paul and Apollos and the John of the Apocalypse, he denies the Davidic descent of Christ-Jesus. Yet he distinguishes Christ from Jesus by asserting that his flesh was given up 'to corruption,' after he had offered it for the sins of his people. Jesus revealed 'the resurrection from the dead,' but it is not said he rose bodily. 'Jesus, who was manifested both by type and in the flesh, is not the Son of man, but the Son of God; since, therefore, they were to say that Christ was the son of David, fearing and understanding the error of the wicked (Jews), he saith: "The Lord said unto my Lord, Sit at my right hand, until I make thine enemies thy footstool."' Thus also Isaiah, by a falsified text, is asserted to have referred words to Christ, recorded to have been addressed to Cyrus the Anointed. Barnabas tries to prove that the wicked Jews cannot be the heirs of the covenant, since 'the tables of the testament of the Lord' were broken, after Moses had received them 'written in the spirit by the finger of the hand of the Lord.' But 'learn now how We (the good Jews) received it. Moses received as a servant, but the Lord himself, having suffered in our behalf, hath given it to us, that we should be the people of inheritance.' In another passage Christ is called 'Lord of all the world, to whom God said at the foundation of the

---

[1] Partly recognised in the Churches under the title of 'The Epistle of Barnabas to the Hebrews,' which is probably the 'Epistle of Barnabas' referred to in the Canon of Muratori (Hilgenfeld, *l. c.* 109).

world, Let us make man after our image, and after our likeness.'[1]

'The prophets, having obtained grace from Him, prophesied concerning Him; and He (since it behoved Him to appear in the flesh), that He might abolish death, and reveal the resurrection from the dead, endured (what and as He did), in order that He might fulfil the promise made unto the fathers, and by preparing a new people for Himself might show, whilst He dwelt on earth, that He, when He has raised mankind, will also judge them. Moreover, teaching Israel, and doing so great miracles and signs, He preached (the truth) to him, and greatly loved him. But when he chose His own apostles who were to preach His gospel (He did so from among those) who were sinners above all sin, that He might show He came "not to call the righteous but sinners to repentance." Then He manifested himself to be the Son of God. For if He had not come in the flesh, how could men have been saved by beholding Him? Since looking upon the sun which is to cease to exist, and is the work of His hands, their eyes are not able to bear his rays. The Son of God therefore came in the flesh with this view, that He might bring to a head the sum of their sins, who had persecuted His prophets to the death. For this purpose, then, He endured.' 'He himself willed thus to suffer, for it was necessary that He should suffer on the tree. For, says he who prophesies regarding Him: "Spare my soul from the sword, fasten my flesh with nails, for the assemblies of the wicked have risen up against me."'[2]

The sufferings of Christ, necessary for salvation, were 'foreshown' by the prophets. Pre-eminently among the numerous references to Messianically inter-

[1] We give the text contained in *The Ante-Nicene Christian Library,* where the *Codex Sinaiticus* and the edition of Hilgenfeld have been consulted.

[2] Barn. xii.–xiv., v. vi.; comp. Ps. xxii. 21, 17, cix. 120.

preted passages in Scripture is that about the servant
of God slain like a lamb, which with the offering up
of Isaac is enumerated among the types of Christ's
vicarious sacrifice on the cross. Barnabas finds the
Messianic cross frequently referred to in the Old
Testament, by the side of the brazen serpent. Those
who have been 'renewed' by the remission of sins,
thus procured, have been 'refashioned,' they belong
to the 'second fashioning' or creation of 'these last
days.' This new creation is described as given over
to Christ before the foundation of the earth, and
as an effect of the Spirit of God, implied to have
been brought down from heaven by the Angel-
Messiah, who will return after 6,000 years, when the
finishing of all things (the Millennium) will take place.
Like the cross, baptism has been prefigured in the Old
Testament. God has described both 'the water (of
baptism) and the cross' in the first Psalm, as also by
Zephaniah and Ezechiel.[1]

Like Apollos in the Epistle to the Hebrews of Alex-
dria, to whom Barnabas seems to have addressed this
Epistle, a more perfect knowledge, a 'more profound
gift,' or 'the engrafted spiritual gift,' a gnosis is referred
to, which Christ has 'put within' the newly created or
newborn, in those who are called the possessors of 'the
Spirit poured forth from the rich Lord of love,' who
brought it. The 'knowledge hid in parables,' about
'things present or future,' the readers of the Epistle
cannot understand, and this 'wisdom and understanding
of secret things' has been 'placed in us' by our blessed

[1] Barn. v. vii. xi. xii. vi. xv.; Ps. i. 3–6; Zeph. iii. 19; Ezek. xlvii.
12. The many irreconcilable quotations from the Old Testament, and later
from the earliest records of the words of Jesus, seem to be best explained by
the assumption that a gnostically reformed version of the Scriptures formed
part of the Scripture-collection of the Essenes and Therapeuts, which was
utilised, as was the Septuagint, in the composition of our Gospels and of
Pauline Epistles, according to Eusebius. Comp. Hebr. vii. 27, ix. 3, 4, and
the quotations in the writings of Justin Martyr.

Lord. Barnabas asserts that these mysteries were not made known to Israelites proper, or Hebrews, who were 'abandoned,' for 'as it is written' (in some Gospel) 'many are called but few are chosen.'[1]

Essenic are the following doctrines in the Epistle of Barnabas. The Angel-Messiah as personal and aboriginal type of humanity; the distinction between a spiritual and a material world, as of a way of light from a way of darkness; the distinction of a celestial from a terrestrial Messiah; the figurative interpretation of Scripture; the secret tradition or gnosis of the Initiated, connected with the Spirit of God brought by the Messiah; the abolition of bloody sacrifices, and the typical interpretation of those commanded by the law; the injunction to be spiritually minded, as a 'perfect temple to God' in which he dwells and prophesies; the injunctions not 'to stretch forth the hand' or to swear; to give alms; to 'communicate in all things' with the neighbour, not calling things one's own, inasmuch as 'partakers in common of things which are incorruptible' ought also to be 'of those things which are corruptible'; not to be hasty with the tongue, and 'as far as possible' to be 'pure in the soul'; to 'preserve' what has been received (the secret things), 'neither adding to it or taking from it'; to 'pacify' those that contend 'by bringing them together'; to 'confess' one's sins, not going 'to prayer with an evil conscience.'

Essenic is the injunction not, 'by retiring apart, to live a solitary life,' as if 'already fully justified,' but to come together 'in one place,' making 'common inquiry' concerning what tends to the general welfare. Essenic in the Epistle of Barnabas is also the water-baptism as a symbol of spiritual purity, and the rigid keeping of the Sabbath, as a type of the seventh thousand of years, of 'the day of the Lord' which shall be 'as a thousand years.' The return of the Son of God will lead to the

---

[1] Barn. ix. I. xvii. vi. iv. Matt. xx. 16; xxii. 14; comp. 4 Esdr. viii. 3.

judgment, to cosmical changes, and to the 'beginning of
the eighth day;' that is, 'a beginning of another world.'
The eighth day was by Barnabas held to be a memorial
of the resurrection of Jesus which took place on that
day, or the first day of the week. Nothing is said of its
having been ' the third day according to the Scriptures,'
but this is indirectly implied by the comparison drawn
between the death of Jesus and the slaying of the ram
or lamb in the place of Isaac, with which the slaying
of the Paschal lamb by Moses seemed to be connected.

We are perhaps justified in regarding the Christology
of Barnabas as identical with that of Paul, and to explain
the separation of the former from the latter exclusively
by the dissension about admitting the Gentiles. Yet by
the denial of the Davidic descent of Jesus, Barnabas
taught a different doctrine than that in Paul's Epistles.
Moreover, he believed either, like Cerinthus, in a
double Messianic personality, one angelic one human,
or, like Simon Magus, in a mere apparent humanity
of Jesus. It is probable enough that both Paul and
Barnabas were pupils of Gamaliel, as reported. We
tried to show that Gamaliel as a leading Rabbi stood
in connection with that Essenic and Medo-Chaldæan
or, Magian tradition of which the Book of Daniel is the
earliest known exponent. Barnabas, the Palestinian Essene, and Paul, the preacher of Therapeutic doctrines, had
this in common, that both regarded Jesus as the Angel of
God who can pardon transgressions, and whose resurrection was typified. Passing over as perhaps unhistorical the
account in the Acts about the first journey of Paul and
Barnabas from Antioch to Jerusalem, of which Paul says
nothing, the well-attested facts remain, that Barnabas, at
the bidding of the Twelve or not, introduced Paul to the
Church at Antioch ; that Barnabas and Peter were at
Antioch by Paul called dissembling Jews ; that when
seventeen years after his conversion to the faith of Stephen
(the Therapeut) Paul was introduced by Barnabas to the

Apostles at Jerusalem, they were all afraid of him, but recognised Paul and Barnabas as Apostles among the Gentiles; and that at Antioch the contention between Paul and Barnabas was 'so sharp, that they parted asunder,' and that Barnabas and Mark returned to Cyprus.

Barnabas seems to have stood nearer to the 'John' of the Apocalypse, to which the Epistle refers indirectly, than to Paul, to whose writings there is not any direct reference. Similarity of expression, and such views as angels of Satan, can be easily traced back to a common source, such as the teaching of Gamaliel. Unlike the Esdras of the Apocalypse, Barnabas wrote in the time of Domitian, whom he regarded as 'the last stumbling-block.' After him he expected the Beloved of God to come to his inheritance, at the end of 6,000 years from the creation of the world. Then 'the temple of God shall be built in glory, in the name of the Lord.'[1]

The Epistles of John.

The distinction between a true and a false knowledge or gnosis can be shown to have been already made in the first century, and to have centred in the denial of the human nature of Christ-Jesus. The Docetics of the second century stood in direct connection with the Essenes whose doctrines were similar to those of Simon Magus and Barnabas. We regard this false doctrine of the Apostolic and of the after-Apostolic age as the original secret doctrine of the Essenes. It was in so far opposed by Paul, as he clearly acknowledged, at least in the Epistle to the Romans, that the same Jesus Christ or Christ-Jesus was Son of God according to the spirit of holiness, and was son of David according to the flesh. On that basis Paul's doctrine was recognised by the Church.

The Apostle John, or rather John the presbyter, as

[1] Barn. iv. xvi. This settles the year 97 for its composition; comp. Hilgenfeld, *l. c.* 544, Note 1.

he called himself, wrote his three Epistles probably from
Ephesus, and perhaps before the destruction of Jerusalem, since he writes, ' it is the last time,' which may
be referred to the Jewish Church and nation.   John's
principal object is to oppose those who in ' the spirit of
Antichrist,' and as ' Antichrists,' denied in those Apostolic days that Christ has come ' in the flesh.'   His contemporaries, Barnabas and Cerinthus, distinguished
between Jesus and Christ, thus denying the presence in
all ages of the Spirit of God in mankind.   The Apostle
calls this the denial of ' the Father and the Son.'

   ' The false teachers went out from us, but were
not of us.'   Thus it seems to be implied that the
Essenes had separated from the recognised Judaism
ever since they formed the third or independent
party among the Jews, which they did at least about
150 years before the birth of Jesus.   As they had
not continued with the Pharisees who sat in the seat of
Moses, so they had not continued with those who, like
John, had ' seen and heard,' who had ' looked upon,' and
whose ' hands handled,' the bodily manifestation or appearing, that is, the incarnation of ' the Word of Life.'
That Word or Logos is by John described as a spiritual
substance, as the seed or sperma, which if it ' abide ' in
man, causes him to be ' born of [from] God,' and prevents
him from sinning.[1]

   The false teachers, the ' many Antichrists ' who had
even then arisen, that is, in the Apostolic age, are described by the Apostle as if they were Essenes.   What
he writes against their doctrine of Christ confirms the
fact we tried to establish, that the secret tradition of
the Essenes included the doctrine of an Angel who
would be manifested on earth as Messiah, but not as a
human embodiment of the Word or Spirit of God.   The
very commencement of the First Epistle of John shows
that the Apostle found it necessary to testify, that he

[1] 1 John ii. 18-22 ; iv. 3 ; iii. 9.

and his fellow-workers had seen Jesus Christ with their eyes, not as a bodiless spirit, as a phantom, but as a human reality, that their hands had ' handled ' the Word of Life, Jesus Christ, the Son of God.

Like James, John does not regard the Word in the heart of man, 'his seed,' as a new spiritual faculty or new gift of God, which had come to man after the incarnation and sacrificial death of Jesus, according to Paul's declaration. The Word of Life is ' the engrafted word ' of which James writes that it is ' able to save the soul ;' it is ' the word of God ' which in the First Epistle of Peter is described as 'the imperishable seed,' living and abiding, by which man is born again, and which Word Peter had preached by the gospel. Neither John, Peter, nor James distinguishes this Word, or Christ, from ' the spirit of promise,' which came not till after the atonement by the death of Jesus on the cross, according to Paul's doctrine.[1]

The heretics against whom John writes his Epistles, especially his First Epistle, denied that Christ had come in flesh and blood ; they held that he came ' in water only,' that is, that Christ or the Spirit of God was not in Jesus at his birth, but descended and rested on him at his baptism. The Apostle declares in opposition to these false teachers, that Christ came also ' in the blood.' Those whom the Apostle John calls Antichrists distinguished Christ from Jesus, as Cerinthus and the writer of the Apocalypse of ' John ' has done. These teachers of a new and false doctrine asserted to possess a knowledge or gnosis of Jesus Christ, but they kept not ' his commandments.' The contents of the First Epistle of John suggest with sufficient clearness, that this gnosis which the Apostle John opposes is the secret tradition of the Essenes. From this high probability we are led to conjecture that the Essenes denied Christ's coming in the flesh. This the writings of Philo con-

[1] I Peter i. 23; James i. 18, 21; Rom. x. 5-9.

firm, who knew all about the Essenes, and held them in high estimation, even if he was not a Therapeutic Essene. Philo says nothing of a Messianic incarnation or atonement. Like Simon and apparently Barnabas, the Essenes denied the human nature of Christ-Jesus, regarding him as the Angel-Messiah, as absolutely supernatural, not as an incarnation of the Angel of God, but as One come down from heaven, 'apparently as man, yet not as man,' as 'Son of God, but not as Son of man.' It is also Essenic what John writes about the false gnostics in his time who hated their brethren. For the separatist Essenes, not the Therapeuts, with whom we connected Paul, hated their brethren the Gentiles, and denied that Christ is also 'a propitiation' for the sins of the whole world.[1]

The false teachers in the time of the Apostle John held, like the Essenes, that they did not transgress against the law according to its literal interpretation, inasmuch as by a figurative and spiritual interpretation of the letter they considered themselves entitled to disregard the Commandments which the letter of the law imposed. By so doing they did not regard themselves as sinning; they said that they had no sin. John opposes these Essenic gnostics by saying, that 'the transgression of the law is sin,' that 'all unrighteousness is sin,' that 'he that doeth sin is of the devil, because the devil sinneth from the beginning; but that he that doeth righteousness is righteous, even as He [Jesus Christ] is righteous.' Every righteous man 'is of God.' Thus the Apostle John acknowledges the existence of the Word from the beginning, and of the devil from the beginning; he regards neither as a personality, but he distinguishes 'the children of God' from 'the children of the devil.' This spiritual dualism, of Oriental origin, was an apostolic doctrine. 'For this purpose the Son

---

[1] John v. 6; ii. 9, 11.

of God was manifested, that he might destroy the works of the devil,' that is, of the evil spirit.[1]

'That which was from the beginning,' Christ, the Word or Spirit of God, was manifested in Jesus, in flesh and blood. God sent that Divine Power, God 'sent His Son as a propitiation for our sins.' As in the Angel, who can pardon sin, so in Jesus was the name or Spirit of God. Therefore he could not sin, he was ' begotten of God ' and ' sinneth not,' for ' he that hath been begotten of God, he keepeth [preserveth] himself, and the wicked one [the evil spirit] toucheth him not.' God abode with Jesus, and the love of him was perfected in him. God had given to Jesus, as he has given to us, ' of his Spirit,' and therein Jesus knew and ' know we, that we abide in him and he in us.'

' This is the witness: that God gave to us eternal life, and this life is in His Son.' The Apostle does not say that this life, the Word of Life, ' that which was from the beginning,' was the premundane Son of God; but he says that this anointing power of God is ' in ' his Son, in Jesus the Anointed. Thus John's testimony on the true doctrine of Christ is in perfect harmony with the confession of Peter, that the man Jesus of Nazareth has by God been anointed ' with the Holy Ghost and with power.' In this sense John testifies ' that the Father hath sent the Son as Saviour of the world.' Jesus is the Son of God because his Spirit or Word abode ' in him and he in God.' So does God abide in every man who confesses this; every such believer abides in God. ' He that believeth on the Son of God hath the witness in him.'[2]

The Divine Sonship is abiding communion and life in the Spirit of God. That Word or Spirit which abides in Jesus, the Son of God, is God; God is a Spirit. In

---

[1] 1 John i. 8; iii. 4–10; comp. for the denial of sin by Gnostics, Clem. Alex. *Excerpta ex-propheticis,* § 15; Opp. p. 993; Hilgenfeld, *l. c.* 688.

[2] 1 John iii. 5; iv. 10–15; v. 18; v. 10.

an evidently genuine passage which is omitted, purposely
or not, in many ancient manuscripts, the Spirit of God
in man is clearly indicated to be the Father and also to
be the Son : ' Whosoever denieth the Son, neither hath
he the Father ; he that confesseth the Son, hath the
Father also.'   Again : ' If that which ye heard from the
beginning abide in you, ye also shall abide in the Son
and in the Father.'   Therefore the Apostle writes : ' We
are in the true One, in his Son Jesus Christ.   This is
the true God, and eternal life.'[1]   It was necessary to
omit these words after the introduction of the doctrine
of the three eternal Persons, of which the Bible knows
nothing.   The Word which was in the beginning, which
was in mankind, and also in Jesus, is the Father.   Its
bodily manifestation in Jesus is called the Son, who
after his resurrection became an advocate with the
Father.

Nothing is said in the Epistles of John about a Personal Word who, as an angel, was with God before the
creation of the world.   The Word of Life which was in
the beginning can abide in man ; his word, his seed,
the incorruptible seed of the word of God, the engrafted
word, is able to save the soul.   Those who have an
' anointing (a Christ) from the Holy One,' from the
Father, require ' no new commandment,' they know all
things,' they need not be taught a figurative interpretation of the Scriptures, a gnosis or deeper and secret
knowledge.   The Word which the readers of this
Epistle ' have heard ' is ' the old commandment,' which
they ' had from the beginning.'   Also in the time of
Moses that Word was in man's heart that he might do it.

But ' the law and the prophets until John,' him
included, had prophesied about the future coming of
that Word to the heart of man, so that the true light,
although actually in man, could not shine.   It was
Jesus who showed by his words and works that the

[1] 1 John ii. 23, 24; v. 20.

Spirit of God is in man, that 'the kingdom of heaven is already come.' The Scribes and Pharisees ' shut up the kingdom of heaven against men,' but some entered in nevertheless, although by force ; they had to press into it, for it suffered violence. Now, after the days of John, and since the days of Jesus, who drove out evil spirits by the Spirit of God, as did others in Israel, his beloved disciple, the Apostle John, could write ' a new commandment, which thing is true in him (in Jesus Christ) and in you, because the darkness is passing away, and the true light now shineth.' [1]

Jesus did follow the promptings of his Word, of his seed, therefore he sinned not, and he was the Saviour of the world, a propitiation for the sins of men. Christ, the Word or Spirit of God, did verily come in flesh and blood ; that power of God became incarnate in the man Jesus, who by his life, not by his sacrificial death, became a propitiation for the sins of mankind. Because the reality of his blood was denied, John writes that ' the blood of Jesus cleanseth us from all sin.' This is not a figurative expression, but a mysterious reality. Whosoever has the Word of Life, the Spirit of God, abidingly in him, is by that light of God enabled to ' walk in the light as he is in the light,' and ' he cannot sin.' For such there is no condemnation, nor need of another Saviour than God himself, inasmuch as that spiritual fellowship or communion with God ' cleanseth us from all sin.' That saving communion with God is the direct result of our walking in the light as God is in the light. Because the great mystery of ' God manifested in the flesh ' was by false teachers in those days denied, because Christ, the Word of God, was declared not to have come in flesh and blood, that is, because the presence of the Word or Spirit of God in man was denied ; therefore the Apostle writes, that ' the blood ' of him in whom is no sin, that is, of him whom God had

[1] 1 John ii. 20, 7, 8.

anointed with his Spirit, that the blood of Jesus Christ the Son of God cleanseth us from all sin. If the truth is in us, and 'if we confess our sins,' then God 'is faithful and just to forgive us our sins, and to cleanse us from all unrighteousness.' Thus it is God himself, he who 'is light,' God manifested in flesh and blood, who 'cleanseth us from all sin,' who is our Saviour. But because Jesus, by his merit, is the perfect organ of God's spirit, is the incarnation of God, therefore what is said of the Father can be said of the Son also. It is God who cleanseth us from all sin and who gives to us eternal life. This forgiveness of sin, this life 'is in his Son,' in Jesus the Christ.

In order to teach by word and deed the old commandment, that the Word of God is in man's heart that he may do it—which commandment had become a dead letter ; in order to teach the new commandment, the thing which is true in him and in mankind ; in order that the self-imposed darkness might pass away and the God-granted true light might shine, Jesus had to tread a forbidden path and to lay down his life for us. Thus he enabled us to perceive the love of God. For God was in him, and God is love. The followers of Jesus ought—if necessary—to lay down their lives 'for the brethren.'

In the Epistles of the Apostle John not a word is said about a sacrificial or vicarious death of Jesus on the cross as the Lamb of God. Like the Epistle of James, the Epistles of John exclude the Paulinic doctrine of atonement, as found in the 'Gospel after John.'

If Paul had already developed in his Epistles the doctrine of Christ's atonement, as a necessary preliminary and condition of the coming of the spirit of promise ; if Paul had declared, before the composition of the Epistles of John, that the words of Moses about the Word in the heart of man were a prophecy of Christ's resurrection, then the Apostle John opposed not only the false doctrines of the Essenes, but also this doctrine of Paul.

Most Gnostics of the Apostolic and after-apostolic age agreed in denying, that Christ, whom they regarded as the Angel-Messiah, came in the flesh. But only Cerinthus and his followers, as later Basilides, believed in a merely temporary abiding of Christ in Jesus, in a double personality of the Messiah, distinguishing the terrestrial Jesus from the celestial Christ. Consequently all Gnostics excluded a corporeal resurrection of Jesus Christ, of which even Paul said nothing. This new or dualistic form of gnosis, which Paul attacked in his Epistle to the Colossians, paved the way for the unlimited co-operation of Paul and the twelve Apostles. Because of this distinction between the Angel Christ and the man Jesus, all Apostles would have opposed the 'Revelation of John,' as also the accounts transmitted to us about the corporeal resurrection of Jesus. These narratives seem to have been invented, not before the composition of the fourth Gospel, perhaps with a view to undermine the doctrine of two contemporaneous Messianic personalities, and to establish the belief in the Oneness of Jesus Christ.

Retrospect.

The conception of a non-material or spiritual from a material world, the cosmic dualism, probably of East-Iranian origin, was in course of time connected with a severe mode of life, with an asceticism which prevailed on the Ganges and on the Euphrates, and of which there is no trace among the East-Iranians or Zoroastrians. Gautama-Buddha, the preacher of a 'tradition from beyond,' from a supermundane world, was regarded as one of the incarnations of the first of seven

Archangels, of Serosh, the vicar of God, and the first among the co-Creators of the universe. The proved connection of Parsism and Buddhism with Essenism led us to the assumption that the Essenes expected as Messiah an incarnate angel, like Buddha, the virgin-son, and that they denied his birth in the flesh by natural means. This hypothesis we found confirmed by what we know about John the Baptist, the Ashai or bather, the Essai or Essene. So mysterious was the apparition of this celestial Messiah among men supposed to be, that Philo, probably an Essene, abstains from even referring to a theory on the subject. 'The Archangelic Word of God,' the 'Highpriest of the profession,' the 'second God,' had appeared to Jacob and others, but the idea is never expressed by Philo, that 'the most ancient Son of God' would come in the flesh, either as son of a virgin, like Buddha, or otherwise. Yet the connection with Philo of Stephen, Paul, and Apollos, the first proclaimers of the doctrine that Christ had become incarnate in Jesus, leads to the almost provable assumption that Philo felt bound to keep back something about the Messianic expectations of the Essenes. If they expected an Angel-Messiah, they were by a special oath bound not to reveal these expectations to the uninitiated. Philo certainly did not, any more than John the Baptist or Josephus, regard his contemporary Jesus as the Messiah, but Elkesai the Essene did.

The Essenic doctrine of an Angel-Messiah, which can be proved to have prevailed at the end of the Apostolic age, must also have been recognised by the Initiated among the Essenes in the time of John the Baptist or Essene, since they were bound to transmit their doctrines in no 'other way' than they had 'received them.' Even in the fourth century, Epiphanius could attest that the Essenes had not changed in anything. When John sent the deputation to Jesus, he wanted to know, whether Jesus was 'he that should come,' the Tathâgata of

Buddhists, the Angel-Messiah. The answer of Jesus, when connected with other recorded sayings of his, implies that he did not regard himself as an Angel, and that he attributed the works which he did to the presence of the Spirit of God in man, which John announced as future. John was a Gnostic, which word has the same meaning as Buddhist.

The gnosis or deeper knowledge of the Essenes is of Eastern origin, and centred in the doctrine of an Angel-Messiah, of which there is no trace in any of those portions of Hebrew Scriptures which were possibly written before the exportation to Babylon, nor in the first three Gospels. We have traced this Oriental and Essenic gnosis, about the Angel-Messiah, in the Book of Daniel and in several Jewish and Christian Scriptures connected with the same. The most important exponents of the new Messianic doctrine are the speech of Stephen, the writings of Paul and Apollos, the Revelation of John, not the Apostle, and the Epistle of Barnabas. But they not all followed Simon Magus in denying that Christ came really in the flesh.

The Oriental and Essenic gnosis of pre-Christian and Christian times, inasfar as it regards the Angel-Messiah, was acknowledged by the Midrashim, the Targums, and the Talmud. It was represented by John the Baptist, opposed by Jesus, yet applied to the latter by Stephen and Paul. The Apostle of the Gentiles coupled the new Messianic doctrine with the Therapeutic principle of universality, for which reason he was opposed by the Gentile-excluding or separatist Essenes. To these seem to have belonged Simon Magus and Barnabas, for also the latter in fact denied the human nature of Jesus, as did the false teachers against whom the Apostle John wrote his First Epistle. Paul promulgated a Gnostic, Essenic, and essentially Buddhistic doctrine of Christ, whilst opposing that form of gnosis which Cerinthus proclaimed, of which the Revelation of John is the fullest exponent. Though issued forth from Judaism, Christianity applied to Jesus, without his authority, a Messianic doctrine unknown to and excluded by the Old Testament.

The fourth Gospel, still unknown to Papias, whilst he knew the First Epistle of John, was assimilated in form to the latter, with the intention of establishing Apostolic authority for the Gospel of the Angel-Messiah and the Lamb.

The Twelve and Paul agreed to work together on the understanding that the kingdom of heaven is the rule of the Spirit of God in mankind, and that by this Divine power Jesus was of God anointed, was made Christ. Thus the difference between the doctrine of the anointed man and that of the anointed Angel was not allowed to stand in the way of the practical purposes, the uniting influences, of Christianity.

General Conclusion.—The Roman Church.

Two different dates are given in the Gospels for the crucifixion. According to the first three Gospels it is the 15th Nisan, not the day when the paschal lamb was killed, but the day following the 14th Nisan, on which latter day, according to the fourth Gospel, the crucifixion took place.[1] This date, and consequently the following 'third day,' the 16th Nisan for the resurrection, Paul must have had in his mind when he wrote about the 'passover slain for us,' and about 'the firstfruits of them that slept,' evidently regarding Jesus Christ as the antitype both of the paschal lamb and of the paschal omer. 'The Gospel after John' is alone in harmony with Paul's Epistles, since the resurrection-day,

---

[1] John xviii. 28; comp. xiii. 1; xviii. 39; xix. 14. The day of the Passover began with the evening of the 14th; Eus. *H.E.* vii. 32, 18.

the first day of the week, is here the third day, whilst that same 'first day of the week' is the second day after the crucifixion according to the first three Gospels. In the latter the narrative of the crucifixion excludes the conception that Jesus, on the day of His death, fulfilled in a literal sense the type of the 14th, and by His resurrection the type of the 16th Nisan, according to a figurative interpretation of the law. Yet in these same Gospels the resurrection-day is referred to as the third day. It is obvious that the first day of the week cannot have been the third after the 15th of the month, and also after the 14th of the month in the same year.

We are therefore led to assume at the outset that the passages in the first three Gospels about the resurrection on the third day may have been inserted after the publication of the fourth Gospel, where alone the narrative of the crucifixion harmonises with the statements of Paul about the resurrection on ' the third day according to the Scriptures.'

It can be rendered probable that this final revision of the Gospels was a necessary consequence of the paschal dispute which broke out in the middle of the second century, when Bishop Polycarp, the associate of the Apostle John and of other apostles, opposed at Rome, in the presence of Pope Anicetus, the Easter-rite of the Western churches, as established by Roman presbyterial tradition, and as supported, in the main point, by the fourth Gospel, which forms part of our Canon, but was not then referred to.

Paul distinguishes between the Jewish and the Christian passover as between the prophesying type and the fulfilling antitype, that is, he connects the slaying of the Jewish paschal lamb with the crucifying of Jesus as the slain passover or paschal lamb of the Christians. Thus Paul prepared the way for the separation of the Jewish from the Christian Passover, as we find it in the account of the Last Supper in the Gospel after Luke.

The Passover or paschal supper having been made ready, Jesus sat down, and the Apostles with Him, round the table on which the paschal lamb was served. 'And He said unto them : " Heartily have I desired to eat this Passover with you before I suffer.   For I say unto you, I will not any more eat it, until it be fulfilled in the Kingdom of God." '   Though not clearly stated,[1] it is implied that Jesus did not refer to a mere spiritual partaking of the Passover, but that He did eat the lamb, on this final occasion, before His death, which would be the fulfilment of the typical Passover, and thus the beginning of the Kingdom of God.   For the kingdom of ' the spirit of promise' would not come till after His death, as Paul had declared.   'And He took a cup, gave thanks and said : take this and divide it among yourselves, for I say unto you, I will not henceforth drink of the fruit of the vine, until the Kingdom of God shall come.'

By reporting that Jesus spoke these words about the fruit of the vine at the end of the supper, not before it, as it is recorded in the first Gospel, the third Gospel implies that Jesus did not Himself drink of the cup. The expression ' fruit of the vine ' seems to have been changed from ' wine.'   For the cup contained wine, to which Paul never referred, and not merely ' liquor of grapes,' which was equally forbidden to the Nasirites, as also, presumably, to the Essenes.   Eating the lamb and drinking the wine at the Passover was an institution so contrary to Essenic principles and rites, that the Essenes, whom Philo calls the first allegorists, must have figuratively interpreted this ordinance of the Law, giving it a merely spiritual sense.   An exceptional permission to eat meat and drink wine at the paschal meal cannot be assumed to have been granted to the Essenes.[2]   By implying that Jesus did not drink of the

---

[1] In Matt. xxvi. 21, 26 it is written: 'and as they [the disciples only ?] were eating, he said.'

[2] According to Justin Martyr (*Apol.* i. 65 comp. 13) the cup of the Last

cup, the third Gospel has approximated Jesus to Essenic rites. Thus a mystic meaning has been given to the cup, apparently connecting the 'cup of blessing,' the third cup of the Jewish paschal supper, with the words attributed to Jesus in the first Gospel, about the cup which He was about to drink, the cup of His last suffering, which He prayed might pass from Him, and which the Apostles were not able to drink. In Mark these words are amplified by a reference to the baptism (of the Holy Ghost) with which Jesus was baptized.[1]

After having narrated the Jewish Passover which Jesus ate with His disciples, the third Gospel gives a separate account of a new sacrament instituted by Jesus, which is almost literally reproduced from Paul's Epistle. It is here clearly implied that the paschal lamb is henceforth, after that Jesus had eaten of it, not to be eaten any more, since its typical meaning was the next day to be fulfilled by the death of Jesus on the cross, as the slain Passover or paschal lamb of the Christians, as Lamb of God. The bread is to be eaten 'in remembrance' of Him, of His body given for them, and as (the symbol of) His body. In like manner the cup, the drinking of which is not referred to, is explained as (the symbol of) 'the new covenant' in His blood, shed for them. According to the Scriptures every covenant required blood, and as the old covenant was confirmed by the blood of the paschal lamb, so it is implied that the new covenant would on the following day be confirmed by the blood of Jesus as the Lamb of God, in a non-literal but imputed fulfilment of the law.

It is obvious that the accounts of the Last Supper in the three Gospels are based on the supposition that Jesus was not crucified on the day of the slaying of the paschal lamb, on the 14th Nisan. Yet this is implied by the

Supper, like the cup at the love feasts of the Christians, may have contained 'wine and water,' in the middle of the second century.
[1] Matt. xx. 22; xxvi. 39; Mark x. 38; comp. *Martyr. Polyc.* 14.

fourth Gospel, which gives no account of the Last Supper, because such narrative in such a place would have led to inextricable confusion. Instead of it, the rite of feet-washing is introduced.

Paul states in his account of the Last Supper that the memorial rite was instituted by Jesus, not in the night of the Passover, but ' in the night in which He was betrayed,' which, according to the fourth Gospel, was the night from the 13th to the 14th Nisan. The Apostle clearly implies, by other statements, that Jesus rose, visible or not, on 'the third day according to the Scriptures,' that His death as the slain Passover took place as antitype of the paschal lamb on the 14th Nisan, and His resurrection as ' the first fruits ' and ' the first born ' took place, as antitype of the paschal firstfruits, on the 16th Nisan. It is therefore certain that Paul refers to the 13th Nisan as to the night of the betrayal, and the same is implied in the fourth Gospel.

We assume here that Paul regarded Jesus as the incarnate Angel of God, or the spiritual Rock which followed the Israelites, in harmony with the almost certain Essenic expectation of an Angel-Messiah, and that the twelve Apostles must have regarded Him as the promised anointed man. It is quite possible that Paul's implied doctrine of Jesus as the paschal lamb was derived, like his Messianic doctrine, from the Essenes.

It has now to be shown that the Essenes had in the first century a Passover-rite similar to that which prevailed in all Christian churches after the Council of Nice, when the paschal dispute was finally decided in favour of the Roman-Alexandrian Easter-rite.

Eusebius connects the Therapeutic ' festival of our Saviour's passion,' described by Philo, the contemporary of Jesus, with what was still in the fourth century ' in vogue among ' the Christians, that is, with ' the customs that are observed by us alone at the present day, particularly the vigils of the great festival.'

According to Philo, the Therapeuts, whom Eusebius reckons among the aboriginal Christians, were accustomed to pass special days of their Easter festival ' in fasting[1] and watching, and in the study of the Divine Word.' Now, this is what the Christians in the fourth century continued to do, as Eusebius testifies, who declares that ' the same customs ' which were observed by the Christians ' alone,' in implied contradistinction to the customs of the Jews, had prevailed in the first century among the Therapeuts, as described by Philo.

It is thus proved that in the fourth century, and after the decisions of the First General Council, the Christian Church recognised the connection of its Easter-rite, as then universally accepted, with that of the Therapeutic Essenes of the first century. From this it necessarily follows that the Christian ' vigils of the great festival of our Lord's passion,' to which Eusebius refers, corresponded with a similar fasting and watching of the Therapeuts, as practised by them before the middle of the first century, that is, probably not later than a few years after the crucifixion of Jesus, and as possibly also practised by Essenes in pre-Christian times.

Philo wrote a treatise ' on the festivals ' of the law, as figuratively interpreted and mystically observed by those who were ' in the habit of turning plain stories into allegory,' that is, by the Therapeuts, the sect which ' first pre-eminently studied ' the ' invisible sense that lies enveloped in the expressions, the soul.' Philo shows that the feast of the 14th Nisan, when ' the people ' of the Hebrews offer sacrifice, which the Therapeuts did not, was by these Essenes regarded as ' figuratively ' representing ' the purification of the soul.'

---

[1] If Jesus has spoken the words attributed to Him in the Gospel after Matthew (ix. 14, 15), He has sanctioned the fasting, which originally was a rite of the disciples of John the Baptist or Essene, as distinguished expressly from that of the disciples of Jesus.

On that day they fulfilled ' their hereditary custom
with prayer and songs of praise.' Instead of eating
the lamb on the 14th Nisan, they connected that day
with a fulfilment to which the type of the paschal lamb
pointed, and to which fulfilment, or deeper and real
meaning of this rite, they looked forward. They expected a fulfilling antitype of the paschal lamb. Did
the lamb without blemish refer to it which, according
to the Law of Moses, was to be offered to God on the
third day after the eating of the paschal lamb?

The great Alexandrian mystic—probably himself a
Therapeut—then describes the meaning of the 15th
Nisan, as a day of ' cheerfulness and giving of thanks
to God,' as the first day of unleavened bread, the day
of ' the great migration' which the Israelites made from
Egypt, the memorial-day of ' the gratitude due for
their deliverance.' He does not refer to the ' holy convocation' which the law orders on this day. Then
Philo explains the subsequent festival, named ' the
sheaf,' which Moses ordered to be solemnised on the
16th Nisan. On this day of the offering of the paschal
omer, on the third day after the slaying of the paschal
lamb, the Therapeuts seem to have held the ' holy convocation' which the law ordains on the day before.
Philo calls the 16th the festival of ' the solemn assembly,' which festival was ' the prelude of another
festival of still greater importance,' of the day of Pentecost, or of the fiftieth day, which was reckoned by the
Therapeuts, and according to the law, from the 16th
Nisan. There can therefore be no doubt that the Therapeuts regarded the 16th Nisan, the day of the offering
of the paschal omer, and of the lamb ' without blemish,' the day of their holy convocation or ' solemn
assembly,' as the day when they expected, in the early
hours of the morning, the fulfilling antitype of the
lamb offered to God the third day after the 14th

Nisan, when 'the people,' but not the Therapeuts, continued to slay the paschal lamb, only as a memorial of the past, not as a type of the future.

This great festival, the day of 'the solemn assembly,' preceded by solemn night-watches, not only by Therapeuts and early Christians, but also by all Christians after the Nicene Council, is what Eusebius calls 'the great festival of our Lord's passion,' which was preceded by vigils. Of course Eusebius refers to the day of the resurrection which, as will be pointed out presently, had just been fixed by the council, for all churches, to be solemnised on the Sunday after the 14th Nisan, in harmony with the Roman-Alexandrian rite. The Church historian might have more correctly called it 'the great festival of our Lord's resurrection,' but already Tertullian had called both days, the day of the crucifixion and the day of the resurrection, 'the day of the Passover.'[1] Without taking cognizance of the days of the month, Eusebius is bent upon connecting the solemnities in Christian Churches on the holy even of Saturday before Easter with the corresponding vigils of the Therapeuts and early Christians.

Philo did not designate the Therapeuts as 'Christians,' and we shall see that this name for the so-called disciples of Jesus was preceded by that of Essaioi, by which name the Alexandrian contemporary of Jesus designates those whom Josephus calls Essenes. Also the Jewish historian does not yet know 'Christians,' or any party distinguished from Essenes as from Pharisees and Sadducees. The connection of Christians and Essenes, darkly implied by Philo and Josephus, is clearly confirmed by Eusebius. He insists on the identity of the Therapeutic Easter-rites and of those of the Christian Church, that is of the 'original practices handed down from the Apostles.' By this statement he would force us to conclude that the twelve Apostles sanctioned the

---

[1] Tert. *de Orat.* 14; *de Cor. Mil.* 3.

Easter-rite as all Christians observed it after the Council of Nice, and that the Apostles either were Essenes, or had accepted the 'hereditary custom' of the Therapeuts respecting the Passover.

It is impossible to assume that the 'hereditary custom' of the Therapeuts, of 'the first' who had found, according to Philo, the deeper sense or gnosis of the Passover-rite and its Messianic fulfilment, did not date from pre-Christian times. They looked forward, long before the crucifixion of Jesus, to whom Philo does not refer, to the fulfilment of what was dimly indicated by the slaying of the paschal lamb on the 14th Nisan; and they must have expected that fulfilment on the 16th Nisan, on the third day, according to their figurative interpretation of the Scriptures. On that day, we are informed by the three first Gospels, the twelve Apostles were surprised by what they considered 'idle tales' of women, by their reports about the visible resurrection of Jesus from the grave. We are told of these women, that they watched at the grave of Jesus, instead of following the Jews to the temple for the solemn offering of the first fruits and of the lamb without blemish. They must be regarded as representatives of Essenic expectation. If on the morning of the third day after His death and after the slaying of the paschal lamb Jesus was visibly raised from the grave, this miracle could only be regarded as the fulfilment and thus the confirmation of what the Essenes expected about the antitype of the lamb offered to God with the firstlings on the third day after the slaying of the paschal lamb.

Could it be asserted that Jesus died contemporaneously with the slaying of the paschal lamb, and that He rose from the grave, as Paul asserts, on the third day, that is, early in the morning of the 16th Nisan, when the paschal omer and the lamb without blemish were offered in the temple to God?

The words 'in the end of the Sabbath, as it began to dawn toward the first day,' or, 'very early in the morning of the first day of the week,' or 'when it was just beginning to dawn,' or, 'on the first day of the week, while it was yet dark,' clearly point to the very day and hour when the paschal omer was offered in the temple, in the early morn of the 16th Nisan. It is the exact time when, after solemn 'vigils,' the Therapeuts, according to the hereditary custom of their sect, began the great festival, the day of 'solemn assembly,' and when we may presume them to have expected the fulfilment of what was prefigured by the offering of the first fruits and the lamb without blemish, on the third day after the slaying of the paschal lamb, on the 16th Nisan. This day of the reported visible resurrection of Jesus was, only according to the fourth Gospel, the third day after his crucifixion, which latter is implied to have taken place on the 14th Nisan.

We shall see that it is this Gospel only which supports the Easter-rite of the Christian West in the second century, whilst the Easter-rite of the Eastern churches is based on the narrative about the crucifixion in the first three Gospels. It will become evident that the paschal dispute which was openly declared about the middle of the second century was founded not only on a difference of ritual, but on the question whether the law was to be literally or figuratively observed. The real question was whether Jesus had died on the 14th Nisan, contemporaneously with the slaying of the paschal lamb, as antitype of the same, or on the 15th Nisan, the day of the liberation from the Egyptian house of servitude, thus pointing to a spiritual exodus from spiritual bondage. It can be shown that the paschal dispute was indirectly connected with the doctrine of Jesus Christ as the Lamb of God.

It was in the year 155 that Bishop Polycarp of Smyrna declared, before Pope Anicetus, that he had solemnised the Passover with the Apostle John, and that, in accordance with this apostolic tradition, the Eastern churches preserved the Jewish Passover, especially the Jewish paschal supper, which they continued to solemnise in the night of the 14th Nisan, as the parting supper of the Lord, whilst on the following day they kept the day of His crucifixion. The Western churches, led by Rome and Alexandria, took no cognisance of the Jewish Passover, and opposed the apostolic rites which Polycarp represented by the tradition which presbyters had transmitted who preceded Pope Anicetus, and by which he was bound.

According to this Roman rite, the 14th and the 15th Nisan might fall respectively as much as five and seven days before the memorial days of the crucifixion and of the resurrection, but these two events of Gospel-narrative could not be solemnised respectively on two successive days. The Roman Church, according to its presbyterial tradition, fixed the Sunday after the 14th Nisan as the day of the resurrection, the preceding Friday as the day of the crucifixion, and thus the Saturday in Easter-week vaguely corresponded to the Jewish great Sabbath of the paschal week, which however was fixed by a day of the month, by the 15th Nisan, the first day of unleavened bread, the week-day of Sabbatical rest.[1]

It is in harmony with this Roman Easter-rite, which was opposed by Polycarp, the associate of John and other Apostles, that the day of the resurrection is described in all four Gospels as the day after the seventh day or Sabbath, and yet as the first day of the week, and as a Sunday, not as a week-Sabbath determined by the 15th Nisan. That day might have fallen on the seventh day or Sabbath, and the 16th Nisan might have fallen on the day after the real Sabbath, on the first day

---

[1] Levit. xxiii. 11, 15.

of the week, according to Jewish reckoning, this being Sunday or the first day of the week according to the Christian week. But if so, the crucifixion had taken place on the day previous to the resurrection, according to the narratives in the first three Gospels. Only according to the fourth Gospel the first day of the week, or resurrection-day, is the third day after the crucifixion.

It is to be remarked that all Gospel accounts about the resurrection, but only the crucifixion account in the fourth Gospel, confirm the Roman Easter-rite. It follows, that the day of the crucifixion, the 15th Nisan as the first three Gospels assert, was the seventh day or Sabbath, and cannot have been the day before the Sabbath as stated in all four Gospels. Only according to the fourth Gospel the crucifixion was on the 14th Nisan, thus on Friday, in harmony with the Paulinic Easter-rite as fixed by Roman presbyters who had preceded Pope Anicetus.

By fixing, for all years to come, week days instead of days of the month for the solemnities in memory of· the crucifixion and the resurrection, the Roman Church obliterated the typical importance of the 14th as well as of the 16th Nisan. Thus the dangerous question was prevented from arising, whether the resurrection of Jesus had taken place on the day after His crucifixion, according to the statements of the first three Gospels, or on ' the third day according to the Scriptures,' as Paul's Epistles and the fourth Gospel clearly assert or imply.

If about the middle of the second century the so-called Gospel after John had been recognised by the Church, whether as an Apostolic work or not, some mention must have been made of it during the paschal dispute. Polycarp must have declared such scripture to be not apostolic and not historical, inasmuch as it asserts what the Eastern churches, the Quartodecimans, could not admit, but what the Roman and the

Western churches held, that Christ was crucified contemporaneously with the slaying of the Jewish paschal
lamb, and as antitype of thé same, as Lamb of God.
Again, Anicetus must have referred to this apostolic
authority for the Western rite, and for the doctrine of
the Lamb of God. If any reference to 'the Gospel
after John' had then been made by either party,
Irenæus and Eusebius must have made the most of it in
their accounts of this dispute. Irenæus informs us that
' Anicetus yielded' in so far to Polycarp, out of respect,
that he permitted him to consecrate the elements in
his presence, and that ' they separated from each other
in peace, all the Church being at peace ; both those that
observed and those that did not observe, maintaining
peace.'

The difference continued. It was not merely a
question of calendar or about ' the manner of fasting,'
whether the fast should be kept one day, two days, or
more. In fact, Polycarp insisted, on the authority of
the twelve Apostles, that the Jewish paschal supper
with the paschal lamb must continue to be solemnised
by the Church of Christ, and that this ought to be
done, according to apostolic custom, on the day when
Jesus ate the lamb with His disciples. In fact, Anicetus insisted, on no other authority than that of some
presbyters who had preceded him in Rome, that Jesus had
not eaten the paschal lamb before He suffered, though
the first three Gospels assert this, but that He was crucified on the day when the Jewish paschal lamb was slain,
and that Jesus was, as Paul had declared, the antitype
and divinely ordered fulfilment of the same. The
difference was essentially one of dogma, and pointed to
the doctrine of Jesus Christ as the Lamb of God, of
which doctrine the first three Gospels say nothing,
whilst it forms the very basis of the fourth Gospel. So
important were the issues of this dispute held to
be about forty years later (196), that when Bishop

Polycrates of Ephesus and the bishops of Asia Minor renewed the dispute, Pope Victor—vainly opposed by the peacemaker Irenæus—excommunicated all who opposed the Western rite, which was then accepted by a few of the Eastern churches.

Was the crucified Jesus, as antitype of the paschal lamb, the fulfilment of what the law in its literal sense could be held to have predicted, or had he not brought about such a fulfilment? Was Jesus crucified on the day when the paschal lamb was slain, on the 14th Nisan, and did He rise from the grave the third day according to a figurative interpretation of the Scriptures, that is, as antitype of the paschal omer and lamb without blemish, offered on the 16th Nisan? Or was this day of the reported visible resurrection from the grave the second day after the crucifixion of Jesus on the 15th Nisan, as the first three Gospels unanimously report? It is certain that these three Gospels record what the twelve Apostles knew about the day of the crucifixion, whilst by the fourth Gospel the doctrine of Paul is conveyed, and falsely attributed to the Apostle John, that is, the doctrine about Jesus having died on the 14th Nisan and having risen the third day 'according to the Scriptures.'

No further evidence is needed for asserting that the Quartodeciman paschal rite was upheld by the Apostle John's Church in Asia, which his associate Bishop Polycarp of Smyrna represented and defended against the Pope at Rome, who represented all the Western churches and Alexandria. But an important confirmation of this assertion is contained in the encyclical letter of the Church of Smyrna concerning the martyrdom of its bishop, Polycarp. Hilgenfeld has incontestably proved[1] that according to this generally

[1] Hilgenfeld, *Der Paschastreit* (1860), comp. *Zeitschrift f. W. T.* 1861, pp. 285-318.

authentic monument of Christian antiquity, Polycarp suffered martyrdom in the year 166, on Tuesday, March 26, that day being 'the great Sabbath,' that is, the 15th Nisan, on which day of the month Jesus had been crucified, according to the first three Gospels. This letter indirectly but clearly points out the above-named and other parallels with the passion of Jesus as related by these Gospels. The letter confirms that the Quarto-decimans, on the authority of John and of other Apostles with whom Polycarp associated, continued, according to the law, to regard the Passover as fixed by the day of the month, and that they would have opposed the solemnisation of Easter on fixed days of the week, as sanctioned by the Church at Rome and the Western churches generally.

Hilgenfeld and his party are in a position trium-phantly to declare that ' critical historical inquiry in the paschal dispute has maintained victoriously, against all raging and stormy attacks, a firm stronghold of the Church, which covers the domain of a free Gospel in-quiry equally well as the right understanding of the most ancient Church history.'

The paschal dispute, in fact, was based on that disagreement between the twelve Apostles on one side, and Paul on the other, which it was the object of the Acts to obliterate, but which the Epistles of Paul clearly establish.[1] To conclude. Jesus is not connected with the type of the paschal lamb in the first three Gospels, and this doctrine is there quite excluded, whilst the fourth Gospel connects it with the testimony of John the Baptist or Essene, and with the fact, there alone implied, that Jesus had not eaten the paschal lamb the day before His death, but had been crucified three days before His resurrection as antitype of the lamb, as the Passover of the Christians, according to Paul's

[1] See Appendix.

definition. Polycarp and Polycrates stood up for the paschal doctrine and rite of the twelve Apostles, the Popes Anicetus and Victor for that of the Apostle Paul, which was finally recognised by the Council of Nice.

Eusebius wrote his Church History up to the year of the council, and as an introduction to the same. He died fifteen years after it, in 340. The paschal dispute was his great difficulty. Even the writings of the peacemaker Irenæus, though intended to show that it was merely a ritual dispute, dimly showed the deeper grounds of dissension. The Arian dispute which had arisen in the time of Irenæus, and which the Council of Nice settled contemporaneously with the paschal dispute, centred in the doctrine of the divinity of Christ and in the doctrine of three Divine Persons in Unity. If Christ was not the pre-existing Angel-Messiah and Lamb of God from the beginning, the doctrine of the Trinity could not be established. But if these new doctrines could be applied to Jesus, the doctrine of the Trinity could not be evaded, and must be acknowledged.

Paul had clearly taught or implied that Jesus Christ was the incarnate Angel of God, ' the spiritual rock' which followed the Israelites, ' the Man from heaven,' and the Creator of the World, ' by' whom all things were made, who had come in the ' likeness ' of sinful flesh, and who was crucified as antitype of the paschal lamb, as Lamb of God. Paul was not directly referred to during the paschal dispute, and yet the tradition of some presbyters who had preceded Pope Anicetus was the Paulinic tradition, whether or not also that of the Essenes. Nor did either party refer to the fourth Gospel, which supports the Paulinic doctrine and the Roman Easter-rite.

Eusebius pleaded the cause of Arius at the Council of Nice, although four years earlier this Alexandrian presbyter had been excommunicated by his bishop, on the ground that according to his doctrine Christ could not be the true God, but only a divine being, whether angelic or human. It is perhaps doubtful whether Arius regarded Christ as an anointed angel, or as an anointed man. But it is certain that Eusebius regarded Jesus as the incarnate Angel of God, 'the Word of God, God of God, Light of light, Life of life, the only begotten Son, born before all creation, begotten of God the Father before all ages, by whom also all things were made; who on account of our salvation became incarnate, and lived among men; and who having suffered and risen again on the third day, ascended to the Father, and shall come again in glory to judge the living and the dead.'

To the form of the creed as drawn up by Eusebius various additions were made, especially the expressions 'of the substance of the Father,' and 'consubstantial with the Father,' and the doctrine of Arius was expressly anathematised : ' But those who say that there was a time when he was not, or that he did not exist before he was begotten, or that he was made of nothing, or assert that he is of other substance or essence than the Father, or that the Son of God is created, or mutable, or susceptible of change, the catholic and apostolic Church of God anathematises.'

Having first objected to these additions, Eusebius afterwards gave his assent to the Nicene Creed as acknowledged by the council, but he explained the additions in the sense of his previous assertions, by saying that 'the condemnation of the assertion that before He was begotten He had no existence, does not involve any incongruity, because all (after the death of Arius) assent to the fact that He was the Son of God before He was begotten, according to the flesh.' [1]

Eusebius, in thus yielding, in form at least, 'having regard to peace, as dreading lest we should lose a right understanding of the matter,' did more than Polycarp

[1] Socrates, *H. E.* i. 8; Theodoret, *H. E.* i. 11, 12.

had done when he confronted Anicetus during the paschal dispute, which was connected with what became the Arian dispute. Both disputes were now closed, and his Church History up to this first general council had to be written with an eye to the compromise then in fact recognised by the Council of Nice. The Church historian undertook to prove that its decrees were in harmony with the one tradition which the twelve Apostles as well as Paul had transmitted. Yet Eusebius cannot bring forward a single fact or argument in favour of his attempt to establish the non-apostolic origin of the tradition represented at the beginning of the paschal dispute by Polycarp, the associate of the Apostles. He does not say who were, in his opinion, the 'simple and inexperienced' authors of the apostolic practice opposed by the presbyters of Rome, who 'did not observe, neither did they permit those after them to observe it.' Already Irenæus could write to Pope Victor that his predecessors did not cast off any one 'merely for the sake of the form.' Like Irenæus, Eusebius is bent upon denying the existence of dogmatic differences in his time, and above all they both are careful not to admit, and they even try to render impossible, the assumption that dogmatic differences can have existed between the twelve Apostles and Paul. Eusebius unhesitatingly declares that 'the very difference in our fasting establishes the unanimity of our faith.'

Eusebius had serious reasons for supporting the apostolic origin of the fourth Gospel by earlier testimony than that of Irenæus. He had to show, if he could, to what testimony, in favour of the composition of that Gospel by the Apostle John Anicetus might have referred; how the Pope could have convinced Polycarp of his error in promulgating 'a remoter tradition' than that of the Western churches, but which had originated in 'simplicity and inexperience,' and could not have been

apostolic, as Polycarp asserted. For this purpose
Eusebius must have cited, in the first place, Papias,
bishop of Hierapolis, whom Irenæus had designated as
a direct disciple of the Apostle John.[1] Eusebius can
only show that Papias, who knew the first Epistle
of John, referred but to two Gospels, of Mark and
Matthew. Eusebius cannot show that Papias referred
—any more than Polycarp—to Paul personally, or to
the third and fourth Gospels. Yet Polycarp in his
epistle (ch. iv.) cites and explains a passage from the
first Epistle of John (iv. 3) the Apostle and his associate.

In the second place, Eusebius had to utilize for his
purpose the writings of Hegesippus. He gives extracts
from this Jewish-Christian's 'Memorials of Apostolic
Doctrine.' He was a born Jew, whose lifetime almost
covers the second century, and of whom he writes that
in his Memorials 'he left a most complete record of
his own views.'[2] Having considered the unhistorical
nature of Eusebius's declaration, that the practices of
the Therapeuts, described by Philo and sanctioned by
Rome, were those which 'the first heralds of the
Gospel' had 'handed down from the Apostles,' we are
bound to accept with great caution what he says
about the private if not peculiar views of Hegesippus.

Referring to 'the ancient heresies prevalent among
the Jews,' Hegesippus stated that 'there were also
different opinions' in Israel 'against the tribe of Judah
and the Messiah.' He distinguishes the Messianic
opinions of the Essenes from those of the Sadducees
and Pharisees. According to Hegesippus, Christianity
had evolved from Judaism, but not by a figurative
interpretation of the Scriptures. For not a word is
attributed to Hegesippus which could be explained as
sanctioning the Essenic mode of interpretation, their

[1] Iren. *Haer.* v. 33, 4 f.; but compare Eus. *H. E.* iii. 39, 1 f.
[2] *Hist. Eccl.* iv. 22; comp. 8; ii. 23; iii. 11.

rites or doctrines. What he says about James, the brother of the Lord, proves that Hegesippus must have regarded Jesus as the anointed man announced by 'the law and the prophets,' not as the anointed angel.

If it can be established that Paul has applied to Jesus, as Stephen had done before him, this new Messianic conception, although Jesus had opposed it, then it will follow that the difference between the twelve Apostles and Paul was based on nothing less than on 'different opinions' about Christ.

After the loss (destruction?) of the work of Hegesippus it cannot be proved, but it is almost certain, that it contained direct attacks against Paul. For one such passage has been cited by Stephanos Gobaros, of the sixth century, who had put together the diverging and contradicting sayings of the Fathers on dogmatic questions. Hegesippus referred to Paul's having written that God had revealed to him through His spirit what eye had not seen, nor ear heard, and which had not entered the heart of man. Yet Jesus had said to the twelve Apostles: 'Blessed are your eyes for they see, and your ears for they hear.' Hegesippus had added that Paul, by such 'vain' saying, had placed himself in 'lying contradiction' to Matthew.[1] It is not likely that this was the only passage which Eusebius found it convenient not to cite in his Church History, calculated to show that the doctrinal unity of the present had always existed in the past.

We saw that Eusebius connects the Roman Easter-rite directly with Essenic practices, as recognised by the Apostles. Moreover, he actually declares it to be 'highly probable' that the Scriptures peculiar to the order of the Therapeuts, which they had received from the founders of their sects, were made use of in the composition of our Gospels and of the Pauline Epistles,

---

[1] *Photius Cod.* 232.

especially that to the Hebrews.[1] So determined was
the Church historian to use every conceivable argument
in his attempt to connect the indubitable and acknowledged Essenic Easter-rite of the Roman Church with
the twelve Apostles as well as with Paul! Can it be true
that the rite in question was indeed transmitted by the
twelve Apostles, although Polycarp declared the contrary? If Peter founded the Roman Church, the
Jewish-Christian origin of which is undisputed, can he
and can John be regarded as having been originally
Essenes, or as having become the promulgators of
Essenic doctrines? If not, are we at liberty to suppose
that anti-Jewish influence in Rome decided the Easter-
rite in that Church sooner or later after the death of
Peter, in accordance with Paulinic and Essenic (Gnostic?)
tradition?

According to Hegesippus it was after the reign of
Trajan (98–117), after the death of the Apostles and of
the direct hearers of Jesus, that 'false teachers,' who up
to this time had been or may have been ' skulking in
dark retreats,' as Hegesippus admits, openly came forward with ' combinations of impious error by fraud and
delusions,' preaching against 'the gospel of truth.'
Before the open and combined attack of these false
Gnostics, the peace in the virgin-Church had not been
disturbed. It seems that already before this time, according to a statement of Polycarp, recorded by Irenæus,
the Apostle John had stood up against Cerinthus, and
designated him as ' the enemy of truth.' But Hegesippus
does not refer to Cerinthus as a disturber of the peace,
perhaps because Cerinthus, whether he wrote the anti-
Paulinic Apocalypse or not, like the Jewish-Christian
historian, did not recognise the Apostle Paul.

Nor does Hegesippus seem to have connected with
the open gnostic conspiracy in the time of Trajan either
Simon Magus nor his ' successor ' Menander, with whom

---

[1] *Hist. Eccl.* ii. 17.

Eusebius connects Basilides and Saturninus, as well as Cerdon, who preceded Marcion. But already in the year of Trajan's accession (97–98) Barnabas, by his Epistle, had crossed the border, the non-overstepping of which had until then kept the peace in the Church. Not only because of Paul's admission of the Gentiles, Barnabas separated from him. It is probable that Hegesippus regarded the anti-Jewish teaching of Barnabas as the beginning of the open attacks on the true Church. For Barnabas represented Essenic-Gnostic doctrines, and opposed by his advanced Paulinism the compromise which Paul tried to accomplish with Judaism. It was not necessary for Hegesippus to consider the moderate and tolerating Judaism expressed in the so-called first Epistle of Clement, whether composed already in 68 or from 93 to 96 or in 120. But the false Gnostics with their ultra-Paulinism followed the advanced Paulinism of the Epistle of Barnabas, and they left in its isolation the Epistle of Clement which first sets up the authority of 'Peter and Paul.' The compromise which the Gnostics intended to bring about was to lead to far greater concessions from the Jewish-Christian party. They did not forget that shortly before his death Paul had been designated as the chief of a sect everywhere spoken against, therefore as a false teacher.

According to Epiphanius it was shortly before the paschal dispute that the leading Gnostics, among them Marcion, the great anti-Judaist, went to Rome and asked the Roman presbyters, whose predecessors had declared Paul to belong to a sect everywhere spoken against, whether the old bottles would do for the new wine. Did the Gnostics point to a revision and amplification of the Gospels? Did they point to the necessity of a new Gospel in which the law of Moses would be openly asserted to be only the law of the Jews, as is done in the fourth Gospel? Did these Gnostics, whose connection with the Essenes and with some of Paul's doctrines we have pointed out—did they plead before the Roman elders the necessity of asserting in the new law of a new Gospel that the Jews always misunderstood the words of Jesus by not interpreting them figuratively, according to Essenic-Gnostic fashion? Was the new Gospel to assert that John the Baptist or Essene had pointed to Jesus as the Lamb of God, that His crucifixion had taken place contemporaneously with the slaying of the paschal lamb, and His resurrection on the third day, according to Paulinic and Essenic tradition? If so, the anti-Jewish fourth Gospel must have become recognised by the churches after the commencement of the paschal dispute, sooner or later after the year 155, and the Essenic character of 'the Gospel after John' as well as of the Pauline Epistles would become probable. Then the otherwise unaccountable statement of Eusebius about the insertion of Essenic tradition in all four Gospels as well as in Pauline Epistles would be confirmed by the fourth Gospel, which is so directly connected with Paul's Epistles.

It must here suffice to state that only according to the fourth Gospel Peter's brother, Andrew, and another disciple, whom tradition identifies with John, were disciples of the Baptist, the 'Ashai or Essai, the Essene, when Jesus called them. Thus it is darkly intimated that the Essenic tradition about Jesus having been crucified as antitype of the paschal lamb, in accordance with the Baptist's testimony and with the Gospel 'after John,' had received the sanction of this Apostle. If so, Andrew's brother, the Apostle Peter, could have sanctioned no other than the Essenic tradition, which he must have transmitted to the presbyters of the Roman Church, as Eusebius clearly indicates that he did. But the accounts of the Passover in the first three Gospels prove that the twelve Apostles cannot possibly have believed Jesus to have been crucified on the day when the Jewish paschal lamb was slain. The twelve must have protested against such a statement, and also against the doctrine of the Lamb of God which was based upon it, if in their time such a statement had been made in any Scripture purporting to represent their knowledge about the views of Jesus on the Passover.

By its Easter-rite, which the fourth Gospel alone supports, and which triumphed finally at the Council of Nice, the Roman Church has certainly not followed the tradition of the Apostle John, but it has represented Essenic and Paulinic tradition. Yet at the end of the so-called Gospel after John it is asserted that the disciple whom Jesus loved has written this Gospel. The unusual attestation is made by several persons, who declare: 'We know that his witness is true.' These persons can only have been the elders of a Church where the Roman Easter-rite prevailed in the second century. They cannot have been representatives of the Churches of Smyrna and of Ephesus, since the bishops of these Churches opposed at Rome the Easter-rite there prevailing, and Polycarp had done this as associate of the Apostle John, with whom he had celebrated the Passover. Nor can those who testify that the Apostle John has composed the fourth Gospel have been the elders of any of the Eastern Churches, who were all represented by Polycarp. It is not to be doubted that this Apostle ministered in Asia Minor, and it is probable that he was buried at Ephesus.

Those who attested the apostolic composition of the fourth Gospel, attributing it to the Apostle John, although Polycarp had claimed, without contradiction, the authority of that Apostle, his associate, for the rite which the Roman Church opposed, may with sufficient reason be regarded as the leading elders of the Church at Rome. That Church must be held responsible for the setting up and the recognition of the fourth Gospel as 'the Gospel after John.' It is the Roman Church which originated the discrepancies in the first three Gospels, which exclude by their narratives of the crucifixion the resurrection on 'the third day according to the Scriptures,' whilst in these Gospels have yet been inserted narratives of the resurrection as having taken place on the third day after the crucifixion. The second day is the only possible day according to the first three Gospels for the event recorded at the end of them, in appendixes of more than doubtful historical credibility.

Among the Gnostics who were in Rome before A.D. 132, and who probably continued there till about twenty years later, must first be mentioned Basilides. He had already recognised Paul, whom Cerinthus had opposed ; after him a gospel was called 'the gospel according to Basilides,' mentioned by Origen and Jerome, and his commentary, of which extracts are preserved, shows that this gospel was akin to that 'according to Luke.' Basilides, who died soon after A.D. 132, according to Jerome, is by Hippolytus, about the year A.D. 225, shown by extracts to have frequently used our canonical fourth Gospel.[1] Valentinus came to Rome about 136 to 140, a few years after the death of Basilides, and remained there beyond 155, when the famous debates took place between Polycarp and Pope Anicetus. It is non-proven whether he knew the fourth Gospel of our Canon, but this is more than probable if Basilides used it, and since disciples of Valentinus before 170 have certainly cited passages we find only there. Valentinus was 'a hearer of Theudas' who 'was the pupil of Paul,' according to Clement of Alexandria. The latter states that this Apostle designates as 'the fulness of the blessings of Christ' which he would bring to the Romans, 'the gnostic communication' or tradition about the

---

[1] Hilgenfeld and Lipsius, *Einleitung in das N. T.* 46, 47, consider it possible that these extracts refer to a later Gnosticism.

mysteries till then hidden (to the Romans), and which the learned father explains were revealed by the Son of God, 'the Teacher who trains the Gnostic by mysteries.'[1] Paul was fully recognised as an Apostle by Valentinus, and since 140 by Marcion as the only Apostle. Asserting that 'Paul alone knew the truth,' Marcion altered Luke's Gospel into the gospel which he alone recognised. Had the Fourth Gospel of our Canon, or one similar to it, been then recognised by the Churches, it would have been easier for the Paulinic gnostic, after some alterations, to recognise the same, although not as composed by the Apostle John.

Since the Gospel after John, or a document containing similar passages to those we find in that gospel only, was known, at least to Gnostics, perhaps already more than 23 years before the arrival of Polycarp at Rome, the more remarkable it is that Pope Anicetus did not refer to that gospel, as to a document in favour of the Western Easter-rite, with which the Gnostics must have sympathised. If it could be asserted that this gospel was composed by the Apostle John, it would have contradicted what Polycarp, his associate, had said about this Apostle's recognition of the Jewish and Christian Passover-rite in the Eastern Churches, and the Paschal dispute would have been over at once.

It can be now asserted, without fear of impartial contradiction, that all the passages which refer to or are connected with the announced resurrection of Jesus on 'the third day,' were certainly added in the first three Gospels, and this not before the recognition of the Fourth Gospel, or possibly with a view to its reception in the Canon. How many more corrections, omissions, or additions seem then to have been effected in the Gospels and the Acts of the Apostles, we have not here to enquire. Suffice it to say, that in the first Gospel of our Canon the aboriginal genealogy of Jesus, showing

[1] Strom. vii. 17; v. 10; vii. 2; Rom. xv. 29.

his human descent, has been undermined ; that his mission as Son of David has been enlarged ; many references to the Old Testament have been cited from the (Essenic?) Septuagint ; the testimony of the (Essenic) Baptist was somewhat harmonised with its record in the Fourth Gospel, diametrically opposed to ' the Gospel according to the Hebrews,' which latter is the groundwork of that according to Matthew.   This Gospel was recast, in part immediately after the destruction of Jerusalem, partly about the middle of the second century, by a Roman Catholic reviser.

It will continue to be a debatable question, to what extent the first three Gospels, as transmitted to us, were composed with an eye to the Fourth Gospel, and to what extent the latter was finally revised with a view of harmonising it, as far as possible, with the earlier propagated Gospels and with Pauline Epistles.   But it can be rendered probable that, by the pressure of the increasingly mighty party of Gnostics, about the middle of the second century, the Roman Church, till then chiefly the representative of Jewish-Christian principles, of those of the twelve Apostles, was offered a compromise based on the full recognition of Paul.   This compromise, which is imperatively demanded by an unprejudiced comparison of the Scriptures forming the New Testament, had become a necessity for the Roman Church, which could not have brought about the peace in the Churches, on the basis of uniformity, without having first brought about and sanctioned the collection of New Testament Scriptures in the very form in which they have been transmitted to us.

The connection of Paul and of the Gnostics with the Essenes being then known, at least to the ' stewards of the mysteries of God,' it became necessary, by Paul's tardy but full recognition of the humanity of Jesus in the Epistle to the Romans—assuming that isolated passage not to be a later interpolation—to separate him from the Gnostics who denied the natural birth of Jesus, the first of whom was Simon of Samaria. The Church having recognised as Apostolic the fourth Paulinic, gnostic, and anti-judaic gospel, Marcion's distinction between the God of the Christians and the God of the Jews had to be authoritatively denied. Jesus is therefore here reported to have said, that his God was the God of the Jews, what neither He nor Paul certainly ever could have denied. To yield in such and similar points was made easy for Marcion and his adherents by the recognition of the new Christian Gospel as a new law, contrasted to the law of Moses, which did not bring 'grace and truth.'

The Fourth Gospel promulgates the Paulinic and Essenic doctrine of Christ as the Angel of God and the world's creator. By the omission of the genealogies and by other passages it draws in question the humanity of Jesus, which the Docetics denied; it confirms the new and Essenic doctrine of Christ as the Lamb of God, and thus the Roman Easter-rite, based on the new assertion that Jesus had been crucified on the 14th Nisan, contemporaneously with the slaying of the paschal lamb. Finally, it qualifies, if it does not oppose, the promise of the keys to Peter, by the promise of another advocate of the Divine Spirit, which promise some of the Paulinic, Essenic, and Gnostic parties may well have regarded as fulfilled by Paul. For in the letters addressed to the brethren in Asia and Phrygia by the Christians in Gaul, which Irenæus may have brought to Rome soon after A.D. 170, it is stated of one of their martyrs, Vettius Epagathus, that 'he had the Paraclete within him, namely the Spirit more abundant than Zacharias,' probably the Father of John the Baptist or Essene. No reference is made to the recorded Pentecostal outpouring of the Spirit. Origen argues that the Paraclete brought the Gnosis, which the Twelve did not know.[1]

[1] Eus. *H.E.* V. 1; Orig. *c. Cels.* II. 2; *de Princ.* I. 3.

Although against all Gnostic doctrines a protest was made about 180 by the so-called Muratorian list of Scriptures which the Roman Church recognised, yet a compromise, based on the introduction of the anti-Jewish Easter-rite by Pope Sixtus I. (about 115–125), seems to have been offered by the Gnostic party. Although the succeeding Popes Hyginus and Pius I. checked the fervour of the Gnostics, it was probably by such a compromise that Anicetus declared himself to be bound. Having accepted it on her own conditions, the Roman Church became the declared enemy of the aboriginal non-Essenic Jewish-Christianity, represented by the twelve Apostles, and which Paul had only in part opposed.

Paul was martyred during the Neronic persecution, in the city in which, till after the middle of the second century, Jewish Christians and Gentile Christians attended different places of worship, according to Justin Martyr;[1] in the city from which Paul could write to the Philippians that some there preached Christ 'even for envy and strife,' and 'out of love of dispute and not in purity'; in the city from whence 'brethren' went to meet Paul 'as far as Appii forum,' and where yet he was connected with a 'sect' which was 'everywhere spoken against.' This was done by 'the chief of the Jews,' including the presbyters of the Christian Church, whom Paul called 'brethren' at Rome as he called Apostles at Antioch 'Jews.'

Paul suffered martyrdom in Rome at a time when the Roman law regarded the Jewish (and Jewish Christian) religion as a lawful one, but where already about the time of Paul's conversion the State had to interfere because of riots occasioned by a Chrestus-party, which, according to Clement of Alexandria, may be termed a Christos-party. The name Christians, by which 'the disciples' were first called at Antioch, was given to those who had been called Jessaioi or

---

[1] Dial. 47 ; Mangold, Der Römerbrief.

Essaioi, that is, to the Essenes and Therapeuts, who were distinguished from the Nazoraioi, as the first disciples of Jesus were called, according to Epiphanius.[1] The separation of Jews and Jewish Christians at Rome from Paulinic (Essenic) or Gentile Christians is proved directly by the Acts, and by Justin Martyr, indirectly by Paul's Epistle. It becomes thus explainable why the harmonising Acts do not refer to the martyrdom of Paul, which seems to have taken place under circumstances which had to be mystified in order to strengthen the bonds of peace in the Churches.

Jews had settled in Rome more than a century before Paul's martyrdom, as the Hebrew cemetery proves. Among them seem to have been Essenes or Therapeuts, since Aquila of Pontus, possibly the Onkelos of Pontus after whom the Targum is called, had left Rome about the time of the edict banishing Jews, it may be in consequence of the Chrestus-dispute among them. These Jewish disputants, the Christians, earlier called Essaioi, were probably Essenes, and Aquila and Priscilla were almost certainly Therapeuts, since these taught Apollos ' the more perfect doctrine,' the gnosis of Essenic origin, whilst only Therapeuts had women among their Initiated. Paul had promised to the Romans to bring them some ' spiritual gift,' that is, the gnosis, according to Clement of Alexandria. The ' chiefs of the Jews ' in Rome, called this gnosis the doctrine of ' a sect everywhere spoken against.' The non-orthodox Jews or Essenes, first called Christians in the centre of Simon Magus's activity, at Antioch, where Paul called Peter and Barnabas dissembling ' Jews,' had different opinions about Jesus the Messiah, considering him the incarnate Angel of God, as the extracts from Elkesai's book prove. During the reign of Nero (5 4-68) they seem to have all expected, like Paul, Christ's return at that time. By their figurative interpretation of Scripture, they had been taught

[1] Hær. xxix.

that Christ's return would be accompanied by great events, ending with the fall of 'Babylon' or Imperial Rome, to be destroyed ' by fire.'

Between four and five years after the burning of Rome the 'revelation' of this Essenic expectation was published, which had been known to the Initiated only. It refers to the martyrs slain by Nero, to 'the souls of them that have been slain for the Word of God, and for the testimony which they bore.' To that testimony belonged the prophecy of the burning of Rome, the fulfilment of which the Essenes in the year 64 must have believed to have come. The accusation that these Essenic Socialists, the 'Christians,' had caused this great conflagration is non-proven. Yet Tacitus writes : ' Those (" Christians ") who confessed (to have set fire to the city), later by their information a vast multitude were convicted, not so much for the crime of incendiarism as for (their) hatred of the human race.'[1] This hatred had found its expression in the symbolical account of contemporaneous events as recorded in the Apocalypse, when Tacitus (born 57, consul 97) received favours from Vespasian. Before the Apocalypse was published, between June 68 and January 69, it may have been known that there were men within the city who in their conventicles whispered into each other's ears : Rome must be effaced, ' delenda est Roma '!

It is the Roman Church which has inculcated on the Christian conscience many recorded facts which are non-proven if historical. Thus Christians were led to believe that the twelve Apostles, who had not expected any miracle at the grave, and who considered the stories of the women as ' idle tales,' became convinced of the visible resurrection of Jesus on 'the third day according to the Scriptures.' Thus the Church was led to believe that it was the sudden conversion of the Apostles from unbelief which overcame their dismay and dejection,

---

[1] Tacitus, *Ann.* **xv.** 44; Suet. *Nero,* 16.

caused by the crucifixion of their Master, whom they had all forsaken, from whom they had fled, because of this apparent frustration of their hopes. To bring about this conversion, which we are told commenced at the grave to which women had called the Apostles, it was necessary that Jesus Christ should appear to them in the same bodily shape in which He had been nailed to the cross, not as a spirit, but in the flesh and with bones which could be and were handled. Thus resuscitated in the human form, though surrounded with an indescribable glory, it is written that Jesus commanded the Apostles to baptize in the name of the Trinity, a doctrine not known to the Old Testament, nor confirmed by those sayings of Jesus which are recorded in the first three Gospels. To these unbelieving Apostles, after their sudden conversion, which preceded the recorded Pentecostal miracle, the command and authority was given to retain or remit sins, that is, to 'pardon transgressions,' like the Angel of the Lord. They saw the risen Lord ascend to the skies, whether on the third or on the fortieth day, and heard the two men in white apparel promise that the same Jesus which was taken up from them into heaven 'shall come' as they had beheld Him go into heaven, that is, with flesh and blood. Yet Paul had said that 'flesh and blood cannot inherit' the kingdom of God, which Christ had entered in this form, as we are told.

The Epistles of Paul prove that, like himself, the twelve Apostles were by apparitions of the Crucified convinced of their Master's life after death, but they do not even imply that the disciples whom Jesus had chosen preached His resurrection on 'the third day according to the Scriptures,' that is, as antitype of the paschal lamb and of the paschal omer. Yet the Twelve gave Paul and Barnabas the hand of fellowship, and recognised them as Apostles among the Gentiles. Though there were essential differences between the doctrines of the Apostles of circumcision and those of the Apostles of uncircumcision, Paul writes that the same God was effectual in both.

'The holy Catholic Church' had to represent not only the tradition of Peter but also the tradition of Paul. It is possible that these traditions had been respectively represented in Rome by the contemporaneous successors of Peter and of Paul, by Cletus and Linus. The latter, surviving Cletus, or more probably Clement, was the first Roman bishop of the united Petrinic and Paulinic Churches, whose pontificate lasted till 86. A great compromise had to be made, not only with regard to doctrine, but with regard to history. Without the establishment of peace in the ancient Church, much less of the truth would have been transmitted by written records, the relative value and the interpretation of which could not have been and was not confided to the people. Mysteries there had always been in every established Church, and mysteries formed necessarily the rock of the Catholic Church. We regard nothing as more historical, though mysterious, than what is conveyed by the words: 'Thou art Peter, and upon this rock will I build my Church, and the gates of hell shall not prevail against it.'

We cannot here examine the genuineness or the meaning of these words, nor shall we attempt to elucidate the question whether the Apostle Peter, personally at Rome or not, can have transmitted to the elders of the Roman Church 'the mysteries of the kingdom of heaven.' Jesus is recorded to have entrusted such mysteries to the safe keeping of the Apostles, probably in the fullest measure to those three to whom Paul refers as pillars of the Church, in which passage James is mentioned before Peter. The primacy of the Roman Church, which was sooner or later an historical fact, may therefore have been originally derived, not from the political pre-eminence of Rome as the city of the world, but it may really have been an institution founded by Jesus Christ for the purpose of transmitting from generation to generation a holy trust. If so, the stewards of these mysteries, whom Jesus did not appoint as bishops, have received the command of Jesus Christ, as recorded in the Gospels, at some future time to preach openly, from the housetops, the mysteries confided to them, to reveal to the nations 'the key of knowledge,' once 'taken away' by the spiritual leaders of Israel. If Jesus has promised to the twelve Apostles that He would in an especial sense be with them 'all the days, even unto the end of the world,' the light from heaven will reveal to their successors the proper time for carrying out that command. Till then holy tradition, 'the memory of the Church,' partly ascertained by free critical inquiry, must be recognised as the source of Holy Scripture, as the key to the lock. There was a Church before the Bible.

Before Paul's martyrdom, he and the twelve Apostles had already initiated and acted upon a compromise which led to their harmonious co-operation. Based upon this compromise, which Paul's Epistle to the Galatians acknowledges, a more far-reaching compromise became necessary, about the middle of the second century, in consequence of the paschal dispute and the increasing power of the Gnostics. To the Roman Church belongs the high honour to have brought about a final compromise, accepting it with all its conditions and consequences, including the enlargement and revision of the New Testament. It is a sad but incontrovertible fact, that only thus, on the supposed necessity of doctrinal uniformity, the peace in the Churches became possible. By acting in the spirit of Peter and Paul, the peace in the Churches will in future be established and maintained.[1]

---

[1] We purpose to show this in a work entitled 'The Peace in the Churches.'

When the seed of the Word of God shall have sufficiently prepared the hearts of mankind, then the Holy Ghost, through the instrumentality of different tongues and forms, will assemble the nations of the whole world, in the unity, not in the uniformity, of the faith, and Christ shall be ' all in all.'

APPENDIX.

.

Notes on Farrar's ' Life and Work of St. Paul.'

1. *Dogmatical difficulty.*—Canon Farrar regards the Acts as 'in all its main outlines a genuine and trustworthy history,' and 'in complete accordance' with Paul's Epistles 'as regards the main facts.' Paul's statement about ' the false brethren secretly introduced,' which certainly refers to main facts, is not mentioned in the Acts. Paul implies that these false brethren were those who ' came from James.' Farrar explains that they ' *represented themselves* as emissaries of James,' probably exaggerating the statement they were authorised to make, if indeed they had ' any express commission,' and did not ' assume' the authority of James. But this is evidently one of those intended omissions in the Acts, so admirably calculated ' to check the strife of parties by showing that there had been no irreconcilable opposition between the views and ordinances of St. Peter and St. Paul.' The former was called a hypocrite by the latter, for having accepted the correction of James, and for having, with Barnabas and ' the other Jews,' separated from Paul. Again, the Canon tells us, ' without hesitation,' that Gal. ii. is Paul's account of the Apostolic Council narrated in Acts xv., that his Second journey was in fact the Third. No doubt, dogmatical difficulties would arise from the admission of two, for a time, hostile parties in the primitive Church, of ' opposition of the leaders, of personal antipathy of St. Paul and the Twelve' (Farrar, l. c. I. 399 f, 7, 8, 405 n, 3, 410 f, 440, 447 ; comp. Jowett, *Romans*, etc., I. 326 ; Bishop Lightfoot on *St. Paul and the Three* ; Gal. 276–346).

St. Paul himself asserts that ' faith' came to Israel from without, not from the Twelve, but by the engrafting of the wild olive branch on the native olive tree, that is, of the Ethiopian or African olive (Oleaster) on the Palestinian olive. Pliny and others state that this was done to strengthen the native olive (*H. N.* xviii. 18 ; Colum. *de re Rust.* v. 9 ; Palladius, etc., see Farrar, l. c. I. 21, 1).

2. *Chronological difficulty.*—Referring to the period of the Judges as given by St. Paul, Farrar admits (I. 370, 2) that the 450 years result from the addition of the respective Scriptural dates, which he calls ' vague and often synchronous,' and that this period is confirmed by Josephus. Yet he clings to the 480 years of the First Book of Kings, and asserts that by accepting Paul's period of 450 years ' we only create chronological difficulties.' But the 14th of Hezekiah ought to be the year B.C. 711 according to Assyrian inscriptions ; and it is so, if the period of 450 years is accepted, together with the traditional year B.C. 2360 for the Flood. All the required synchronisms, hitherto regarded as difficulties, or rather impossibilities, can be thus established (*The Chronology of the Bible* ; comp. *Trans. Society of Biblical Archæology*, VI. 100–106).

Corrigenda and Addenda.

Page   v, line 6, *Bereshith Rabah* I., on Dan. ii. 22.
  „   9, „ 12, *for* though, *read* through.

  „   18, „   9, ⎧ *for* Tathâgatha *read* Tathâgata. Turnour, in his Introduction to the *Mahawanso*, p. 56, decides that Tathâgata may mean 'he who had come in the same manner as the other Buddha's.' Childers in his *Pali Dict.* identifies Tathâgata
  „   25, „ 14, ⎨ with the expression 'the son of man.' The Chinese ju lai (Tathâgata) is explained by Medhurst in his *Chinese*
  „ 151, „ 21, ⎩ *Dict.* as 'the coming' (Buddha). For these reasons Professor Beal (in a letter) translates Tathâgata by 'the coming One' (comp. Ezek. xxi. 27; Is. ix. 6; xvi. 5; Jer. xxiii. 5).

  „   23, „ 21, *for* sign   *read* constellation.
  „   28, „   6, „ variableness   „ parallax.
  „   36, „ 13, „ unbearing,   „ unbaring.
  „   48, note, *read* Köppen, *Die Religion des Buddha I.*
  „   58, line 19, *for* vhû *read* bhû.
  „   „   „ 20, „ vhûvar „ bhûvar.
  „   78, „ 27, *read* in the 27th year about B.C. 259.
  „   82, „ 11, *read*, and enjoins reverence for one's own faith, and no reviling nor injury.
  „ 104, note, *for* Jehovah *read* Elohim.
  „ 106, line 23, *read* seven walls of Ecbatana.
  „ 109, „ 22, „ which fact Clement of Alexandria designates as non-proven.
  „ 109, note, *read* puerperal state, though she was not; for some say, that after she brought forth she was found, when examined, to be a virgin.
  „ 167, line 5, *for* redemption *read* liberation.
  „ 182, „ 19, „ Rome *read* Cæsarea.
  „ 187, note 1, *read* Rom. viii. 3, 4.
  , 193, line 23, *for* mankind *read* the new creation.
  „   „   „ 26, „ all men are *read* 'all things,' and, in a special sense, 'we' are.
  „ 225, „ 28, *for* 14th Nisan *read* 13th Nisan.
  „ 226, „   3, „ . . . .
  „ 252, „ 19, „ Hebrews *read* Hebrew.
  „ 253, „ 19, „ tribal *read* scribal.
  „ 272, „ 10, *read* by the Sadducees, not by the Pharisees.
  „ 276, „ 12, „ a later date has been supported.
  „ 287, „ 13, „ Çtutgar.
  „ 229, „ 20, „ 1776–75.
  „ 300, „ 22, „ Enoch, and already then.

TABLE OF PRINCIPAL CONTENTS.

39 PATERNOSTER ROW, E.C.
LONDON, *April* 1880.

GENERAL LISTS OF WORKS

PUBLISHED BY

MESSRS. LONGMANS, GREEN & CO.

———◦•ᦞ•◦———

HISTORY, POLITICS, HISTORICAL MEMOIRS, &c.

Russia Before and After

the War. By the Author of 'Society in St. Petersburg' &c. Translated from the German (with later Additions by the Author) by EDWARD FAIRFAX TAYLOR. Second Edition. 8vo. 14s.

Russia and England from

1876 to 1880; a Protest and an Appeal. By O. K. Author of 'Is Russia Wrong?' With a Preface by J. A. FROUDE, M.A. Portrait and Maps. 8vo. 14s.

History of England from

the Conclusion of the Great War in 1815. By SPENCER WALPOLE. 8vo. VOLS. I. & II. 1815-1832 (Second Edition, revised) price 36s. VOL. III. 1832-1841, price 18s.

History of England in the

18th Century. By W. E. H. LECKY, M.A. VOLS. I. & II. 1700-1760. Second Edition. 2 vols. 8vo. 36s.

The History of England

from the Accession of James II. By the Right Hon. Lord MACAULAY.

STUDENT'S EDITION, 2 vols. cr. 8vo. 12s.
PEOPLE'S EDITION, 4 vols. cr. 8vo. 16s.
CABINET EDITION, 8 vols. post 8vo. 48s.
LIBRARY EDITION, 5 vols. 8vo. £4.

Lord Macaulay's Works.

Complete and uniform Library Edition. Edited by his Sister, Lady TREVELYAN. 8 vols. 8vo. with Portrait, £5. 5s.

Critical and Historical

Essays contributed to the Edinburgh Review. By the Right Hon. Lord MACAULAY.

CHEAP EDITION, crown 8vo. 3s. 6d.
STUDENT'S EDITION, crown 8vo. 6s.
PEOPLE'S EDITION, 2 vols. crown 8vo. 8s.
CABINET EDITION, 4 vols. 24s.
LIBRARY EDITION, 3 vols. 8vo. 36s.

The History of England

from the Fall of Wolsey to the Defeat of the Spanish Armada. By J. A. FROUDE, M.A.

CABINET EDITION, 12 vols. crown, £3. 12s.
LIBRARY EDITION, 12 vols. demy, £8. 18s.

The English in Ireland

in the Eighteenth Century. By J. A. FROUDE, M.A. 3 vols. 8vo. £2. 8s.

Journal of the Reigns of

King George IV. and King William IV. By the late C. C. F. GREVILLE, Esq. Edited by H. REEVE, Esq. Fifth Edition. 3 vols. 8vo. price 36s.

The Life of Napoleon III.

derived from State Records, Unpublished Family Correspondence, and Personal Testimony. By BLANCHARD JERROLD. In Four Volumes, 8vo. with numerous Portraits and Facsimiles. VOLS. I. to III. price 18s. each.

A

The Constitutional History
tory of England since the Accession of George III. 1760–1870. By Sir THOMAS ERSKINE MAY, K.C.B. D.C.L. Sixth Edition. 3 vols. crown 8vo. 18s.

Democracy in Europe;
a History. By Sir THOMAS ERSKINE MAY, K.C.B. D.C.L. 2 vols. 8vo. 32s.

Introductory Lectures on
Modern History delivered in 1841 and 1842. By the late THOMAS ARNOLD, D.D. 8vo. 7s. 6d.

On Parliamentary Government in England; its Origin,
Development, and Practical Operation. By ALPHEUS TODD. 2 vols. 8vo. 37s.

History of Civilisation in
England and France, Spain and Scotland. By HENRY THOMAS BUCKLE. 3 vols. crown 8vo. 24s.

Lectures on the History
of England from the Earliest Times to the Death of King Edward II. By W. LONGMAN, F.S.A. Maps and Illustrations. 8vo. 15s.

History of the Life &
Times of Edward III. By W. LONGMAN, F.S.A. With 9 Maps, 8 Plates, and 16 Woodcuts. 2 vols. 8vo. 28s.

History of the Life and
Reign of Richard III. Including the Story of PERKIN WARBECK. By JAMES GAIRDNER. Second Edition, Portrait and Map. Crown 8vo. 10s. 6d.

Memoirs of the Civil
War in Wales and the Marches, 1642-1649. By JOHN ROLAND PHILLIPS, of Lincoln's Inn, Barrister-at-Law. 8vo. 16s.

History of England under the Duke of Buckingham and
Charles I. 1624–1628. By S. R. GARDINER. 2 vols. 8vo. Maps, 24s.

The Personal Government
ment of Charles I. from the Death of Buckingham to the Declaration in favour of Ship Money, 1628–1637. By S. R. GARDINER. 2 vols. 8vo. 24s.

Memorials of the Civil
War between King Charles I. and the Parliament of England as it affected Herefordshire and the Adjacent Counties. By the Rev. J. WEBB, M.A. Edited and completed by the Rev. T. W. WEBB, M.A. 2 vols. 8vo. Illustrations, 42s.

Popular History of
France, from the Earliest Times to the Death of Louis XIV. By Miss SEWELL. Crown 8vo. Maps, 7s. 6d.

A Student's Manual of
the History of India from the Earliest Period to the Present. By Col. MEADOWS TAYLOR, M.R.A.S. Third Thousand. Crown 8vo. Maps, 7s. 6d.

Lord Minto in India;
Correspondence of the First Earl of Minto, while Governor-General of India, from 1807 to 1814. Edited by his Great-Niece, the COUNTESS of MINTO. Completing Lord Minto's Life and Letters published in 1874 by the Countess of Minto, in Three Volumes. Post 8vo. Maps, 12s.

Indian Polity; a View of
the System of Administration in India. By Lieut.-Col. G. CHESNEY. 8vo. 21s.

Waterloo Lectures; a
Study of the Campaign of 1815. By Col. C. C. CHESNEY, R.E. 8vo. 10s. 6d.

The Oxford Reformers—
John Colet, Erasmus, and Thomas More; a History of their Fellow-Work. By F. SEEBOHM. 8vo. 14s.

History of the Romans
under the Empire. By Dean MERIVALE, D.D. 8 vols. post 8vo. 48s.

General History of Rome
from B.C. 753 to A.D. 476. By Dean MERIVALE, D.D. Crown 8vo. Maps, price 7s. 6d.

The Fall of the Roman
Republic; a Short History of the Last Century of the Commonwealth. By Dean MERIVALE, D.D. 12mo. 7s. 6d.

The History of Rome.
By WILHELM IHNE. VOLS. I. to III. 8vo. price 45s.

Carthage and the Carthaginians.
By R. BOSWORTH SMITH, M.A. Second Edition. Maps, Plans, &c. Crown 8vo. 10s. 6d.

The Sixth Oriental Monarchy;
or, the Geography, History, and Antiquities of Parthia. By G. RAWLINSON, M.A. With Maps and Illustrations. 8vo. 16s.

The Seventh Great Oriental Monarchy;
or, a History of the Sassanians. By G. RAWLINSON, M.A. With Map and 95 Illustrations. 8vo. 28s.

The History of European Morals
from Augustus to Charlemagne. By W. E. H. LECKY, M.A. 2 vols. crown 8vo. 16s.

History of the Rise and Influence of the Spirit of Rationalism in Europe.
By W. E. H. LECKY, M.A. 2 vols. crown 8vo. 16s.

The History of Philosophy,
from Thales to Comte. By GEORGE HENRY LEWES. Fifth Edition. 2 vols. 8vo. 32s.

A History of Classical Greek Literature.
By the Rev. J. P. MAHAFFY, M.A. Trin. Coll. Dublin. 2 vols. crown 8vo. price 7s. 6d. each.

Zeller's Stoics, Epicureans, and Sceptics.
Translated by the Rev. O. J. REICHEL, M.A. New Edition revised. Crown 8vo. 15s.

Zeller's Socrates & the Socratic Schools.
Translated by the Rev. O. J. REICHEL, M.A. Second Edition. Crown 8vo. 10s. 6d.

Zeller's Plato & the Older Academy.
Translated by S. FRANCES ALLEYNE and ALFRED GOODWIN, B.A. Crown 8vo. 18s.

'Aristotle and the Elder Peripatetics' and 'The Præ-Socratic Schools,' completing the English Edition of ZELLER'S Work on Ancient Greek Philosophy, are preparing for publication.

Epochs of Modern History.
Edited by C. COLBECK, M.A.

Church's Beginning of the Middle Ages, 2s. 6d.
Cox's Crusades, 2s. 6d.
Creighton's Age of Elizabeth, 2s. 6d.
Gairdner's Houses of Lancaster and York, 2s. 6d.
Gardiner's Puritan Revolution, 2s. 6d.
——— Thirty Years' War, 2s. 6d.
Hale's Fall of the Stuarts, 2s. 6d.
Johnson's Normans in Europe, 2s. 6d.
Ludlow's War of American Independence, 2s. 6d.
Morris's Age of Anne, 2s. 6d.
Seebohm's Protestant Revolution, 2/6.
Stubbs's Early Plantagenets, 2s. 6d.
Warburton's Edward III. 2s. 6d.

Epochs of Ancient History.
Edited by the Rev. Sir G. W. COX, Bart. M.A. & C. SANKEY, M.A.

Beesly's Gracchi, Marius & Sulla, 2s. 6d.
Capes's Age of the Antonines, 2s. 6d.
——— Early Roman Empire, 2s. 6d.
Cox's Athenian Empire, 2s. 6d.
——— Greeks & Persians, 2s. 6d.
Curteis's Macedonian Empire, 2s. 6d.
Ihne's Rome to its Capture by the Gauls, 2s. 6d.
Merivale's Roman Triumvirates, 2s. 6d.
Sankey's Spartan & Theban Supremacies, 2s. 6d.

Creighton's Shilling History
of England, introductory to 'Epochs of English History.' Fcp. 8vo. 1s.

Epochs of English History.
Edited by the Rev. MANDELL CREIGHTON, M.A. Fcp. 8vo. 5s.

Browning's Modern England, 1820-1874, 9d.
Cordery's Struggle against Absolute Monarchy, 1603-1688, 9d.
Creighton's (Mrs.) England a Continental Power, 1066-1216, 9d.
Creighton's (Rev. M.) Tudors and the Reformation, 1485-1603, 9d.
Rowley's Rise of the People, 1215-1485, price 9d.
Rowley's Settlement of the Constitution, 1688-1778, 9d.
Tancock's England during the American & European Wars, 1778-1820, 9d
York-Powell's Early England to the Conquest, 1s.

The Student's Manual of
Ancient History; the Political History,
Geography and Social State of the
Principal Nations of Antiquity. By W.
COOKE TAYLOR, LL.D. Cr. 8vo. 7s. 6d.

The Student's Manual of
Modern History; the Rise and Progress of the Principal European Nations.
By W. COOKE TAYLOR, LL.D. Crown
8vo. 7s. 6d.

BIOGRAPHICAL WORKS.

The Life of Henry Venn,
B.D. Prebendary of St. Paul's, and
Hon. Sec. of the Church Missionary
Society; with Extracts from his Letters
and Papers. By the Rev. W. KNIGHT,
M.A. With an Introduction by the
Rev. J. VENN, M.A. [*Just ready.*

Memoirs of the Life of
Anna Jameson, Author of 'Sacred and
Legendary Art' &c. By her Niece,
GERARDINE MACPHERSON. 8vo. with
Portrait, 12s. 6d.

Isaac Casaubon, 1559-
1614. By MARK PATTISON, Rector
of Lincoln College, Oxford. 8vo. 18s.

The Life and Letters of
Lord Macaulay. By his Nephew,
G. OTTO TREVELYAN, M.P.
CABINET EDITION, 2 vols. crown 8vo. 12s.
LIBRARY EDITION, 2 vols. 8vo. 36s.

The Life of Sir Martin
Frobisher, Knt. containing a Narra-
tive of the Spanish Armada. By the
Rev. FRANK JONES, B.A. Portrait,
Maps, and Facsimile. Crown 8vo. 6s.

The Life, Works, and
Opinions of Heinrich Heine. By
WILLIAM STIGAND. 2 vols. 8vo.
Portrait, 28s.

The Life of Mozart.
Translated from the German Work of
Dr. LUDWIG NOHL by Lady WALLACE.
2 vols. crown 8vo. Portraits, 21s.

The Life of Simon de
Montfort, Earl of Leicester, with
special reference to the Parliamentary
History of his time. By G. W.
PROTHERO. Crown 8vo. Maps, 9s.

Felix Mendelssohn's Let-
ters, translated by Lady WALLACE.
2 vols. crown 8vo. 5s. each.

Autobiography. By JOHN
STUART MILL. 8vo. 7s. 6d.

Apologia pro Vitâ Suâ;
Being a History of his Religious
Opinions by JOHN HENRY NEWMAN,
D.D. Crown 8vo. 6s.

Leaders of Public Opi-
nion in Ireland; Swift, Flood,
Grattan, O'Connell. By W. E. H.
LECKY, M.A. Crown 8vo. 7s. 6d.

Essays in Ecclesiastical
Biography. By the Right Hon. Sir J.
STEPHEN, LL.D. Crown 8vo. 7s. 6d.

Cæsar; a Sketch. By JAMES
ANTHONY FROUDE, M.A. formerly
Fellow of Exeter College, Oxford.
With Portrait and Map. 8vo. 16s.

Life of the Duke of Wel-
lington. By the Rev. G. R. GLEIG,
M.A. Crown 8vo. Portrait, 6s.

Memoirs of Sir Henry
Havelock, K.C.B. By JOHN CLARK
MARSHMAN. Crown 8vo. 3s. 6d.

Vicissitudes of Families.
By Sir BERNARD BURKE, C.B. Two
vols. crown 8vo. 21s.

Maunder's Treasury of
Biography, reconstructed and in great
part re-written, with above 1,600 ad
ditional Memoirs by W. L. R. CATES.
Fcp. 8vo. 6s.

MENTAL and POLITICAL PHILOSOPHY.

Comte's System of Positive Polity, or Treatise upon Sociology :—

VOL. I. **General View of Positivism** and Introductory Principles. Translated by J. H. BRIDGES, M.B. 8vo. 21*s.*

VOL. II. **The Social Statics,** or the Abstract Laws of Human Order. Translated by F. HARRISON, M.A. 8vo. 14*s.*

VOL. III. **The Social Dynamics,** or the General Laws of Human Progress (the Philosophy of History). Translated by E. S. BEESLY, M.A. 8vo. 21*s.*

VOL. IV. **The Theory of the Future of Man** ; with COMTE's Early Essays on Social Philosophy. Translated by R. CONGREVE, M.D. and H. D. HUTTON, B.A. 8vo. 24*s.*

De Tocqueville's Democracy in America, translated by H. REEVE. 2 vols. crown 8vo. 16*s.*

Analysis of the Phenomena of the Human Mind. By JAMES MILL. With Notes, Illustrative and Critical. 2 vols. 8vo. 28*s.*

On Representative Government. By JOHN STUART MILL. Crown 8vo. 2*s.*

On Liberty. By JOHN STUART MILL. Post 8vo. 7*s.* 6*d.* crown 8vo. 1*s.* 4*d.*

Principles of Political Economy. By JOHN STUART MILL. 2 vols. 8vo. 30*s.* or 1 vol. crown 8vo. 5*s.*

Essays on some Unsettled Questions of Political Economy. By JOHN STUART MILL. 8vo. 6*s.* 6*d.*

Utilitarianism. By JOHN STUART MILL. 8vo. 5*s.*

The Subjection of Women. By JOHN STUART MILL. Fourth Edition. Crown 8vo. 6*s.*

Examination of Sir William Hamilton's Philosophy. By JOHN STUART MILL. 8vo. 16*s.*

A System of Logic, Ratiocinative and Inductive. By JOHN STUART MILL. 2 vols. 8vo. 25*s.*

Dissertations and Discussions. By JOHN STUART MILL. 4 vols. 8vo. £2. 7*s.*

The A B C of Philosophy ; a Text-Book for Students. By the Rev. T. GRIFFITH, M.A. Prebendary of St. Paul's. Crown 8vo. 5*s.*

Philosophical Fragments written during intervals of Business. By J. D. MORELL, LL.D. Crown 8vo. 5*s.*

Path and Goal ; a Discussion on the Elements of Civilisation and the Conditions of Happiness. By M. M. KALISCH, Ph.D. M.A. 8vo. price 12*s.* 6*d.*

The Law of Nations considered as Independent Political Communities. By Sir TRAVERS TWISS, D.C.L. 2 vols. 8vo. £1. 13*s.*

A Systematic View of the Science of Jurisprudence. By SHELDON AMOS, M.A. 8vo. 18*s.*

A Primer of the English Constitution and Government. By S. AMOS, M.A. Crown 8vo. 6*s.*

Fifty Years of the English Constitution, 1830-1880. By SHELDON AMOS, M.A. Crown 8vo. 10*s.* 6*d.*

Principles of Economical Philosophy. By H. D. MACLEOD, M.A. Second Edition in 2 vols. VOL. I. 8vo. 15*s.* VOL. II. PART I. 12*s.*

Lord Bacon's Works, collected & edited by R. L. ELLIS, M.A. J. SPEDDING, M.A. and D. D. HEATH. 7 vols. 8vo. £3. 13*s.* 6*d.*

Letters and Life of Francis Bacon, including all his Occasional Works. Collected and edited, with a Commentary, by J. SPEDDING. 7 vols. 8vo. £4. 4*s.*

The Institutes of Justinian;
with English Introduction, Translation, and Notes. By T. C. SANDARS, M.A. 8vo. 18s.

The Nicomachean Ethics
of Aristotle, translated into English by R. WILLIAMS, B.A. Crown 8vo. price 7s. 6d.

Aristotle's Politics, Books
I. III. IV. (VII.) Greek Text, with an English Translation by W. E. BOLLAND, M.A. and Short Essays by A. LANG, M.A. Crown 8vo. 7s. 6d.

The Politics of Aristotle;
Greek Text, with English Notes. By RICHARD CONGREVE, M.A. 8vo. 18s.

The Ethics of Aristotle;
with Essays and Notes. By Sir A. GRANT, Bart. LL.D. 2 vols. 8vo. 32s.

Bacon's Essays, with Annotations. By R. WHATELY, D.D. 8vo. 10s. 6d.

Picture Logic; an Attempt
to Popularise the Science of Reasoning. By A. SWINBOURNE, B.A. Post 8vo. 5s.

Elements of Logic. By
R. WHATELY, D.D. 8vo. 10s. 6d. Crown 8vo. 4s. 6d.

Elements of Rhetoric.
By R. WHATELY, D.D. 8vo. 10s. 6d. Crown 8vo. 4s. 6d.

On the Influence of Authority in Matters of Opinion. By the late Sir. G. C. LEWIS, Bart. 8vo. 14s.

The Senses and the Intellect. By A. BAIN, LL.D. 8vo. 15s.

The Emotions and the Will. By A. BAIN, LL.D. 8vo. 15s.

Mental and Moral Science; a Compendium of Psychology and Ethics. By A. BAIN, LL.D. Crown 8vo. 10s. 6d.

An Outline of the Necessary Laws of Thought; a Treatise on Pure and Applied Logic. By W. THOMSON, D.D. Crown 8vo. 6s.

Essays in Political and Moral Philosophy. By T. E. CLIFFE LESLIE, Hon. LL.D. Dubl. of Lincoln's Inn, Barrister-at-Law. 8vo. 10s. 6d.

Hume's Philosophical Works. Edited, with Notes, &c. by T. H. GREEN, M.A. and the Rev. T. H. GROSE, M.A. 4 vols. 8vo. 56s. Or separately, Essays, 2 vols. 28s. Treatise on Human Nature, 2 vols. 28s.

Lectures on German Thought. Six Lectures on the History and Prominent Features of German Thought during the last Two Hundred Years, delivered at the Royal Institution of Great Britain. By KARL HILLEBRAND. Rewritten and enlarged. Crown 8vo. 7s. 6d.

MISCELLANEOUS & CRITICAL WORKS.

Selected Essays, chiefly
from Contributions to the Edinburgh and Quarterly Reviews. By A. HAYWARD, Q.C. 2 vols. crown 8vo. 12s.

Miscellaneous Writings
of J. Conington, M.A. Edited by J. A. SYMONDS, M.A. 2 vols. 8vo. 28s.

Short Studies on Great
Subjects. By J. A. FROUDE, M.A. 3 vols. crown 8vo. 18s.

Literary Studies. By the
late WALTER BAGEHOT, M.A. Fellow of University College, London. Edited, with a Prefatory Memoir, by R. H. HUTTON. Second Edition. 2 vols. 8vo. with Portrait, 28s.

Manual of English Literature, Historical and Critical. By T. ARNOLD, M.A. Crown 8vo. 7s. 6d.

The Wit and Wisdom of
the Rev. Sydney Smith. Crown 8vo. 3s. 6d.

Lord Macaulay's Miscellaneous Writings :—

LIBRARY EDITION, 2 vols. 8vo. 21s.
PEOPLE'S EDITION, 1 vol. cr. 8vo. 4s. 6d.

Lord Macaulay's Miscellaneous Writings and Speeches.

Student's Edition. Crown 8vo. 6s.

Speeches of the Right

Hon. Lord Macaulay, corrected by Himself. Crown 8vo. 3s. 6d.

Selections from the Writings of Lord Macaulay.

Edited, with Notes, by G. O. TREVELYAN, M.P. Crown. 8vo. 6s.

Miscellaneous and Post-

humous Works of the late Henry Thomas Buckle. Edited by HELEN TAYLOR. 3 vols. 8vo. 52s. 6d.

Miscellaneous Works of

Thomas Arnold, D.D. late Head Master of Rugby School. 8vo. 7s. 6d.

The Pastor's Narrative;

or, before and after the Battle of Wörth, 1870. By Pastor KLEIN. Translated by Mrs. F. E. MARSHALL. Crown 8vo. Map, 6s.

German Home Life; a

Series of Essays on the Domestic Life of Germany. Crown 8vo. 6s.

Realities of Irish Life.

By W. STEUART TRENCH. Crown 8vo. 2s. 6d. boards, or 3s. 6d. cloth.

Two Lectures on South

Africa delivered before the Philosophical Institute, Edinburgh, Jan. 6 & 9, 1880. By JAMES ANTHONY FROUDE, M.A. 8vo. 5s.

Cetshwayo's Dutchman;

the Private Journal of a White Trader in Zululand during the British Invasion. By CORNELIUS VIJN. Translated and edited with Preface and Notes by the Right Rev. J. W. COLENSO, D.D. Bishop of Natal. Crown 8vo. Portrait, 5s.

Apparitions; a Narrative

of Facts. By the Rev. B. W. SAVILE, M.A. Second Edition. Crown 8vo. price 5s.

Max Müller and the

Philosophy of Language. By LUDWIG NOIRÉ. 8vo. 6s.

Lectures on the Science

of Language. By F. MAX MÜLLER, M.A. 2 vols. crown 8vo. 16s.

Chips from a German

Workshop; Essays on the Science of Religion, and on Mythology, Traditions & Customs. By F. MAX MÜLLER, M.A. 4 vols. 8vo. £2. 18s.

Language & Languages.

A Revised Edition of Chapters on Language and Families of Speech. By F. W. FARRAR, D.D. F.R.S. Crown 8vo. 6s.

The Essays and Contri-

butions of A. K. H. B. Uniform Cabinet Editions in crown 8vo.

Recreations of a Country Parson, Three Series, 3s. 6d. each.

Landscapes, Churches, and Moralities, price 3s. 6d.

Seaside Musings, 3s. 6d.

Changed Aspects of Unchanged Truths, 3s. 6d.

Counsel and Comfort from a City Pulpit, 3s. 6d.

Lessons of Middle Age, 3s. 6d.

Leisure Hours in Town, 3s. 6d.

Autumn Holidays of a Country Parson, price 3s. 6d.

Sunday Afternoons at the Parish Church of a University City, 3s. 6d.

The Commonplace Philosopher in Town and Country, 3s. 6d.

Present-Day Thoughts, 3s. 6d.

Critical Essays of a Country Parson, price 3s. 6d.

The Graver Thoughts of a Country Parson, Three Series, 3s. 6d. each.

DICTIONARIES and OTHER BOOKS of REFERENCE.

One-Volume Dictionary
of the English Language. By R. G. LATHAM, M.A. M.D. Medium 8vo. 24s.

Larger Dictionary of
the English Language. By R. G. LATHAM, M.A. M.D. Founded on Johnson's English Dictionary as edited by the Rev. H. J. TODD. 4 vols. 4to. £7.

Roget's Thesaurus of
English Words and Phrases, classified and arranged so as to facilitate the expression of Ideas, and assist in Literary Composition. Revised and enlarged by the Author's Son, J. L. ROGET. Crown 8vo. 10s. 6d.

English Synonymes. By
E. J. WHATELY. Edited by R. WHATELY, D.D. Fcp. 8vo. 3s.

Handbook of the English
Language. By R. G. LATHAM, M.A. M.D. Crown 8vo. 6s.

Contanseau's Practical
Dictionary of the French and English Languages. Post 8vo. price 7s. 6d.

Contanseau's Pocket
Dictionary, French and English, abridged from the Practical Dictionary by the Author. Square 18mo. 3s. 6d.

A Practical Dictionary
of the German and English Languages. By Rev. W. L. BLACKLEY, M.A. & Dr. C. M. FRIEDLÄNDER. Post 8vo. 7s. 6d.

A New Pocket Diction-
ary of the German and English Languages. By F. W. LONGMAN, Ball. Coll. Oxford. Square 18mo. 5s.

Becker's Gallus ; Roman
Scenes of the Time of Augustus. Translated by the Rev. F. METCALFE, M.A. Post 8vo. 7s. 6d.

Becker's Charicles;
Illustrations of the Private Life of the Ancient Greeks. Translated by the Rev. F. METCALFE, M.A. Post 8vo. 7s 6d.

A Dictionary of Roman
and Greek Antiquities. With 2,000 Woodcuts illustrative of the Arts and Life of the Greeks and Romans. By A. RICH, B.A. Crown 8vo. 7s. 6d.

A Greek-English Lexi-
con. By H. G. LIDDELL, D.D. Dean of Christchurch, and R. SCOTT, D.D. Dean of Rochester. Crown 4to. 36s.

Liddell & Scott's Lexi-
con, Greek and English, abridged for Schools. Square 12mo. 7s. 6d.

An English-Greek Lexi-
con, containing all the Greek Words used by Writers of good authority. By C. D. YONGE, M.A. 4to. 21s. School Abridgment, square 12mo. 8s. 6d.

A Latin-English Diction-
ary. By JOHN T. WHITE, D.D. Oxon. and J. E. RIDDLE, M.A. Oxon. Sixth Edition, revised. Quarto 21s.

White's College Latin-
English Dictionary, for the use of University Students. Royal 8vo. 12s.

M'Culloch's Dictionary
of Commerce and Commercial Navigation. Re-edited, with a Supplement shewing the Progress of British Commercial Legislation to the Year 1880, by HUGH G. REID. With 11 Maps and 30 Charts. 8vo. 63s. The SUPPLEMENT separately, price 5s.

Keith Johnston's General
Dictionary of Geography, Descriptive, Physical, Statistical, and Historical ; a complete Gazetteer of the World. Medium 8vo. 42s.

The Public Schools Atlas
of Ancient Geography, in 28 entirely new Coloured Maps. Edited by the Rev. G. BUTLER, M.A. Imperial 8vo. or imperial 4to. 7s. 6d.

The Public Schools Atlas
of Modern Geography, in 31 entirely new Coloured Maps. Edited by the Rev. G. BUTLER, M.A. Uniform, 5s.

ASTRONOMY and METEOROLOGY.

Outlines of Astronomy.
By Sir J. F. W. HERSCHEL, Bart. M.A. Latest Edition, with Plates and Diagrams. Square crown 8vo. 12s.

Essays on Astronomy.
A Series of Papers on Planets and Meteors, the Sun and Sun-surrounding Space, Stars and Star Cloudlets. By R. A. PROCTOR, B.A. With 10 Plates and 24 Woodcuts. 8vo. 12s.

The Moon; her Motions,
Aspects, Scenery, and Physical Condition. By R. A. PROCTOR, B.A. With Plates, Charts, Woodcuts, and Lunar Photographs. Crown 8vo. 10s.6d.

The Sun; Ruler, Light, Fire,
and Life of the Planetary System. By R. A. PROCTOR, B.A. With Plates & Woodcuts. Crown 8vo. 14s.

The Orbs Around Us;
a Series of Essays on the Moon & Planets, Meteors & Comets, the Sun & Coloured Pairs of Suns. By R. A. PROCTOR, B.A. With Chart and Diagrams. Crown 8vo. 7s. 6d.

Other Worlds than Ours;
The Plurality of Worlds Studied under the Light of Recent Scientific Researches. By R. A. PROCTOR, B.A. With 14 Illustrations. Cr. 8vo. 10s. 6d.

The Universe of Stars;
Presenting Researches into and New Views respecting the Constitution of the Heavens. By R. A. PROCTOR, B.A. Second Edition, with 22 Charts (4 Coloured) and 22 Diagrams. 8vo. price 10s. 6d.

The Transits of Venus;
A Popular Account of Past and Coming Transits. By R. A. PROCTOR, B.A. 20 Plates (12 Coloured) and 27 Woodcuts. Crown 8vo. 8s. 6d.

Saturn and its System.
By R. A. PROCTOR, B.A. 8vo. with 14 Plates, 14s.

The Moon, and the Condition and Configurations of its Surface.
By E. NEISON, F.R.A.S. With 26 Maps & 5 Plates. Medium 8vo. 31s. 6d.

A New Star Atlas, for the
Library, the School, and the Observatory, in 12 Circular Maps (with 2 Index Plates). By R. A. PROCTOR, B.A. Crown 8vo. 5s.

Larger Star Atlas, for the
Library, in Twelve Circular Maps, with Introduction and 2 Index Plates. By R. A. PROCTOR, B.A. Folio, 15s. or Maps only, 12s. 6d.

A Treatise on the Cycloid,
and on all forms of Cycloidal Curves, and on the use of Cycloidal Curves in dealing with the Motions of Planets, Comets, &c. and of Matter projected from the Sun. By R. A. PROCTOR, B.A. With 161 Diagrams. Crown 8vo. 10s. 6d.

Dove's Law of Storms,
considered in connexion with the Ordinary Movements of the Atmosphere. Translated by R. H. SCOTT, M.A. 8vo. 10s. 6d.

Air and Rain; the Beginnings of a Chemical Climatology.
By R. A. SMITH, F.R.S. 8vo. 24s.

Schellen's Spectrum Analysis,
in its Application to Terrestrial Substances and the Physical Constitution of the Heavenly Bodies. Translated by JANE and C. LASSELL, with Notes by W. HUGGINS, LL.D. F.R.S. 8vo. Plates and Woodcuts, 28s.

NATURAL HISTORY and PHYSICAL SCIENCE.

Professor Helmholtz'
Popular Lectures on Scientific Subjects. Translated by E. ATKINSON, F.C.S. With numerous Wood Engravings. 8vo. 12s. 6d.

Professor Helmholtz on
the Sensations of Tone, as a Physiological Basis for the Theory of Music. Translated by A. J. ELLIS, F.R.S. 8vo. 36s.

Ganot's Natural Philo-
sophy for General Readers and Young Persons ; a Course of Physics divested of Mathematical Formulæ and expressed in the language of daily life. Translated by E. ATKINSON, F.C.S. Third Edition. Plates and Woodcuts. Crown 8vo. 7s. 6d.

Ganot's Elementary
Treatise on Physics, Experimental and Applied, for the use of Colleges and Schools. Translated by E. ATKINSON, F.C.S. Ninth Edition. Plates and Woodcuts. Large crown 8vo. 15s.

Arnott's Elements of Phy-
sics or Natural Philosophy. Seventh Edition, edited by A. BAIN, LL.D. and A. S. TAYLOR, M.D. F.R.S. Crown 8vo. Woodcuts, 12s. 6d.

The Correlation of Phy-
sical Forces. By the Hon. Sir W. R. GROVE, F.R.S. &c. Sixth Edition, revised and augmented. 8vo. 15s.

Weinhold's Introduction
to Experimental Physics ; including Directions for Constructing Physical Apparatus and for Making Experiments. Translated by B. LOEWY, F.R.A.S. 8vo. Plates & Woodcuts 31s. 6d.

A Treatise on Magnet-
ism, General and Terrestrial. By II. LLOYD, D.D. D.C.L. 8vo. 10s. 6d.

Elementary Treatise on
the Wave-Theory of Light. By H. LLOYD, D.D. D.C.L. 8vo. 10s. 6d.

Fragments of Scienc
By JOHN TYNDALL, F.R.S. Six Edition, revised and augmented. 2 vo crown 8vo. 16s.

Heat a Mode of Motio
By JOHN TYNDALL, F.R.S. Fi Edition in preparation.

Sound. By JOHN TYNDAL
F.R.S. Third Edition, includi Recent Researches on Fog-Signallii Crown 8vo. price 10s. 6d.

Contributions to Mol
cular Physics in the domain Radiant Heat. By JOHN TYNDA F.R.S. Plates and Woodcuts. 8vo. 1

Professor Tyndall's R
searches on Diamagnetism a Magne-Crystallic Action ; includi Diamagnetic Polarity. New Edit in preparation.

Professor Tyndall's Le
tures on Light, delivered in Amer in 1872 and 1873. With Portrait, Pl & Diagrams. Crown 8vo. 7s. 6d.

Professor Tyndall's Le
sons in Electricity at the Ro Institution, 1875-6. With 58 Wo cuts. Crown 8vo. 2s. 6d.

Professor Tyndall's Not
of a Course of Seven Lectures Electrical Phenomena and Th ries, delivered at the Royal Instituti Crown 8vo. 1s. sewed, 1s. 6d. cloth

Professor Tyndall's Not
of a Course of Nine Lectures Light, delivered at the Royal Insti tion. Crown 8vo. 1s. swd., 1s. 6d. clo

Principles of Animal M
chanics. By the Rev. S. HAUGHTC F.R.S. Second Edition. 8vo. 21s

Text-Books of Science,

Mechanical and Physical, adapted for the use of Artisans and of Students in Public and Science Schools. Small 8vo. with Woodcuts, &c.

Abney's Photography, 3s. 6d.

Anderson's (Sir John) Strength of Materials, 3s. 6d.

Armstrong's Organic Chemistry, 3s. 6d.

Barry's Railway Appliances, 3s. 6d.

Bloxam's Metals, 3s. 6d.

Goodeve's Mechanics, 3s. 6d.

———— Mechanism, 3s. 6d.

Gore's Electro-Metallurgy, 6s.

Griffin's Algebra & Trigonometry, 3/6.

Jenkin's Electricity & Magnetism, 3/6.

Maxwell's Theory of Heat, 3s. 6d.

Merrifield's Technical Arithmetic, 3s. 6d.

Miller's Inorganic Chemistry, 3s. 6d.

Preece & Sivewright's Telegraphy, 3/6.

Rutley's Study of Rocks, 4s. 6d.

Shelley's Workshop Appliances, 3s. 6d.

Thomé's Structural and Physiological Botany, 6s.

Thorpe's Quantitative Analysis, 4s. 6d.

Thorpe & Muir's Qualitative Analysis, price 3s. 6d.

Tilden's Chemical Philosophy, 3s. 6d.

Unwin's Machine Design, 3s. 6d.

Watson's Plane & Solid Geometry, 3/6.

Light Science for Leisure

Hours ; Familiar Essays on Scientific Subjects, Natural Phenomena, &c. By R. A. PROCTOR, B.A. 2 vols. crown 8vo. 7s. 6d. each.

An Introduction to the

Systematic Zoology and Morphology of Vertebrate Animals. By A. MACALISTER, M.D. With 28 Diagrams. 8vo. 10s. 6d.

The Comparative Anatomy

and Physiology of the Vertebrate Animals. By RICHARD OWEN, F.R.S. With 1,472 Woodcuts. 3 vols. 8vo. £3. 13s. 6d.

Homes without Hands

a Description of the Habitations o Animals, classed according to thei Principle of Construction. By the Rev J. G. WOOD, M.A. With about 14 Vignettes on Wood. 8vo. 14s.

Wood's Strange Dwell

ings ; a Description of the Habitation of Animals, abridged from 'Home without Hands.' With Frontispiec and 60 Woodcuts. Crown 8vo. 7s. 6d.

Wood's Insects at Home;

a Popular Account of British Insects, their Structure, Habits, and Trans. formations. 8vo. Woodcuts, 14s.

Wood's Insects Abroad ;

a Popular Account of Foreign Insects, their Structure, Habits, and Transformations. 8vo. Woodcuts, 14s.

Wood's Out of Doors ; a

Selection of Original Articles on Practical Natural History. With 6 Illustrations. Crown 8vo. 7s. 6d.

Wood's Bible Animals ; a

description of every Living Creature mentioned in the Scriptures, from the Ape to the Coral. With 112 Vignettes. 8vo. 14s.

The Sea and its Living

Wonders. By Dr. G. HARTWIG. 8vo. with many Illustrations, 10s. 6d.

Hartwig's Tropical

World. With about 200 Illustrations. 8vo. 10s. 6d.

Hartwig's Polar World ;

a Description of Man and Nature in the Arctic and Antarctic Regions of the Globe. Maps, Plates & Woodcuts. 8vo. 10s. 6d.

Hartwig's Subterranean

World. With Maps and Woodcuts. 8vo. 10s. 6d.

Hartwig's Aerial World ;

a Popular Account of the Phenomena and Life of the Atmosphere. Map, Plates, Woodcuts. 8vo. 10s. 6d.

Kirby and Spence's Introduction to Entomology, or Elements of the Natural History of Insects. Crown 8vo. 5s.

A Familiar History of Birds. By E. STANLEY, D.D. Fcp. 8vo. with Woodcuts, 3s. 6d.

Rural Bird Life ; Essays on Ornithology, with Instructions for Preserving Objects relating to that Science. By CHARLES DIXON. With Coloured Frontispiece and 44 Woodcuts by G. Pearson. Crown 8vo. 7s. 6d. cloth extra, gilt edges.

Rocks Classified and Described. By BERNHARD VON COTTA. An English Translation, by P. H. LAWRENCE, with English, German, and French Synonymes. Post 8vo. 14s.

The Geology of England and Wales; a Concise Account of the Lithological Characters, Leading Fossils, and Economic Products of the Rocks. By H. B. WOODWARD, F.G.S. Crown 8vo. Map & Woodcuts, 14s.

Keller's Lake Dwellings of Switzerland, and other Parts of Europe. Translated by JOHN E. LEE, F.S.A. F.G.S. With 206 Illustrations. 2 vols. royal 8vo. 42s.

Heer's Primæval World of Switzerland. Edited by JAMES HEYWOOD, M.A. F.R.S. With Map, 19 Plates, & 372 Woodcuts. 2 vols. 8vo. 16s.

The Puzzle of Life and How it Has Been Put Together ; a Short History of Praehistoric Vegetable and Animal Life on the Earth. By A. NICOLS, F.R.G.S. With 12 Illustrations. Crown 8vo. 3s. 6d.

The Origin of Civilis tion, and the Primitive Condition Man ; Mental and Social Condition Savages. By Sir J. LUBBOCK, Ba M.P. F.R.S. 8vo. Woodcuts, 18s.

A Dictionary of Scienc Literature, and Art. Re-edited the late W. T. BRANDE (the Auth and the Rev. Sir G. W. COX, Bart. M. 3 vols. medium 8vo. 63s.

Hullah's Course of Le tures on the History of Mod Music. 8vo. 8s. 6d.

Hullah's Second Cour of Lectures on the Transition Per of Musical History. 8vo. 10s. 6d

Loudon's Encyclopæd of Plants ; comprising the Spec Character, Description, Culture, tory, &c. of all the Plants found Great Britain. With upwards 12,000 Woodcuts. 8vo. 42s.

De Caisne & Le Maou Descriptive and Analytical Bota Translated by Mrs. HOOKER ; . edi and arranged by J. D. HOOKER, M. With 5,500 Woodcuts. Imperial 8 price 31s. 6d.

Rivers's Orchard-Hous or, the Cultivation of Fruit Trees un Glass. Sixteenth Edition, re-edited T. F. RIVERS. Crown 8vo. with Woodcuts, 5s.

The Rose Amateu Guide. By THOMAS RIVERS. Lat Edition. Fcp. 8vo. 4s. 6d.

Town and Window Ga dening, including the Structure, Hal and Uses of Plants. By Mrs. BUCKTC With 127 Woodcuts. Crown 8vo.

CHEMISTRY and PHYSIOLOGY.

Practical Chemistry; the Principles of Qualitative Analysis. By W. A. TILDEN, D.Sc. Lond. F.C.S. Professor of Chemistry in Mason's College, Birmingham. Fcp. 8vo. 1s. 6d.

Miller's Elements of Chemistry, Theoretical and Practical. Re-edited, with Additions, by H. MACLEOD, F.C.S. 3 vols. 8vo.

PART I. CHEMICAL PHYSICS. 16s.
PART II. INORGANIC CHEMISTRY, 24s.
PART III. ORGANIC CHEMISTRY, 31s. 6d.

Annals of Chemical Medicine; including the Application of Chemistry to Physiology, Pathology, Therapeutics, Pharmacy, Toxicology, and Hygiene. Edited by J. L. W. THUDICHUM, M.D. VOL. I. 8vo. 14s.

Health in the House: Twenty-five Lectures on Elementary Physiology in its Application to the Daily Wants of Man and Animals. By Mrs. BUCKTON. Crown 8vo. Woodcuts, 2s.

A Dictionary of Chemistry and the Allied Branches of other Sciences. By HENRY WATTS, F.C.S. assisted by eminent Scientific and Practical Chemists. 7 vols. medium 8vo. £10. 16s. 6d.

Third Supplement, completing the Record of Chemical Discovery to the year 1877. PART I. 8vo. 36s. PART II. completion, in the press.

Select Methods in Chemical Analysis, chiefly Inorganic. By WM. CROOKES, F.R.S. With 22 Woodcuts. Crown 8vo. 12s. 6d.

The History, Products, and Processes of the Alkali Trade, including the most recent Improvements. By CHARLES T. KINGZETT, F.C.S. With 32 Woodcuts. 8vo. 12s.

Animal Chemistry, or the Relations of Chemistry to Physiology and Pathology: a Manual for Medical Men and Scientific Chemists. By CHARLES T. KINGZETT, F.C.S. 8vo. price 18s.

The FINE ARTS and ILLUSTRATED EDITIONS.

In Fairyland; Pictures from the Elf-World. By RICHARD DOYLE. With 16 coloured Plates, containing 36 Designs. Folio, 15s.

Lord Macaulay's Lays of Ancient Rome. With Ninety Illustrations on Wood from Drawings by G. SCHARF. Fcp. 4to. 21s.

Miniature Edition of Macaulay's Lays of Ancient Rome, with Scharf's 90 Illustrations reduced in Lithography. Imp. 16mo. 10s. 6d.

Moore's Lalla Rookh. TENNIEL's Edition, with 68 Woodcut Illustrations. Crown 8vo. 10s. 6d.

Moore's Irish Melodies, MACLISE's Edition, with 161 Steel Plates. Super-royal 8vo. 21s.

Lectures on Harmony, delivered at the Royal Institution. By G. A. MACFARREN. 8vo. 12s.

Sacred and Legendary Art. By Mrs. JAMESON. 6 vols. square crown 8vo. £5. 15s. 6d.

Jameson's Legends of the Saints and Martyrs. With 19 Etchings and 187 Woodcuts. 2 vols. 31s. 6d.

Jameson's Legends of the Monastic Orders. With 11 Etchings and 88 Woodcuts. 1 vol. 21s.

Jameson's Legends of the Madonna. With 27 Etchings and 165 Woodcuts. 1 vol. 21s.

Jameson's History of the Saviour, His Types and Precursors. Completed by Lady EASTLAKE. With 13 Etchings and 281 Woodcuts. 2 vols. 42s.

The Three Cathedrals dedicated to St. Paul in London. By W. LONGMAN, F.S.A. With numerous Illustrations. Square crown 8vo. 21s.

The USEFUL ARTS, MANUFACTURES, &

The Art of Scientific
Discovery. By G. GORE, LL.D. F.R.S. Crown 8vo. 15s.

The Amateur Mechanics'
Practical Handbook; describing the different Tools required in the Workshop. By A. H. G. HOBSON. With 33 Woodcuts. Crown 8vo. 2s. 6d.

The Engineer's Valuing
Assistant. By H. D. HOSKOLD, Civil and Mining Engineer. 8vo. price 31s. 6d.

Industrial Chemistry; a
Manual for Manufacturers and for Colleges or Technical Schools; a Translation (by Dr. T. H. BARRY) of Stohmann and Engler's German Edition of PAYEN's 'Précis de Chimie Industrielle;' with Chapters on the Chemistry of the Metals, &c. by B. H. PAUL, Ph.D. With 698 Woodcuts. Medium 8vo. 42s.

Gwilt's Encyclopædia of
Architecture, with above 1,600 Woodcuts. Revised and extended by W. PAPWORTH. 8vo. 52s. 6d.

Lathes and Turning, Simple, Mechanical, and Ornamental. By W. H. NORTHCOTT. Second Edition, with 338 Illustrations. 8vo. 18s.

The Theory of Strains in
Girders and similar Structures, with Observations on the application of Theory to Practice, and Tables of the Strength and other Properties of Materials. By B. B. STONEY, M.A. M. Inst. C.E. Royal 8vo. with 5 Plates and 123 Woodcuts, 36s.

A Treatise on Mills and
Millwork. By the late Sir W. FAIRBAIRN, Bart. C.E. Fourth Edition, with 18 Plates and 333 Woodcuts. 1 vol. 8vo. 25s.

Useful Information for
Engineers. By the late Sir W. FAIRBAIRN, Bart. C.E. With many Plates and Woodcuts. 3 vols. crown 8vo. 31s. 6d.

The Application of Ca
and Wrought Iron to Buildi Purposes. By the late Sir W. FAIRBAIRN, Bart. C.E. With 6 Plates a 118 Woodcuts. 8vo. 16s.

Hints on Househol
Taste in Furniture, Upholste and other Details. By C. L. EAS LAKE. Fourth Edition, with 100 Ill trations. Square crown 8vo. 14s.

Handbook of Practic
Telegraphy. By R. S. CULLE Memb. Inst. C.E. Seventh Editio Plates & Woodcuts. 8vo. 16s.

A Treatise on the Stea
Engine, in its various applications Mines, Mills, Steam Navigation, Ra ways and Agriculture. By J. BOURN C.E. With Portrait, 37 Plates, a 546 Woodcuts. 4to. 42s.

Recent Improvements i
the Steam Engine. By J. BOURN C.E. Fcp. 8vo. Woodcuts, 6s.

Catechism of the Stea
Engine, in its various Applicatio By JOHN BOURNE, C.E. Fcp. 8v Woodcuts, 6s.

Handbook of the Stea
Engine, a Key to the Author's Cat chism of the Steam Engine. By BOURNE, C.E. Fcp. 8vo. Woodcuts, 9

Examples of Steam an
Gas Engines of the most recent A proved Types as employed in Mine Factories, Steam Navigation, Railwa and Agriculture, practically describe By JOHN BOURNE, C.E. With 5 Plates and 356 Woodcuts. 4to. 70s.

Cresy's Encyclopædia o
Civil Engineering, Historical, Theo retical, and Practical. With abov 3,000 Woodcuts. 8vo. 42s.

Ure's Dictionary of Arts
Manufactures, and Mines. Seventh Edition, re-written and enlarged by R HUNT, F.R.S. assisted by numerou contributors. With 2,604 Woodcuts 4 vols. medium 8vo. £7. 7s.

Practical Treatise on Metallurgy.
Adapted from the last German Edition of Professor KERL'S Metallurgy by W. CROOKES, F.R.S. &c. and E. RÖHRIG, Ph.D. 3 vols. 8vo. with 625 Woodcuts. £4. 19s.

Anthracen; its Constitution,
Properties, Manufacture, and Derivatives, including Artificial Alizarin, Anthrapurpurin, &c. with their Applications in Dyeing and Printing. By G. AUERBACH. Translated by W. CROOKES, F.R.S. 8vo. 12s.

On Artificial Manures,
their Chemical Selection and Scientific Application to Agriculture; a Series of Lectures given at the Experimental Farm at Vincennes in 1867 and 1874–75. By M. GEORGES VILLE. Translated and edited by W. CROOKES, F.R.S. With 31 Plates. 8vo. 21s.

Practical Handbook of
Dyeing and Calico-Printing. By W. CROOKES, F.R.S. &c. With numerous Illustrations and specimens of Dyed Textile Fabrics. 8vo. 42s.

The Art of Perfumery,
and the Methods of Obtaining the Odours of Plants; the Growth and general Flower Farm System of Raising Fragrant Herbs; with Instructions for the Manufacture of Perfumes for the Handkerchief, Scented Powders, Odorous Vinegars and Salts, Snuff, Dentifrices, Cosmetics, Perfumed Soap, &c. By G. W. S. PIESSE, Ph.D. F.C.S. Fourth Edition, with 96 Woodcuts. Square crown 8vo. 21s.

Mitchell's Manual of
Practical Assaying. Fourth Edition, revised, with the Recent Discoveries incorporated, by W. CROOKES, F.R.S. Crown 8vo. Woodcuts, 31s. 6d.

Loudon's Encyclopædia
of Gardening; the Theory and Practice of Horticulture, Floriculture, Arboriculture & Landscape Gardening. With 1,000 Woodcuts. 8vo. 21s.

Loudon's Encyclopædia
of Agriculture; the Laying-out, Improvement, and Management of Landed Property; the Cultivation and Economy of the Productions of Agriculture. With 1,100 Woodcuts. 8vo. 21s.

RELIGIOUS and MORAL WORKS.

A Handbook to the Bible,
or, Guide to the Study of the Holy Scriptures derived from Ancient Monuments and Modern Exploration. By F. R. CONDER, and Lieut. C. R. CONDER, R.E. late Commanding the Survey of Palestine. Second Edition; Maps, Plates of Coins, &c. Post 8vo. price 7s. 6d.

Four Lectures on some
Epochs of Early Church History. By the Very Rev. C. MERIVALE, D.D. Dean of Ely. Crown 8vo. 5s.

A History of the Church
of England; Pre-Reformation Period. By the Rev. T. P. BOULTBEE, LL.D. 8vo. 15s.

Sketch of the History of
the Church of England to the Revolution of 1688. By T. V. SHORT, D.D. Crown 8vo. 7s. 6d.

The English Church in
the Eighteenth Century. By CHARLES J. ABBEY, late Fellow of University College, Oxford; and JOHN H. OVERTON, late Scholar of Lincoln College, Oxford. 2 vols. 8vo. 36s.

An Exposition of the 39
Articles, Historical and Doctrinal. By E. H. BROWNE, D.D. Bishop of Winchester. Eleventh Edition. 8vo. 16s.

A Commentary on the
39 Articles, forming an Introduction to the Theology of the Church of England. By the Rev. T. P. BOULTBEE, LL.D. New Edition. Crown 8vo. 6s.

Sermons preached mostly in the Chapel of Rugby School
by the late T. ARNOLD, D.D. Collective Edition, revised by the Author's Daughter, Mrs. W. E. FORSTER. 6 vols. crown 8vo. 30s. or separately, 5s. each.

Historical Lectures on
the Life of Our Lord Jesus Christ. By C. J. ELLICOTT, D.D. 8vo. 12s.

The Eclipse of Faith ; or
a Visit to a Religious Sceptic. By HENRY ROGERS. Fcp. 8vo. 5s.

Defence of the Eclipse of
Faith. By H. ROGERS. Fcp. 8vo. 3s. 6d.

Nature, the Utility of
Religion and Theism. Three Essays by JOHN STUART MILL. 8vo. 10s. 6d.

A Critical and Gram-
matical Commentary on St. Paul's Epistles. By C. J. ELLICOTT, D.D. 8vo. Galatians, 8s. 6d. Ephesians, 8s. 6d. Pastoral Epistles, 10s. 6d. Philippians, Colossians, & Philemon, 10s. 6d. Thessalonians, 7s. 6d.

Conybeare & Howson's
Life and Epistles of St. Paul. Three Editions, copiously illustrated.

Library Edition, with all the Original Illustrations, Maps, Landscapes on Steel, Woodcuts, &c. 2 vols. 4to. 42s.

Intermediate Edition, with a Selection of Maps, Plates, and Woodcuts. 2 vols. square crown 8vo. 21s.

Student's Edition, revised and condensed, with 46 Illustrations and Maps. 1 vol. crown 8vo. 9s.

The Jewish Messiah ;
Critical History of the Messianic Idea among the Jews, from the Rise of the Maccabees to the Closing of the Talmud. By J. DRUMMOND, B.A. 8vo. 15s.

Bible Studies. By M. M.
KALISCH, Ph.D. PART I. *The Prophecies of Balaam.* 8vo. 10s. 6d. PART II. *The Book of Jonah.* 8vo. price 10s. 6d.

Historical and Critical
Commentary on the Old Testament; with a New Translation. By M. M. KALISCH, Ph.D. Vol. I. Genesis, 8vo. 18s. or adapted for the General Reader, 12s. Vol. II. Exodus, 15s. or adapted for the General Reader, 12s. Vol. III. Leviticus, Part I. 15s. or adapted for the General Reader, 8s. Vol. IV. Leviticus, Part II. 15s. or adapted for the General Reader, 8s.

Ewald's History of Isra
Translated from the German by J. CARPENTER, M.A. with Preface by MARTINEAU, M.A. 5 vols. 8vo. 63

Ewald's Antiquities
Israel. Translated from the Germ by H. S. SOLLY, M.A. 8vo. 12s. 6

The Types of Genesi
briefly considered as revealing Development of Human Nature. A. JUKES. Crown 8vo. 7s. 6d.

The Second Death a
the Restitution of all Things; w some Preliminary Remarks on Nature and Inspiration of Holy Scr ture. By A. JUKES. Crown 8vo. 3s.

The Gospel for the Nin
teenth Century.   Third Editi 8vo. price 10s. 6d.

Supernatural Religio
an Inquiry into the Reality of vine Revelation. Complete Editi thoroughly revised. 3 vols. 8vo. 36

Lectures on the Orig
and Growth of Religion, as ill trated by the Religions of Indi being the Hibbert Lectures, delivel at the Chapter House, Westmins Abbey, in 1878, by F. MAX MÜLL M.A. 8vo. 10s. 6d.

Introduction to the Sc
ence of Religion, Four Lectures (livered at the Royal Institution ; w Essays on False Analogies and t Philosophy of Mythology. By F. M MÜLLER, M.A. Crown 8vo. 10s.

The Four Gospels 1
Greek, with Greek-English Lexic By JOHN T. WHITE, D.D. Ox Square 32mo. 5s.

Passing Thoughts o
Religion. By Miss SEWELL. Fcp. 8 price 3s. 6d.

Thoughts for the Ag
By Miss SEWELL. Fcp. 8vo. 3s. 6d

Preparation for the Hol
Communion ; the Devotions chie from the works of Jeremy Taylor, Miss SEWELL. 32mo. 3s.

Bishop Jeremy Taylor's
Entire Works; with Life by Bishop Heber. Revised and corrected by the Rev. C. P. EDEN. 10 vols. £5. 5s.

Hymns of Praise and
Prayer. Corrected and edited by Rev. JOHN MARTINEAU, LL.D. Crown 8vo. 4s. 6d. 32mo. 1s. 6d.

Spiritual Songs for the
Sundays and Holidays throughout the Year. By J. S. B. MONSELL, LL.D. Fcp. 8vo. 5s. 18mo. 2s.

Christ the Consoler; a
Book of Comfort for the Sick. By ELLICE HOPKINS. Second Edition. Fcp. 8vo. 2s. 6d.

Lyra Germanica; Hymns
translated from the German by Miss C. WINKWORTH. Fcp. 8vo. 5s.

The Temporal Mission
of the Holy Ghost; or, Reason and Revelation. By HENRY EDWARD MANNING, D.D. Crown 8vo. 8s. 6d.

Hours of Thought on
Sacred Things; Two Volumes of Sermons. By JAMES MARTINEAU, D.D. LL.D. 2 vols. crown 8vo. 7s. 6d. each.

Endeavours after the
Christian Life; Discourses. By JAMES MARTINEAU, D.D. LL.D. Fifth Edition. Crown 8vo. 7s. 6d.

The Pentateuch & Book
of Joshua Critically Examined. By J. W. COLENSO, D.D. Bishop of Natal. Crown 8vo. 6s.

Lectures on the Penta-
teuch and the Moabite Stone; with Appendices. By J. W. COLENSO, D.D. Bishop of Natal. 8vo. 12s.

TRAVELS, VOYAGES, &c.

Sunshine and Storm in
the East, or Cruises to Cyprus and Constantinople. By Mrs. BRASSEY. With 2 Maps and 114 Illustrations engraved on Wood by G. Pearson, chiefly from Drawings by the Hon. A. Y. Bingham; the Cover from an Original Design by Gustave Doré. 8vo. 21s.

A Voyage in the 'Sun-
beam,' our Home on the Ocean for Eleven Months. By Mrs. BRASSEY. Cheaper Edition, with Map and 65 Wood Engravings. Crown 8vo. 7s. 6d.

One Thousand Miles up
the Nile; a Journey through Egypt and Nubia to the Second Cataract. By Miss AMELIA B. EDWARDS, Author of 'Untrodden Peaks and Unfrequented Valleys,' 'Barbara's History,' &c. With Facsimiles of Inscriptions, Ground Plans, Two Coloured Maps of the Nile from Alexandria to Dongola, and 80 Illustrations engraved on Wood from Drawings by the Author; bound in ornamental covers designed also by the Author. Imperial 8vo. 42s.

Wintering in the Ri-
viera; with Notes of Travel in Italy and France, and Practical Hints to Travellers. By WILLIAM MILLER, S.S.C. Edinburgh. With 12 Illustrations. Post 8vo. 12s. 6d.

San Remo and the Wes-
tern Riviera; comprising Bordighera, Mentone, Monaco, Beaulieu, Villefranche, Nice, Cannes, Porto Maurizio, Marina, Alassio, Verezzi, Noli, Monte Grosso, Pegli, Cornigliano, Genoa, and other Towns—climatically and medically considered. By A. HILL HASSALL, M.D. Map and Woodcuts. Crown 8vo. 10s. 6d.

Eight Years in Ceylon.
By Sir SAMUEL W. BAKER, M.A. Crown 8vo. Woodcuts, 7s. 6d.

The Rifle and the Hound
in Ceylon. By Sir SAMUEL W. BAKER, M.A. Crown 8vo. Woodcuts, 7s. 6d.

Himalayan and Sub-

Himalayan Districts of British India, their Climate, Medical Topography, and Disease Distribution; with reasons for assigning a Malarious Origin to Goître and some other Diseases. By F. N. MACNAMARA, M.D. F.R.G.S. Surgeon-Major (retired) Indian Medical Service, late Professor of Chemistry, Calcutta Medical College, and Medical Inspector of Inland Labour Transport, Calcutta. 8vo.   [*In the press.*

The Alpine Club Map of

Switzerland, with parts of the Neighbouring Countries, on the scale of Four Miles to an Inch. Edited by R. C. NICHOLS, F.R.G.S. 4 Sheets in Portfolio, 42s. coloured, or 34s. uncoloured.

The Alpine Guide.   I

JOHN BALL, M.R.I.A.   Post 8vo. w Maps and other Illustrations :—

The Eastern Alps, 10s. 6

Central Alps, including (

the Oberland District, 7s. 6d.

Western Alps, includi

Mont Blanc, Monte Rosa, Zermatt, Price 6s. 6d.

On Alpine Travelling an

the Geology of the Alps.   Price Either of the Three Volumes or Parts the 'Alpine Guide' may be had w this Introduction prefixed, 1s. extra.

WORKS of FICTION.

Novels and Tales. By the

Right Hon. the EARL of BEACONSFIELD, K.G. Cabinet Editions, complete in Ten Volumes, crown 8vo. 6s. each.

Lothair, 6s.	Venetia, 6s.
Coningsby, 6s.	Alroy, Ixion, &c. 6s.
Sybil, 6s.	Young Duke &c. 6s.
Tancred, 6s.	Vivian Grey, 6s.

Henrietta Temple, 6s.

Contarini Fleming, &c. 6s.

Tales from Euripides;

Iphigenia, Alcestis, Hecuba, Helen, Medea.   By VINCENT K. COOPER, M.A. late Scholar of Brasenose College, Oxford.   Fcp. 8vo. 3s. 6d.

Whispers from Fairy-

land. By the Right Hon. E. H. KNATCHBULL-HUGESSEN, M.P. With 9 Illustrations.   Crown 8vo. 3s. 6d.

Higgledy-Piggledy; or,

Stories for Everybody and Everybody's Children. By the Right Hon. E. H. KNATCHBULL-HUGESSEN, M.P. With 9 Illustrations. Cr. 8vo. 3s. 6d.

Stories and Tales.   I

ELIZABETH M. SEWELL.   Cabii Edition, in Ten Volumes, each conta ing a complete Tale or Story —

Amy Herbert, 2s. 6d.   Gertrude, 2s. The Earl's Daughter, 2s. 6d.   T Experience of Life, 2s. 6d.   Cle Hall, 2s. 6d.   Ivors, 2s. 6d.   Kathari Ashton, 2s. 6d.   Margaret Perciv 3s. 6d.   Laneton Parsonage, 3s. Ursula, 3s. 6d.

The Modern Novelist

Library.   Each work complete in itse price 2s. boards, or 2s. 6d. cloth :—

By Lord BEACONSFIELD.

Lothair.	Henrietta Temple.
Coningsby.	Contarini Fleming.
Sybil.	Alroy, Ixion, &c.
Tancred.	The Young Duke,
Venetia.	Vivian Grey.

By ANTHONY TROLLOPE.

Barchester Towers.
The Warden.

THE MODERN NOVELIST'S LIBRARY—*continued.*

By Major WHYTE-MELVILLE.

Digby Grand. | Good for Nothing.
General Bounce. | Holmby House.
Kate Coventry. | The Interpreter.
The Gladiators. | Queen's Maries.

By the Author of 'The Rose Garden.'
Unawares.

By the Author of 'Mlle. Mori.'
The Atelier du Lys.
Mademoiselle Mori.

By Various Writers.
Atherstone Priory.
The Burgomaster's Family.
Elsa and her Vulture.
The Six Sisters of the Valleys.

The Novels and Tales of the Right Honourable the Earl of Beaconsfield, K.G. Complete in Ten Volumes, crown 8vo. cloth extra, gilt edges, 30s.

POETRY and THE DRAMA.

Lays of Ancient Rome; with Ivry and the Armada. By LORD MACAULAY. 16mo. 3s. 6d.

Horatii Opera. Library Edition, with English Notes, Marginal References & various Readings. Edited by Rev. J. E. YONGE, M.A. 8vo. 21s.

Poetical Works of Jean Ingelow. New Edition, reprinted, with Additional Matter, from the 23rd and 6th Editions of the two volumes respectively; with 2 Vignettes. 2 vols. fcp. 8vo. 12s.

Poems by Jean Ingelow. FIRST SERIES, with nearly 100 Woodcut Illustrations. Fcp. 4to. 21s.

The Poem of the Cid: a Translation from the Spanish, with Introduction and Notes. By JOHN ORMSBY. Crown 8vo. 5s.

Festus, a Poem. By PHILIP JAMES BAILEY. 10th Edition, enlarged & revised. Crown 8vo. 12s. 6d.

The Iliad of Homer, Homometrically translated by C. B. CAYLEY. 8vo. 12s. 6d.

The Æneid of Virgil. Translated into English Verse. By J. CONINGTON, M.A. Crown 8vo. 9s.

Bowdler's Family Shak- speare. Genuine Edition, in 1 vol. medium 8vo. large type, with 36 Woodcuts, 14s. or in 6 vols. fcp. 8vo. 21s.

Southey's Poetical Works, with the Author's last Corrections and Additions. Medium 8vo. with Portrait, 14s.

RURAL SPORTS, HORSE and CATTLE MANAGEMENT, &c.

Annals of the Road; or, Notes on Mail and Stage-Coaching in Great Britain. By Captain MALET. With 3 Woodcuts and 10 Coloured Illustrations. Medium 8vo. 21s.

Down the Road; or, Reminiscences of a Gentleman Coachman. By C. T. S. BIRCH REYNARDSON. Second Edition, with 12 Coloured Illustrations. Medium 8vo. 21s.

Blaine's Encyclopædia of
Rural Sports; Complete Accounts, Historical, Practical, and Descriptive, of Hunting, Shooting, Fishing, Racing, &c. With 600 Woodcuts. 8vo. 21s.

A Book on Angling ; or,
Treatise on the Art of Fishing in every branch ; including full Illustrated Lists of Salmon Flies. By FRANCIS FRANCIS. Post 8vo. Portrait and Plates, 15s.

Wilcocks's Sea-Fisher-
man : comprising the Chief Methods of Hook and Line Fishing, a glance at Nets, and remarks on Boats and Boating. Post 8vo. Woodcuts, 12s. 6d.

The Fly-Fisher's Ento-
mology. By ALFRED RONALDS. With 20 Coloured Plates. 8vo. 14s.

Horses and Riding. By
GEORGE NEVILE, M.A. With 31 Illustrations. Crown 8vo. 6s.

Youatt on the Horse.
Revised and enlarged by W. WATSON, M.R.C.V.S. 8vo. Woodcuts, 12s. 6d.

Youatt's Work on the
Dog. Revised and enlarged. 8vo. Woodcuts, 6s.

The Dog in Health a
Disease. By STONEHENGE. T Edition, with 78 Wood Engravin Square crown 8vo. 7s. 6d.

The Greyhound.
STONEHENGE. Revised Edition, w 25 Portraits of Greyhounds, ‹ Square crown 8vo. 15s.

Stables and Stable Fi
tings. By W. MILES. Imp. 8 with 13 Plates, 15s.

The Horse's Foot, a
How to keep it Sound. By MILES. Imp. 8vo. Woodcuts, 12s.

A Plain Treatise o
Horse-shoeing. By W. MILES. P 8vo. Woodcuts, 2s. 6d.

Remarks on Horse
Teeth, addressed to Purchasers. W. MILES. Post 8vo. 1s. 6d.

The Ox, his Diseases a
their Treatment ; with an Essay Parturition in the Cow. By J. DOBSON, M.R.C.V.S. Crown 8ᵛ Illustrations, 7s. 6d.

WORKS of UTILITY and GENERAL INFORMATION.

Maunder's Treasury of
Knowledge and Library of Reference ; comprising an English Dictionary and Grammar, Universal Gazetteer, Classical Dictionary, Chronology, Law Dictionary, Synopsis of the Peerage, Useful Tables, &c. Fcp. 8vo. 6s.

Maunder's Biographical
Treasury. Latest Edition, reconstructed and partly re-written, with above 1,600 additional Memoirs, by W. L. R. CATES. Fcp. 8vo. 6s.

Maunder's Treasury of
Natural History ; or, Popular Dictionary of Zoology. Revised and corrected Edition. Fcp. 8vo. with 900 Woodcuts, 6s.

Maunder's Scientific an
Literary Treasury; a Popular F cyclopædia of Science, Literature, a Art. Latest Edition, partly re-writt with above 1,000 New Articles, by Y. JOHNSON. Fcp. 8vo. 6s.

Maunder's Treasury
Geography, Physical, Historic Descriptive, and Political. Edited W. HUGHES, F.R.G.S. With 7 Ma and 16 Plates. Fcp. 8vo. 6s.

Maunder's Historic
Treasury; Introductory Outlines Universal History, and Separate H tories of all Nations. Revised by t Rev. Sir G. W. COX, Bart. M. Fcp. 8vo. 6s,

The Treasury of Botany,

or Popular Dictionary of the Vegetable Kingdom ; with which is incorporated a Glossary of Botanical Terms. Edited by J. LINDLEY, F.R.S. and T. MOORE, F.L.S. With 274 Woodcuts and 20 Steel Plates. Two Parts, fcp. 8vo. 12s.

The Treasury of Bible

Knowledge ; being a Dictionary of the Books, Persons, Places, Events, and other Matters of which mention is made in Holy Scripture. By the Rev. J. AYRE, M.A. Maps, Plates & Woodcuts. Fcp. 8vo. 6s.

A Practical Treatise on

Brewing ; with Formulæ for Public Brewers & Instructions for Private Families. By W. BLACK. 8vo. 10s. 6d.

The Theory of the Mo-

dern Scientific Game of Whist. By W. POLE, F.R.S. Tenth Edition. Fcp. 8vo. 2s. 6d.

The Correct Card ; or,

How to Play at Whist ; a Whist Catechism. By Major A. CAMPBELL-WALKER, F.R.G.S. Latest Edition. Fcp. 8vo. 2s. 6d.

The Cabinet Lawyer ; a

Popular Digest of the Laws of England, Civil, Criminal, and Constitutional. Twenty-Fifth Edition, corrected and extended. Fcp. 8vo. 9s.

Chess Openings. By F.W.

LONGMAN, Balliol College, Oxford. New Edition. Fcp. 8vo. 2s. 6d.

Pewtner's Compre-

hensive Specifier ; a Guide to the Practical Specification of every kind of Building-Artificer's Work. Edited by W. YOUNG. Crown 8vo. 6s.

Modern Cookery for Pri-

vate Families, reduced to a System of Easy Practice in a Series of carefully-tested Receipts. By ELIZA ACTON. With 8 Plates and 150 Woodcuts. Fcp. 8vo, 6s,

Food and Home Cookery.

A Course of Instruction in 'Practical Cookery and Cleaning, for Children in Elementary Schools. By Mrs. BUCKTON. Woodcuts. Crown 8vo. 2s.

Hints to Mothers on the

Management of their Health during the Period of Pregnancy and in the Lying-in Room. By THOMAS BULL, M.D. Fcp. 8vo. 2s. 6d.

The Maternal Manage-

ment of Children in Health and Disease. By THOMAS BULL, M.D. Fcp. 8vo. 2s. 6d.

The Farm Valuer. By

JOHN SCOTT, Land Valuer. Crown 8vo. 5s.

Rents and Purchases ; or,

the Valuation of Landed Property, Woods, Minerals, Buildings, &c. By JOHN SCOTT. Crown 8vo. 6s.

Economic Studies. By

the late WALTER BAGEHOT, M.A. Fellow of University College, London. Edited by RICHARD HOLT HUTTON. 8vo. 10s. 6d.

Economics for Beginners

By H. D. MACLEOD, M.A. Small crown 8vo. 2s. 6d.

The Elements of Bank-

ing. By H. D. MACLEOD, M.A. Fourth Edition. Crown 8vo. 5s.

The Theory and Practice

of Banking. By H. D. MACLEOD, M.A. 2 vols. 8vo. 26s.

The Resources of Mod-

ern Countries ; Essays towards an Estimate of the Economic Position of Nations and British Trade Prospects. By ALEX. WILSON. 2 vols. 8vo. 24s.

The Patentee's Manual ;

a Treatise on the Law and Practice of Letters Patent, for the use of Patentees and Inventors. By J. JOHNSON, Barrister-at-Law ; and J. H. JOHNSON, Assoc. Inst. C.E. Solicitor and Patent Agent, Lincoln's Inn Fields and Glasgow. Fourth Edition, enlarged. 8vo. price 10s. 6d.

INDEX.

322 Depths of Satan 1st Epistles to
Corinthians confirmed by
hidden ref to deep things of
depths (deep things) depths
of the Knowledge of God
to the Gnosis which Paul
preached & led to the Depths
of Satan.